MILLER'S COLLECTORS CARS

Yearbook & Price Guide 2001

MILLER'S COLLECTORS CARS
Yearbook & Price Guide 2001

General Editor
Dave Selby

Foreword by
Charles Morgan

MILLER'S COLLECTORS CARS YEARBOOK AND PRICE GUIDE 2001

Created and designed by
Miller's Publications
The Cellars, High Street
Tenterden, Kent TN30 6BN
Telephone: 01580 766411
Fax: 01580 766100

General Editor: Dave Selby
Editorial and Production Co-ordinator: Ian Penberthy
Editorial Assistants: Carol Gillings, Lalage Johnstone
Designers: Philip Hannath, Kari Reeves
Advertisement Designer: Simon Cook
Advertising Executive: Jo Hill
Advertising Assistant: Melinda Williams
Production Assistants: Elaine Burrell, Gillian Charles
Additional Photography: Haynes Motor Museum, Robin Saker,
Jacques Chevalier, GPL, Guy Griffiths, Brian Jocelyne
Indexer: Rosemary Appleyard

First published in Great Britain in 2000
by Miller's, a division of Mitchell Beazley,
imprints of Octopus Publishing Group Ltd,
2–4 Heron Quays, London E14 4JP

© 2000 Octopus Publishing Group Ltd

A CIP catalogue record for this book is
available from the British Library

ISBN 1 84000 313 8

Black and white Illustrations and film output by CK Litho, Whitstable, Kent
Colour origination by Pica Colour Separation Overseas Pte Ltd, Singapore
Printed and bound by Toppan Printing Co (HK) Ltd, China

Front cover illustration:

1956 Jaguar XK140 Drophead Coupé **£57,000–65,000 TWY**

Contents

Acknowledgements

The publishers would like to acknowledge the great assistance given by our consultants:

Malcolm Barber   81 Westside, London SW4 9AY Tel: 0171 228 8000

Tom Falconer   Claremont Corvette, Snodland, Kent ME6 5NA

Simon Johnson   Military Vehicle Trust, 7 Carter Fold, Mellor,
                            Lancs BB2 7ER

Brian Page   Classic Assessments, Stonechat House,
                            Moorymead Close, Watton-at-Stone, Herts SG14 3HF

Mike Penn CEI,   Haynes Motor Museum, Sparkford,
Tech Eng ITE, Mairso   Nr Yeovil, Somerset BA22 7LH

Mike Smith   Chiltern House, Ashendon, Aylesbury, Bucks HP18 0HB

Neil Tuckett   Marstonfields, North Marston, Bucks MK18 3PG

We would like to extend our thanks to all auction houses, their press offices, and dealers who have assisted us in the production of this book, along with the organisers and press offices of the following events:

Beaulieu September Autojumble & Automart
Louis Vuitton Classic
Goodwood Festival of Speed
Foster's British Grand Prix
Coys International Historic Festival
Rétromobile, Paris

Classic & Prestige Vehicle Auctions

Serving London, the South West, Central and South East of England

---

Barons offer regular sales throughout the year at the prestigious Sandown Park venue. With extensive free car parking, on site hotel, full restaurant and bar facilities and the 10,000 square foot Esher Hall, this venue offers unrivalled facilities and easy access.

Entering your car into a Barons auction is simplicity itself.

We can send you our information pack and entry form.

You may enter a car by Fax or Telephone.

You can enter a car via our Web Site.

Whichever method you choose, you can be assured of the highest levels of service and promotion, with a data base running into many thousands, our interactive web site and targeted advertising, your car will be seen by the largest possible audience.

Barons not only offer unrivalled levels of service, we also offer some of the most competitive rates in the business, with an entry fee of only £75.00 + VAT and commissions of 5% + VAT.

Visit Barons Web Site at www.barons-auctions.com

Fax-U-Back information line: 09067 110060
(Calls charged at 50p per minute)
Email: info@barons-auctions.com
Call Laurence Sayers Gillan or Ian Murray on
(023 80) 840081 or 741314   Fax: (023 80) 840124

Barons (Specialist Vehicle Auctioneers) Ltd – Brooklands House – 33 New Road
Hythe – Southampton SO45 6BN

How to use this book

It is our aim to make the guide easy to use. Marques are listed alphabetically and then chronologically. Commercial Vehicles, Children's Cars, Replica Vehicles, Restoration Projects, Racing & Rallying and Military Vehicles are located after the marques, toward the end of the book. In the Automobilia section objects are grouped alphabetically by type. If you cannot find what you are looking for please consult the index which starts on page 348.

1947 Volkswagen Type 11 Saloon, air-cooled flat-4 engine, retaining many original features including semaphore indicators, left-hand drive, finished in black, beige cloth interior believed of later origin, good condition throughout.
£7,500–9,000 **S**

1979 Volkswagen Beetle Cabriolet, fitted with GT wheels, factory optional air conditioning and heated rear window, left-hand drive, finished in Diamond silver, black hood and interior.
£8,000–9,000 **COYS**

Caption
provides a brief description of the vehicle or item, and could include comments on its history, mileage, any restoration work carried out and current condition.

1972 Volkswagen 1600E Fastback, 1584cc, fuel injection, finished in metallic turquoise, black interior trim, little use in last 4 years, 26,000 miles recorded, original condition throughout.
£6,000–7,000 **H&H**

Cross Reference
See Colour Review

Volkswagen Beetle
Plans for a Volksauto, with distinctive aerodynamic body and a rear-mounted, flat-four engine to save space, were announced as early as 1934. Dr Porsche designed the 'People's Car' along the lines of his famous rear-engined GP Auto Union, and no model has ever had a longer production life than the Beetle, produced continuously from 1945 and outselling even the Model T Ford.

Miller's Starter Marque

Starter Volkswagen: *Beetle, 1945–70.*
- The Volkswagen Beetle is one bug they just can't find a cure for; it has been produced continuously from 1945.
- The fact that the Beetle is still in production means that cheap spares are readily available for most models other than very early cars. That buzzing, air-cooled, four-cylinder engine is well nigh unburstable too, and in mechanical terms, the cars are easy to work on. One fact says it all: the world record for an engine swap – drive up to drive away – is just over three minutes.
- If you're a classic purist, there's first-of-breed purity of either the 1131cc, 1945–53 split-screen cars or the 1953–57, oval-window 1200cc cars. For driveability and less-onerous ownership costs, a good mid-way motor is the 1500cc Bug produced from 1966 to 1970. It's old enough to be a classic, fast enough to keep up and still pure in design.
- The body's the Beetle's bug, though. Although the wings bolt on and virtually every body panel is available, there are a lot of Beetle bodywork bodgers. Check very closely where the body attaches to the floorpan, just behind the front wheels and immediately ahead of the rear wheels: severe rust here can make the vehicle unsafe.

◄ **1962 Volkswagen Microbus,** 1192cc, flat-4 engine, 40bhp, 4-speed manual gearbox, 4-wheel hydraulic drum brakes, Safari windows, original luggage rack, tip-out windscreens, California roof, completely restored, finished in sky blue with a white roof.
£15,000–18,000 **RM**

Source Code
refers to the 'Key to Illustrations' on page 330 which lists the details of where the item was photographed, and whether a dealer or auction house. Advertisers are also indicated on this page.

Miller's Starter Marque
refers to selected marques that offer affordable, reliable and interesting classic motoring.

Information Box
covers relevant information on marques, designers, racing drivers and special events.

VOLKSWAGEN Model	ENGINE cc/cyl	DATES	CONDITION 1	2	3
Beetle (split rear window)	1131/4	1945–53	£5,000	£3,500	£2,000
Beetle (oval rear window)	1192/4	1953–57	£4,000	£2,000	£1,000
Beetle (sloping headlamps)	1192/4	1957–68	£2,500	£1,000	£600
Beetle Cabriolet	1192/4	1954–60	£6,000	£4,500	£2,000
Beetle 1500	1493/4	1966–70	£3,000	£2,000	£1,000
Beetle 1302 LS	1600/4	1970–72	£2,500	£1,850	£850
Beetle 1303 S	1600/4	1972–79	£3,000	£2,000	£1,500
1500 Variant/1600	1493/				
	1584/4	1961–73	£2,000	£1,500	£650
1500/1600	1493/				
	1584/4	1961–73	£3,000	£2,000	£800
Karmann Ghia/I	1192/4	1955–59	£5,000	£3,000	£1,000
Karmann Ghia/I DHC	1192/4	1957–59	£8,000	£5,000	£3,500
Karmann Ghia/I	1192/4	1960–74	£5,500	£3,000	£1,800
Karmann Ghia/I DHC	1192/4	1960–74	£7,000	£4,500	£2,000
Karmann Ghia/3	1493/4	1962–69	£4,000	£2,500	£1,250

VOLKSWAGEN 259

Price Guide
these are worked out by a team of trade and auction house experts, and are based on actual prices realised. Remember that Miller's is a PRICE GUIDE not a PRICE LIST and prices are affected by many variables such as location, condition, desirability and so on. Don't forget that if you are selling it is quite likely you will be offered less than the price range. Price ranges for items sold at auction include the buyer's premium.

Price Boxes
give the value of a particular model, dependent on condition and are compiled by our team of experts, car clubs and private collectors.
Condition 1 refers to a vehicle in top class condition, but not concours d'élégance standard, either fully restored or in very good original condition.
Condition 2 refers to a good, clean roadworthy vehicle, both mechanically and bodily sound.
Condition 3 refers to a runner, but in need of attention, probably to both bodywork and mechanics. It must have a current MOT.
Restoration projects are vehicles that fail to make the Condition 3 grading.

11

Foreword

S ome people are kind enough to say that every handbuilt Morgan that emerges from our works in Malvern is an 'instant classic'. Certainly it cannot be denied that tradition means a great deal to us and we're thankful that it is also valued by our discerning customers, who appreciate the unique qualities of our cars and are prepared to wait patiently as their new car is handcrafted to suit their individual tastes and driving needs. However, although we cherish tradition, I also like to think that we are not stuck in the past. Motoring has to move with the times and so do Morgans. One thing that's rarely mentioned about our cars, but of which we are quietly proud, is that 35 new Morgans now put out the same amount of carbon monoxide as one did ten years ago. I like to think we take our social and ecological responsibilities very seriously, and in some ways are even taking a lead. For example, nothing cleans the air better than a 30-year-old tree, and we need to keep planting new trees to furnish the raw materials for our ash-framed cars. Also, as you read this, we are poised to enter one of the most exciting phases in the company's history with the new Aero 8, which blends the traditional with thoroughly modern practices, including a race-derived aluminium tub. With a history dating back over 90 years, Morgan is one of the longest-established motor manufacturers in the world. A browse through the *Miller's Collectors Cars Price Guide* charts a fascinating story of marques that have grown to greatness and others that have wilted and faded away. It's the story of the first full motoring century, and who can say whether the motor car will survive another? In the meantime, though, we should appreciate what we have, for at our fingertips is a kaleidoscopic variety of motoring choices. It's my hope that this edition of *Miller's Collectors Cars Price Guide* will help some of you make that choice to drive the past into the future and keep it alive – lest we forget.

Charles Morgan

State of the Market

The past 12 months have seen some important changes in the auction scene, some of them exciting and some rather sad. After 35 years, Sotheby's has closed its London-based car department, although the company has formed an alliance with Paris-based Poulain le Fur, and several sales have been held in France. Coy's has also announced that it is relinquishing its sponsorship and auction at the Silverstone Historic Festival after the 2000 event, and Brooks will officiate in future.

Christie's held a few select sales in the UK, but its results at Pebble Beach, Tarrytown (New York) and at the Petersen Museum in Los Angeles have helped to make it one of the strongest auction houses in the USA. Significantly its competitor, Kruse, was sold to eBay, the Internet auction group, and both in the UK and USA there has been increased Internet auction activity.

Among the provincial auctioneers, H & H in Buxton continues to do well, consistently turning in results around the 70 per cent sold mark, and had a marvellous result with the ex-Rob Walker Lotus 49, realising £367,500. Newcomer Barons, at Sandown Park, is beginning to make good headway, its most recent sale topping £100,000. In Southend, Purely Classics has made a good start, holding regular sales and catering for the lower end of the market, while BCA (formerly ADT) has continued to hold satisfactory sales at Blackbushe and its purpose-built venues, again catering mainly for lower-priced classics.

Brooks' Summer Vintage sale at Beaulieu in July 1999 topped £1 million, and Coy's at Silverstone achieved several six-figure sums, including the £286,725 paid for the ex-James Cagney 1957 Ferrari California 250 Spyder. Brooks was back at Nürburgring with a sale that nudged £1 million in August 1999, and also consolidated its position in the USA with its second major sale at Quail Lodge, California, which totalled approximately $10 million. Highlights included the £1.2 million paid for the 1952 works Mercedes-Benz 300SL coupé, which won that year's Le Mans race, while the £837,025 paid for a 1938 Delahaye 135M Competition model must be some kind of record.

Christie's Pebble Beach sale did well, totalling £11,340,000, of which £2,565,675 was accounted for by the 1937 Alfa Romeo 8C 2900 B cabriolet, while 27 other vehicles exceeded £60,000 each.

Echoing the success of its sales at Beaulieu Autojumble, Brooks held a sale during Hershey week in Pennsylvania in October 1999, at which a 1959 BMW 507 brought £161,515, three other cars topped six-figure dollar prices, and 85 per cent of 350 lots of automobilia found buyers. Brooks was also back at Earl's Court during Motor Show week with a series of sales that topped £1.23 million. Highest price was the £85,100 paid for the Cord 810 of Led Zeppelin's Jimmy Page. Christie's has held some excellent selective sales at Nine Elms in London, and in its November 1999 event achieved £1,706,500 for the 1956 ex-Ecurie Ecosse, Le Mans-winning Jaguar D-Type.

Coy's 'True Greats' sale in November 1999 achieved some notable prices, including £504,638 for a 1962 Ferrari 250 SWB and £113,513 for a 1964 330 GTO replica. H & H's sale in December totalled £400,000, while Brooks' Olympia sale series totalled £1.7 million, and its popular Ferrari sale at Gstaad in Switzerland topped £5.6 million, with a 1957 Ferrari 250 GT Zagato 'Double Bubble' Berlinetta leading the field at £1,088,340.

Brooks' Monaco 2000 total was £4.25 million during the Historic Grand Prix weekend. Poulain le Fur and Barrett Jackson/Coys also held sales during Grand Prix week.

In the UK, BCA, Barons and H & H held successful sales in the early part of 2000, and Brooks took over Sotheby's old slot at the RAF Museum, Hendon, in February for a record £800,000 sale for that time of year.

A new innovation for Brooks was an Aston Martin sale held at the Newport Pagnell factory, which topped £2 million, while its Rolls-Royce sale, held in conjunction with the RREC annual concours at Towcester, also saw a high percentage of sales. A 1913 Rolls-Royce Silver Ghost made £159,900 and a Phantom 1 Barker tourer £139,000. Coy's was back at its prestigious Chiswick house venue in May and achieved six-figure sums on several cars, including a 1955 Mercedes-Benz 300SL Gullwing at £105,000.

Dealers report good business generally, with overseas buyers forming quite a high proportion, despite the strong pound. Prices are quite firm and not fluctuating, but interest is slightly higher perhaps than a couple of years ago.

As if to underline the buoyant state of the market at the moment, Brooks' sale at the Goodwood Festival of Speed in June 2000 totalled an excellent £3.2 million, with the 1997 McLaren F1 GTR Longtail Coupé (the World GT Championship car) highest seller at £276,500, closely followed at £271,000 by the ex-Bruce McLaren 1961 3.8-litre E-Type Jaguar Competition model. Ferraris are still strong too, a 1990 F40 Berlinetta making £159,000, followed closely by the ex-Tom Walkinshaw Racing 1990 Jaguar XJR II at £150,000. At a more down-to-earth level, it was encouraging to see a 1948 MG TC Midget making £13,500 plus premium – the T-series cars have been in the doldrums a bit – while a very good 1966 Mk II Jaguar 3.8 manual with overdrive, chrome wire wheels and Harvey Bailey handling kit justified its £21,500.

Signs that the Japanese recession is easing were evidenced by Japanese buyers at Goodwood, and private buyers are generally on the increase. There are no indications that this present state of the market is likely to alter in the near future.

Malcolm Barber

A Golden Age

Phew, we made it! This time last year, the British classic-car community was becoming jittery about the impending disappearance of leaded fuel. As the world celebrated the new millennium, it was also the dawn of a new lead-free age as leaded petrol was removed from forecourt petrol pumps.

What happened next? Well, not a lot, really. The world carried on and so did our classic cars. After the holidays, when it came time for the first post-millennium top up, cars that could stomach unleaded did, and those that couldn't filled up with lead-replacement petrol (LRP). In fact, leaded petrol didn't quite disappear, because a few independent retailers were given dispensation to supply a trickle of the leaded stuff. And that was that. The wheels of the classic car world kept turning and, although there was little to mark the occasion, motoring celebrated the end of its first full century.

Whatever your thoughts on the motor car – and if you're reading this I'm guessing you're a fan – there can be no denying that the internal-combustion engine was the greatest instrument of social change in the 20th century.

Consider this. It was only a little over a century ago that the very few motor cars on Britain's roads were restricted to 2mph in built-up areas and 4mph in open country. Then, in 1896, the law was changed in a piece of legislation termed by intrepid automobilists of the day as the 'Emancipation Act' and Britain's horseless-carriage age was unleashed to gallop along at a heady 12mph. Just over a century later, in 1997, RAF Squadron Leader Andy Green drove Richard Noble's Thrust SSC to set a new land-speed record of 763.035mph.

And now where are we? Almost back where we began, because traffic in London now travels at an average speed of 10mph, not just in the rush hours, but throughout the day. And that is actually slower than in the early years of the 20th century, when horses were the predominant means of travel. In some ways, the motor car has become a victim of its own success, for back in 1904 there were fewer than 29,000 cars on Britain's roads. Today there are around 23 million, and some informed estimates suggest that the figure will rise to more than 33 million by the year 2031.

It's possible that the great revolution created by the motor car is beginning to run out of steam, that the pace of change effected by the internal-combustion engine is slowing down, perhaps even going into reverse. Back in 1890, the average distance a Briton travelled from his home in a year was 13 miles. A century later, that was the average distance of the daily commute, with most of those 13 miles covered in the motor car. Now, though, there's another shift, with increasing numbers of people avoiding commuting altogether, thanks to modern electronic communications.

As for the good old internal-combustion engine, its days are surely numbered in mass transport. At current rates of consumption, fossil fuels would run dry somewhere around 2050. But the reality is that not only are cars becoming more fuel efficient, but also more reserves of oil are being discovered. Strangely, though, the end of fossil fuels is a kind of non-issue. As one expert put it to me, 'The stone age didn't end because we ran out of stone and you could say the same about oil.'

In other words, long before the world's oil reserves dwindle to critical levels, we will have moved on to other power sources. In fact it's happening already. Honda's 'tomorrow-car-today' is the Insight coupé, which has hybrid drive from an internal-combustion engine and an electric motor. Just a few years down the line, Daimler Chrysler is promising the NECAR 4, based on an A-Class Mercedes-Benz powered by a liquid-hydrogen fuel cell, which mixes the hydrogen with oxygen across a catalytic surface to produce electrical energy and pure water as the only emission.

There are other things going on that should also command your attention. Have you noticed that the world's ultimate sports cars are actually becoming slower. These days, in an act of collective responsibility, quite a few manufacturers have restricted the top speed of their top-flight models to 155mph. That will be the limit imposed by BMW on the £86,000 Z8. Now if you look at the Jaguar section of this book, for example, you'll see that just a fraction of that amount will buy you an E-Type with a top speed just a few mph shy of that limit.

There's one more vision of the future. In the long term, a lot of motor industry analysts see a shift away from private motor cars to public transport, and if you take that thought to its logical conclusion there may come a day when the only way to enjoy motoring will be in costly private track sessions. And just as it was a century ago, private motoring may once more become a pursuit enjoyed by the privileged few.

These are a few of the reasons why I think the golden age of the motor car is over. For the enthusiast, though, it's a different matter, because at our finger tips we have a rich seam a century deep to mine for our motoring pleasure. That's why *The Miller's Collectors Car Price Guide* exists, to help enthusiasts tap into our world-wide motoring heritage and drive the past into the future. Let's hope that for many of you that journey starts right here. Happy hunting.

Dave Selby

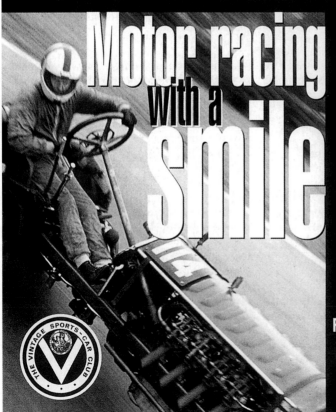

Don't Throw Away A Fortune!
Invest In
Miller's Price Guides

Please send me the following editions

❑ **Miller's Chinese & Japanese Antiques Buyer's Guide** – £19.99
❑ **Miller's Collectables Price Guide 2000/2001** – £17.99
❑ **Miller's Ceramics Buyer's Guide** – £19.99
❑ **Miller's Antiques Price Guide 2001** – £22.99
❑ **Miller's Late Georgian to Edwardian Furniture Buyer's Guide** – £19.99

If you do not wish your name to be used by Miller's or other carefully selected organisations for promotional purposes, please tick this box ❑

I enclose my cheque/postal order for £.................. Please make cheques payable to '*Octopus Publishing Group Ltd*' or please debit my Access/Visa/Amex/Diners Club account number | | | | | | | | | | | | | | | | | Expiry Date............/............

p&p is free in the UK, but please add £3.50 if you are ordering from overseas.

NAME *Title_____ Initial_____ Surname*_____

ADDRESS_____

_____ *Postcode*_____

SIGNATURE_____

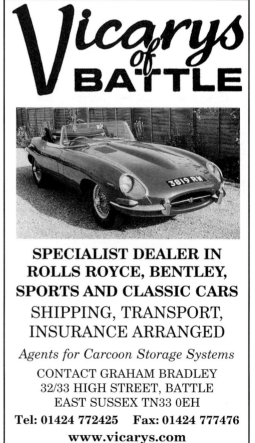

Abarth

◄ **1959 Abarth 750 Berlinetta,** coachwork by Zagato, restored 1991–92, finished in red, original black interior, running gear in excellent condition.
£14,000–16,000 BKS

In the late 1950s, small-capacity Abarths racked up win after win and among them was the pretty Abarth 750 Zagato. The stroke of genius was its distinctive 'double bubble' roof, which gave the driver and passenger adequate headroom without the penalty of a tall windscreen. The 750 was based on the chassis of the Abarth Fiat 600, but the customer had so much choice of specification, including engines, that it is rare to find two identical cars.

▶ **1961 Abarth 750 Berlinetta,** coachwork by Zagato, left-hand drive, completely restored 1993, finished in red, black upholstery.
£11,000–13,000 BKS

In 1960, the organisers of the Sebring 12-hour race added a four-hour race for cars up to 1 litre. It was the first endurance race for such cars and attracted a large entry, including a special Austin-Healey Sprite driven by Stirling Moss. It was won by a private Abarth 750 driven by an amateur team. The Sebring race was run four times in all, and on every occasion an Abarth won.

AC

For some enthusiasts, the legend and myth of the awesome Anglo-American Cobra eclipses all ACs before or since. Certainly the company had come a long way since 1907, when it had produced its first utility vehicles under the company name Auto-Carriers. After WW1, ACs began to take on a sporting character, and in 1922 an AC became the first 1500cc car to cover 100 miles in one hour. After 1945, ACs continued to appeal to discerning and necessarily well-healed sporting drivers, but the car that really brought the company to wider notice was the lovely Ace of 1954, which American racer Carroll Shelby transformed into the fearsome Cobra. Although the first incarnation of the Cobra expired in 1968, its legend has given rise to a later series of 'continuation' Cobras and spawned a thriving kit-car industry producing 'fake-snakes', as the pretenders are termed by those who are lucky enough to own the real thing.

◄ **1939 AC 16/60 Ace 2–4–6 Coupé,** 1991cc, 6-cylinder engine, synchromesh gearbox, underslung chassis, top-hinged conventional boot in place of dickey, sunroof, good condition.
£18,500–21,000 BKS

Fewer than 600 post-1933 standard 16hp cars are thought to have been built before production ended in 1939. The 2–4–6 Coupé was so named because it could carry two passengers in the front, two on a hammock back seat, which could be rolled up to admit luggage, and two in the dickey.

AC Model	ENGINE cc/cyl	DATES	CONDITION 1	2	3
Sociable	636/1	1907–12	£10,500	£9,000	£4,500
12/24 (Anzani)	1498/4	1919–27	£14,000	£11,500	£7,500
16/40	1991/6	1920–28	£18,000	£15,000	£11,000
16/60 Drophead/Saloon	1991/6	1937–40	£24,000	£21,000	£15,500
16/70 Sports Tourer	1991/6	1937–40	£35,000	£26,000	£18,000
16/80 Competition 2-Seater	1991/6	1937–40	£55,000	£45,000	£35,000

AC Model	ENGINE cc/cyl	DATES	CONDITION 1	2	3
2 litre	1991/6	1947–55	£7,000	£4,000	£1,500
Buckland	1991/6	1949–54	£8,500	£5,500	£2,500
Ace	1991/6	1953–63	£30,000	£25,000	£18,000
Ace Bristol	1971/6	1954–63	£45,000	£30,000	£25,000
Ace 2.6	1553/6	1961–62	£38,000	£32,000	£29,000
Aceca	1991/6	1954–63	£22,000	£16,000	£11,000
Aceca Bristol	1971/6	1956–63	£28,000	£20,000	£12,000
Greyhound Bristol	1971/6	1961–63	£16,000	£12,000	£8,000
Cobra Mk II 289	4735/8	1963–64	£90,000	£80,000	£60,000
Cobra Mk III 427	6998/8	1965–67	£125,000	£100,000	£80,000
Cobra Mk IV	5340/8	1987–	£55,000	£40,000	£28,000
428 Frua	7014/8	1967–73	£19,000	£15,000	£10,000
428 Frua Convertible	7014/8	1967–73	£28,000	£20,000	£16,000
3000 ME	2994/6	1976–84	£15,000	£10,000	£8,000

Racing history for Cobra will put the price to £100,000–120,000+.

1954 AC Aceca-Bristol, original AC engine replaced by more powerful Bristol unit, brakes rebuilt, resprayed, new tan leather interior, very good condition apart from noisy gearbox.
£13,000–15,000 BKS

The Aceca was essentially a fastback coupé version of the AC Ace and shared the latter's race-bred chassis. The Ace/Aceca's story began when John Tojeiro built an MG-engined special for racing. A fellow enthusiast saw the twin-tube chassis with its all-independent suspension and made him an offer he couldn't refuse. Tojeiro never did become a racing driver, but became a constructor instead. One of his customers, Cliff Davis, fitted a Bristol engine and had a bodyshop create a copy of Touring's Ferrari 166 *barchetta* body. This impressed AC Cars, who put it into production as the Ace, using AC's 1991cc straight-six engine.

◄ **1961 AC Aceca-Ford,** 6-cylinder Ford Zephyr engine, triple Weber carburettors, 170bhp, c140mph top speed, recently restored, top end overhauled, new carburettors, exhaust, starter motor and radiator, finished in British Racing green, interior in need of some cosmetic attention.
£19,000–21,000 COYS

► **1962 AC Greyhound,** 1991cc, 4-speed manual gearbox, overdrive on 2nd, 3rd and top gears, front disc brakes, Alfin rear drums, bare-metal respray 1996, finished in metallic green, chrome wire wheels, stainless steel exhaust system, original grey leather interior trim in very good condition, 1 of only 6 examples with AC 6-cylinder engine, original condition.
£11,000–13,000 H&H

1958 AC Ace-Bristol, completely restored 1990, bare-metal respray in Rolls Royce silver, reupholstered in black hide, new weather equipment including tonneau and sidescreens, 2,000 miles covered since 1993.
£48,000–53,000 COYS

When new, this particular car was raced in SCCA Production Class events in the hands of Dick Hayes and Dick Schraeder.

AC Cobra (1962–68)

Engine: V8, 289cu.in (4727cc); 427cu.in (6997cc).
Power output: 289, 271–370bhp; 427, 355–425bhp.
Transmission: Four-speed manual.
Brakes: Discs all-round.
Top speed: 289, 136+mph; 427, 165mph.
0–60mph: 289, 5.2–5.5 seconds; 427, 4.2 seconds.
Production: Estimates vary from 560 to 580 for the 289 model, and 316 to 510 for the 427.

The story of the AC Cobra began in Surrey in 1954, with the launch of AC's neat, lean and agile Ace, an expensive, bespoke sports car powered by a rather vintage six-cylinder unit. In 1962, American Carroll Shelby gave it a massive shot of steroids, pumping up the chassis, suspension, brakes and aluminium

body to cope with a series of fire-breathing Ford V8s. The first 75 cars used 4.2 litre engines, then grew to 4.7 litres to create the 289 – the engine's capacity in cubic inches. Performance figures were shattering, but still Shelby wanted more, and in an attempt to achieve his goal of winning Le Mans, he squeezed in a stonking 7 litre V8 and beefed up the chassis even more to create the Cobra 427. It never did win Le Mans, but competition Cobras won races in other categories all over the world, and on the streets the car, marketed as 'the fastest production car ever sold to the public' was – and still is – just about the loudest, proudest, most raucous and primal four-wheeled projectile around.

◀ **1963 AC Cobra Mk II,** 4727cc Ford V8 engine, 4-speed manual gearbox, 4-wheel disc brakes, completely restored, finished in red with white racing stripe, black interior trim, roll bar, racing harnesses, history file, original, excellent condition throughout.
£70,000–77,000 COYS

1965 AC Cobra, 4.7 litre Ford V8 engine, 330bhp, lightweight aluminium body, 4-wheel disc brakes, 165mph top speed.
£80,000–90,000 HMM

1986 AC 3000 ME, 3000cc Ford V6 engine, 5-speed manual gearbox, finished in red, black interior trim, wheels in need of repolishing, 550 miles recorded, unregistered.
£9,000–10,500 H&H

Alfa Romeo

The Milanese company began life in 1909 as ALFA (*Anonima Lombardo Fabbrica Automibili*), produced its first cars in 1910 and became Alfa Romeo when industrialist Nicolo Romeo took control in 1915. In the 1920s, Alfa Romeo produced some exquisite sporting machines and dominated Grand Prix racing for a decade, before being overwhelmed by the might of the Mercedes and Auto Union teams in the mid-1930s. Post-1945 Alfas became more accessible and many models from the 1960s onward have sometimes been tagged 'poor man's Ferraris'. That may sound like a put-down, but it should be regarded as a compliment – albeit a little backhanded – for there are very few poor-handling Alfa Romeos, and most have all the characteristics to engage keen drivers with their lithe, lean and sure-footed agility.

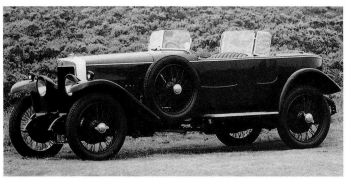

1925 Alfa Romeo 22/90 RLSS (Super Sport) Four-Seater Boat-Tail Tourer, coachwork by Thornton Engineering, 2996cc, 6-cylinder engine, dry-sump lubrication, twin carburettors, Dewandre vacuum servo-assisted braking, restored, finished in maroon over black, black leather upholstery and weather equipment, very good condition.
£47,000–55,000 BKS

A late 1920s Alfa Romeo dealer shield, only given to the most successful dealers, few pre-war examples known to survive, excellent condition.
£3,500–4,250 BKS

1929 Alfa Romeo Gran Tourismo 17/75, 1750cc, double overhead camshafts, supercharged, 85bhp, 95mph top speed.
£80,000–90,000 HMM

A known continuous history can add value to and enhance the enjoyment of a car.

1932 Alfa Romeo 8C 2300 Cabriolet, coachwork by Pinin Farina, 2336cc, 8-cylinder inline engine, double overhead camshafts, Roots-type supercharger, 140+bhp, 4-speed manual gearbox, 4-wheel drum brakes, 1 of only 47 8C 2300s built in 1932, 1 owner for 42 years, good condition.
£500,000+ BKS

This particular car's Pinin Farina *due posti* cabriolet coachwork appears to date from 1937–39, making it a later modification upon the original (and then still much admired) 1932 mechanicals.

ALFA ROMEO Model	ENGINE cc/cyl	DATES	CONDITION 1	2	3
24HP	4084/4	1910–11	£25,000	£16,000	£12,000
12HP	2413/4	1910–11	£18,000	£11,000	£8,000
40–60	6028/4	1913–15	£32,000	£24,000	£14,000
RL	2916/6	1921–22	£30,000	£24,000	£14,000
RM	1944/4	1924–25	£28,000	£17,000	£13,000
6C 1500	1487/6	1927–28	£50,000*	£20,000+	£10,000+
6C 1750	1752/6	1923–33	£100,000+	£80,000+	
6C 1900	1917/6	1933	£18,000	£15,000	£12,000
6C 2300	2309/6	1934	£30,000+	£18,000	£15,000
6C 2500 SS Cabriolet/Spider	2443/6	1939–45	£100,000	£50,000	£40,000
6C 2500 SS Coupé	2443/6	1939–45	£60,000	£40,000	£30,000
8C 2300 Monza/Short Chassis	2300/8	1931–34	£1,000,000+	£400,000+	£200,000
8C 2900	2900/8	1935–39	£1,500,000	£1,000,000	-

Value is very dependent on sporting history, body style and engine type.
*The high price of this model is dependent on whether it is 1500 supercharged/twin overhead cam, and with or without a racing history.

ALFA ROMEO Model	ENGINE cc/cyl	DATES	CONDITION 1	2	3
2000 Spider	1974/4	1958–61	£14,000	£9,000	£4,000
2600 Sprint	2584/6	1962–66	£11,000	£7,500	£4,000
2600 Spider	2584/6	1962–65	£13,000	£8,000	£5,000
Giulietta Sprint	1290/4	1955–62	£10,000	£7,000	£4,000
Giulietta Spider	1290/4	1956–62	£12,000	£6,000	£4,500
Giulia Saloon	1570/4	1962–72	£5,000	£3,000	£1,500
Giulia Sprint (rhd)	1570/4	1962–68	£10,500	£6,000	£2,000
Giulia Spider (rhd)	1570/4	1962–65	£11,000	£8,000	£4,000
Giulia SS	1570/4	1962–66	£16,000	£11,000	£5,000
GT 1300 Junior	1290/4	1966–77	£7,000	£5,500	£2,000
Giulia Sprint GT	1570/4	1962–68	£7,500	£5,000	£2,000
1600GT Junior	1570/4	1972–75	£7,000	£4,000	£2,000
1750/2000 Berlina	1779/ 1962/4	1967–77	£4,000	£2,000	£1,000
1750GTV	1779/4	1967–72	£7,000	£6,000	£2,000
2000GTV	1962/4	1971–77	£6,500	£4,000	£2,000
1600/1750 (Duetto)	1570/ 1779/4	1966–67	£10,000	£7,500	£5,000
1750/2000 Spider (Kamm)	1779/ 1962/4	1967–78	£9,000	£6,000	£3,000
Montreal	2593/8	1970–77	£10,000	£8,000	£5,000
Junior Zagato 1300	1290/4	1968–74	£7,000	£5,000	£3,000
Junior Zagato 1600	1570/4	1968–74	£8,000	£6,000	£4,000
Alfetta GT/GTV (chrome)	1962/4	1972–86	£4,000	£2,500	£1,000
Alfasud	1186/ 1490/4	1972–83	£2,000	£1,000	£500
Alfasud ti	1186/ 1490/4	1974–81	£2,500	£1,200	£900
Alfasud Sprint	1284/ 1490/4	1976–85	£3,000	£2,000	£1,000
GTV6	2492/6	1981–	£4,000	£2,500	£1,000

1934 Alfa Romeo 6C 2300 Gran Turismo Drophead Coupé, 4-seater coachwork by Pinin Farina, 2309cc, double-overhead-camshaft, 6-cylinder engine, 76bhp, supplied with a new cylinder head and valve gear (not fitted), history file, little use since 1965.
£40,000–45,000 BKS

First registered in England in 1939, this Gran Turismo was acquired almost by accident in 1965 by a previous owner who visited his local scrapyard to buy a battery and came away with the Alfa and a Delage 6/70 as well.

1961 Alfa Romeo Giulietta SZ Coupé, coachwork by Zagato, engine rebuilt, new clutch and fuel pump, bare-metal respray in dark blue with yellow centre stripe, well maintained.
£29,000–33,000 BKS

Alfa Romeo launched the Giuletta range in 1954 and, from the beginning, it was a runaway success. The standard Giulietta won races and rallies. By 1960, however, it was facing stiffer competition, so Alfa commissioned Zagato to build a lightweight aerodynamic version. The short-chassis Sprint Zagato (SZ) was pared to the bone and tipped the scales at only 785kg which, together with a tuned engine, helped it to a top speed of over 125mph.

1954 Alfa Romeo 1900 Super Sprint Coupé, coachwork by Touring, 1975cc, double-overhead-camshaft, tuned replacement engine, 115bhp, independent front suspension, excellent condition throughout.
£25,000–28,000 BKS

Alfa Romeo's first all-new offering of the post-war era, the 1900, was also the first Alfa to employ unitary construction.

1963 Alfa Romeo Giulia Spider, 1570cc, 4-cylinder, double-overhead-camshaft engine, 92bhp, 5-speed gearbox, independent front suspension, 109mph top speed, restored, finished in blue, good condition.
£9,500–11,000 Pou

1964 Alfa Romeo 2600 Spider, 2584cc, steering
and brakes overhauled, finished in red, chip on bonnet,
driver's door resprayed, reupholstered in black leather
1988, otherwise original, 63,700 miles recorded,
1 of only 103 right-hand-drive examples built.
£8,500–10,500 H&H

1965 Alfa Romeo Giulia SS, coachwork by Bertone,
1574cc, 4-cylinder engine, finished in red,
good condition.
£17,000–20,000 LOM

1966 Alfa Romeo 2600 SZ Coupé, coachwork by Zagato, 2584cc, double-overhead-camshaft, 6-cylinder engine,
145bhp, 5-speed gearbox, servo-assisted 4-wheel disc brakes, completely restored 1992, finished in white,
original alloy wheels, dark red leather upholstery, very good condition throughout.
£21,000–24,000 BKS

1973 Alfa Romeo Montreal Coupé, coachwork by Bertone, 2593cc, double-overhead-camshaft, fuel-injected V8,
200bhp, 5-speed ZF gearbox, 0–60mph in 7.6 seconds, 137mph top speed, engine rebuilt 1991, 620 miles covered
since, finished in white, grey cloth upholstery, bodywork good, interior very good, excellent mechanical condition.
£5,000–6,000 BKS

The Montreal came about when Alfa Romeo was asked to build a car for Canada's Expo '67 to represent
all that was best in the automotive industry. It was a superb car, with attractive styling and a motor racing
pedigree, and it should have sold well. However, Alfa Romeo did virtually nothing to promote it, and in the
end a mere 3,925 were made between 1971 and 1977.

Alfa Romeo Montreal (1970–77)

Engine: Double-overhead-camshaft V8, 2593cc.
Power output: 200bhp at 6,550 rpm.
Transmission: Five-speed ZF manual gearbox.
Brakes: Servo-assisted ventilated discs all-round.

Top speed: 137mph.
0–60mph: 7.5 seconds.
Production: 3,925.
Price in 1972: £5,077 (£800 less than BMW 3.0CSi).

1973 Alfa Romeo Junior Z Coupé, coachwork by Zagato, 1570cc, double-overhead-camshaft engine, 109bhp, 5-speed gearbox, 4-wheel disc brakes, 118mph top speed, finished in blue, tan upholstery, 1 of only 402 made, good condition throughout.
£6,500–8,000 BKS

The Alfa Romeo Junior was a lively performer even as a standard four-seat saloon. When fitted with Zagato's lightweight, two-seat coupé bodywork, it was much more nimble and responsive.

1967 Alfa Romeo 1600 Spider Duetto Cabriolet, 1570cc, double-overhead-camshaft, 4-cylinder engine, twin carburettors, 5-speed gearbox, finished in red.
£3,750–4,500 Pou

When the new Spider was first seen at the Geneva motor show in 1966, Alfa launched a competition to name the car. After ploughing through 140,000 entries with suggestions like Lollobrigida, Bardot and Nuvolari, they chose Duetto, which neatly summed up the two's-company-three's-a-crowd image.

1968 Alfa Romeo Duetto Spider, 1750cc, 4-cylinder engine, factory hardtop, finished in white, black interior, new carpets, soft top in need of renewal, otherwise good condition.
£5,000–6,000 BRIT

Perspex headlamp covers give smoother airflow and raise top speed a little. However, they were banned in the USA.

Miller's Starter Marque

Starter Alfa Romeos: *1750 and 2000 GTV; 1300 Junior Spider, 1600 Duetto Spider, 1750 and 2000 Spider Veloce; 1300 and 1600 GT Junior; Alfasud ti & Sprint.*

- Responsive, eager and sweet twin-cam engines, finely-balanced chassis, nimble handling and delightful looks are just some of the character traits of classic Alfas from the mid-1960s onward. They are also eminently affordable. For the kind of money that gets you an MGB or TR Triumph, you could be a little more adventurous and acquire an engaging Alfa Romeo sporting saloon or convertible.
- That's the good news; the bad news is that the unfortunate reputation Alfas of the 1960s and 1970s earned for rusting was deserved.
Even that has its up-side, because the suspicion still lingers and helps keep prices comparatively low. In fact, most of the Alfas you will be looking at now will have had major surgery at least once, so you should be able to find one with plenty of metal. Even so, take a magnet along.
Classic Alfa owners – or *Alfisti* as they prefer to call themselves – have a saying: you pay for the engineering and the engine, but the body comes free. Bear in mind too that maintenance costs are likely to be pricier than those of an MG or Triumph TR.

Auction prices

Miller's only includes cars declared sold. Our guide prices take into account the buyer's premium, VAT on the premium, and the extent of any published catalogue information relating to condition and provenance. To identify cars sold at auction, cross-refer the source codes at the ends of photo captions with the Key to Illustrations on page 330.

1968 Alfa Romeo Spider, 1750cc, double-overhead-camshaft, 4-cylinder engine, 5-speed gearbox, 125mph top speed.
£8,000–10,000 HMM

Originally, Spiders were only offered in red and white; 4,672 were made for the UK market.

▶ **1974 Alfa Romeo Spider 2000,** 1962cc, double-overhead-camshaft engine, Spica fuel injection, Montreal-style alloy wheels, US export model, left-hand drive, new floorpans and sills, finished in silver.
£3,500–4,000 BARO

The Kamm-tail Spyder was introduced in 1967 and went on to 1978, taking over from the boat-tailed Duetto.

1984 Alfa Romeo Spider Mk III LS, coachwork by Pininfarina, alloy wheels, finished in red, beige interior.
£10,000–12,000 LOM

▶ **1986 Alfa Romeo Spider Mk III LS,** coachwork by Pininfarina, alloy wheels, finished in red, beige interior.
£14,000–16,000 LOM

The Alfa Romeo Spider has enjoyed a cult following ever since one was driven by Dustin Hoffman to the strains of Simon and Garfunkel in the film The Graduate.

◀ **1989 Alfa Romeo Spider,** 1962cc, double-overhead-camshaft, 4-cylinder engine, finished in white, black interior, excellent condition throughout.
£6,000–7,000 BRIT

1991 Alfa Romeo Spider S4 2000, coachwork by Pininfarina, 1962cc, finished in red, beige interior.
£11,000–13,000 **LOM**

1983 Alfa Romeo Alfetta 2000 GTV, finished in red, black interior, good condition.
£4,000–4,500 **LOM**

1986 Alfa Romeo GTV 6, alloy wheels, finished in red, cream interior.
£8,500–9,500 **LOM**

1991 Alfa Romeo SZ 'Double Bubble' Coupé, coachwork by Zagato, supercharged engine, 320bhp, rebuilt with 'double bubble' roof, smoothed bodywork and revised air intakes, Tecnomagnesio wheels, finished in Zagato blue, tan leather interior, 15,000km recorded, minor fibreglass stress marks, otherwise excellent condition throughout.
£22,000–25,000 **BKS**

Reviving its tradition of building special-bodied Alfa Romeos, Zagato unveiled the SZ in 1989. The aggressive-looking two-seater eschewed Zagato's traditional smoothly rounded styling and aluminium coachwork in favour of an angular shell in lightweight fibreglass. Race-developed suspension endowed the SZ with superlative handling and roadholding, while its very respectable 243km/h top speed was achieved courtesy of a 206bhp version of Alfa's 3 litre V6.

1991 Alfa Romeo SZ Coupé, coachwork by Zagato, 3 litre, double-overhead-camshaft V6 engine, 206bhp, 243km/h top speed, finished in red, Havana leather interior, 2,200km recorded, excellent condition throughout.
£19,000–23,000 **BKS**

Allard

Long before he became a car maker in his own right, Sydney Herbert Allard had built up a wealth of valuable experience by competing widely in various forms of motorsport. At the age of 19, in 1929, he was already racing three-wheeled Morgans and selling cars at his family's south London Ford dealership. In the 1930s, he was a major force in trials and hillclimbs, and by 1936 he had built his first Allard special, based on a Ford V8 chassis with a sparse body that even included bits of a Bugatti Type 57. These early specials developed into the big, hairy-chested sports cars that were the company's staple offerings, but were produced only in limited numbers. Sydney Allard drove his own creations to win the 1949 British Hillclimb Championship and the 1952 Monte Carlo Rally.

◀ **1947 Allard K1,** Ford sidevalve V8 engine, restored, good condition.
£22,000–25,000 HMM

This particular car is the only surviving works rally K1 and also the only good K1 known to exist in a state other than completely rebuilt. It was the blue car of the red, white and blue team entered in the 1947 Alpine Rally, and came fifth in the hands of Leonard Potter.

1950 Allard J2, 5.4 litre Cadillac V8 engine, 160bhp, 3-speed close-ratio gearbox, hydraulic Alfin drum brakes, mounted inboard at the rear, finished in red, red leather interior, fewer than 10,000 miles recorded.
£70,000–77,000 BKS

Introduced in 1950, the J2 was based on a 100in-wheelbase, box-section chassis with independent front suspension by a split beam axle and transverse leaf spring. At the rear, however, the J2 was the first Allard to use a de Dion rear axle, which was suspended on coil springs, and located by radius arms.

◀ **1951 Allard P1A,** 3622cc, Ford sidevalve V8 engine, gearbox, torque tube and rear axle, box-section chassis, split-axle independent front suspension, transverse leaf springs front and rear, completely restored, finished in Gunmetal grey, new chrome, new grey leather interior.
£8,000–10,000 COYS

The P1 saloon entered production in 1949, some 500 examples being produced between 1949 and 1952. They proved versatile performers, one achieving success on the 1952 Monte Carlo Rally in the hands of Sydney Allard himself.

ALLARD Model	ENGINE cc/cyl	DATES	CONDITION 1	2	3
K/K2/L/M/M2X	3622/8	1947–54	£18,500+	£12,000	£8,000
K3	var/8	1953–54	£24,000	£15,000	£11,000
P1	3622/8	1949–52	£19,500	£13,000	£8,000
P2	3622/8	1952–54	£22,000	£18,000	£11,500
J2/J2X	var/8	1950–54	£60,000+	£50,000	£35,000
Palm Beach	1508/4, 2262/6	1952–55	£12,000	£10,000	£5,500
Palm Beach II	2252/ 3442/6	1956–60	£25,000+	£20,000	£11,000

Alvis

Always sporting in nature, generally elegant and occasionally surprisingly innovative, Alvis trickled along from 1919 to 1966 aloof from the automotive mainstream, producing a select strain of often memorable vehicles. The Coventry company was an early proponent of front-wheel drive, which appeared in 1928 on the 12/75. In the 1930s, the handsome and fast Speed 20 tourers were never so extrovert as to be bold, but were assuredly self-confident. Initially, some early post-war offerings were a little wayward – for example, the whale-like TB14 and TB21 – but perhaps no Alvis models were ever more elegant than the last-of-line TD, TE and TF21, which brought car making to a close when Rover took control in 1966.

1931 Alvis 12/50 TJ Beetleback Sports, 2-seat coachwork by Carbodies, completely overhauled, engine rebuilt, new radiator, rechromed, rewired, gearbox rebuilt, new clutch and propshaft, new dynamo, starter overhauled, finished in green and black, disappearing hood, original steps under the doors, green interior.
£17,000–19,000 BKS

The Alvis 12/50 was officially discontinued in 1929, but reintroduced in September 1930 incorporating lessons learned from its six-cylinder derivative, the Silver Eagle. The revived TJ 12/50 was essentially a touring model, and the lack of a sports version was remedied in March 1931 with the new high-compression TK12/60. This car is believed to be an interim model built before the announcement of the 12/60 with TK-style twin carburettors.

1932 Alvis Firefly Tourer, coachwork by Cross and Ellis, 1496cc, 4-cylinder engine, restored 1989–92, engine rebuilt, all auxiliary components repaired as necessary, clutch renewed, kingpins renewed, new springs, pins and bushes, coachwork rebuilt, all aluminium panels and timber framework renewed as required, retrimmed in red hide, black double-duck weather equipment including tonneau, correct Firefly radiator mascot, fewer than 1,500 miles since restoration, unused since 1996.
£13,500–16,000 BRIT

Continuing the theme established by the legendary 12/50 and 12/60 models, Alvis introduced the Firefly late in 1932. It was of exceptionally sturdy construction, the chassis effectively being a scaled-down version of the contemporary Speed 20. The Firefly was available as a sports tourer, drophead coupé, or four- or six-light saloon. Arguably the most attractive was the Cross and Ellis tourer. In fact, this car began life as a saloon, but was rebodied with Cross and Ellis tourer coachwork in the 1950s.

◀ **1934 Alvis Speed 20 Type SB,** 4-seat coachwork by Martin and King, good condition.
£31,000–34,500 UMC

ALVIS Model	ENGINE cc/cyl	DATES	CONDITION 1	2	3
12/50	1496/4	1923–32	£20,000	£13,000	£7,000
Silver Eagle	2148	1929–37	£16,000	£12,000	£8,000
Silver Eagle DHC	2148	1929–37	£18,000	£13,000	£9,000
12/60	1645/4	1931–32	£15,000	£10,000	£7,000
Speed 20 (tourer)	2511/6	1932–36	£35,000+	£28,000	£18,000
Speed 20 (closed)	2511/6	1932–36	£25,000	£18,000+	£11,000
Crested Eagle	3571/6	1933–39	£10,000	£7,000	£4,000
Firefly (tourer)	1496/4	1932–34	£14,000+	£10,000	£6,000
Firefly (closed)	1496/6	1932–34	£7,000	£5,000	£4,000
Firebird (tourer)	1842/4	1934–39	£13,000	£10,000	£6,000
Firebird (closed)	1842/4	1934–39	£7,000	£5,000	£4,000
Speed 25 (tourer)	3571/6	1936–40	£38,500	£30,000	£20,000
Speed 25 (closed)	3571/6	1936–40	£23,000	£17,000	£12,000
3.5 litre	3571/6	1935–36	£35,000	£25,000	£18,000
4.3 litre	4387/6	1936–40	£44,000	£30,000	£22,000
Silver Crest	2362/6	1936–40	£14,000	£10,000	£7,000
TA	3571/6	1936–39	£18,000	£12,000	£8,000
12/70	1842/4	1937–40	£10,000	£8,000	£6,000

ALVIS Model	ENGINE cc/cyl	DATES	CONDITION 1	2	3
TA14	1892/4	1946–50	£9,500	£8,000	£4,500
TA14 DHC	1892/4	1946–50	£14,000	£11,000	£5,000
TB14 Roadster	1892/4	1949–50	£15,000	£10,000	£8,000
TB21 Roadster	2993/6	1951	£16,000	£10,000	£7,000
TA21/TC21	2993/6	1950–55	£12,000	£9,000	£5,000
TA21/TC21 DHC	2993/6	1950–55	£17,000	£13,000	£10,000
TC21/100 Grey Lady	2993/6	1953–56	£13,000	£11,000	£5,000
TC21/100 DHC	2993/6	1954–56	£19,000	£15,000	£9,000
TD21	2993/6	1956–62	£11,000	£8,000	£4,000
TD21 DHC	2993/6	1956–62	£22,000	£16,000	£10,000
TE21	2993/6	1963–67	£15,000	£10,000	£7,000
TE21 DHC	2993/6	1963–67	£22,000	£16,000	£8,000
TF21	2993/6	1966–67	£16,000	£12,000	£8,000
TF21 DHC	2993/6	1966–67	£28,000	£17,000	£13,000

◄ **1935 Alvis Speed 20 Tourer,** 4-seat coachwork by Vanden Plas, 2762cc, 6-cylinder engine, high-ratio axle, engine rebuilt early 1990s, steering rebuilt, bodywork restored 1980s, finished in British Racing green, double-duck hood, burgundy red interior, excellent condition throughout.
£40,000–44,000 BKS

The Silver Eagle series was superseded in 1932 by the Speed 20, powered by a similar engine. For a car that could reach 90mph, the new model was excellent value at under £700. Its low chassis made it ideal for sporting coachwork, and that built by Vanden Plas was among the finest seen on any 1930s sports car.

1954 Alvis TC21/100 Drophead Coupé, coachwork by Tickford, very original, recent new hood and carpets.
£11,500–13,500 UMC

1950s Alvis Owners' Club car badge, enamel good, 3 x 5in (7.5 x 12.5cm).
£70–80 LE

Alvis TD21, TE21 & TF21 (1958–67)

Engine: Overhead-valve straight-six, 2993cc.
Power output: 103–150bhp.
Transmission: Four-speed manual; five-speed manual from 1962, along with optional automatic.
Brakes: Drums all-round to 1959; then front discs; discs all-round from 1962.
Top speed: 105–120mph.
0-60mph: 11.5–14 seconds.
Production: 1,528.
Prices in 1958: Saloon, £2,993.17s including purchase tax; drophead coupé, £3,293.17s including purchase tax.
Better looking than Bristols – some say – priced on a par with Aston Martins, but less flashy, and with an interior as sumptuous as a Bentley or a Rolls-Royce, Alvis's final flourish was a quintessential understatement of quiet, British establishment old-money confidence. The Duke of Edinburgh owned a TD drophead; actor James Mason also

owned a drophead, while WWII flying ace Douglas Bader had a TD and then a TE. You can't get more British than that, yet the shape actually came from Swiss coachbuilder Hermann Graber, who took an Alvis TC21 chassis and transformed it into a restrained two-door sporting coupé for the 1955 Paris motor show. The result was the very pricey, 100mph, hand-built TC108G, of which only 16 or 17 were made, with bodies produced under licence in the UK. In 1958, Park Ward took over body production and the lightly revised model was named the TD21, evolving gently through the TE to the final TF version. By then, Rover had taken control of Alvis and when, shortly after, Rover was absorbed into British Leyland in 1967 there was no longer a place for anything so individual as an Alvis.
Pick of the bunch: The last-of-the-line TF21; it's the fastest, with triple-carb 150bhp power, all-round disc brakes and other modernities.

1958 Alvis TD21 Saloon, coachwork by Park Ward, 3 litre, 6-cylinder engine, 4-speed manual gearbox, chrome knock-off wire wheels, finished in 2-tone grey, red leather interior trim and upholstery, first example built, unrestored, 38,800 miles recorded, very good original condition.
£6,000–7,000 H&H

1960 Alvis TD21 Series I Drophead Coupé, 6-cylinder, overhead-valve engine, 115bhp, front disc brakes, restored, good condition.
£17,000–20,000 HMM

▶ **1964 Alvis TE21 Saloon,** 2993cc, 6-cylinder engine, manual gearbox, wire wheels, Webasto sunroof, finished in silver, navy leather trim.
£4,000–5,000 BRIT

With the exception of the TA14 of 1946–49, all the post-war offerings from Alvis were powered by the excellent 3 litre engine that first appeared in the TA21 of 1950. The final variants were the TE and TF21 series, distinguishable from the previous TD21 by quadruple headlamps. In all other respects, the styling remained basically unchanged. Production of all Alvis motor cars ceased in 1967.

Amilcar

◀ **1921 Amilcar Type CC Roadster,** 1000cc, 4-cylinder sidevalve engine, 3-speed gearbox, right-hand drive, quarter-elliptic springing, staggered seating, restored 1995, finished in red with black wings, interior retrimmed in black leather.
£5,000–6,000 BKS

The 1920s saw European manufacturers keen to exploit the increasing demand for small sports cars, France's foremost exponents of the *voiturette* being Amilcar and Salmson. Established in Paris, Amilcar introduced its first car, the Type CC, in 1921. It would develop into Types CS and 4C. The successor CGS and CGSS (*Surbaissé*) models helped establish the company's reputation world-wide, but by 1930 Amilcar had turned its attention to touring cars.

Armstrong-Siddeley

1947 Armstrong-Siddeley Hurricane Three-Position Drophead Coupé, 1991cc, 6-cylinder engine, 4-speed manual gearbox, restored, finished in black and yellow, new beige double-duck hood, much brightwork rechromed, new magnolia leather interior.
£10,000–12,000 H&H

1959 Armstrong-Siddeley Star Sapphire, 4 litre, 6-cylinder engine, 1 of only 902 built.
£8,000–10,000 HMM

Aimed at the Jaguar market, the Star Sapphire's engine was claimed to provide matching performance, while the car's handling was said to be equal or better.

Aryathis

1989 Aryathis Cabriolet, 5083cc, Chevrolet V8 engine, fuel injection, twin Garrett turbochargers, electronic ignition, 404bhp, 4-speed automatic transmission, 4-wheel disc brakes, alloy wheels, left-hand drive, finished in Tahitian blue metallic, ivory interior, very good condition throughout.
£13,000–16,000 Pou

Aston Martin

Many people equate Aston Martin's glory years with the heyday of James Bond: those classic years when Bond was Connery and 007 drove a DB Aston. But it was only a few years before silver-screen stardom that Aston Martin was also creating a name for itself in international motor racing with a vigorous works programme that culminated in a Le Mans win, in 1959, for the DBR1. Those dizzy heights were a long way from the day, in 1913, when Robert Bamford and Lionel Martin set up Bamford & Martin Ltd, in London's South Kensington, and set about tuning and developing Singer 10s. In 1919, the first prototype Aston Martins were produced – the name had been inspired by the Aston Clinton Hill Climb and Lionel Martin's surname.

Since then, production has always remained limited, and it was not until 1984 that the 10,000th Aston Martin, a V8 model, was built. For much of its life, Aston Martin's existence has been precarious: it went bankrupt in 1925; then, in 1947, industrialist David Brown took over, heralding the era of the glamorous DB – or David Brown – Astons, which came to full bloom in the 1960s. On the road, the DB4, 5 and 6 models were the stuff of dreams – literally – with a DB4 costing approximately the equivalent of two E-Type Jaguars. Yet the company still struggled financially. In 1972, David Brown gave up the struggle – losses were reckoned at £1 million a year – and after several changes of ownership, the company's future became secure when Ford took over in 1987.

1954 Aston Martin DB2/4 Drophead Coupé, coachwork by Tickford, converted to left-hand drive, restored 1988, suspension, brakes and gearbox overhauled 1991, finished in dark blue, original Azure blue leather upholstery, excellent condition throughout.
£52,000–57,500 BKS

The DB2/4 of 1953 was a more sophisticated version of the DB2 with occasional rear seats. It had a top speed of 120mph and 0–60mph acceleration in 11.1 seconds.

ASTON MARTIN Model	ENGINE cc/cyl	DATES	CONDITION 1	2	3
Lionel Martin Cars	1486/4	1921–25	£26,000+	£18,000	£16,000
International	1486/4	1927–32	£36,000	£20,000	£16,000
Le Mans	1486/4	1932–33	£60,000	£40,000	£32,000
Mk II	1486/4	1934–36	£40,000	£30,000	£25,000
Ulster	1486/4	1934–36	£80,000+	£50,000	–
2 litre	1950/4	1936–40	£40,000	£25,000	£18,000

Value is dependent upon racing history, originality and completeness.
Add 40% if a competition winner or works team car.

1954 Aston Martin DB2/4, 2580cc, double-overhead-camshaft Vantage engine, 125bhp, Borrani wire wheels, engine overhauled, little mileage since, rewired, finished in Bluebird blue, interior partially reupholstered, 70,350 miles recorded.
£13,000–15,000 BKS

Donald Campbell, destined to become the holder of the World Land Speed Record at 403.1mph and the World Water Speed Record at 276.33mph, took delivery of this car in May 1954.

1958 Aston Martin DB2/4 Mk III, 2922cc engine, 178bhp, manual gearbox with overdrive, restored at a cost of £30,000, stainless steel exhaust, finished in red, grey and red interior, 74,500 miles recorded, excellent condition throughout.
£23,000–26,000 H&H

1962 Aston Martin DB4 Series IV Vantage, coachwork by Touring, 3.7 litre, 'Special Series' engine, triple carburettors, 266bhp, wide-ratio gearbox, 3.3:1 final drive, completely restored, 6,000 miles covered since mechanical rebuild, finished in Wedgwood blue, grey leather interior.
£47,000–52,000 BKS

Introduced in 1958, the DB4 was a completely new model, and every inch bore testimony to Aston's racing programme. The straight-six, double-overhead-camshaft engine had been proven in the DBR2 sports-racer, and Brown, whose fortune was founded on gear making, specified a new four-speed gearbox with overdrive. The elegant Superleggera body was the work of Touring of Milan. With 240bhp on tap, even in the basic model, the DB4 was the world's fastest four-seat production car. It could top 140mph, sprint to 60mph in 8.5 seconds and, even more impressively, thanks to four-wheel disc brakes, it was the first production car ever that could go from rest to 100mph and back to rest in under 20 seconds.

◀ **1963 Aston Martin DB4 Convertible,** 3670cc 6-cylinder, double-overhead-camshaft engine, 240bhp, 4-speed, all-synchromesh gearbox, restored 1988–91, engine rebuilt, oil cooler, overdrive extended to 2nd and 3rd gears, limited-slip differential, chassis overhauled, suspension uprated, handling kit, brakes upgraded to dual-circuit DB4GT spec., finished in Ascot grey, red leather upholstery refurbished, 64,000 miles recorded, 1 of 70 built, good condition throughout.
£60,000–66,000 BKS

▶ **1963 Aston Martin DB4 Series V Vantage GT,** coachwork by Touring, double-overhead-camshaft, 6-cylinder engine, 266bhp, finished in Flame red, black leather interior, 1 of 6 Series V DB4s built with twin-plug GT power units, very good condition.
£69,000–76,000 COYS

Although the David Brown era is considered by many to be Aston Martin's golden period, the company struggled to make a profit on its cars. A friend once asked David Brown if he could buy an Aston Martin at cost price. David Brown replied: 'I would love to sell it to you at cost, but I couldn't possibly charge you that much.'

◀ 1967 Aston Martin DB6 Mk I, finished in Dubonnet Rosso, black hide interior, very good condition. £28,000–32,000 KING

The DB6 may ooze pure-bred Bulldog Britishness, but the styling is an evolution of the Touring of Milan-designed DB4. Prince Charles owns a DB6 Volante. At top speeds, the upturned tail was said to reduce aerodynamic lift by half. Six DB6 estates were built by coachbuilder Harold Radford.

Aston Martin DB6 (1965–71)

Engine: Double-overhead-camshaft, straight-six, 3995cc.
Power output: 282–325bhp (325bhp was Aston's claimed output for Vantage-spec. engine).
Transmission: Five-speed ZF manual or Borg-Warner automatic.
Brakes: Four-wheel discs.
Top speed: 148+mph.
0–60mph: 6.1–6.7 seconds.
0–100mph: 15 seconds.
Production: 1,753.
Price in 1967: £5,084 for Vantage saloon.
If James Bond had ever hung up his Walther PPK

and settled down with a wife and kids, the DB6, with its characteristic uplifted Kamm tail, would have been the Aston for him. With four proper seats, the option of automatic transmission and power steering, it was almost practical. Of the classic DB series, which started with the DB4 in 1958, the DB6 is also the fastest, but in the eyes of some enthusiasts is a little softer and less sporting than its forebears. Consequently the DB6, although the most civilised of the classic DB Aston saloons, is the least prized and most affordable; in today's market, it is something of an Aston bargain.

1969 Aston Martin DB6 Vantage Volante Convertible, 3995cc, 6-cylinder engine, triple SU carburettors, 325bhp, 5-speed ZF gearbox, restored 1990–93, fitted with power-assisted steering, finished in black, black Connolly leather upholstery, 1 of only 9 long-wheelbase DB6 Volantes built, very good condition throughout.
£67,000–75,000 BKS

After 37 Volante convertibles had been completed on the short-wheelbase DB5 chassis, the model adopted the DB6 chassis in October 1966. Distinguishable by its flared wheel arches and DBS wheels, the Mk II DB6, introduced in 1969, was available with AE Brico electronic fuel injection. In all 1,575 DB6s were made between 1965 and 1970, plus 140 long-wheelbase Volantes.

▶ 1968 Aston Martin DBS, 6-cylinder engine, automatic transmission, finished in light metallic green, black hide interior, low mileage.
£10,000–12,000 LEW

1969 Aston Martin DBS Vantage, 3995cc, 6-cylinder engine, 5-speed ZF manual gearbox, wire wheels, left-hand drive, finished in Silver Birch, original black leather interior, 60,000km recorded.
£28,000–32,000 BKS

Introduced in October 1967, the DBS employed a widened and lengthened version of the DB6's chassis adapted to accept a de Dion rear axle. Aston Martin had always intended the DBS to house its new V8, but the car first appeared with the 3995cc six of the DB6. Bigger and more luxuriously appointed than the latter, the standard DBS was slightly slower, although the Vantage version's 140+mph top speed and 15-second standing quarter-mile time were very impressive.

◄ **1971 Aston Martin DBS V8,** manual gearbox, finished in blue, black leather interior, 2 owners, 41,000 miles recorded, very good condition throughout
£14,000–17,000 VIC

ASTON MARTIN Model	ENGINE cc/cyl	DATES	CONDITION 1	2	3
DB1	1970/4	1948–50	£30,000+	£20,000	£16,000
DB2	2580/6	1950–53	£30,000+	£18,000	£14,000
DB2 Conv	2580/6	1951–53	£45,000+	£28,000+	£17,000
DB2/4 Mk I/II	2580/2922/6	1953–57	£30,000	£18,000	£14,000
DB2/4 Mk II Conv	2580/2922/6	1953–57	£45,000	£30,000	£15,000
DB Mk III Conv	2922/6	1957–59	£45,000	£28,000	£18,000
DB Mk III	2922/6	1957–59	£30,000	£20,000	£15,000
DB4	3670/6	1959–63	£40,000	£25,000	£16,000
DB4 Conv	3670/6	1961–63	£60,000	£35,000	–
DB4 GT	3670/6	1961–63	£140,000+	£100,000	–
DB5	3995/6	1964–65	£45,000	£30,000	£20,000
DB5 Conv	3995/6	1964–65	£55,000+	£38,000	–
DB6	3995/6	1965–69	£30,000	£20,000	£16,000
DB6 Mk I auto	3995/6	1965–69	£28,000	£18,000	£14,000
DB6 Mk I Volante	3995/6	1965–71	£50,000+	£32,000	£28,000
DB6 Mk II Volante	3995/6	1969–70	£60,000	£40,000	£30,000
DBS	3995/6	1967–72	£15,000+	£15,000	£9,000
AM Vantage	5340/8	1972–73	£15,000	£12,000	£9,000
V8 Vantage Oscar India	5340/8	1978–82	£30,000+	£20,000	£10,000
V8 Volante	5340/8	1978–82	£40,000	£30,000	£25,000
Works/competition history is an important factor as is Vantage specification.					

◄ **1971 Aston Martin DBS V8,** 5340cc, manual gearbox, resprayed in British Racing green, good condition. **£9,500–11,000 BRIT**

Introduced in 1969, the DBS V8 was almost identical in appearance to the six-cylinder DBS, but it boasted a 5.3 litre, aluminium V8 engine of an entirely new design. Although Aston Martin never officially quoted power outputs, it gave about 345bhp.

1971 Aston Martin DBS V8, 5340cc, double overhead camshafts, Bosch electronic fuel injection, 160+mph top speed, suspension, wheels and tyres uprated to Vantage specification, finished in dark blue, ivory Connolly hide interior, history file.
£11,000–13,000 COYS

1971 Aston Martin DBS Vantage, manual gearbox, chrome wire wheels, 48,000 miles recorded.
£12,000–15,000 VIC

► **1972 Aston Martin Vantage,** 3995cc, 6-cylinder engine, restored 1997–98, bumpers replaced, wheels rebuilt, stainless steel exhaust system, bare-metal respray in Imperial blue, dark blue hide interior, 32nd car built, very good condition.
£13,000–15,000 BRIT

The Vantage was basically a revised DBS with a redesigned front that featured two 7in quartz-iodine headlamps, rather than the four lamps of the previous model. Only 70 were built before production concentrated on the Aston Martin V8.

◄ **1973 Aston Martin V8,**
4 Weber carburettors,
electronic ignition, manual gearbox,
air conditioning, 160mph top speed,
restored early 1990s, rear axle
rebuilt, new sills, finished in metallic
blue, blue-piped parchment
upholstery, some corrosion and
cosmetic blemishes, history file.
£9,000–11,000 BKS

► **1973 Aston Martin V8,**
5340cc V8 engine,
automatic transmission,
finished in Tudor grey,
black leather upholstery
and trim, 2 owners since
1977, 77,388 miles
recorded, excellent
condition throughout.
£10,000–12,000 H&H

Restored values

The cost of a professional
restoration will have an
influence on, but no direct
relation to, a car's market
value. A restored car can have
a market value lower than the
cost of its restoration.

◄ **1974 Aston Martin V8,**
5340cc V8 engine, 4 twin-choke
carburettors, automatic transmission,
restored at a cost of over £30,000,
finished in red, beige leather
upholstery, 60,000 miles recorded,
excellent condition throughout.
£13,000–15,000 H&H

1979 Aston Martin V8 Osca India, automatic transmission, BBS alloy wheels, air conditioning, finished in Florida
blue, blue hide interior, very good condition throughout.
£22,000–25,000 KING

◀ **1979 Aston Martin V8 Volante,** 5340cc, double-overhead-camshaft V8 engine, manual gearbox, all-independent suspension, 4-wheel disc brakes, finished in dark red, beige interior, 21,000 miles recorded, excellent original condition.
£50,000–55,000 MEE

1988 Aston Martin Vantage Volante, factory 6.3 litre engine, 14,000 miles recorded, excellent condition.
£80,000–90,000 MEE

1989 Aston Martin Vantage, 5340cc V8 engine, 21,000 miles recorded, excellent condition throughout.
£65,000–75,000 MEE

▶ **1989 Aston Martin PoW Vantage Volante,** 5340cc, double-overhead-camshaft V8 engine, well maintained, 12,000 miles recorded, excellent condition.
£120,000–132,000 MEE

This car is one of 22 built to the same specification as the Vantage Volante supplied to HRH Prince of Wales.

◀ **1982 Aston Martin V8 Volante Convertible,** converted to Vantage specification, Weber carburettors, manual gearbox, sports exhaust system, front and rear handling kits, finished in crimson, cream leather interior and beige carpets, over £28,000 spent since 1997, 60,700 miles recorded.
£30,000–34,000 BKS

▶ **1987 Aston Martin V8,** 5340cc aluminium 8-cylinder engine, fuel injection, automatic transmission, alloy wheels, driving lamps, 45,000 miles recorded, excellent condition throughout.
£45,000–50,000 MEE

1982 Aston Martin Lagonda, coachwork by Tickford, 5340cc, double-overhead-camshaft, aluminium V8 engine, 4 Weber carburettors, 280bhp, 3-speed automatic transmission, independent front suspension by wishbones and coil springs, de Dion rear axle on coil springs, 4-wheel ventilated disc brakes, mounted inboard at the rear, digital cathode-ray-tube instrumentation, 148mph top speed, 0–60mph in 7.9 seconds, finished in Salisbury blue, black upholstery, very good condition.
£9,500–11,000 COYS

The launch of the Aston Martin Lagonda in 1974 marked a return of the Lagonda name, which had remained dormant since the Rapide ceased production in 1964. It employed a DBS V8 chassis stretched to accommodate four doors and increased rear legroom, otherwise sharing the same mechanical specification as the smaller car. Only seven cars were built, but before production ended in June 1976, William Towns had penned a completely new Series 2 version, which was launched in October 1976.

◀ **1983 Aston Martin Lagonda,** 5340cc, double-overhead-camshaft V8, 3-speed automatic transmission, New York motor show car and demonstrator, fitted with US emission-control engine, left-hand drive, finished in blue, matching Connolly hide interior, walnut trim, 35,368km recorded, 2 owners, good condition throughout.
£16,000–18,000 BKS

1989 Aston Martin Zagato Volante Convertible, coachwork by Zagato, 5.3 litre, double-overhead-camshaft V8 engine, fuel injection, 320bhp, 5-speed gearbox, left-hand drive, finished in Gladiator red, black leather interior, 7,200km recorded, supplied with original Vantage front end.
£55,000–61,000 BKS

With the introduction of the Zagato Vantage in 1986, Aston Martin renewed its association with one of Italy's most illustrious coachbuilders, the latter having been responsible for the desirable DB4GT Zagato. Part of Zagato's brief had been to shed some of the standard Vantage's weight, which was achieved by shortening the wheelbase by a little over 17cm to create Aston's first production two-seater since the DB4GT. Given the success of the coupé, a Zagato Volante convertible was not long in coming, the first example being shown in 1987. Restyled, the Volante's rather bland frontal grille was not to everyone's taste, and a number were fitted with Vantage front ends by the factory. Only 35 Zagato Volantes were sold between 1987 and 1989.

1990 Aston Martin Virage, automatic transmission, finished in Suffolk red, magnolia leather interior, 30,000 miles recorded, accident damaged and repaired, chassis realigned by recognised Aston Martin repairers.
£29,000–34,000 BKS

After almost 20 years in production, Aston's V8 was updated for the 1990s as the Virage. The existing Lagonda chassis and suspension were used in revised form for the new car, while engine development was entrusted to Callaway Engineering, of Connecticut. Immensely strong, the old V8's bottom half was retained, but fitted with new cylinder heads boasting four valves per cylinder and hydraulic tappets. With 330bhp on tap, it was good for a top speed of almost 160mph and a 0–60mph time of under seven seconds.

1990 Aston Martin Virage, 6.3 litre V8 engine, 5-speed manual gearbox, suspension modified, fitted with 18in road wheels, converted to wide-body spec. to accommodate 6.3 litre performance package, over £40,000 spent on refurbishment and conversion to 6.3 litres, factory-modified front grille, resprayed metallic green, interior retrimmed in green-piped Parchment leather, fewer than 37,000 miles recorded, history file.
£45,000–50,000 BKS

Ahead of its twin-supercharged Vantage, Aston Martin offered a 6.3 litre conversion for the existing 5340cc, V8-engined Virage. The extensive modifications boosted maximum power from 330 to 500bhp and increased top speed from 155 to a staggering 174mph.

Auburn

◀ **1929 Auburn Boat-Tail Speedster,** right-hand drive, recent complete restoration, engine rebuilt, gearbox overhauled, new kingpins, shackle pins and bearings throughout, body rebuilt to original specification, tan leather upholstery.
£40,000–45,000 KI

Restored values

The cost of a professional restoration will have an influence on, but no direct relation to, a car's market value. A restored car can have a market value lower than the cost of its restoration.

▶ **1932 Auburn 8–100 Four-Door Saloon,** 8-cylinder engine, 37,000 miles recorded, good condition.
£7,000–8,000 KI

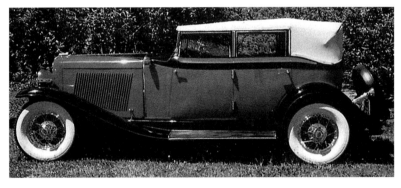

◀ **1933 Auburn Phaeton,** engine rebuilt and resprayed 1993, 150 miles covered since, finished in orange-red to match original leather upholstery, knock-off wire spoke wheels overhauled and rechromed 1996, after-market bonnet holder, rear seat pull-down armrest.
£38,000–43,000 KI

Audi

1984 Audi 200 Turbo Saloon, full electric pack, climate control, finished in Graphite grey, well maintained, good original condition.
£800–1,000 BARO

1985 Audi Quattro, 2 litre, 5-cylinder engine, over 215bhp, left-hand drive, braking system, steering and drivetrain completely overhauled, finished in turquoise blue, grey upholstery, good condition throughout.
£3,800–4,200 COYS

The Quattro took the rallying world by storm, being the first car to use a turbocharged engine in conjunction with four-wheel drive. This was a formula that other manufacturers had to follow to remain competitive.

Austin

Even before the young Herbert Austin set up car manufacturing under his own name in 1905, he had already built up considerable practical knowledge and valuable experience in the fledgling motor industry. In 1894, the young engineer had seen his first horseless carriage, a three-wheeled Bollée, and a year or so later he built his own vehicle along broadly similar lines. In 1900, after producing further prototypes, he set Wolseley on the road to car manufacturing with a capable four-wheeled voiturette, but left in 1905 after a dispute with the company's directors. In 1906, the Austin Motor Company Limited produced its first car, a 25/30hp touring model,

at Longbridge on the outskirts of Birmingham. Then, for 80 years, it remained a major player at the core of the British motor industry until, in 1987, the Austin name was finally dropped from the renamed Rover Group. At various times in its history, Austin was the largest British car maker. As for the cars, Austin's greatest legacy must surely be the two modest machines that transformed British motoring on each side of a world war. The Austin 7 of 1922 brought motoring en masse to the middle classes, and in 1959 the new Austin Se7en, as it was originally badged, brought motoring to millions in a pocket-sized world-beater better known as the Mini.

1927 Austin 'Heavy' 12/4 Tourer, restored, finished in dark green/black, green leather interior, stored for the last 7 years, black wet-weather gear, in need of recommissioning, excellent condition.
£9,000–10,000 CGC

1930 Austin 7 Saloon, finished in dark blue over black, good condition.
£4,500–5,000 CC

▶ **1931 Austin 7 Two-Seat Special,** 747.5cc, 4-cylinder engine, 3-speed gearbox, cycle wings, restored, good condition.
£6,000–7,000 HMM

Herbert Austin's baby car was offered in many different styles during its 17-year production run. Very popular were the Ulster, Speedy and Nippy sporting cars. After WWII, when most of the sports cars built were being sold to America to repay war debts, motoring enthusiasts began a cult of building Austin 7 specials.

AUSTIN Model	ENGINE cc/cyl	DATES	CONDITION 1	2	3
25/30	4900/4	1906	£35,000	£25,000	£20,000
20/4	3600/4	1919–29	£20,000	£12,000	£6,000
12	1661/4	1922–26	£8,000	£5,000	£2,000
7/Chummy	747/4	1924–39	£7,000	£5,000	£2,500
7 Coachbuilt/Nippy/Opal, etc	747/4	1924–39	£10,000	£9,000	£7,000
12/4	1861/4	1927–35	£5,500	£5,000	£2,000
16	2249/6	1928–36	£9,000	£7,000	£4,000
20/6	3400/6	1928–38	£12,500	£10,000	£8,000
12/6	1496/6	1932–37	£6,000	£4,000	£1,500
12/4	1535/4	1933–39	£5,000	£3,500	£1,500
10 and 10/4	1125/4	1932–47	£4,000	£3,000	£1,000
10 and 10/4 Tourer	1125/4	1933–47	£5,000	£3,500	£1,000
18	2510/6	1934–39	£8,000	£5,000	£3,000
14	1711/6	1937–39	£6,000	£4,000	£2,000
Big Seven	900/4	1938–39	£4,000	£2,500	£1,500
8	900/4	1939–47	£3,000	£2,000	£1,000
28	4016/6	1939	£6,000	£4,000	£2,000
Prices for early Austin models are dependent on body style – landaulette, tourer, etc.					

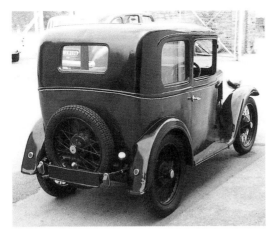

1934 Austin 7 Saloon, 747.5cc sidevalve engine, synchromesh gearbox, restored, good condition.
£4,000–5,000 HMM

1936 Austin 7 Saloon, 747.5cc, Pytchley sunshine roof, finished in green with black wings, original green leather interior trim, 60,000 miles recorded, history file, very original.
£3,000–3,500 BKS

1937 Austin 7 Opal Tourer, finished in blue and black, 3 owners, good condition throughout.
£3,500–4,000 BARO

◄ **1933 Austin 7 Box Saloon,** 747.5cc, 4-speed gearbox, finished in blue and black, good mechanics, poor paintwork, retrimmed seats.
£3,750–4,250 UMC

> A known continuous history can add value to and enhance the enjoyment of a car.

1934 Austin 7 Saloon, 747.5cc, 4-speed gearbox, 81in wheelbase, restored, finished in red, red leather interior, driver's door in need of attention to achieve a perfect fit, otherwise good condition throughout.
£2,500–3,000 BKS

The Austin 7 was a huge success from the moment deliveries began in January 1923, and eventually it dominated the light car market in Britain. In essence, it changed little in the course of production, retaining the A-frame chassis, transverse front spring, rear quarter-elliptics and four-cylinder sidevalve engine to the end. There were many detail improvements along the way, including a longer wheelbase, roomier bodies, coupled brakes and a three-bearing crankshaft.

◀ **1938 Austin Big 7 Saloon,** 900cc, 4-cylinder engine, finished in blue with black wings, full sunshine roof, original blue interior, very good condition throughout.
£2,500–3,000 H&H

Restored values

The cost of a professional restoration will have an influence on, but no direct relation to, a car's market value. A restored car can have a market value lower than the cost of its restoration.

1947 Austin 8, 900cc, 4 cylinders, rewired, finished in black, brown interior trim, good mechanical condition.
£800–1,000 BRIT

Miller's Starter Marque

- **Starter Austins:** *Austin 7; A55/A60 Cambridge; A90/95/99/105/110 Westminster; Nash Metropolitan; A30/35/40; 1100 and 1300.*
- Although, in general, post-war Austin models were pretty populous, not all are in plentiful supply. Those listed above are blessed with a good survival rate, spares and club support, and normally possess those Austin virtues of durability.
- From the pre-war period, the Austin 7 is eminently viable as a run-while-you-restore car, with little to baffle the DIY mechanic.
- One of the most engaging Austins of the post-war era is the Austin/Nash Metropolitan. They should really have called it the Neopolitan, for this quaint little dolly-mixture of a car came in a choice of dazzling ice-cream colours: red, yellow and turquoise over white. The hardtop versions had white roofs and lower bodies, making them resemble a sliced-white sandwich with a variety of sickly fillings. Initially, the Metropolitan was built by Austin for the American Nash company as a 'sub-compact', or two-thirds-scale Yank tank. It was available in the UK from 1957.

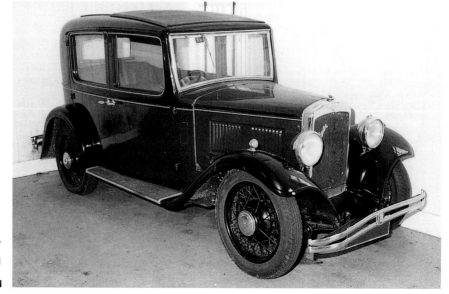

▶ **1933 Austin 10/4 Saloon,** 1125cc engine, finished in green with black wings, green interior, good mechanical condition.
£5,000–6,000 VIN

▶ **1934 Austin 10/4 Saloon,** 1125cc, Ace Avion wheel discs, auxiliary lamps, finished in blue and black, original blue leather interior, good condition throughout.
£4,500–5,000 BRIT

At its introduction in April 1932, the Austin 10/4 filled the gap between the 7hp range and the recently introduced Light 12/6. Well received, it went on to become a best-seller and was developed progressively, a 10hp model remaining in Austin catalogues until 1947. Today, the earlier chrome-radiator models, produced between 1932 and 1934, are the most sought after.

1938 Austin 10 Cambridge, 1125cc, 4-cylinder, sidevalve engine, Girling mechanical brakes, Easiclene wheels, finished in black, brown interior trim, partially refurbished, unused since 1997, in need of recommissioning.
£1,000–1,200 BRIT

1930 Austin 12/4 Two-Seater with Dickey, 1861cc, 4-cylinder engine, completely restored.
£8,500–9,500 AS

1939 Austin 12 New Ascot, 1535cc, 4-cylinder engine, partially refurbished, rewired, finished in black, retrimmed brown interior, new carpets, good mechanical condition.
£2,000–2,500 BRIT

The redoubtable Austin 12 received styling alterations similar to the Austin 10 range in August 1936, being given the title 'New Ascot' to differentiate it from the earlier model with its perpendicular styling. The Austin 12 was always noted for its reliability, and many saw service as taxis, including this example.

1951 Austin Sheerline, 3993cc, 6-cylinder engine, finished in dark green, tan interior, good condition throughout.
£5,000–6,000 PM

Austin A40 (1958–67)

Engine: Overhead-valve, four-cylinder, 948cc; 1098cc from October 1962.
Power output: 34–37bhp for 948cc; 48bhp for 1098cc.
Transmission: Four-speed manual.
Brakes: Hydro-mechanical drums; full hydraulic drums from October 1961.
Top speed: 73–75+mph for 948cc; 83mph for 1098cc.
0–60mph: 29–30 seconds for 948cc; 23 seconds for 1098cc.
Production: 340,000
Price in 1958: £676.7s.

Now nearly forgotten and rarely seen on the roads, in its day the Austin A40 represented something of a quiet revolution. It was launched to replace the cute, peanut-shaped A35 and, by comparison, offered crisp modern looks thanks to its Italian Pininfarina styling. Austin ads touted the new A40 as 'the world's most advanced small car', a bold claim that didn't quite stack up at the launch and certainly couldn't be justified in any way when the Mini was launched a year later. Nevertheless, the A40 was roomy for its size, pleasant to drive, predictable in handling and perky enough. These last qualities attracted the motorsport crowd, who raced and rallied the car with verve, but where the A40 really scored was as a family carry-all. One of its handiest features were the fold-flat rear seats, which made it a really versatile load carrier with reasonably easy access from the drop-down boot lid. A year later, the Countryman version featured a split tailgate with lift-up rear window to create a first-generation small hatchback, the concept and execution of which are still recognizable in modern offerings. For a brief period, the A40 was thoroughly modern, but the competition soon massed around it in the shape of outside rivals like the Triumph Herald and Ford Anglia, as well as in-house competitors from BMC's advanced front-wheel-drive 1100 range. By 1967, the once modern A40 looked decidedly dated and gently faded away. Today, it remains largely overlooked and humbly priced, and is all the more appealing for that, because for near banger money you could have an easily-maintained, about-town classic carry-all. Out of town, on the M40, an A40 could even lose you your licence – if you're really trying and the cop who stops you has an unreasonable loathing of A40s.
For: Cheaper and more capable all-round than the obviously cuter Austin A30/35.
Against: Low survival rate; rust prone; no problem with mechanical parts, but some body parts and trim scarce.

◀ **1959 Austin A40 Farina Saloon,** 948cc, 4-cylinder engine, 34bhp, restored, good condition.
£1,300–1,500 HMM

The fourth generation of A40, introduced by BMC in 1958, was a radical departure from previous models, the estate-car-like body having been styled by Pininfarina. In 1959, a true A40 estate was announced as the Countryman, and in 1961 the Mk II model, with a slightly longer wheelbase and more power, was introduced. The Mk II was further updated in 1962, when it received the Morris Minor's 1098cc engine, and it continued in production until 1967.

Austin Cambridge A55/A60 & Morris Oxford V/VI (1959–71)

Engine: Overhead-valve, four-cylinder, 1489 and 1622cc.
Power output: 53–68bhp.
Transmission: Four-speed manual; optional automatic on some models.
Brakes: Girling hydraulic drums all-round.
Top speed: 80–90mph.
0–60mph: 19.5–24 seconds.
Production: 1,207,000.
Prices in 1960: Austin A55, £801; Morris Oxford, £815; Wolseley 15/60, £936; MG Magnette, £1,012; Riley 4/68, £1028.

The names above are only a sample from BMC's biblical model christening book. Lump them together, mix in the Wolseley, MG and Riley four-cylinder variants, with their own mystic-rune model names and/or numbers, and the only generic term anyone's ever been able to come up with is 'Big Farinas', on account of the fact that the design was penned by Italy's Pininfarina studio. That's what they came to be called by banger racers, who drove droves of them to destruction, little appreciating the nuances that once had served as slight social distinctions in the pecking order of the suburban driveway. One thing, the banger boys did appreciate, though, was the hefty monocoque hull and the fact that, for a while, there were hordes of them at scrap prices. In the early 1960s, these Big Farinas also earned praise for their compliant ride, and owners would also have considered their straightforward mechanics, capacious boot and spacious family accommodation of more note than outright pace or the fact that the Big Farinas persisted with drum brakes to the last.

Austins and Morrises were the plain-Jane motors with no frills. The Wolseley added wood and leather garnish; the MG offered a more peppy engine; and the Riley combined the MG's performance with the Wolseley's trim.

An Austin A55 Cambridge brochure, c1960, 8¼ x 11in (21 x 28cm).
£3–4 PC

1962 Austin Westminster Saloon, 2912cc, automatic transmission, finished in black with red trim, 51,000 miles from new, bodywork and brightwork in good condition, leather upholstery and trim in excellent condition.
£2,000–2,500 H&H

1962 Austin Gypsy, 2286cc, finished in Limestone over green, beige interior trim, fewer than 8,000 miles from new, very good running order.
£4,000–4,500 H&H

1973 Austin 1300 Countryman, 1275cc, 4-cylinder engine, 4-speed manual gearbox, front-wheel drive, finished in blue, olive green interior trim and upholstery, original plastic covers on front seats, 91 miles recorded.
£1,400–1,650 H&H

AUSTIN Model	ENGINE cc/cyl	DATES	CONDITION 1	2	3
16	2199/4	1945–49	£3,000	£2,000	£1,000
A40 Devon	1200/4	1947–52	£2,000	£1,200	£750
A40 Sports	1200/4	1950–53	£6,000	£4,000	£2,000
A40 Somerset	1200/4	1952–54	£2,000	£1,500	£750
A40 Somerset DHC	1200/4	1954	£5,000	£4,000	£2,500
A40 Dorset 2-door	1200/4	1947–48	£2,000	£1,500	£1,000
A70 Hampshire	2199/4	1948–50	£3,000	£1,500	£1,000
A70 Hereford	2199/4	1950–54	£3,000	£1,500	£1,000
A90 Atlantic DHC	2660/4	1949–52	£10,000	£6,000	£4,000
A90 Atlantic	2660/4	1949–52	£6,000	£4,000	£3,000
A40/A50 Cambridge	1200/4	1954–57	£1,200	£750	£500
A55 Mk I Cambridge	1489/4	1957–59	£1,000	£750	£500
A55 Mk II	1489/4	1959–61	£1,000	£750	£500
A60 Cambridge	1622/4	1961–69	£1,000	£750	£500
A90/95 Westminster	2639/6	1954–59	£2,000	£1,500	£750
A99 Westminster	2912/6	1959–61	£1,500	£1,000	£500
A105 Westminster	2639/6	1956–59	£3,000	£1,500	£750
A110 Mk I/II	2912/6	1961–68	£2,000	£1,500	£750
Nash Metropolitan	1489/4	1957–61	£3,500	£2,000	£750
Nash Metropolitan DHC	1489/4	1957–61	£6,000	£3,000	£1,500
A30	803/4	1952–56	£1,500	£800	-
A30 Countryman	803/4	1954–56	£1,500	£1,000	-
A35	948/4	1956–59	£1,000	£500	-
A35 Countryman	948/4	1956–62	£1,500	£1,000	-
A40 Farina Mk I	948/4	1958–62	£1,250	£750	£200
A40 Mk I Countryman	948/4	1959–62	£1,500	£1,000	£400
A40 Farina Mk II	1098/4	1962–67	£1,000	£750	-
A40 Mk II Countryman	1098/4	1962–67	£1,200	£750	£300
1100	1098/4	1963–73	£1,000	£750	-
1300 Mk I/II	1275/4	1967–74	£750	£500	-
1300 GT	1275/4	1969–74	£1,800	£1,000	£750
1800/2200	1800/2200/4	1964–75	£1,500	£900	£600
3 Litre	2912/6	1968–71	£3,000	£1,500	£500

Austin-Healey

In 1946, Donald Healey, engineer and former rally driver, became a car manufacturer in his own right, producing Healey cars in Warwick. His offerings were bespoke, produced in limited numbers and always sporting in character, but Healey also had a vision of an affordable, true 100mph sports car that would fill a gap in the American market between the Jaguar XK120 and the cheap and cheerful MG T-series. The Healey Hundred was one of the brightest stars of the 1952 Earls Court Motor Show, and literally overnight it became the Austin-Healey when Austin boss Leonard Lord decided that his company – which had already agreed to supply engines – wanted to build the car

everyone was talking about. The Austin-Healey 100 fulfilled its brief superbly, with about 80 per cent of all production going to the USA. The original four-cylinder Austin-Healey 100/4 became the 100/6 in 1956, when it received a six-cylinder, 2639cc engine; then in 1959, it gained a 2912cc engine, which gave the model name Austin-Healey 3000. Meanwhile, in 1958, Austin-Healey addressed the budget sports car market with the Sprite, which became known and loved throughout the world as the Frog-eye Sprite or, as the Americans prefer, the Bug-eye. The Sprite Mk II was, in effect, a rebadged MG Midget and ran concurrently with the MG offering until 1971.

1953 Austin-Healey 100/4, 2660cc, 4-speed manual gearbox with overdrive, completely restored, minimal use since, finished in pale metallic blue, grey wire wheels, dark blue hood, tonneau cover, dark blue upholstery and carpets, dent to offside rear wing, otherwise excellent condition.
£16,000–18,000 BKS

1956 Austin-Healey 100/4, 2660cc, 4-cylinder engine, overdrive gearbox, heater, tonneau cover and full weather equipment, left-hand drive, restored, 1,800 miles covered since, finished in Reno red and black, red upholstery.
£13,000–15,000 COYS

▶ **1965 Austin-Healey 3000 Mk III BJ8,** 3000cc, restored 1991 at a cost of over £18,000, 4,700 miles covered since, finished in red, black interior trim, very good condition throughout.
£17,000–19,000 H&H

1966 Austin-Healey 3000 Mk III, older restoration, engine rebuilt 1995, overdrive unit reconditioned, stainless steel exhaust system, electrical system renewed as required, finished in Ice blue and Old English white, new blue vynide hood.
£18,000–20,000 BRIT

The final version of the Austin-Healey 3000, the Mk III, was introduced in 1964 and enjoyed a four-year production run. The power output of 150bhp gave a top speed of 120mph and vivid acceleration, while the braking system benefited from a servo. The interior trim was more luxurious than that of its predecessor.

1967 Austin-Healey 3000 Mk III Phase 2 BJ8 2+2, completely restored, converted to right-hand drive, concours condition.
£18,000–20,000 Mot

> A known continuous history can add value to and enhance the enjoyment of a car.

1958 Austin-Healey Sprite Mk I, completely restored, c1,000 miles covered since, replacement engine and gearbox, fitted with optional front bumpers and heater, finished in Pageant blue, black interior.
£5,000–6,000 COYS

The Austin-Healey Sprite was the right car for its time. When it arrived in the spring of 1958, the economy had grown sufficiently for there to be a large number of buyers who yearned for the spiritual heir to the MG Midgets of the 1930s. The Sprite was the car. It had style, it was a proper driver's car, it had a respected badge and it was thoroughly practical with proven running gear. Above all else, it was fun. Its cheeky looks made people smile, and it is one of the rare cars that not only won respect, but affection, gaining the nickname 'Frog-eye'.

1958 Austin-Healey Sprite Mk I, 997cc, completely restored 1990–92, about 2,000 miles covered since, finished in red, black and red interior trim, very good condition throughout.
£2,500–3,000 H&H

1959 Austin-Healey Sprite Mk I, completely restored 1994–95, later 1275cc engine and associated gearbox, wider wheels, fibreglass bonnet, halogen headlights, rear panel modified to accept a roll-cage, finished in Old English white, red interior, BMIHT certificate.
£7,500–8,500 BKS

1961 Austin-Healey Sprite Mk I, completely restored early 1990s, 1275cc engine, front disc brakes, wire wheels, original bonnet, finished in white, full hood, tonneau cover, new sidescreens, red interior trim, good condition.
£3,750–4,500 H&H

1968 Austin-Healey Sprite Mk IV, mildly tuned 1275cc, 4-cylinder engine, 114mph top speed, finished in green, black interior trim, mostly original, good mechanical condition.
£3,000–3,500 BRIT

AUSTIN HEALEY Model	ENGINE cc/cyl	DATES	CONDITION 1	2	3
100 BN 1/2	2660/4	1953–56	£20,000	£14,000	£8,000
100/6, BN4/BN6	2639/6	1956–59	£18,000	£13,500	£8,000
3000 Mk I	2912/6	1959–61	£20,000	£13,000	£8,500
3000 Mk II	2912/6	1961–62	£22,000	£15,000	£9,000
3000 Mk IIA	2912/6	1962–64	£23,000	£15,000	£11,000
3000 Mk III	2912/6	1964–68	£24,000	£17,000	£11,000
Sprite Mk I	948/4	1958–61	£10,000	£7,000	£4,000
Sprite Mk II	948/4	1961–64	£5,000	£3,000	£2,000
Sprite Mk III	1098/4	1964–66	£4,500	£3,000	£1,500
Sprite Mk IV	1275/4	1966–71	£5,000	£3,000	£1,500

Bentley

After working as a railway engineer, Walter Owen Bentley undertook his first commercial automotive venture in 1912, when he took over an agency selling three makes of French car just off London's Baker Street. During WWI, he worked on aero-engines, and in 1919 founded Bentley Motors. The first 3 Litre prototype took to the road in 1920, production getting under way at Cricklewood in north-west London in 1922. Two years later, a 3 Litre won Le Mans, and the legend was cemented with further Le Mans victories in 1927, 1928, 1929 and 1930. Yet Bentley's formidable racing reputation wasn't enough to keep the company in the black, and it fell into receivership in 1931, to be taken over by Rolls-Royce in 1933. The subsequent refined, Derby-built, Rolls-Royce-designed

Bentleys became known as 'the silent sports car', and many were graced with supremely elegant bodies. After WWII, production resumed at Crewe. The Mk VI Bentley of 1946 represented a turning point, as it was the first Rolls-Bentley product to be offered with an off-the-shelf factory body, although special coachbuilt bodies were still available. By 1955, the standard-bodied Bentley S-series was little more than a Rolls-Royce with a Bentley radiator. However, in the 1980s, Bentley began to emerge from the shadows of Rolls-Royce and regain its true sporting identity. In today's market, S-series and T-series Bentleys can often be slightly cheaper than their Rolls-Royce counterparts. In its independent existence from 1919 to 1931, total Bentley production amounted to only 3,024 cars.

1922 Bentley 3 Litre Sports Two-Seater, 2996cc, overhead-camshaft, 4-cylinder inline engine, 4 valves per cylinder, 4-speed A-type gearbox, rear-wheel drum brakes, suspension by semi-elliptic leaf springs front and rear, cycle wings, side-mounted spare, matching chassis and engine nos, coachwork thought to be original, restored, correct beaded-edge wheels, black double-duck hood, finished in blue, brown leather interior excellent condition throughout.
£50,000–60,000 C

W.O. Bentley launched the 3 litre car that bore his name in 1919. In only mildly developed form, this was the model that became a legend in motor racing and which, with its leather-strapped bonnet, classic radiator design and British Racing green livery has become the archetypal vintage sports car.

After Terence Cuneo, Bentley at Le Mans 1929, colour print, showing the Erlanger-Benjafield 4½ Litre refuelling in the pits as the Dunfee-Kidston 4½ Litre roars by.
£85–100 BKS

1924 3 Litre Bentley Dual-Cowl Four-Seat Tourer, coachwork by Vanden Plas, twin sloper carburettors, B-type gearbox, correct beaded-edge wheels, twin side-mounted spares, complete weather equipment including tonneau, engine rebuilt early 1990s, finished in green over black, black leather interior, well maintained.
£50,000–60,000 BKS

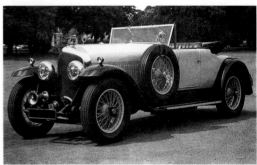

1926 Bentley 6½ Litre Short-Chassis Simplex Coupé, coachwork by Mulliner, 6597cc, 6-cylinder engine, plate clutch, 11ft short-wheelbase chassis, raked windscreen, front quarter-lights, glass side windows, twin side-mounted spares, Stephan Grebel headlamps, screen-mounted swivel spotlamps, front-mounted electric klaxon.
£110,000–121,000 BKS

By 1924, it was becoming increasingly obvious to W.O. Bentley that even in long-chassis form, the 3 Litre model would not cope with the demands for ever grander coachwork, and work began that year on developing a new car to address the problem. The new chassis and engine were developed in time to launch the 6½ Litre at Olympia in October 1925.

BENTLEY Model	ENGINE cc/cyl	DATES	CONDITION		
			1	2	3
3 Litre	2996/4	1920–27	£100,000	£75,000	£40,000
Speed Six	6597/6	1926–32	£300,000	£250,000	£160,000
4½ Litre	4398/4	1927–31	£175,000	£125,000	£80,000
4½ Litre Supercharged	4398/4	1929–32	£600,000+	£300,000	£200,000
8 Litre	7983/6	1930–32	£350,000	£250,000	£100,000
3½ Litre Saloon & DHC	3699/6	1934–37	£70,000	£30,000	£15,000
4¼ litre Saloon & DHC	4257/6	1937–39	£70,000	£35,000	£20,000
Mk V	4257/6	1939–41	£45,000	£25,000	£20,000

Prices are dependent on engine type, chassis length, matching chassis and engine nos, body style and coachbuilder, and original extras like supercharger, gearbox ratio, racing history and originality.

1934 Bentley 3½ Litre Sports Saloon, coachwork by Barker, restored, finished in red and cream, beige leather interior, concours winner.
£29,000–32,000 BKS

The continuation of the Bentley name was assured when the financially troubled company was acquired by Rolls-Royce in 1931. In 1933, the new 'Silent Sports Car' was announced, having been developed from the experimental Rolls-Royce 18hp Peregrine chassis with an all-new six-cylinder, overhead-valve engine. The Bentley sporting tradition was maintained, the new car having a top speed of 90mph, but now it was much quieter, which was directly attributable to Rolls-Royce engineering.

◀ **1934 Bentley 3½ Litre Drophead Coupé,** coachwork by Park Ward, finished in black, tan hide upholstery, well maintained, variety of mechanical spares, including sump, starter motor, rocker box cover with cams, crankshaft, flywheel, steering box and column.
£40,000–45,000 COYS

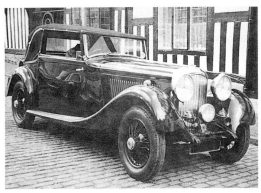

1934 Bentley 3½ Litre Drophead Coupé, coachwork by Park Ward, engine rebuilt 1997, Wintone horns, Notek centre spotlamp, rear-mounted spare wheel, finished in black with red coachlines, interior trimmed in red leather, front seats reupholstered 1998, good overall condition.
£30,000–34,000 S

1939 Bentley 4¼ Litre MX Lightweight Tourer, 4257cc, 6-cylinder engine, overdrive, mechanics overhauled, original factory specification in all major respects, finished in cream and blue, blue leather interior.
£28,000–32,000 BKS

The MX was introduced in 1939, and the overdrive top gear gave the car the extra performance necessary for long-distance touring. This car was fitted with James Young Coupé coachwork originally, but was rebodied in later years with lightweight aluminium tourer coachwork.

BENTLEY Model	ENGINE cc/cyl	DATES	CONDITION 1	2	3
Abbreviations: HJM = H J Mulliner; PW = Park Ward; M/PW = Mulliner/Park Ward					
Mk VI Standard Steel	4257/4566/6	1946–52	£16,000	£10,000	£5,000
Mk VI Coachbuilt	4257/4566/6	1946–52	£25,000	£20,000	£12,000
Mk VI Coachbuilt DHC	4566/6	1946–52	£40,000+	£30,000	£20,000
R-Type Standard Steel	4566/6	1952–55	£12,000	£10,000	£7,000
R-Type Coachbuilt	4566/6	1952–55	£25,000	£20,000	£15,000
R-Type Coachbuilt DHC	4566/4887/6	1952–55	£50,000	£35,000	£25,000
R-Type Cont (HJM)	4887/6	1952–55	£80,000+	£40,000	£29,000
S1 Standard Steel	4887/6	1955–59	£15,000	£10,000	£7,000
S1 Cont 2-door (PW)	4877/6	1955–59	£30,000	£25,000	£20,000
S1 Cont Drophead	4877/6	1955–59	£80,000+	£75,000	£50,000
S1 Cont F'back (HJM)	4877/6	1955–58	£50,000	£35,000	£25,000
S2 Standard Steel	6230/8	1959–62	£15,000	£9,000	£6,000
S2 Cont 2-door (HJM)	6230/8	1959–62	£60,000	£40,000	£30,000
S2 Flying Spur (HJM)	6230/8	1959–62	£45,000	£33,000	£22,000
S2 Conv (PW)	6230/8	1959–62	£60,000+	£50,000	£35,000
S3 Standard Steel	6230/8	1962–65	£16,000	£11,000	£9,000
S3 Cont/Flying Spur	6230/8	1962–65	£45,000	£30,000	£25,000
S3 2-door (M/PW)	6230/8	1962–65	£30,000	£25,000	£10,000
S3 Conv (modern conversion – only made one original)	6230/8	1962–65	£40,000	£28,000	£20,000
T1	6230/6, 6750/8	1965–77	£10,000	£8,000	£4,000
T1 2-door (M/PW)	6230/6, 6750/8	1965–70	£15,000	£12,000	£9,000
T1 Drophead (M/PW)	6230/6, 6750/8	1965–70	£30,000	£20,000	£12,000

1949 Bentley Mk VI Two-Door Saloon, coachwork by James Young, 4257cc, 6-cylinder engine, chassis in good condition, finished in silver over lilac, light grey leather upholstery in good condition, stored since 1997, in need of mechanical attention.
£11,500–13,000 BKS

1949 Bentley Mk VI Sedanca Coupé, coachwork by Gurney Nutting, 4257cc, 6-cylinder engine, left-hand drive, finished in black and red, red leather interior, cocktail cabinet, well maintained, 76,000 miles recorded.
£40,000–45,000 BKS

Bentley's all-new post-war model combined sporting flair and engineering finesse. A departure for the new model was the availability of factory-built coachwork, although the Mk VI remained available in chassis form for those who wanted bespoke coachwork from the dwindling band of traditional coachbuilders, such as Gurney Nutting. The R-ROC publication *The Flying Lady* described the Sedance Coupé as 'combining elegance and sporty open-air motoring in a tasteful, yet flamboyant package'.

1949 Bentley Mk VI Special, aluminium bodywork on ash frame, pre-war Derby Bentley bonnet, 15 gallon rear-mounted fuel tank, restored 1997, engine and gearbox overhauled, finished in British Racing green, black trimmed seats and tonneau cover.
£22,000–25,000 COYS

This Mk VI has been rebodied following the traditional design and construction of the vintage machines that were so successful during the 1920s and 1930s.

1949 Bentley Mk VI Two-Door Drophead Coupé, coachwork by Park Ward, 4257cc, converted to full oil filter system, finished in maroon, power-operated burgundy hood, beige hide interior, paintwork and chrome in very good condition, well maintained, 1 of 45 drophead coupés built.
£42,000–46,500 BKS

1950 Bentley Mk VI Drophead Coupé, coachwork by Abbott, 4257cc, 6-cylinder engine, overhead inlet and side exhaust valves, twin SU carburettors, belt-driven dynamo and water pump, independent front suspension by wishbones and coil springs, live leaf-sprung rear axle, 4-wheel drum brakes with mechanically-driven servo, 90mph top speed, finished in cream and red, cream upholstery.
£19,000–23,000 COYS

1950 Bentley Donington V8 Roadster, coachwork by Johnard, 6.2 litre V8 engine, alloy wheels, finished in claret, black hide interior, 1,301 miles recorded, 1 of only 2 V8-engined models built, formerly owned by Elton John, excellent condition throughout.
£22,000–25,000 BKS

This two-seater Bentley special was built in 1978 on a Mk VI chassis by Dorset based Johnard Vintage Car Repairs. It was fitted with a later S2 V8 engine and front disc brakes, while the bodywork was a combination of fibreglass and aluminium panels.

1951 Bentley Mk VI Standard Steel Saloon, 4566cc, 6-cylinder F-head engine, SU carburettors, restored 1980–85 at a cost of c£30,000, recent engine overhaul, fewer than 50 miles covered since, finished in 2-tone grey, original grey Connolly hide interior piped in navy blue.
£10,000–12,000 BKS

1951 Bentley Mk VI Lightweight Sports Saloon, coachwork by Mulliner, 4257cc, 6-cylinder F-head engine, original beige leather upholstery and interior fittings, period radio, folding picnic tables to rear, 1 family ownership for 44 years, 47,500 miles recorded, original apart from later rear lamps.
£13,500–15,000 BKS

◄ **1952 Bentley Mk VI Saloon,** 4566cc, fitted with Rolls-Royce grille and hub caps, finished in silver, beige trim, good condition throughout.
£9,500–11,000 **H&H**

1952 Bentley R-Type Saloon, coachwork by James Young, 4566cc, manual gearbox, sound chassis, finished in 2-tone green, green leather interior, unused for some time, recently recommissioned.
£14,000–16,000 **RCC**

► **1954 Bentley R-Type Saloon,** coachwork by James Young, factory fitted with twin foglamps, Continental radiator shell and bumpers, front screen demister, stored 1971–90, restored over 4 years, new exhaust system, finished in black over grey, red interior.
£12,000–14,000 **BKS**

1954 Bentley R-Type Saloon, coachwork by Mulliner, 4566cc, 6-cylinder F-head engine, independent front suspension by wishbone and coil springs, live leaf-sprung rear axle, 4-wheel drum brakes with mechanical servo assistance, left-hand drive, finished in Tudor grey.
£12,000–14,000 **COYS**

1955 Bentley R-Type Continental, coachwork by Mulliner, 4.9 litre, 6-cylinder engine, manual gearbox, c120mph top speed, well maintained, completely restored, original.
£68,000–75,000 COYS

Although the Derby Bentley preserved a distinctive identity compared to its Rolls-Royce cousins, most of this was lost in the early post-war years when the difference between the Mk VI Bentley and the Silver Dawn was reduced to a matter of mild tuning. However, this state of affairs was corrected in 1952 with the introduction of what was to become the greatest sporting post-war Bentley of all, the R-Type Continental. In most cases fitted with fastback coupé coachwork by Mulliner, it was the fastest production four-seater in the world.

1955 Bentley R-Type Continental, coachwork by Mulliner, 4887cc, 6-cylinder F-head engine, manual gearbox with right-hand change, air conditioning, alarm, seat belts, fire extinguisher, rear-wheel spats, restored, finished in black, brown leather upholstery and trim, 92,000 miles recorded, bodywork very sound.
£71,000–79,000 BKS

1956 Bentley S1 Saloon, 4887cc, 6-cylinder engine, new exhaust system, finished in black, beige leather interior, good mechanical condition.
£5,000–6,000 BRIT

The S1 was introduced in September 1955 and proved a success in the export market, particularly North America.

1956 Bentley S1 Saloon, resprayed in dark grey over light grey, original blue and grey leather upholstery in good condition, well maintained.
£13,000–15,000 RCC

1958 Bentley S1 Empress Line Saloon, coachwork by Hooper, 4887cc, 6-cylinder, inlet-over-exhaust engine, automatic transmission, power-assisted steering, finished in Pearl grey, bench front seat, beige leather upholstery, ebony veneers, paintwork and chrome in good condition, history file.
£14,000–17,000 BKS

1958 Bentley S1 Drophead Coupé, coachwork by Mulliner, 4887cc, 6-cylinder engine, 4-speed automatic transmission, left-hand drive, 119mph top speed, interior in excellent condition.
£185,000–204,000 RM

◄ **1959 Bentley S2 Saloon,** 6230cc V8 engine, automatic transmission, Radford conversion with raised aluminium bootlid, Webasto sunroof, adjustable Reutter front seats with picnic tables, folding split rear seats, concealed vanity units and storage lockers, picnic table in the boot, £4,000 spent on gearbox rebuild, new rear springs, stainless steel exhaust, bodywork completely restored, new sills and wings, all chrome renewed, bare-metal respray in grey over blue, sunroof re-covered, interior woodwork restored, grey leather upholstery.
£14,000–16,000 H&H

► **1960 Bentley S2 Continental,** 6230cc, automatic transmission, completely restored early 1990s at a cost of about £60,000, finished in Dawn blue, pale blue interior trim, as-new condition.
£42,000–48,000 H&H

► **1964 Bentley S3 Saloon,** 6230cc, 6-cylinder engine, resprayed in Sand, burgundy hide interior, very good original condition.
£14,000–16,000 BRIT

The ultimate development of the S-series Bentley, the S3 retained similar coachwork to its predecessors, but was instantly recognisable by its twin headlamps.

1965 Bentley S3 Saloon, coachwork by James Young, finished in Oxford blue, 116mph top speed.
£9,000–11,000 BKS

This car carries one of the last bodies made by James Young, itself one of the last two independent British coachbuilders. Shortly after Rolls-Royce and Bentley introduced unitary construction, James Young ceased making bodies, ending a continuous history of more than 100 years.

1967 Bentley T1 Saloon, 6750cc V8, left-hand drive, finished in 2-tone grey, good condition.
£7,000–9,000 PALM

Dealer prices

Miller's guide prices for dealer cars take into account the value of any guarantees or warranties that may be included in the purchase. Dealers must also observe additional statutory consumer regulations, which do not apply to private sellers. This is factored into our dealer guide prices. To identify dealer cars cross-refer the source codes at the ends of photo captions with the Key to Illustrations on page 330.

1968 Bentley T1, 6230cc V8, bare-metal respray in green at a cost of almost £5,000, original grey leather interior trim, all mechanical components and brightwork in good condition.
£7,000–9,000 BRIT

Successor to the S3, the T-series Bentley appeared in 1965, together with its Rolls-Royce counterpart, the Silver Shadow. It was of monocoque construction and featured self-levelling, fully independent suspension, plus dual-circuit servo-assisted disc brakes. The Bentley was built in considerably fewer numbers than the Rolls-Royce and, therefore, is comparatively rare.

◄ **1969 Bentley T1 Coupé,** coachwork by Mulliner Park Ward, 6230cc, finished in Regal red, tan interior trim, little recent use, recommissioned at a cost of £4,000, excellent condition.
£10,000–12,000 H&H

◄ **1972 Bentley T1 Saloon,**
6750cc V8, new suspension leveller units, brake and suspension pipes, bodywork restored, bare-metal respray in Seychelles blue, magnolia hide interior, good mechanical condition.
£5,500–6,500 BRIT

▶ **1978 Bentley T2 Saloon,**
6750cc V8, automatic transmission, finished in brown with matching trim, 98,900 miles recorded, good condition throughout.
£6,000–7,000 LF

The T1 and T2 were Bentley's equivalents of the Rolls-Royce Silver Shadow I and II. Although virtually identical, apart from the distinctive radiator, Bentley versions can often be cheaper than Rolls-Royce counterparts, despite the fact that Bentley versions are far rarer.

◄ **1979 Bentley T2 Saloon,** 6750cc, rack-and-pinion steering, split-level air conditioning, finished in blue, blue interior trim, 70,000 miles recorded, very good condition throughout.
£9,500–11,000 H&H

Only 558 examples of the Bentley T2 were built.

1980 Bentley T2 Saloon, converted to 7 litres capacity by Harvey Bailey Engineering at a cost of £15,000, 25,000 miles covered since, high-performance pistons, 4-barrel Holley carburettor, stainless steel exhaust system, fitted with same company's handling kit, finished in Pewter, blue Connolly hide interior, very good condition throughout.
£12,000–14,500 BKS

This car was featured in Harvey Bailey's advertising and served as the company's demonstrator, before being sold in 1993.

1984 Bentley Mulsanne Turbo Saloon, 6750cc V8, Garrett AiResearch turbocharger, 135mph top speed, 60mph in about 8 seconds, finished in green, Stone leather interior, good condition throughout.
£12,000–14,000 BKS

Launched in 1982, the Bentley Mulsanne Turbo provoked a rash of headlines proclaiming the return of the Blower Bentley.

◀ **1987 Bentley Turbo R Saloon,** 6750cc, electronic fuel injection, turbocharger, ABS braking, twin-headlamp conversion, finished in Larkspur blue, light blue interior trim, leather top and bottom dash rolls and headlining, 70,000 miles recorded, well maintained, excellent condition.
£16,000–18,000 H&H

▶ **1987 Bentley Turbo R Saloon,** electronic fuel injection, turbocharger, finished in light grey, red-piped leather interior, sports seats, drinks compartment with crystal tumblers and leather-covered flasks, very good condition throughout.
£16,500–18,500 BKS

Introduced in 1985, the Bentley Turbo R continued the theme of the preceding Mulsanne Turbo, but with suspension better suited to the car's increased performance. Outwardly, the R differed by sporting alloy wheels shod with low-profile Pirelli tyres, while inside there was a revised fascia with rev-counter.

◀ **1988 Bentley Turbo R Saloon,** 6750cc, 320bhp, 135mph top speed, 0–60mph in 6.6 seconds, finished in Graphite, beige leather interior, sports seats, well maintained good condition throughout.
£18,000–20,000 BKS

Benz

◀ **1894 Benz Velo 1½hp Two-Seater,** single-cylinder, rear-mounted horizontal engine, belt transmission with chain final drive to the rear wheels, Crypto (extremely low) third speed, spoon braking on rear wheels, copper water tanks, finished in black with red coachlining, folding leather hood, central oil headlamp, twin candle side lamps, twin oil rear lamps, black leather upholstery, own trailer, excellent condition.
£70,000–80,000 BKS

Karl Benz is credited as the man who designed and built the first workable motor car driven by an internal-combustion engine. His company began making gas engines in 1883, built its first car in 1885, and from the outset concentrated on the construction of a complete chassis and engine assembly, rather than the motorisation of a horse-drawn carriage. The earliest Benz cars were three-wheelers, the engine driving the two rear wheels. The first four-wheeler, the Victoria (introduced in 1893), formed the basis of the earliest motorised van and bus in 1895, while the Velo of 1894 followed the same mechanical concept.

Berkeley

1959 Berkeley Sports, 492cc, 3-cylinder engine, 30bhp, front-wheel drive, fibreglass bodywork, good condition.
£3,500–4,000 BERK

1959 Berkeley B105 Sports, 700cc, air-cooled, twin-cylinder Royal Enfield engine, 50bhp, fibreglass bodywork, finished in metallic blue.
£3,500–4,000 BERK

Berliet

◀ **1933 Berliet Type 944 Four-Door Saloon,** 2000cc, overhead-valve engine, 4-speed manual gearbox, finished in blue over black, original black leatherette interior trim in need of refurbishment, otherwise good condition, last model to be produced.
£3,500–4,000 H&H

BMW

Bayerische Flugzeug Werke, as the company was originally called, was founded in 1916 to make aero engines, becoming *Bayerische Motoren Werke* in 1922 with the beginning of motorcycle production. Car production followed in 1928 with the Dixi, an Austin 7 built under licence. The first true BMW, the four-cylinder, 800cc 3/20 appeared in 1932, followed by a range of fine touring and sports cars. The pinnacle of the company's pre-war achievements was the lithe 2 litre 328 which, fitted with a beautiful streamlined body, won the 1940 Mille Miglia. The streamlined 328 undoubtedly had a strong influence on the shape of William Lyons' post-war Jaguar XK120. After the war, BMW survived the nationalisation of its Eisenach factory, by then in East Germany, and several financial crises. The 507 V8-engined roadster – aimed at the Yankee dollar – was beautiful, but extortionately over-priced. The Isetta microcars at first brought salvation, then threatened oblivion as sales slumped in the late 1950s. The turn-around came in 1961 with the launch of the neat Michelotti-styled 1500 and 1800 models, which helped create BMW's modern reputation for superbly-built prestige cars.

BMW Model	ENGINE cc/cyl	DATES	CONDITION 1	2	3
Dixi	747/4	1927–32	£7,000	£3,000	£2,000
303	1175/6	1934–36	£11,000	£8,000	£5,000
309	843/4	1933–34	£6,000	£4,000	£2,000
315	1490/6	1935–36	£9,000	£7,000	£5,000
319	1911/6	1935–37	£10,000	£9,000	£6,000
326	1971/6	1936–37	£12,000	£10,000	£8,000
320 series	1971/6	1937–38	£12,000	£10,000	£8,000
327/328	1971/6	1937–40	£30,000+	£18,000	£10,000
328	1971/6	1937–40	£60,000+	-	-

◀ **1951 BMW 327 Coupé,** 1998cc, 4-speed manual gearbox, finished in cream and black, tan interior trim and upholstery, very good condition throughout. **£13,500–15,000 H&H**

1947 BMW Type 321 Two-Door Saloon, finished in black and white, brown leather interior, good condition. **£1,500–1,800 BKS**

With its factories destroyed by Allied bombing, BMW struggled to re-establish itself after WWII, beginning in 1946 with the manufacture of metal household goods. Car production did not resume for another seven years. However, at the firm's Eisenach factory in the Soviet-controlled eastern zone, production of the 2 litre BMW 321 had resumed almost immediately under the supervision of the Russian Autovelo organisation. Production of these 'counterfeit' BMWs continued until 1955, by which time BMW had successfully challenged the use of its name and badge, forcing the East German company to rename itself Eisenacher Motoren Werke – EMW. About 10,000 BMW/EMW Type 321s were built at Eisenach between 1945 and 1950.

BMW Model	ENGINE cc/cyl	DATES	CONDITION 1	CONDITION 2	CONDITION 3
501	2077/6	1952–56	£9,000	£7,000	£3,500
501 V8/502	2580, 3168/8	1955–63	£10,000+	£5,000	£3,000
503 FHC/DHC	3168/8	1956–59	£25,000+	£20,000	£15,000
507	3168/8	1956–59	£100,000+	£70,000	£50,000
Isetta (4 wheels)	247/1	1955–62	£7,000	£3,000	£1,200
Isetta (3 wheels)	298/1	1958–64	£8,000	£2,500	£1,500
Isetta 600	585/2	1958–59	£3,000	£1,800	£500
1500/1800/2000	var/4	1962–68	£1,800	£800	£500
2000CS	1990/4	1966–69	£5,500	£4,000	£1,500
1500/1600/1602	1499/ 1573/4	1966–75	£3,000+	£1,500	£800
1600 Cabriolet	1573/4	1967–71	£6,000	£4,500	£2,000
2800CS	2788/6	1968–71	£5,000	£4,000	£1,500
1602	1990/4	1968–74	£3,000	£1,500	£1,000
2002	1990/4	1968–74	£3,000	£2,000	£1,000
2002 Tii	1990/4	1971–75	£4,500	£2,500	£1,200
2002 Touring	1990/4	1971–74	£3,500	£2,000	£1,000
2002 Cabriolet	1990/4	1971–75	£5,000+	£3,000	£2,500
2002 Turbo	1990/4	1973–74	£10,000	£6,000	£4,000
3.0 CSa/CSi	2986/6	1972–75	£8,000	£6,000	£4,000
3.0 CSL	3003/ 3153/6	1972–75	£16,000	£10,000	£7,500
MI	3500/6	1978–85	£60,000	£40,000	£30,000
633/635 CS/CSI	3210/3453/6	1976–85	£7,000	£3,000	£2,000
M535i	3453/6	1979–81	£4,500	£3,000	£2,500

Miller's Starter Marque

Starter BMWs: *1502, 1602, 2002, 2002 Touring.*

- The '02 series two-door saloons made BMW's fortune in the late 1960s and established the marque's modern reputation for sporty, stylish saloons. Today, these spirited machines make an awful lot of sense as usable, every-day classics with a dash of real class. What's more, BMW has a deserved reputation for looking after its older cars in terms of mechanical and body spares; neither are the BMW parts particularly pricey.

- All of the '02 series are reassuringly solid and robust, as you'll notice when you sit behind the wheel and pull the door closed with a good solid 'thunk'. All except the 1502 'oil-crisis' model are good for 100mph, while the fuel-injected 2002 Tii offered a class-leading 0–60mph time of 8.2 seconds in 1971. This and the twin-carb 2002 Ti are probably the best buys, while the 1602, plain 2002 and 1502 make sensible down-market alternatives.

- Rust problems are no worse than any other steel monocoque saloon, although particular points to watch include the jacking points, which can eventually fall out and leave the sills prone to rotting from the inside out.

- The overhead-camshaft engine has an alloy cylinder head on a cast-iron block. It's generally long-lived, but the more you know about the car's history, the better. Regular oil changes will promote long life and year-round anti-freeze will help prevent corrosion inside the alloy head, reducing the chance of it warping through overheating.

- All in all, this Beemer's pretty straightforward, but there are a couple of more exotic options. Cabriolets are undoubtedly desirable, but have some nasty rust-traps, particularly behind the rear seat where the hood is stowed. If you're not careful, Cabriolet restoration costs could spiral beyond reach.

- Likewise, the rare 2002 Turbo is an enthusiast's car rather than an every-day user. For a start, only 51 were sold in the UK. If you can find one, you'll get performance – and shattering bills to match.

1973 BMW 2002, 1990cc, overhead-camshaft engine, aluminium crossflow cylinder head, good condition.
£2,500–3,000 HMM

1973 BMW 3.0 CSL Coupé, restored 1990, finished in blue, black interior, Scheel lightweight front bucket seats, original.
£7,500–8,500 BKS

1973 BMW 3.0 CSL Coupé, restored, finished in pale blue, very good condition throughout.
£6,000–7,000 BKS

1975 BMW 2002 Turbo, new clutch, Koni shock absorbers, finished in silver, original Turbo transfers, black interior trim, good condition throughout.
£3,500–4,000 **BKS**

The 2002 Turbo was Europe's first turbocharged car. In fact, when it was launched in 1973, it was the world's only turbocharged production model. Unfortunately, its arrival coincided with the OPEC oil crisis, which restricted sales and its production life.

1984 BMW Alpina B9-3.5, 3430cc, 6-cylinder engine, 245bhp, manual gearbox, progressive-rate coil springs, adjustable Bilstein dampers, limited-slip differential, 16in alloy wheels, large front air dam, rubber boot spoiler, tinted glass, bucket seats, air conditioning, 153+mph top speed, 0–60mph in 6.8 seconds, history file, original condition.
£5,000–6,000 **COYS**

Bristol

Nestling at the end of London's Kensington High Street, hard by the Hilton Hotel, there's a tiny showroom that proclaims in red neon, 'Bristol Cars Ltd'. This is the single retail outlet of what has to be the most British car you can buy. The story of Bristol Cars began in 1947 when the Bristol Aeroplane Company branched out into car manufacture with an anglicised version of the pre-war BMW 327. Bristol's famed six-cylinder engine was derived from a pre-war BMW unit. Combining this with handcrafted coachwork and luxury appointments, Bristols earned the appellation 'The Businessman's Express'. In the early 1960s, Bristol Cars Ltd, as it had become, adopted Chrysler V8 power to endow its luxury sports saloons with extra urge. At their best, the V8 Bristols could offer near Jaguar or Ferrari performance, but with most un-Ferrari-like quiet.

1948 Bristol 400 Saloon, 1971cc, 6-cylinder engine, triple carburettors, oil cooler, 85bhp, engine and brakes rebuilt, converted to unleaded fuel, extra spare wheel, finished in black, interior recently retrimmed in cream hide piped in black, competition harnesses, fire extinguisher, concours winner, excellent condition.
£14,000–16,000 **H&H**

1950 Bristol 401 Saloon, finished in blue with matching leather interior, good condition throughout.
£7,500–9,000 **BKS**

With the introduction of the 401, Bristol began to move away from the pre-war design inherited from BMW. The bodywork was built using Touring's Superleggera method of construction, alloy panels being attached to a lightweight tubular-steel framework, while the low-drag shape was achieved after hours of experimentation in Bristol's wind tunnel. The 401 continued to use its predecessor's running gear and BMW-based, 2 litre, six-cylinder engine with its pushrod-operated, inclined valves.

◀ **1959 Bristol 406 Saloon,** 2200cc, double-overhead-camshaft, 6-cylinder inline engine, triple Solex carburettors, 4-speed manual gearbox, transverse leaf-spring front suspension, live rear axle with Watts linkage and torque arm, 90mph top speed, refurbished as necessary, finished in green, beige leather upholstery, original HMV radio, well maintained, good condition.
£6,250–6,900 **C**

Introduced in 1958, the 406 was the last of the Bristol line to be equipped with engines from the company's Filton plant. Some 300 examples were built up to 1961, when production of the model ceased.

BRISTOL Model	ENGINE cc/cyl	DATES	CONDITION 1	2	3
400	1971/6	1947–50	£18,000	£14,000	£8,000
401 FHC/DHC	1971/6	1949–53	£28,000	£14,000	£8,000
402	1971/6	1949–50	£22,000	£19,000	£12,000
403	1971/6	1953–55	£20,000	£14,000	£10,000
404 Coupé	1971/6	1953–57	£22,000	£15,000	£12,000
405	1971/6	1954–58	£17,000	£13,000	£10,000
405 Drophead	1971/6	1954–56	£25,000	£22,000	£18,000
406	2216/6	1958–61	£15,000	£11,000	£7,000
407	5130/8	1962–63	£15,000	£8,000	£6,000
408	5130/8	1964–65	£14,000	£10,000	£8,000
409	5211/8	1966–67	£14,000	£11,000	£7,000
410	5211/8	1969	£14,000	£10,000	£6,000
411 Mk 1–3	6277/8	1970–73	£16,000	£11,000	£8,000
411 Mk 4–5	6556/8	1974–76	£12,500	£9,500	£7,000
412	5900/ 6556/8	1975–82	£15,000	£9,000	£6,000
603	5211/ 5900/8	1976–82	£12,000	£8,000	£5,000

1965 Bristol 409 Saloon, 5211cc, Chrysler V8 engine, new stainless steel silencer, new coil, battery immobiliser switch, Girling disc brakes, new windscreen, finished in blue, grey interior trim refurbished, front seats reupholstered, new door pulls, new carpets, period Radiomobile radio, 1 of only 74 produced, would benefit from some rechroming and a respray, otherwise good condition throughout.
£5,000–6,000 H&H

1985 Bristol Brigand, 5900cc V8, new transmission, finished in British Racing green, grey leather upholstery, well maintained, 88,300 miles recorded.
£12,000–14,000 BRIT

Although outwardly very similar to the Britannia, the Brigand, which was introduced in 1983, differed by being fitted with the turbocharged engine, as used in the Beaufighter. The excellent Bristol chassis was more than capable of handling the additional power, enabling the traditionally high standard of roadholding to be maintained.

▶ **1970 Bristol 411 Mk 1,** power-assisted steering, power windows, sunroof, finished in burgundy, brightwork in excellent condition, upholstered in Stone leather, 65,131 miles recorded, concours winner, excellent condition.
£14,000–16,000 S

Bristol 400 (1947–50)

Engine: Overhead-valve, six-cylinder, 1971cc.
Power output: 85bhp at 4,500rpm.
Transmission: Four-speed manual.
Top speed: 94mph.
0–60mph: 17.4 seconds.
Price in 1948: £2,723.14s.6d (including purchase tax).
When the Bristol Aeroplane Company decided to branch out into car manufacture, it just so happened that Bristol had a set of plans of the exotic pre-war BMW 327, along with several examples of the car itself. If you doubt the lineage, take a look at the double-kidney grille. The box-section chassis was based on the earlier BMW's, and Bristol engineers refined the already highly-efficient 2 litre BMW engine still further. As for the body style, although it still had faint echoes of the earlier BMW, the Bristol's streamlined, teardrop form was one of the first to be developed in a wind-tunnel. Bristol's stated aim had been to build a 'high-speed luxury motor car for the connoisseur, a powerful elegant model worthy of the "Bristol" reputation'. Neither did it disappoint, with advanced rack-and-pinion steering, crisp handling, eager performance, aircraft-quality construction and a luxury interior. But all this precision came at quite a price, considerably more than any Jaguar or Daimler saloon, and even pricier than the Aston Martin DB1. Only 700 Bristol 400s were built – actually quite a high production figure for a Bristol – but the 400 set the company on the path it would continue to take to this day. Ever since, Bristols have continued to be made in small numbers, providing exclusive, handcrafted luxury for those who could afford them.

◀ **1927 AC Royal 12hp Two-Seat Tourer,** finished in green with black wings, dickey seat, green interior trim, retaining many original parts, engine rebuilt, replacement differential.
£8,000–9,000 H&H

▶ **1962 AC Ace Ruddspeed,** 2.6 litre, Ken Rudd-modified, 6-cylinder Ford Zephyr engine, alloy head, big valves, triple Weber carburettors, special pistons, reprofiled camshaft, balanced bottom end, restored over 10 years, finished in red, chrome wire wheels, original red leather interior, 1 of 36 built, excellent condition.
£55,000–60,000 COYS

This particular car was used by the works to homologate the model for use in international GT racing during the early 1960s. At that time, AC was on the verge of becoming a dominant force in that branch of motor racing.

1930 Alfa Romeo 6C-1750, coachwork by Castagna, 1752cc, 6-cylinder, normally-aspirated engine, dickey seat, right-hand drive, completely restored, finished in red, light tan leather upholstery, excellent condition.
£100,000–120,000 BKS

1953 Alfa Romeo 1900 CS Farina Coupé, coachwork by Pininfarina, 1844cc, 4-cylinder engine, 100bhp, completely restored, little use since, trimmed in black leather, Zagato seats, Nardi wood-rimmed steering wheel, Borrani wire wheels, 1 of only 11 known to exist, excellent condition.
£24,000–27,000 COYS

◀ **1954 Alfa Romeo 1900 Super Sprint Coupé,** coachwork by Touring, double-overhead-camshaft engine, 115bhp, 5-speed gearbox, 112mph top speed, original Borrani wheels, finished in red, light tan interior, 1 of about 299 made.
£32,000–36,000 BKS

This car is believed to have competed in the 1955 or 1956 Mille Miglia road race. At the 1998 Nürburgring Oldtimer Grand Prix, it was voted Best of Show of 300 Alfa Romeos present.

► **1935 Armstrong-Siddeley 12/6 Six-Light Saloon,** 1479cc, 6-cylinder engine, finished in maroon and black, plum interior, history file, very good condition throughout.
£6,750–7,500 H&H

1955 Aston Martin DB2/4, 2992cc, double-overhead-camshaft, 6-cylinder engine, 140bhp at 5,000rpm, 0–60mph in 10 seconds, restored early 1990s, finished in red, black leather upholstery, matching carpets.
£24,000–27,000 COYS

Fine car though the Aston Martin DB2 was, its sales had been affected by the limitations of its two seats and minimal luggage space. As a result, Aston Martin redesigned the rear of the car to incorporate two occasional rear seats, at the same time raising the roof line slightly to increase headroom and fitting a larger rear window in an opening lid. This Aston, the DB2/4, was arguably the world's first hatchback.

1959 Aston Martin DB3, 3 litre, double-overhead-camshaft, 6-cylinder DBD engine, triple carburettors, 180bhp, 4-speed manual gearbox, independent front suspension, live rear axle, Girling front disc brakes, Alfin rear drums, original black leather interior, DB4-style instrument cluster, Borrani wire wheels, left-hand drive, 29,000 miles recorded.
£26,000–29,000 RM

Of the 550 DB3s built, only 47 were fitted with the high-performance DBD engine.

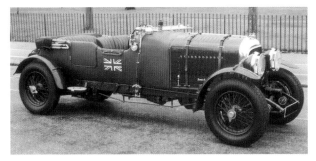

◄ **1928 Bentley 4½ Litre Tourer,** overhead-camshaft engine, 4 valves/2 spark plugs per cylinder, retaining all original major mechanical components, finished in British Racing green, green hide interior, well maintained.
£145,000–160,000 COYS

This car was delivered new with a two-seater body by the small coachbuilder Progressive, which was responsible for bodying just two 4½ Litre models. Subsequently, the body was replaced by a Vanden Plas-style Le Mans body by Robinson.

► **1934 Bentley 3½ Litre Three-Position Drophead Coupé,** coachwork by Vincents, recently restored, finished in off-white, blue and grey leather interior in very good condition, black hood, very sound structural condition, 1 of only 2 Derby Bentleys bodied by Vincents.
£35,000–39,000 RCC

1935 Bentley 4¼ Litre Pillarless Saloon, coachwork by Vanden Plas, 4257cc, 6-cylinder engine, finished in blue over silver, grey interior, removable trafficators to the bumpers, very good condition throughout.
£18,000–21,000 H&H

◄ **1959 BMW 507,** 3168cc V8, 150bhp, 135mph top speed, 0–60mph in 8.8 seconds, restored over 4 years at a cost of £120,000, 1,200km covered since, finished in red, black interior and top, Rudge knock-off wheels, 1 of only 253 made.
£160,000–170,000 BKS

► **1937 Bugatti Type 57 Stelvio Cabriolet,** coachwork by Gangloff, chassis no. 57435, semi-elliptic front springs, quarter-elliptic rear springs, cable-operated brakes, lightweight aluminium bodywork, restored, finished in Bugatti blue, blue top, tan interior, recent £10,000 spent on further work.
£150,000–170,000 COYS

The Type 57 was a landmark car for Bugatti because it was engineered specifically for road use. Most of the company's previous output had consisted of dual-purpose road/competition cars.

◄ **1931 Cadillac V16 All-Weather Phaeton,** 452cu.in, overhead-valve V16, 175hp, 3-speed synchromesh gearbox, 4-wheel power-assisted brakes, 148in wheelbase, complete body-off restoration, pilot ray lights, stainless-steel spoked wheels, correct 'lo-boy' trunk.
£105,000–115,000 RM

1954 Chevrolet Corvette, 235cu.in, overhead-valve, 'Blue Flame' 6-cylinder engine, triple carburettors, 150hp, 2-speed Powerglide automatic transmission, older restoration, good condition.
£24,000–27,000 RM

Production of the two-seat Corvette roadster began in June 1953, and by year's end a total of 300 had been built. Corvette production signified an important technical milestone: GM was the first American car manufacturer to mass-produce a vehicle with a bodyshell made entirely of fibreglass.

1938 Delahaye 135 Competition 'Géo Ham' Roadster No. 700, coachwork by Figoni & Falaschi, rebuilt triple-Solex carburettor engine, nominal mileage since, rebuilt 4-speed manual gearbox, right-hand drive, finished in black with orange coachlining, interior retrimmed in Cognac leather, new carpets.
£800,000+ BKS

Géo Ham – born Georges Hamel – was France's top motoring artist in the 1920s and 1930s. His wonderful sense of line and shape were vividly brought to life at the 1936 Paris Salon. There, the centrepiece of the Delahaye stand was a stunning orange and cream roadster created by the coachbuilding partnership of Figoni & Falaschi on the short-wheelbase, 3.5-litre, six-cylinder Type 135 Competition Court chassis. With dramatic fully-spatted wings concealing the front and rear wheels, and housing the headlamps, the 'Géo Ham' roadster created a sensation. It was bought for 150,000 francs by the playboy prince Aly Khan. Figoni built a further ten roadsters to this voluptuous design, only three of which are known to survive; this car is the sole long-wheelbase example. It was discovered in 1992 in a remote farmyard in the Algerian mountains, with its bodywork intact apart from the boot lid. It also retained its original power unit.

◄ **1952 Ferrari 212 Inter Berlinetta,** coachwork by Touring, chassis no. 0215EL, engine no. 0193EL, original 2562cc engine replaced by an identical 212 unit, triple carburettors, 170bhp, gearbox overhauled, 1,000km covered since, finished in Rosso Ferrari, original black leather upholstery, red carpets, good condition throughout. **£140,000–160,000 BKS**

The Inter was the long-wheelbase version of the 212 series. Only 80 were made, few of them receiving Touring's attractive *Superleggera* body.

► **1953 Ferrari 212 Europa Coupé,** coachwork by Vignale, chassis no. 0287EU, engine no. 0287EU, 2562cc V12, triple carburettors, 160bhp, 5-speed close-ratio gearbox, 120mph top speed, aluminium bodywork, finished in Rosso Rubino, leather upholstery, heater, recent engine rebuild, largely original, good condition throughout. **£150,000–170,000 BKS**

Both the Inter and Europa used the 2.6m-wheelbase chassis. The main difference was that it ran under the back axle on most Inters, and above the axle on the late Europas.

1961 Ferrari 250 GT SWB Lightweight Berlinetta, coachwork by Scaglietti, chassis no. 3067GT, engine no. 3067GT, V12, 240bhp, triple 40DCL6 downdraught Weber twin-choke carburettors, short-wheelbase chassis, aluminium bodywork, aluminium bumpers, engine overhauled at a cost of £20,000, 13,509 miles from new, history file, original. **£500,000+ BKS**

This late-production lightweight car is believed to be one of only four right-hand-drive versions built – two of which were the Rob Walker/Dick Wilkins/Stirling Moss Goodwood TT-winning cars of 1960/61.

1962 Ferrari 250 GT SWB Berlinetta Reproduction, chassis no. 2835, engine no. 2835, engine rebuilt and uprated, triple Weber carburettors, 4-speed gearbox rebuilt, large-capacity radiator, Borrani wire wheels, aluminium fuel tank, trimmed in blue-grey leather. **£70,000–80,000 BKS**

Launched in 1959, the competition SWB proved well-nigh unbeatable in GT racing in the early 1960s. Cars were built for road or track as required, competition versions boasting aluminium bodywork and up to 280bhp. This reproduction, on a 250GTE chassis, features competition-style aluminium coachwork.

1962 Ferrari 250 GT Spyder California, 3000cc, overhead-camshaft V12, triple Weber carburettors, 260bhp, 4-speed manual gearbox, 4-wheel disc brakes, 1 of only 37 covered-headlight cars built.
£700,000+ RM

By 1957, the 250GT 'Tour de France' Lightweight Berlinetta was winning GT races wherever it appeared and was equally at home as a very fast road car. Luigi Chinetti, Ferrari's US agent, foresaw a demand for a convertible version and pressed Enzo Ferrari to build such a car. The result, called the Spyder California, proved an instant success. When the long-wheelbase 250GT 'Tour de France' Berlinetta was phased out in 1959, it was replaced by the SWB (short-wheelbase) Berlinetta fitted with disc brakes. California Spyders were built on the new chassis with more powerful, outside-plug engines.

◀ 1967 Ferrari 275 GTB/4 Berlinetta, chassis no. 09887, engine no. 09887, 165mph top speed, bodywork completely restored, resprayed in original Pino Verde, Borrani wire wheels, original alloy wheels included, reupholstered in tan Connolly hide, fewer than 70,000km recorded.
£190,000–210,000 BKS

The 275GTB/4 appeared in 1966, and apart from a bonnet bulge was virtually identical in appearance to the existing 'long-nose' 275GTB, but its 3.3 litre V12 sported four overhead camshafts, six Weber 40DCN carburettors and a dry-sump lubrication system. The engine gave 300bhp at 8,000rpm. In total, only 350 275GTB/4s were produced.

▶ Fiat Jolly 500, 479cc, overhead-valve, twin-cylinder engine, 16.5bhp, 4-speed gearbox, 4-wheel independent suspension, hydraulic brakes, completely restored, finished in turquoise, authentic Jolly decals, wicker seats, fringed 'surrey' top, completely original.
£13,000–15,000 RM

Intended as a leisure vehicle, the Fiat Jolly was built by Ghia and based on the popular Fiat 500.

◀ 1970 Fiat Dino 2400 Spyder, coachwork by Pininfarina, 2.4 litres, restored 1995/96, 3,000km covered since, finished in silver, black upholstery, excellent condition.
£24,000–28,000 BKS

The Fiat Dino was introduced in 1966 with a 2 litre, four-camshaft V6 engine, being built as a Spyder by Pininfarina and a 2+2 coupé by Bertone. The 2.4 Dino appeared in 1969, assembly having been switched to the Ferrari works in Maranello, improving build quality. The new car featured independent rear suspension, improved braking and cooling, greater power and a new ZF gearbox. Only 424 2.4 litre Spyders were made, compared to 1,133 2 litre Spyders.

◀ **1935 Ford DeLuxe Phaeton,** 221cu.in sidevalve V8, 85bhp, 3-speed manual gearbox, 4-wheel mechanical brakes, completely restored, finished in navy blue, tan cloth hood, rear-mounted spare wheel, dark grey leather interior, concours condition.
£17,000–19,000 RM

1937 Ford V8-78 Utility Car, finished in black, black fabric roof, interior trimmed in beige, period radio, right-hand drive, concours condition.
£20,000–23,000 BKS

Launched in Britain in January 1937, the streamlined 'split-screen' Ford V8-78 bore a resemblance to its upmarket cousin, the Lincoln-Zephyr. 'Easy-action self-energising' cable brakes replaced the rod-operated brakes of earlier V8s. Most expensive of the V8-78 range was the handsome wood-bodied, seven-seat Utility Car, which sold for £265 (the basic saloon was £240). Its bodywork was produced at Ford's Iron Mountain woodworking plant in Michigan, using maple framing and birch panelling from the company's own hardwood forests.

1931 Invicta 4½ Litre S-Type Low Chassis, inline 6-cylinder Meadows engine, 115bhp, semi-elliptic springs and hydraulic dampers front and rear, engine, gearbox and rear axle overhauled, completely restored chassis fitted with new bearings, bolts and trunnions at a cost of £4,000, finished in black, new burgundy interior trim.
£140,000–150,000 COYS

When the Invicta S-Type was unveiled in 1930, it caused a sensation; it was the lowest, sleekest car in the world. In fact, it was so low that some pundits predicted that it would be uncontrollable and would break away when driven hard. However the S-Type proved them wrong, winning the 1931 Monte Carlo Rally (it was second the following year), returning clean sheets in the 1931 and 1932 International Alpine Trials, and performing with distinction on tight and twisty hill climbs like Shelsley Walsh and Prescott.

▶ **1936 Jaguar SS100 2½ Litre,** original engine, completely restored, finished in metallic sand, black upholstery, restored, very good condition throughout.
£70,000–80,000 COYS

This car was supplied new to the Mayor of Prague. Due to the poor road conditions throughout Czechoslovakia at the time, he had its wings modified to shroud the wheels more closely to prevent loose stones and chippings from being thrown up by the wheels. The modified wings remain on the car today.

1938 Jaguar SS 2½ Litre Drophead Coupé, 2663cc, 6-cylinder engine, 100bhp, restored 1990–99, 154 miles covered since, engine, gearbox and axles rebuilt, new stainless steel exhaust system, all ancillary and electrical components rebuilt or replaced as necessary, rewired, body panels replaced or repaired as necessary, interior retrimmed in red leather, new headlining and hood, woodwork refurbished, 'as new' condition.
£53,000–63,000 BKS

1949 Jaguar XK120 Lightweight Roadster, chassis No. 660002, restored 1990, original block, gearbox, rear axle and propshaft, replacement cylinder head, all original panels except new hand-made bonnet, reconstructed ash body frame, finished in original shade of cream, red/beige interior, beige hood, tonneau and sidescreens, 'as new' condition.
£85,000–95,000 BKS

Conceived as a low-volume model, the XK120 proved considerably more popular than expected, with the result that the expensive-to-produce, ash-framed alloy bodywork was replaced by steel after only 240 cars had been completed. This car, the very first of the batch of handbuilt, lightweight cars, exhibits a number of differences from its counterparts, indicating that at the time of its construction not all the fine details of the design had been finalised.

◀ **1964 Jaguar Mk II 3.8 Saloon,** 3781cc, 6 cylinders, manual gearbox with overdrive, independent front suspension by wishbones and coil springs, leaf-sprung live rear axle, 4-wheel disc brakes, 125mph top speed, restored at a cost of £25,000, all mechanical components overhauled or replaced as necessary, Jaguar-approved XJ6 power-assisted rack-and-pinion steering conversion, bare-metal respray in maroon, new wire wheels, new beige leather interior, excellent condition throughout.
£33,000–37,000 BKS

▶ **1964 Jaguar E-Type Roadster,** 3781cc, double-overhead-camshaft, 6-cylinder engine, triple SU carburettors, 265bhp, 4-speed manual gearbox, 4-wheel independent suspension and disc brakes, completely restored, only 60 miles covered since, original fog lamps and radio.
£35,000–40,000 RM

◀ **1971 Jaguar E-Type Series II Roadster,** 4235cc, double-overhead-camshaft, 6-cylinder engine, twin Stromberg carburettors, 177bhp, all-synchromesh gearbox, 4-wheel independent suspension and disc brakes, finished in black, matching black leather upholstery, US-market export model, left-hand drive, 500km covered since 1994.
£15,000–18,000 COYS

BSA

◀ **1933 BSA 10hp Four-Door Saloon,** 1185cc, 4-cylinder engine, fluid flywheel, Daimler-type pre-selector gearbox, standard factory coachwork, completely restored, finished in maroon and black, maroon leather upholstery.
£6,500–7,500 BKS

The Birmingham Small Arms Company, better known for manufacturing motorcycles, offered a sturdy 10hp car in 1933, exhibiting no less than six different body styles at Olympia that year. These embraced the work of Mulliner, Holbrook and Salmon; the standard factory saloon coachwork was by Pressed Steel.

Restored values

The cost of a professional restoration will have an influence on, but no direct relation to, a car's market value. A restored car can have a market value lower than the cost of its restoration.

▶ **1937 BSA 10hp Scout Coupé,** 1203cc, 4-cylinder engine, finished in black, red interior trim, good condition throughout.
£2,750–3,500 BRIT

Bugatti

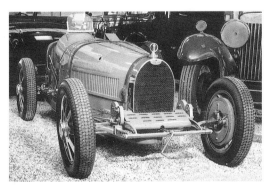

◀ **1926 Bugatti T35B,** chassis no. 4748, 2262cc, 8-cylinder engine, supercharged, restored, good condition throughout.
£250,000+ HMM

Lithe, elegant and without an ounce of surplus material, the T35 Bugatti was outstandingly successful in competition, winning more than 3,000 awards in sporting events, including 12 major Grand Prix wins in 1926 alone.

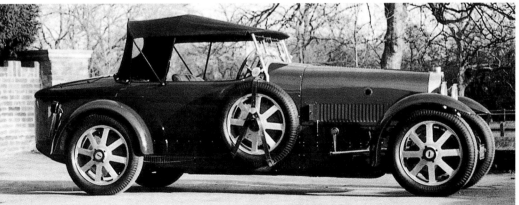

1927 Bugatti Type 43 Grand Sport, chassis no. 43182, engine no. 21, 8-cylinder inline engine, overhead camshaft, 2 inlet valves and 1 exhaust valve per cylinder, Roots-type supercharger, Bosch magneto, standard Grand Sport coachwork, very good condition.
£250,000+ BKS

Introduced in March 1927, the Type 43 was a high-performance four-seater fitted with the supercharged engine of the Type 35B Grand Prix car. It was the first such machine available to the general motoring public capable of sustainable speed in excess of 100mph. Type 43s contested all the major sports car events of their period, including Le Mans, the Tourist Trophy, the Alpine Trial, the Spa 24 hours and the Brooklands Double Twelve, although for a variety of reasons they never achieved the success on the track that their performance warranted.

BUGATTI Model	ENGINE cc/cyl	DATES	CONDITION 1	2	3
13/22/23	1496/4	1919–26	£40,000	£32,000	£25,000
30	1991/8	1922–36	£45,000	£35,000	£30,000
32	1992/8	1923	£45,000	£35,000	£30,000
35A	1991/8	1924–30	£110,000+	£90,000	£80,500
38 (30 update)	1991/8	1926–28	£44,500	£34,000	£28,000
39	1493/8	1926–29	£120,000	£90,000	£80,000
39A Supercharged	1496/8	1926–29	£140,000+	-	-
35T	2262/8	1926–30	£140,000+	-	-
37 GP Car	1496/4	1926–30	£110,000+	£90,000	£75,000
40	1496/4	1926–30	£50,000	£42,000	£35,000
38A	1991/8	1927–28	£48,000	£40,000	£35,000
35B Supercharged	2262/8	1927–30	£300,000+	£170,000+	-
35C	1991/8	1927–30	£170,000+	-	-
37A	1496/4	1927–30	£125,000+	-	-
44	2991/8	1927–30	£60,000+	£40,000	£35,000
45	3801/16	1927–30	£150,000+	-	-
43/43A Tourer	2262/8	1927–31	£180,000+	-	-
35A	1991/8	1928–30	£140,000	£110,000	£90,000
46	5359/8	1929–36	£140,000	£110,000	£90,000
40A	1627/4	1930	£55,000	£45,000	£35,500
49	3257/8	1930–34	£60,000+	£45,000	£35,500
57 Closed	3257/8	1934–40	£60,000+	£35,000	£30,000
57 Open	3257/8	1936–38	£90,000+	£60,000	£55,000
57S	3257/8	1936–38	£250,000+	-	-
57SC Supercharged	3257/8	1936–39	£250,000+	-	-
57G	3257/8	1937–40	£250,000+	-	-
57C	3257/8	1939–40	£140,000+	-	-

Racing history is an important factor with the GP cars.

1933 Bugatti Type 49 Torpedo Tourer, chassis no. 49542, engine no. 49542, 3257cc, 8-cylinder, overhead-camshaft engine, 2 inlet valves and 1 exhaust valve per cylinder, twin plugs, 85bhp, dry-plate clutch, helical gears, semi-elliptic front springs, quarter-elliptic rear springs, restored 1980s, new torpedo coachwork, further mechanical restoration at a cost of £19,000, finished in blue over black.
£44,000–50,000 BKS

◀ **1939 Bugatti Type 57 Stelvio Drophead Coupé,** coachwork by Gangloff, chassis no. 57725, engine no. 533, 3257cc, double-overhead-camshaft, 8-cylinder inline engine, 135bhp, 4-speed manual gearbox, beam front axle on semi-elliptic leaf springs, reversed quarter-elliptic rear springs, 4-wheel hydraulic drum brakes, finished in 2-tone blue, tan leather interior, 'as new' condition.
£188,500–207,500 C

Buick

BUICK Model	ENGINE cc/cyl	DATES	CONDITION 1	2	3
Veteran	various	1903–09	£18,500	£12,000	£8,000
18/20	3881/6	1918–22	£12,000	£5,000	£2,000
Series 22	2587/4	1922–24	£9,000	£5,000	£3,000
Series 24/6	3393/6	1923–30	£9,000	£5,000	£3,000
Light 8	3616/8	1931	£18,000	£14,500	£11,000
Straight 8	4467/8	1931	£22,000	£18,000	£10,000
50 Series	3857/8	1931–39	£18,500	£15,000	£8,000
60 Series	5247/8	1936–39	£19,000	£15,000	£8,000
90 Series	5648/8	1934–35	£20,000	£15,500	£9,000
40 Series	4064/8	1936–39	£19,000	£14,000	£10,000
80/90	5247/8	1936–39	£25,000	£20,000	£15,000
McLaughlin	5247/8	1937–40	£22,000	£15,000	£10,000

Various chassis lengths and bodies will affect value. Buick chassis fitted with British bodies prior to 1916 were called Bedford-Buicks. Right-hand drive can have an added premium of 25%.

A known continuous history can add value to and enhance the enjoyment of a car.

◀ **1940 Buick Roadmaster,** 8-cylinder inline engine, ex-military staff car, resprayed green and cream, tan interior, in need of refurbishment. **£500–1,000 BKS**

1953 Buick Skylark Convertible, 322cu.in, overhead-valve V8, 188bhp, automatic transmission, servo-assisted 4-wheel hydraulic brakes, power steering, electric windows, seats and aerial, completely restored, finished in white, black hood, concours condition. **£40,000–45,000 RM**

Based on a Roadmaster chassis, the Skylark was intended to give European sports cars a run for their money. With the convertible top in place, the car was less than 5ft tall. The low-slung Buick not only looked the part, but also came equipped with a luxurious interior. All told, 1,690 Skylarks were built in 1953.

BUICK Model	ENGINE cu in/cyl	DATES	CONDITION 1	2	3
Special/Super 4 Door	248/ 364/8	1950–59	£6,000	£4,000	£2,000
Special/Super Riviera	263/ 332/8	1050–56	£8,000	£6,000	£3,000
Special/Super Convertible	263/ 332/8	1950–56	£8,500	£5,500	£3,000
Roadmaster 4 door	320/ 365/8	1950–58	£11,000	£8,000	£6,000
Roadmaster Riviera	320/ 364/8	1950–58	£9,000	£7,000	£5,000
Roadmaster Convertible	320/ 364/8	1950–58	£14,500	£11,000	£7,000
Special/Super Riviera	364/8	1957–59	£10,750	£7,500	£5,000
Special/Super Convertible	364/8	1957–58	£13,500	£11,000	£6,000

Cadillac

Almost from its very beginnings in 1902, the name Cadillac has stood for prestige motoring, and in the luxury car market this General Motors flagship marque has often set the standards for others to follow. In 1912, Cadillac fitted electric lighting as standard on its 5.5 litre (336cu.in) four-cylinder model; in 1914, it introduced its first V8 engine, which has remained a feature of the marque ever since. In 1930, the extravagant V16 arrived, followed closely by the V12 models, in both cases styled by Harley Earl, who went on to create the ultimate American post-war automotive styling statements with fins, lavish chrome and bullet-shaped bumpers.

1929 Cadillac Series 341B Convertible Coupé, coachwork by Fisher, 341cu.in V8 engine, 90bhp, 3-speed manual gearbox, semi-elliptic leaf springs front and rear, 4-wheel mechanical drum brakes, left-hand drive, older restoration, finished in brown with black wings, brown leather interior, good condition.
£40,750–44,850 C

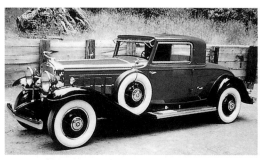

1930 Cadillac V16 Coupé with Dickey, 452cu.in, overhead-valve V16, 175hp, 3-speed synchromesh gearbox, 4-wheel servo-assisted brakes, Madame X-style windscreen, restored, new interior, excellent condition.
£55,000–65,000 RM

1930 Cadillac V16 Fleetwood Roadster, coachwork by Fleetwood, 7.4 litre, overhead-valve V16 engine, 165bhp, 148in wheelbase, finished in black, red interior, original, excellent condition throughout.
£90,000–100,000 BKS

In 1930, no fewer than 71 body chassis combinations were offered for the Cadillac V16, few of them reaching three figures in terms of units produced. This car began life as a four-door saloon, but during the 1960s it was fitted with a period roadster body (from an eight-cylinder Cadillac), which had been built by Fleetwood, one of America's finest coachbuilders.

◀ **1934 Cadillac V16 Convertible Coupé,** 452cu.in, overhead-valve V16 engine, 185hp, 3-speed gearbox, 4-wheel servo-assisted brakes, Hotchkiss steering, restored.
£200,000+ RM

Cadillac predicted that 400 V16 models would be built in 1934, but the orders never came, and only 60 were sold that year, signalling the end of the ultra-luxury automobile market in the USA. Because of its steep $8,150 price tag at the time, only one of these striking five-passenger convertible coupés was built on the 452-D V16 chassis.

CADILLAC (pre-war) Model	ENGINE cc/cyl	DATES	CONDITION 1	2	3
Type 57–61	5153/8	1915–23	£20,000+	£14,000	£6,000
Series 314	5153/8	1926–27	£22,000	£15,000	£6,000
Type V63	5153/8	1924–27	£20,000	£13,000	£5,000
Series 341	5578/8	1928–29	£22,000	£15,000	£6,000
Series 353–5	5289/8	1930–31	£50,000+	£30,000	£18,000
V16	7406/16	1931–32	£80,000+	£50,000+	£20,000
V12	6030/12	1932–37	£42,000+	£25,000	£15,000
V8	5790/8	1935–36	£30,000+	£15,000	£6,000
V16	7034/16	1937–40	£50,000+	£30,000	£18,000

◄ **1949 Cadillac 62 Series Fastback,** completely restored, finished in black, interior trimmed in brown, excellent condition throughout.
£7,500–10,000 PALM

1957 Cadillac Series 62 Convertible, finished in white with white interior, all new paint, chrome, rubber seals, weather-stripping and badges, rebuilt transmission and radio, new rams and electric motor for hood, excellent condition.
£22,000–25,000 AC

1961 Cadillac Sedan De Ville, 390cu.in V8 engine, 4-speed automatic transmission, finished in black, grey interior, 53,178 miles recorded, very good condition throughout.
£4,000–6,000 H&H

▶ **1975 Cadillac Eldorado Convertible,** front-wheel-drive, cruise control, air conditioning, finished in Old English white with matching hood bag, black vinyl interior, burgundy dashboard, 23,243 miles recorded, in need of minor cosmetic attention, good mechanical condition.
£4,750–6,000 BKS

CADILLAC Model	ENGINE cu in/cyl	DATES	CONDITION 1	2	3
4 door sedan	331/8	1949	£8,000	£4,500	£3,000
2 door fastback	331/8	1949	£10,000	£8,000	£5,000
Convertible coupé	331/8	1949	£22,000	£12,000	£10,000
Series 62 4 door	331/ 365/8	1950–55	£7,000	£5,500	£3,000
Sedan de Ville	365/8	1956–58	£8,000	£6,000	£4,000
Coupé de Ville	331/ 365/8	1950–58	£12,500	£9,500	£3,500
Convertible coupé	331/ 365/8	1950–58	£25,000	£20,000	£10,000
Eldorado	331/8	1953–55	£35,000	£30,000	£18,000
Eldorado Seville	365/8	1956–58	£11,500	£9,000	£5,500
Eldorado Biarritz	365/8	1956–58	£30,000	£20,000	£15,000
Sedan de Ville	390/8	1959	£12,000	£9,500	£5,000
Coupé de Ville	390/8	1959	£15,000	£9,000	£5,500
Convertible coupé	390/8	1959	£28,000	£20,000	£10,000
Eldorado Seville	390/8	1959	£13,000	£10,000	£6,000
Eldorado Biarritz	390/8	1959	£30,000	£20,000	£14,000
Sedan de Ville	390/8	1960	£10,000	£8,000	£4,500
Convertible coupé	390/8	1960	£27,000+	£14,000	£7,500
Eldorado Biarritz	390/8	1960	£25,000+	£17,000	£10,000
Sedan de Ville	390/ 429/8	1961–64	£7,000	£5,000	£3,000
Coupé de Ville	390/ 429/8	1961–64	£8,000	£6,000	£4,000
Convertible coupé	390/ 429/8	1961–64	£20,000	£9,000	£7,000
Eldorado Biarritz	390/ 429/8	1961–64	£19,500	£14,000	£9,000

Caterham

◀ **1984 Caterham Super 7 S4,** long-wing example, uprated 1830cc, dry-sumped, pushrod Kent engine, twin 48mm Dell'Orto carburettors, 'Prisoner' alloy wheels, finished in red, full weather equipment, black interior, competition harnesses, roll bar, history file. **£10,500–12,000 BKS**

Sole authorised manufacturer of the Lotus 7 since 1973, Caterham began by building the Series 4 version, but soon switched to the more traditionally styled Series 3. Ford engines, both pushrod and twin-cam, provided the power until the 1990s, when a Vauxhall engine was specified.

Charron

◀ **1912 Charron BA 10hp Torpedo,** 1590cc, 4-cylinder engine, semi-elliptic leaf springs front and rear, finished in green with black wings, black cloth hood, seats and interior trimmed in black leather. **£18,000–22,000 Pou**

Chevrolet

General Motors' mainstay brand takes its name from Swiss-born racing driver Louis Chevrolet. In the early years of the 20th century, he also worked for, among others, de Dion Bouton in New York and played a part in designing the first Chevrolet. But the real prime mover behind Chevrolet was the charismatic chancer William C. Durant, who in 1919 had lost control of General Motors, the firm he'd founded in 1908, and immediately set about making his comeback. In 1911, he set up his new company, naming it after Louis Chevrolet. The latter had left the business by 1913, but by 1916 Durant's fortunes had soared so dramatically that his company actually bought General Motors. However, by 1920, as the post-war Depression took hold, Durant had lost both Chevrolet and General Motors. His legacy is a marque that, ever since, has run a steady course through the mainstream of American motoring.

1933 Chevrolet Deluxe Eagle Cabriolet, 3180cc, 6-cylinder inline engine, finished in tan with brown wings, museum displayed for some time, excellent condition throughout. **£20,000–23,000 KI**

1938 Chevrolet Master Four-Door Saloon, 3548cc, 6-cylinder inline engine, worm-and-roller steering, right-hand drive, restored, finished in dark green, green interior trim, very good condition throughout. **£4,750–5,500 BRIT**

CHEVROLET Model	ENGINE cc/cyl	DATES	CONDITION 1	2	3
H4/H490 K Series	2801/4	1914–29	£9,000	£5,000	£2,000
FA5	2699/4	1918	£8,000	£5,000	£2,000
D5	5792/8	1918–19	£10,000	£6,000	£3,000
FB50	3660/4	1919–21	£7,000	£4,000	£2,000
AA	2801/4	1928–32	£5,000	£3,000	£1,000
AB/C	3180/6	1929–36	£6,000	£4,000	£2,000
Master	3358/6	1934–37	£9,000	£5,000	£2,000
Master De Luxe	3548/6	1938–41	£9,000	£6,000	£4,000

1947 Chevrolet Fleetmaster Saloon, 3500cc, 6-cylinder inline engine, right-hand drive, restored, finished in copper over cream, good overall condition. **£2,500–3,500 BRIT**

1947 Chevrolet SD Fleetline Aerosedan, 3500cc, 6-cylinder inline engine, 3-speed gearbox, right-hand drive, restored, very good condition. **£7,000–8,000 HMM**

► **1951 Chevrolet Fleetline Saloon,** 3500cc, 6-cylinder inline engine, 3-speed manual gearbox, restored, 1,200 miles covered since, finished in red, red and white interior trim and upholstery, excellent condition throughout. **£9,500–11,000 H&H**

CHEVROLET Model	ENGINE cu.in/cyl	DATES	CONDITION 1	2	3
Stylemaster	216/6	1942–48	£8,000	£4,000	£1,000
Fleetmaster	216/6	1942–48	£8,000	£4,000	£1,000
Fleetline	216/6	1942–51	£8,000	£5,000	£2,000
Styleline	216/6	1949–52	£8,000	£6,000	£2,000
Bel Air 4-door	235/6	1953–54	£6,000	£4,000	£3,000
Bel Air Sport Coupe	235/6	1953–54	£7,000	£4,500	£3,500
Bel Air Convertible	235/6	1953–54	£12,500	£9,500	£6,000
Bel Air 4-door	283/8	1955–57	£8,000	£4,000	£3,000
Bel Air Sport Coupe	283/8	1955–56	£11,000	£7,000	£4,000
Bel Air Convertible	283/8	1955–56	£16,000	£11,000	£7,000
Bel Air Sport Coupe	283/8	1957	£11,000	£7,500	£4,500
Bel Air Convertible	283/8	1957	£22,000+	£15,000+	£8,000
Impala Sport Sedan	235/6, 348/8	1958	£12,500	£9,000	£5,500
Impala Convertible	235/6, 348/8	1958	£14,500	£11,000	£7,500
Impala Sport Sedan	235/6, 348/8	1959	£8,000	£5,000	£4,000
Impala Convertible	235/6, 348/8	1959	£14,000	£10,000	£5,000
Corvette Roadster	235/6	1953	£18,000+	£14,000	£10,000
Corvette Roadster	235/6, 283/8	1954–57	£20,000+	£13,000	£9,000
Corvette Roadster	283, 327/8	1958–62	£24,000+	£16,000	£9,000
Corvette Sting Ray	327, 427/8	1963–67	£15,500+	£12,000	£10,000
Corvette Sting Ray Roadster	327, 427/8	1963–66	£22,000+	£15,000	£8,000
Corvette Sting Ray Roadster	427/8	1967	£20,000+	£13,000	£10,000

Value will also be affected by build options, rare coachbuilding options, de luxe engine specifications etc.

1957 Chevrolet Bel Air Convertible, 283cu.in V8 engine, twin 4-barrel carburettors, 245bhp, power-assisted steering, servo-assisted brakes, continental kit, electric windows, completely restored, finished in blue, white top.
£27,000–33,000 BKS

Originally applied to a two-door hardtop coupé version of Chevrolet's Styleline Deluxe in 1950, the Bel Air name was subsequently used to signify a top-of-the-range luxury trim level rather than a separate, distinct body style. Seven Bel Airs formed the 1957 line-up, but the bewildering multitude of engine, transmission and accessory options allowed buyers to tailor cars to meet their specific tastes. The Bel Air's basic engines comprised a 235.5cu.in, overhead-valve straight-six and a 265 cu.in overhead-valve V8. Power output depended on the transmission specified, and if the stock V8's 170bhp wasn't enough, performance options available ranged from the 185bhp Turbo-Fire V8 to the fuel-injected 283bhp Corvette V8, both of which were 283cu.in engines.

◀ **1967 Chevrolet Camaro SS Convertible,** 350cu.in V8 engine, restored, very good condition.
£13,000–15,000 HMM

The Camaro respresented Chevrolet's challenge to the Ford Mustang. It was launched two years after the latter and soon displaced Chevrolet's existing sporty compact, the rear-engined Corvair, which had been unable to compete with the 'pony car'.

1970 Chevrolet Chevelle SS454 LS6, 454cu.in, overhead-valve V8 engine, forced cowl induction, 450bhp, 4-speed manual gearbox, front disc brakes, electric windows and roof, tilt steering column with sports wheel, correct instrument package, bucket seats, original.
£45,000–50,000 RM

In 1970, the SS454 LS6 was the biggest engine choice for Chevelle models. Everything was uprated either to help achieve the extra torque and horsepower, or to deal with it: forged-crank with four-bolt main bearings, four-barrel carburettors, 12-bolt rear axle and F41 suspension package, which included a rear anti-roll bar. Customers had a choice of either the four-speed 'rock crusher' manual gearbox or the Turbo-Hydramatic automatic. Among the other options was a forced cowl induction system: a flap located under the bulge on the bonnet would open under heavy acceleration, creating a vacuum and forcing cold air into the carburettors.

Chevrolet Corvette (1953–)

The fibreglass 'plastic fantastic' was born in 1953 and began as a creeper, slowly gathering momentum and mutating with moving tastes through four decades of manufacture. In 1992, the 'Vette notched up a million sales and is still going strong. What's more, unlike Ford's Mustang and Thunderbird, the curvy Corvette has kept faith with its sports car roots. Today, the latest Corvette is a true modern supercar, yet with its long nose and aggressive lines, it reveals its lineage as surely as any sporting Jaguar. Whether it's a 1960s Sting Ray or a definitive, flame-red 1950s model, these fibreglass fantasies proudly wave the star-spangled banner as America's native sports car.

Pick of the bunch: All Corvette fanciers have their favourite eras: for some, it's the purity of the very first generation from 1953; others favour the glamorous 1956–62 models; but for many, the Corvette came of age in 1963 with the birth of the menacing Sting Ray. Most valuable are the early and very rare 1953–54 cars, although they're mechanically mundane with an ancient 'stove-bolt' six-cylinder engine and automatic transmission.

For: Just about any classic Corvette will have bystanders cooing at its curves. It has the advantage too of mass-produced mechanicals clothed in an exotic show-car skin.

Against: They're strictly for extroverts and can bring on a fit of anti-American fervour. In short, they're over-sexed, over-thirsty and over here.

Famous Corvette owners: John Wayne, Dinah Shore, William Shatner, Swedish former World Heavyweight Boxing Champion Ingemar Johansson, Shirley Bassey, all of The Beach Boys, all of the original Mercury 7 astronauts, the crew of Apollo 12, Jools Holland.

1953 Chevrolet Corvette, 235cu.in, 6-cylinder inline engine, triple carburettors, dual exhaust system, 190bhp, 2-speed automatic transmission, finished in white, red leather interior, completely restored, only 16 miles covered since.
£50,000–60,000 RM

Production of the two-seat Corvette Roadster began in June 1953, and by year's end, a total of 300 Corvettes had rolled off the assembly line. Corvette production signified an important technical milestone: GM was the first American car manufacturer to successfully mass-produce a vehicle with an underpan and bodyshell made entirely of fibreglass. Zora Arkus-Duntov – developer, designer and acknowledged father of the Corvette – signed this particular car on the underside of the bonnet.

1958 Chevrolet Corvette, 6-cylinder inline engine, 160bhp, factory hardtop, restored, very good condition.
£25,000–27,000 HMM

Restored values

The cost of a professional restoration will have an influence on, but no direct relation to, a car's market value. A restored car can have a market value lower than the cost of its restoration.

1960 Chevrolet Corvette, 283cu.in, V8 engine, fuel injection, 315bhp, 4-speed manual gearbox, 4-wheel hydraulic drum brakes, completely restored, original heavy-duty Harrison aluminium radiator, all fibreglass original and never repaired.
£30,000–35,000 RM

Although the first-series cars (1953–55) introduced the Corvette to America, it was the second series, launched in 1956, that earned the Corvette the title 'America's Sports Car'. The clean, good looks of Harley Earl's new body struck a chord with the American public, and the new design was soon outselling the older style – even at its peak – by a margin of three to one. This example is one of only 11 cars built with a special high-output, aluminium-head version of the fuel-injected 283cu.in V8. It was probably intended for racing, since it came without a radio or heater and was equipped with metallic brakes, blackwall tyres, 4:11 posi-traction rear end and a hardtop only.

► **1965 Chevrolet Corvette Sting Ray Roadster,** 396cu.in V8 engine, 425bhp, side-exit exhaust system, 4-speed manual gearbox, telescopic steering column, electric windows and aerial, finished in Nassau blue, original AM/FM radio, cream leather interior, engine rebuilt at a cost of $4,500, clutch in need of attention, otherwise good condition throughout.
£14,000–18,000 BKS

The heavily revised Corvette, the Sting Ray, arrived in 1963, and for the first time there was a coupé. Chevrolet's 327cu.in standard V8 was joined by an optional 396cu.in 'big block' engine for 1965 only, then a 427 until the end of Sting Ray production in 1967.

1967 Chevrolet Corvette Sting Ray Roadster, 427cu.in L71 V8 engine, fuel injection, off-road exhaust system, 435bhp, close-ratio 4-speed manual gearbox, servo-assisted 4-wheel disc brakes, all-independent suspension, knock-off wheels, hardtop, telescopic steering column with teak-rimmed wheel, completely restored 1996, fewer than 100 miles covered since, completely original, concours winner.
£45,000–50,000 RM

◄ **1968 Chevrolet Corvette Stingray,** 5358cc V8 engine, 5-spoke alloy wheels, original wheels and hubcaps included, finished in silver, black leather interior, very good condition.
£8,000–10,000 BRIT

For 1968, the Corvette underwent a dramatic redesign. The new shape retained the low, ground-hugging stance, but the roof line, which previously had been of the fastback style, was now notched, the rear deck terminating in a Kamm-type panel incorporating a spoiler.

► **1968 Chevrolet Corvette Stingray,** 5700cc V8, high-compression heads, Holley double-pumper carburettor, Muncie close-ratio 4-speed manual gearbox, uprated rear springs, Appliance chrome wheels, T-roof, finished in vermilion, bodywork in excellent condition apart from small mark on driver's door, very good mechanical condition.
£5,500–6,500 BRIT

1972 Chevrolet Corvette Stingray Roadster, 5700cc V8, pre-emission-control engine, hardtop, chrome luggage rack, finished in white, very good condition throughout.
£8,500–10,000 BRIT

1977 Chevrolet Corvette, 5.7 litre V8, 4-speed manual gearbox, T-roof, alloy wheels, luggage rack, air conditioning, completely restored, finished in red, leather-trimmed interior, excellent condition.
£16,000–20,000 COR

1973 Chevrolet Corvette Stingray, Automotion replica, 7.4 litre V8, engine rebuilt, chromed Hooker side exhaust pipes, automatic transmission uprated, finished in Elkhart green with cream centre stripe, black leather interior.
£15,000–17,000 COR

1984 Chevrolet Corvette, 5.7 litre V8, automatic transmission, finished in red, Charcoal grey leather interior.
£6,000–7,000 COR

Chrysler

1931 Chrysler CG Imperial Town Car, coachwork by LeBaron, restored, completely original, excellent condition.
£200,000+ BLK

In 1931, Walter P. Chrysler commissioned LeBaron to build this one-off town car for his wife.

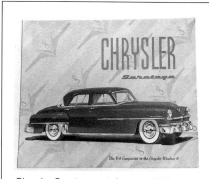

Chrysler Saratoga catalogue, c1949.
£20–25 PMB

1941 Chrysler Newport Dual-Cowl Phaeton, 323cu.in, 8-cylinder, inline sidevalve engine, 143bhp, 4-speed automatic transmission, resprayed, reupholstered in dark green leather.
£175,000+ RM

The Newport was a dream car intended to showcase future automotive styling trends. Its dual-cowl phaeton body style harked back to the Chrysler Imperials of the 1930s, but the car was revolutionary as an example of streamlining and aerodynamics; objects that normally protruded from the main body – such as door handles – were removed. Newports were displayed publicly across the USA, but the marque's shining moment came in 1941, when this particular car was used as the official pace car of the Indianapolis 500 race.

Cisitalia

1947 Cisitalia 202 Gran Sport Berlinetta, coachwork by Pinin Farina, restored, engine rebuilt, 500km covered since, correct Plexiglas side and rear windows, finished in metallic blue, beige cloth interior, excellent condition.
£55,000–65,000 BKS

Originally a manufacturer of sports equipment, in 1946 Cisitalia offered an inexpensive Fiat-powered, single-seat racing car. This was followed by two-seat open and coupé competition cars. In 1947, the ground-breaking 202 Gran Sport road car was launched as a berlinetta and spyder. Like its competition sisters, it had a spaceframe chassis, but what set it apart was the Pinin Farina body, which was hailed as a masterpiece of modern design. In 1951, New York's Museum of Modern Art nominated the Gran Sport as one of the ten greatest automobile designs to that date.

Citroën

André Citroën founded his own firm in 1919 in the former Mors factory, where previously he had worked as chief engineer. Initially, his cars were fairly orthodox and quickly proliferated on French roads. The famed Traction Avant of 1934 was a rare piece of genuine and pioneering mass-market innovation, with its front-wheel drive and unitary hull. After the war, the unconventional ideas continued with the wonderfully idiosyncratic 2CV, which reduced the motor car to its bare essence. The DS19 of 1955 went the other way, raising technical innovation to a new level with its hydro-pneumatic, self-levelling suspension, power-assisted brakes and semi-automatic transmission, not to mention its revolutionary shape. In 1976, Citroën was taken over by Peugeot, since when Citroën cars have largely been more conventional.

CITROËN Model	ENGINE cc/cyl	DATES	CONDITION 1	2	3
A	1300/4	1919	£4,000	£2,000	£1,000
5CV	856/4	1922–26	£7,000	£4,000	£2,000
11	1453/4	1922–28	£4,000	£2,000	£1,000
12/24	1538/4	1927–29	£5,000	£3,000	£1,000
2½ Litre	2442/6	1929–31	£5,000	£3,000	£1,500
13/30	1628/4	1929–31	£5,000	£3,000	£1,000
Big 12	1767/4	1932–35	£7,000	£5,000	£2,000
Twenty	2650/6	1932–35	£10,000	£5,000	£3,000
Ten CV	1452/4	1933–34	£5,000	£3,000	£1,000
Ten CV	1495/4	1935–36	£6,000	£3,000	£1,000
11B/Light 15/Big 15/7CV	1911/4	1934–57	£9,000	£5,000	£2,000
Twelve	1628/4	1936–39	£5,000	£3,000	£1,000
F	1766/4	1937–38	£4,000	£2,000	£1,000
15/6 and Big Six	2866/6	1938–56	£7,000	£4,000	£2,000

1952 Citroën 11 Légère (Light 15) Saloon, French-built model, left-hand drive, recored radiator, finished in black, original grey interior, excellent condition throughout.
£4,500–5,500 BKS

Citroën's 7C Traction Avant broke new ground in almost every aspect of production car engineering when launched in 1934. Unitary construction, front-wheel drive, all-independent torsion-bar suspension, hydraulic brakes, synchromesh gearbox and a four-cylinder, overhead-valve, wet-liner engine were all incorporated in the new car. The 1.3 litre original was soon superseded by larger-engined versions, the 1.9 litre 11 Légère model being known in Britain from 1938 as the Light 15.

◄ **1934 Citroën 8CV Rosalie Saloon,** 1453cc engine, Slough-built example, completely restored, finished in black and burgundy, red leather interior trim, 4 owners, 'as new' condition throughout.
£8,000–9,000 H&H

Miller's Starter Marque

Starter Citroën: *2CV 1948–91.*

- In 1935, Citroën's managing director, Pierre-Joules Boulanger, visited the French market town where he was born and returned to Paris with an attack of conscience and a great idea. He decreed, 'Design me a car to carry two people and 50 kilos of potatoes at 60km/h, using no more than three litres of fuel per 100km. It must be capable of running on the worst roads, of being driven by a debutante and must be totally comfortable.' The project Toute Petite Voiture also had to be like 'a settee under an umbrella', and capable of 'crossing a field carrying a basket of eggs without breaking any'. The rest, as they say, is history. From its Paris launch in 1948 to the end of production in 1991, over seven million 2CVs and its various derivatives have hit the road, making it France's very own people's car.

- It's an undeniable classic, yet a frugal utility vehicle at the same time; fun, too. The fabric roof rolls right back like a sardine can, and you can take the seats out for a family picnic. A rare wonder these days is that all the body panels simply unbolt. In fact, even the main bodyshell is only held in place by a mere 16 bolts. That means it's easy to repair rust- or crash-damaged panels; it also means that fresh panels can hide serious rot on the old-style separate chassis. Inspect the sills – especially at the base of the B-posts – front floorpan, chassis members and chassis rails running to the rear of the car. One indicator of chassis trouble is the appearance of wide gaps around the triangular body section in front of the doors.

- As for that legendary twin-pot, air-cooled engine, it's a remarkably robust unit. Citroën designed it in the knowledge that it was likely to be hammered pretty much all the time and given no more routine maintenance than a farmyard pitchfork. In most cases, you'll be looking at a car with the 602cc engine, and the one thing these need is an oil change every 3,000 miles or so. Neglect here will be revealed by big-end knocking.

- There are two types of gearbox: one for drum-brake cars up to 1982, and another for later disc-braked models. The 'drum' box is very robust, and only if it sounds like a lorry will there be any trouble with the bearings. The 'disc' box is a little more fragile, having a tendency to unwind the second-gear selector ring –– and that may mean a new one. Again, listen for excessive noise.

- Brakes are usually trouble-free, but on disc-braked cars open up the reservoir to see if it's filled with the correct Citroën LHM clear green fluid. If not, the master-cylinder rubbers will soon go – if they haven't dissolved already – and that's £300–400 to rectify.

- Naturally, for a car that's been in production until so recently, parts and spares are plentiful, the supply being aided by a number of 2CV specialists and a healthy club network.

1954 Citroën 15/6H, 2867cc, 6-cylinder inline engine, 76bhp, 3-speed gearbox, 135km/h top speed, finished in black with cream wheels, good condition.
£7,000–10,000 Pou

1954 Citroën 11B Berline, front-wheel drive, restored 1995–97, finished in black, grey cloth interior, very good condition throughout.
£4,000–5,000 BKS

1973 Citroën SM, 2670cc, 6-cylinder engine, 5-speed manual gearbox, suspension overhauled, new spheres, 23,000km recorded, restored, finished in bronze, concours winner.
£7,000–8,000 BRIT

Produced between 1970 and 1975, the SM bristled with innovations, being an amalgamation of Citroën and Maserati technology. A large vehicle, being 16ft long, the SM's styling was delightfully unorthodox, a particularly noteworthy feature being the headlamps, which turned with the steering.

CITROËN Model	ENGINE cc/cyl	DATES	CONDITION 1	2	3
2CV	375/2	1948–54	£1,000	£500	£250
2CV/Dyane/Bijou	425/2	1954–82	£1,000	£800	£500
DS19/ID19	1911/4	1955–69	£5,000	£3,000	£800
Sahara	900/4	1958–67	£5,000	£4,000	£3,000
2CV6	602/2	1963 on	£750	£500	£250
DS Safari	1985/4	1968–75	£6,000	£3,000	£1,000
DS21	1985/4	1969–75	£6,000	£3,000	£1,000
DS23	2347/4	1972–75	£6,000	£4,000	£1,500
SM	2670/ 2974/6	1970–75	£9,000	£6,000	£4,500

Clément

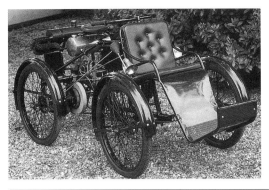

◀ **1900 Clément 3½hp Quadricycle,** 327cc, water-cooled single-cylinder De Dion engine, atmospheric inlet valve, mechanical exhaust valve, trembler-coil ignition, demountable fore-seat, good condition. **£19,000–23,000 BKS**

A successful maker of bicycles and pneumatic tyres, Adolphe Clément diversified into automobile manufacture in 1899, taking an interest in the existing Gladiator concern. Rear-engined tricycles and quadricycles were made at the Gladiator works in Levallois-sur-Seine, before Clément began building a conventional front-engined light car around 1901. Like those of many of its contemporaries, Clément's early vehicles were powered by De Dion engines.

Cord

◀ **1931 Cord L-29 Roadster,** 298.6cu.in, 8-cylinder, sidevalve engine, 3-speed gearbox, front-wheel drive, restored, very good condition throughout. **£45,000–55,000 KI**

▶ **1937 Cord 812 Phaeton,** 269cu.in, sidevalve V8 engine, centrifugal supercharger, 190bhp, 4-speed electric pre-selector gearbox, front-wheel drive, completely restored, fewer than 500 miles since, excellent condition. **£90,000–110,000 RM**

To boost sales after the 1929 stock-market crash, Cord introduced the 810, which combined style, performance and reasonable price. Introduced in 1935, Gordon Buehrig's coffin-nose, retractable-headlight design would create a standard. The 1937 Cord, designated 812, was similar to the 1936 model, except for the supercharger option, which gave 185–195bhp.

DAF

◀ **1971 Daf 44,** 844cc, flat-twin engine, 40bhp, Variomatic transmission, 75mph top speed, restored, good condition. **£750–850 HMM**

The first DAF passenger car went into production in 1959. It incorporated the ingenious and jerk-free Variomatic transmission, a fully automatic system using a centrifugal clutch and V-belt drive with a limited-slip differential.

Daimler

Throughout much of its long career, Daimler's name and fluted radiator have moved in the highest echelons of British society. Yet the marque owes its name to a German inventor. The British Daimler company's origins go back to 1891, when British inventor and businessman Frederick Simms acquired British rights to Gottleib Daimler's engines. The Daimler Motor Company Ltd was formed in 1896, and the first car – which took 60 workers to produce – emerged in March 1897. In 1910, Daimler was given welcome stability and capital with its acquisition by Birmingham Small Arms (BSA), later world renowned for its motorcycles. In the 1920s, Daimler's engines matched Rolls-Royce's for smoothness and silent running, and in 1926 Daimler produced Britain's first series-production V12. After WWII, Daimler struggled to retain its pre-war eminence and certainly, for a while, lost direction. In 1960, the company was acquired by Jaguar, the last distinct true Daimler model being the DS420 limousine (1968–92). Today, the marque lives on as a flagship brand under Jaguar's patronage.

1905 Daimler Detachable-Top Limousine, restored, good condition throughout.
£38,000–42,000 HMM

A hallmark of Daimler cars was the fluted radiator, which was introduced in 1904. The whole of the roof and upper rear quarter of this model can be removed using a bar-and-winch arrangement.

1937 Daimler DB 17/1, 2.2 litre, 6-cylinder engine, pre-selector gearbox, interior fitted with picnic table, footrests and braided handpulls, older restoration, engine and gearbox overhauled, finished in maroon over black, interior retrimmed in red leather, new carpets and headlining.
£5,750–6,500 Mot

1954 Daimler Conquest Roadster, coachwork by Carbodies, gearbox overhauled 1991–92, tonneau and hood in excellent condition, finished in red and cream, maroon leather interior, 23,500km since 1991.
£15,000–17,000 BKS
The Conquest debuted in 1953 and featured a new 2.4 litre, overhead-valve, six-cylinder engine coupled to the familiar Daimler fluid flywheel and pre-selector gearbox. It retained a separate chassis incorporating independent front suspension and Girling hydro-mechanical brakes. Also new was the lightweight Conquest Roadster, which could top 100mph and accelerate from rest to 60mph in 14.5 seconds. Intended for export at first, the Roadster was built in limited numbers, only 118 being produced between 1953 and 1957.

1938 Daimler DB18 Fixed-Head Coupé, coachwork by Windovers, 2522cc, 6-cylinder engine, 4-speed pre-selector gearbox, restored 1990, dry-stored since 1997, finished in silver and maroon, maroon and grey interior trim and upholstery, only example built, in need of tidying.
£2,500–3,000 H&H

DAIMLER Model	ENGINE cc/cyl	DATES	CONDITION 1	2	3
Veteran (Coventry built)	var/4	1897–1904	£75,000	£60,000	£30,000
Veteran	var/4	1905–19	£35,000	£25,000	£15,000
30hp	4962/6	1919–25	£40,000	£25,000	£18,000
45hp	7413/6	1919–25	£45,000+	£30,000	£20,000
Double Six 50	7136/12	1927–34	£40,000	£30,000	£20,000
20	2687/6	1934–35	£18,000	£14,000	£12,000
Straight 8	3421/8	1936–38	£20,000	£15,000	£12,000
Value is dependent on body style, coachbuilder and condition of the sleeve valve engine.					

DAIMLER Model	ENGINE cc/cyl	DATES	CONDITION 1	2	3
DB18	2522/6	1946–49	£6,000	£3,000	£1,000
DB18 Conv S/S	2522/6	1948–53	£14,000	£7,000	£2,000
Consort	2522/6	1949–53	£5,000	£3,000	£1,000
Conquest/Con.Century	2433/6	1953–58	£4,000	£2,000	£1,000
Conquest Roadster	2433/6	1953–56	£16,000	£10,000	£4,000
Majestic 3.8	3794/6	1958–62	£5,000	£2,000	£1,000
SP250	2547/8	1959–64	£12,000	£10,000	£4,500
Majestic Major	4561/8	1961–64	£6,000	£4,000	£1,000
2.5 V8	2547/8	1962–67	£8,000	£5,250	£2,500
V8 250	2547/8	1968–69	£8,000	£4,000	£2,000
Sovereign 420	4235/6	1966–69	£6,500	£3,500	£1,500

1960 Daimler SP250, 2548cc, overhead-valve V8 engine, 4-wheel disc brakes, recently restored, finished in burgundy, tan interior trim and hood.
£12,750–14,500 BRIT

The SP250, which was announced in 1959, represented a move into hitherto uncharted territory for Daimler, well-known for large, high-quality saloons and limousines. The new sports car was powered by a superb 2.5 litre V8 engine, which gave tremendous performance with a top speed approaching 125mph. The car saw service with several constabularies for motorway patrol use.

1962 Daimler SP250, 2547cc V8, completely restored 1990, 3,600 miles covered since, finished in maroon, hard and soft tops, tonneau cover, interior trimmed in black and red.
£8,500–10,000 H&H

1968 Daimler V8 250 Saloon, 2547cc, finished in black, original cream leather interior in good condition, excellent brightwork, good mechanical condition, 68,000 miles recorded.
£7,500–9,000 BRIT

The V8 250 utilised the bodyshell of the Jaguar Mk II saloon and was powered by the excellent Edward Turner designed 2.5 litre engine, as used in the SP250 sports car, albeit with a redesigned sump to clear the Jaguar front suspension assembly.

1968 Daimler V8 250 Saloon, 2547cc V8, Borg Warner automatic transmission, 110mph top speed, braking system overhauled, chassis front-end replaced, sills and jacking points strengthened, finished in gold, red leather interior, good original condition.
£6,500–7,500 BKS

A known continuous history can add value to and enhance the enjoyment of a car.

Daimler Conquest & Century (1954–57)

Body styles: Roadster and drophead coupé.
Engine: Straight-six, 2433cc.
Power output: 100bhp at 4,400rpm.
Transmission: Four-speed, pre-selector manual, fluid flywheel.
Brakes: Drums all-round.
Top speed: 100mph.
0–60mph: 14.5 seconds.
Production: 65 roadsters, 54 drophead coupés.
Price new: £1,673.
Announced in late 1953, for production the following year, this aluminium-bodied faux sportster is nothing if not quirky. In fact, unkinder automobile critics have suggested that it looks as if every panel came from a different car. In its day, it fitted in with few people's conventional notion of what a sports car should be, and was further hampered by its high price – twice that of sporting stalwarts like the Triumph TR2, and a little more costly than Jaguar's sporting thoroughbred, the XK120. Late in 1955, Daimler discontinued the roadster and replaced it with a drophead coupé with a third sideways seat in the rear. If you fancy a rare curio, there are few rarer or curiouser, but beware the public reaction. If you are hoping for a 'What'll she do, mister?', don't be too upset if all you get is, 'Did you make it yourself?'

1967 Daimler Sovereign Saloon, 6-cylinder engine, 248bhp, 125mph top speed, left-hand drive, finished in Old English white, original blue leather interior, 2 owners, 42,000km recorded.
£4,000–5,000 BKS

Sister to the Jaguar 420, and only distinguishable by its traditional fluted radiator grille and a more luxurious interior, the Daimler Sovereign was launched in 1967.

1984 Daimler Double Six Series III Saloon, 5.3 litre, overhead-camshaft V12 engine, automatic transmission, stainless steel exhaust, alloy wheels, finished in metallic dark grey, tinted glass, interior refurbished and retrimmed 1997 in red and grey leather, TV and video recorder installed in rear passenger compartment, 31,247 miles recorded, good condition throughout.
£5,750–6,500 S

1977 Daimler Sovereign LWB Saloon, 4235cc, manual gearbox with overdrive, finished in brown, beige interior trim and upholstery, very good condition.
£1,200–1,500 H&H

1983 Daimler DS420 Limousine, automatic transmission, finished in black, black tinted glass, electric division, 67,000 miles recorded, good condition throughout.
£2,500–3,500 BKS

Intended as a replacement for the ageing Majestic Major Limousine, the DS420 was introduced in 1968. It was based on a stretched Jaguar 420G floorpan and running gear, the latter's all-independent suspension providing excellent handling and ride characteristics, while the 4.2 litre, six-cylinder XK engine ensured that there was no shortage of power.

► **1989 Daimler DS420 Limousine,** 4235cc, 6-cylinder engine, good condition throughout.
£8,000–9,000 BRIT

Darracq

◄ **1903 Darracq Type L 8hp Rear-Entrance Tonneau,** single-cylinder engine, atmospheric inlet valve, mechanical exhaust valve, restored, good condition.
£40,000–50,000 HMM

Darracq began by making cycles in 1891, but its founder, Alexandre Darracq, sold out to British interests in 1896. Although the cars were always designed and built in France, the company was financed in England. Then the company merged with a French concern to make Italian cars, and subsequently acquired American affiliations.

Datsun

A known continuous history can add value to and enhance the enjoyment of a car.

◄ **1973 Datsun 240Z,** restored 1990, fitted with 5735cc Chevrolet V8 engine, full body kit, Compomotive alloy wheels, finished in orange.
£3,500–4,500 BRIT

Datsun 240Z (1969–73)

Engine: Overhead-camshaft straight-six, 2393cc.
Power output: 151bhp at 5,600rpm.
Transmission: All-synchromesh four- or five-speed manual gearbox; or automatic.
Brakes: Discs front/drums rear.
Top speed: 125mph.
0–60mph: 8 seconds.
Production: 156,076.

Throughout the 1960s, Japanese car makers were teetering on the brink of a sports car breakthrough. The revolution came with the Datsun 240Z which, at a stroke, established Japan on the world sports car stage. The E-Type Jaguar wasn't in its first flush of youth and, at the lower level, the Austin-Healey was on its last legs; neither was the MGB exactly factory-fresh. There was a gaping hole in the market, particularly in America, and the Datsun 240Z filled it handsomely. In fact, where many European sports cars made unwilling concessions for the Americans, the 240Z was aimed straight at

them. It was even launched in the US in October 1969, a month before its official Japanese release and, on a rising tide of Japanese exports to the US, it scored a massive hit. It had the looks, vigorous performance, nimble handling and high equipment levels. In its day, it was a great-value sporting package that outsold all rivals. Today, the Datsun 240Z gives plenty of show and go for not much dough, offering all the right sporting sensations for less than half the price of an E-Type Jag, which it once presumptuously attempted to rival.

Pick of the bunch: The sporting Datsun gained weight and girth and slowed down as it mutated through the 260Z and on to the 280ZX. Consequently, many Datsun Z fans favour the original incarnation, the 240Z, for its purity and performance. The ultimate 240Z was the Samurai performance package, with triple Weber carbs, special head and other mods, which gave six-second 0-60mph acceleration.

► **1975 Datsun 260Z,** 2800cc engine, completely restored, 2,000 miles covered since, engine rebuilt, Janspeed manifold, stainless steel exhaust, engine bay detailed to concours standard, gearbox and clutch rebuilt, new body panels, resprayed in red with black bonnet, black powder-coated wheels, black interior.
£4,250–4,750 H&H

De Dion Bouton

◄ **1913 De Dion Bouton 14hp Coupé De Ville,** finished in dark brown, brass fittings including Rushmore headlamps and Rotax side lamps, wire wheels, rear compartment upholstered in beige cloth, chauffeur's compartment with removable canopy upholstered in black leather, fold-down occasional seats, wind-down division, speaking tube to driver, VCC dating certificate.
£11,500–14,000 BKS

De Dion Bouton established its name by building efficient single-cylinder cars and supplying engines to other manufacturers. In 1913, the company offered a wide range of multi-cylinder cars, ranging from the diminutive 7hp twin to the gargantuan 50hp, 7.8 litre, eight-cylinder cars. The mid-range 12 and 14hp cars, however, contributed most to the company's coffers.

Delage

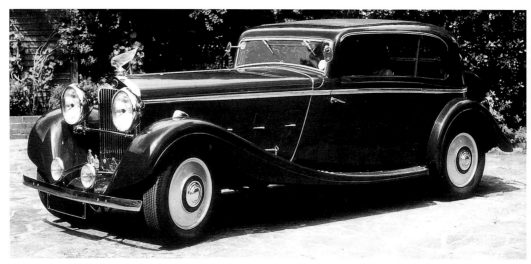

1934 Delage D8 15S Close-Coupled Sports Saloon, coachwork by Chapron, 2667cc, 8-cylinder engine, older restoration, finished in blue, grey hide interior in excellent condition, bodywork, chassis and mechanical components in good condition.
£25,000–28,000 BRIT

From the early 1920s, Delage's mainstay models were the D1 and DM series cars, powered by four- and six-cylinder engines respectively. However, the real *tour de force* came in 1929 with the appearance of the magnificent 4.1 litre, straight-eight D8 series, which was available with a choice of two chassis lengths and invariably clad with exotic coachwork from the likes of Figoni et Falaschi, Henri Chapron and Fernandes et Darrin. In 1933, the D8 was joined by a slightly smaller straight-eight model displacing 2.7 litres – the D8 15.

Delahaye

1946 Delahaye Type 135M Guillore Coach, restored, finished in blue, chromed wire wheels, sunroof, 1 of 3 built, concours winner, excellent condition throughout.
£90,000–110,000 BLK

1949 Delahaye 135M Three-Position Drophead Coupé, coachwork by Chapron, 3557cc, 6-cylinder engine, boot-mounted spare wheel, finished in black, polished aluminium wing edging, ribbed and polished wheel discs, Art Deco-style instrumentation, tan leather-trimmed interior in good condition.
£40,000–45,000 COYS

Throughout the 1920s and early 1930s, Delahaye built unremarkable small family cars and commercial vehicles. The company gained a reputation for strong, soundly engineered machines, well suited to the post-Depression market. It was not until 1936, in the hope of better times ahead, that the splendid 135 model changed that image overnight. With a strong 3.5 litre, six-cylinder engine driving through a Cotal pre-selector gearbox, performance was at the head of its class. The chassis layout was no less sophisticated, with independent, transverse-leaf front suspension and a live, leaf-sprung rear axle. After WWII, Delahaye resumed production of the 135, which is generally acknowledged as the company's finest model.

1952 Delahaye 235MS Sunroof Coupé, coachwork by Chapron, 3557cc, triple-carburettor, 6-cylinder engine, 152bhp, Cotal electrically-controlled gear-change, chromed wire wheels, restored, finished in Diamond black, red leather interior, well maintained, 1 of only 84 built.
£37,000–42,000 BKS

This particular car was displayed at the 1952 Salon de Paris and then was delivered to the French ambassador in Canada.

DeLorean

▶ **1981 DeLorean DMC-12,** 2849cc, rear-mounted, overhead-camshaft V6, 3-speed automatic transmission, fuel injection, electronic ignition, gullwing doors, good condition.
£11,000–13,000 HMM

Originally, the DeLorean was to have had a chassis made from a lightweight composite material, known as ERM. However, this idea was eventually dropped and the chassis constructed from steel, using standard Lotus construction techniques.

DeLorean DMC-12 (1981–82)

Construction: Y-shaped backbone chassis, fibreglass body with brushed stainless steel outer skin.
Engine: Overhead-camshaft V6, 2849cc.
Power output: 130bhp at 5,500rpm.
Transmission: Five-speed manual; optional three-speed automatic.
Top speed: 130mph claimed.
0–60mph: 8.5 seconds claimed.
Production: 8,800.
The ill-fated DeLorean DMC-12 ranks right up there with the Ford Edsel as one of the auto industry's greatest failures. A high-flyer who'd risen to the height of Vice-President of General Motors, John Zachary DeLorean launched his own venture in 1974. By 1982, the short flight of his gull-winged sports car was over and his reputation in tatters. With a design by Giorgetto

Giugiaro's Ital Design, chassis and manufacturing development by Lotus, a unique brushed stainless steel body and fancy gullwing doors, the DeLorean was intended as a glimpse of the future. But with a complex series of capital-raising exercises that eventually saw the company settle in Northern Ireland, production only finally got under way early in 1981. By then, the design was outdated, and those who did buy DeLoreans suffered a litany of quality-control problems. Performance was also disappointing. Like the Edsel before it, the DeLorean bombed against wildly optimistic sale forecasts, and DeLorean Motor Cars foundered in a mire of court cases. Today, there is a small group of DeLorean devotees who find the fascination of the story behind the car almost worth the frustration of owning one.

Miller's is a price GUIDE not a price LIST

◀ **1982 DeLorean DMC-12,** left-hand drive, brushed stainless steel body, black upholstery.
£6,500–7,500 BKS

Desande

1981 Desande Caprice Roadster, Chevrolet V8 engine and automatic transmission, Ford Mustang suspension components, power steering, box-section chassis, finished in dark red and black, interior trimmed in leather, walnut dashboard, fewer than 20 built, formerly owned by HRH The King of Malaysia, good condition throughout.
£11,000–13,000 COYS

De Soto

◄ **1934 De Soto Airflow,** 241cu.in, 6-cylinder engine, 100bhp, restored finished in dark green, good condition. **£3,500–5,000 BKS**

Walter P. Chrysler took 20 years to rise from floor sweeper to motor magnate on a million-dollar salary at Willys, and there was no shortage of backers when he set out to create his own brand in 1923. Chrysler made such an impact on the market that, after five years, De Soto was launched to compete against the likes of Oldsmobile and Pontiac. The Airflow combined a glimpse of the future with aerodynamic efficiency. Controversial at the time, today it is regarded as a landmark in automotive design.

1956 De Soto Fireflyte Convertible, 341cu.in V8 'Pace Car' engine, dual 4-barrel carburettors, 'batwing' air filters, dual exhausts, power steering, servo-assisted brakes, original wire wheels, electric seats, all-signal-seeking radio with optional Hiway Hi Fi, completely restored, finished in yellow over black, 1 of 42 built with 320bhp engine, good to excellent condition. **£30,000–34,000 BKS**

De Tomaso

◄ **1979 De Tomaso Longchamps,** 5796cc V8 engine, 330bhp, 5-speed ZF manual gearbox, all-independent suspension, 4-wheel disc brakes, 238km/h top speed, finished in metallic blue, 1 of 412 built, very good condition. **£13,000–15,000 Pou**

De Tomaso Pantera (1971–93)

Body style: Two-seater sports coupé.
Construction: Unitary with pressed-steel chassis, aluminium and steel body panels.
Engine: Mid-mounted, cast-iron Ford V8, 5763cc.
Transmission: ZF five-speed manual.
Power output: 350bhp at 6,000rpm.
Suspension: Independent all-round: upper and lower, unequal-length wishbones, coil springs, anti-roll bars.
Brakes: Vacuum-assisted discs all-round.
Top speed: 159mph.
0–60mph: 5.5 seconds.
Average fuel consumption: 14mpg.
Few cars descend from more mixed parentage than the De Tomaso Pantera. It's not just the Ford V8 and the Italian styling, courtesy of Ghia; the company's founder, Alejandro de Tomaso, was an Argentinian racing driver turned supercar builder. His first serious effort was the mid-engined, Ford-powered Mangusta of 1967; in 1971, the Pantera developed the theme into an awesome supercar. The project was strongly supported by Ford in the USA, where the company's Lincoln-Mercury division was pushing its performance image hard – the Pantera gave glamour to the showrooms as a plausible Ford GT40 successor. Somewhere between 5,000 and 6,000 were sold in the USA from 1971 to 1974 – no-one knows for sure – but after that, Ford withdrew showroom support and production continued at a trickle until 1993. Nevertheless, the gloriously brawny Pantera continued to evolve into GTS and GT5 versions, sprouting wings, spoilers, flared wheel arches and other appendages like a bodybuilder on steroids. The Pantera is a flawed supercar certainly, with annoying little foibles, like the tendency for the front end to lift and the steering to lighten alarmingly above 120mph, although the later spoilers and wings helped keep it down. But forget the flaws, and just look at and listen to this primal expression of unleashed power. It's evil, beautifully evil.

Duesenberg

1929 Duesenberg Model J Sports Sedan, coachwork by Murphy, 420cu.in, overhead-camshaft, 8-cylinder inline engine, 265hp, 3-speed manual gearbox, 4-wheel vacuum-assisted brakes, Bijur chassis lubrication, restored, finished in dark blue, grey leather upholstery, 1 of 2 Murphy-bodied cars, excellent condition.
£300,000+ RM

Priced at $8,500 for the chassis alone, the Model J was by far the most expensive car in America, and with the economic successes of the 1920s, America's wealthy were ready to indulge themselves. The announcement of the Model J shook the industry and even momentarily halted trading on the floor of the New York stock exchange.

1930 Duesenberg Model J, coachwork by Hibbard & Darrin, 6882cc, 8-cylinder inline engine, restored, excellent condition.
£750,000+ BLK

1931 Duesenberg Model J Tourer, coachwork by Derham, 6816cc, double-overhead-camshaft, 8-cylinder inline engine, restored, 1 of 8 built, very good condition throughout.
£600,000+ HMM

◄ **1935 Duesenberg Model J,** coachwork by Judkins, 6882cc, 8-cylinder inline engine, restored, finished in 2-tone grey, chromed wire wheels, very good condition.
£400,000+ BLK

Erskine

1927 Erskine Roadster, 2392cc, 6-cylinder Continental engine, right-hand drive, restored, engine rebuilt, new vinyl hood, finished in yellow and brown, brown leathercloth interior trim, good mechanical condition.
£2,000–3,000 BRIT

First shown in 1926, the Erskine was a new compact line from Studebaker and took its name from Albert Russell Erskine, then President of the Studebaker Corporation. The Erskine proved successful on the export market, finding particular favour in Britain, Australia and New Zealand. The range continued in production until 1930, offering tourer, saloon, roadster and fixed-head coupé body styles.

Facel Vega

1958 Facel Vega Excellence, Chrysler V8 engine, finished in Midnight blue, original red Connolly hide upholstery, 3 owners, fewer than 87,000km recorded, good condition.
£13,000–15,500 BKS

This example was bought new by the actress Ava Gardner.

1960 Facel Vega HK500, 6.3 litre Chrysler V8 engine, 390bhp, automatic transmission, right-hand drive, 145mph top speed, good condition.
£25,000–28,000 HMM

Ferrari

Enzo Ferrari died in 1988, but his spirit lives on in the exquisite road and race cars produced at Maranello in Italy. The origins of the famous prancing horse emblem date from long before any road cars bore the name. The badge was based on a racing trophy presented to Enzo Ferrari in the 1920s, when the young Italian raced Alfa Romeos. In 1929, he set up Scuderia Ferrari, racing Alfa Romeos with considerable success through the 1930s. The first true Ferrari car – although it didn't bear the name – was a Fiat-based racer built for the 1940 GP di Brescia. The first car to carry the Ferrari name was the 1.5 litre, V12-engined 125, which evolved into the 1995cc 166. A coupé version of the 166 won the 1948 Mille Miglia, ushering in a new era of accomplishments on the track and the road. Since 1969, Fiat has been in control of Ferrari, but to this day the passion for the marque from Maranello remains as hot-blooded as the scarlet livery that is still the choice of 70 per cent of Ferrari buyers.

1952 Ferrari 212 Inter Coupé, coachwork by Ghia, chassis no. 0191EL, engine no. 0191EL, 5-speed gearbox, completely restored 1989–94 at a cost of c$700,000, 100km covered since, finished in original yellow and black, black seats and carpets, formerly owned by Argentinian President Juan Péron.
£200,000+ BKS

This car was exhibited, with a right-hand-drive cabriolet body by Ghia, at the 1952 Turin motor show and was sold in July of that year. Three months later, it was returned to Ghia, where it was reclothed with a striking left-hand-drive coupé body. Painted yellow and black, it was displayed at the 1952 Paris Salon, after which it was shipped to the USA and on to its new owner, President Péron, in 1953.

◄ **1959 Ferrari 250 GT Tour de France Replica,** chassis no. 1657GT, standard 250 GT rebuilt to Tour de France spec., correct inside-plug V12 engine, aluminium calipers, new fuel system, 14-louvre Tour de France-style body.
£120,000–140,000 COYS

Of all the 250 derivatives, the Tour de France long-wheelbase berlinetta remains a milestone in Ferrari history, being the first definitive road-racing berlinetta and the car that contributed most significantly in the mid-to-late 1950s to Ferrari's reputation as the car to beat.

FERRARI Model	ENGINE cc/cyl	DATES	CONDITION 1	2	3
250 GTE	2953/12	1959–63	£32,000	£22,000	£20,000
250 GT SWB (steel)	2953/12	1959–62	£400,000+	£200,000+	-
250 GT Lusso	2953/12	1962–64	£85,000+	£65,000+	£50,000
250 GT 2+2	2953/12	1961–64	£32,000	£24,000	£18,000
275 GTB	3286/12	1964–66	£120,000	£80,000	£70,000
275 GTS	3286/12	1965–67	£90,000	£70,000	£50,000
275 GTB 4–cam	3286/12	1966–68	£190,000+	£150,000	£100,000
330 GT 2+2	3967/12	1964–67	£27,000+	£18,000	£11,000
330 GTC	3967/12	1966–68	£55,000+	£40,000+	£25,000
330 GTS	3967/12	1966–68	£80,000+	£70,000+	£60,000
365 GT 2+2	4390/12	1967–71	£30,000	£20,000	£15,000
365 GTC	4390/12	1967–70	£40,000	£35,000	£30,000
365 GTS	4390/12	1968–69	£150,000+	£100,000+	£80,000
365 GTB (Daytona)	4390/12	1968–74	£80,000	£60,000	£50,000
365 GTC4	4390/12	1971–74	£45,000+	£38,000	£30,000
365 GT4 2+2/400GT	4390/ 4823/12	1972–79	£25,000	£20,000	£10,000
365 BB	4390/12	1974–76	£45,000	£35,000	£25,000
512 BB/BBi	4942/12	1976–81	£50,000+	£40,000	£28,000
246 GT Dino	2418/6	1969–74	£40,000	£30,000	£20,000
246 GTS Dino	2418/6	1972–74	£50,000	£32,000	£20,000
308 GT4 2+2	2926/8	1973–80	£15,000	£10,000	£8,000
308 GTB (fibreglass)	2926/8	1975–76	£25,000	£18,000	£12,000
308 GTB	2926/8	1977–81	£22,000	£16,000	£10,000
308 GTS	2926/8	1978–81	£22,000	£18,000	£11,000
308 GTBi/GTSi	2926/8	1981–82	£24,000	£17,000	£10,000
308 GTB/GTS QV	2926/6	1983–85	£21,500	£16,500	£9,500
400i manual	4823/12	1981–85	£14,000	£11,000	£10,000
400i auto	4823/12	1981–85	£14,000	£11,000	£8,000

1960 Ferrari 250 GT Cabriolet Series II, coachwork by Pininfarina, chassis no. 1797, engine no. 1797, 3 litre, overhead-camshaft, aluminium V12 engine, 240bhp, 4-speed gearbox with overdrive, coil-spring independent front suspension, leaf-sprung live rear axle, 4-wheel disc brakes, multi-tubular frame, partially restored, finished in silver-grey, black hood, red leather interior, good condition throughout.
£55,000–65,000 BKS

Effectively an open-top version of the Pininfarina-built 250 GT Coupé, whose chassis and mechanics it shared, the Cabriolet was built alongside its closed cousin until 1962.

1961 Ferrari 250 GT SWB Spyder California, 2953cc, outside-plug, overhead-camshaft V12, 260bhp, 4-speed manual gearbox, independent wishbone-and-coil spring front suspension, live rear axle on semi-elliptic leaf springs, 4-wheel disc brakes, tubular-steel ladder frame, steel body with aluminium doors, bonnet and boot lid, restored 1993, finished in red, beige interior, 1 of 37 covered-headlamp cars built.
£650,000+ RM

This 250 GT Spyder California is believed to be the only road car fitted with a competition external fuel filler.

Cross Reference
See Colour Review

1962 Ferrari 250 GT SWB, chassis no. 3565, 2953cc V12, downdraught Weber carburettors, GTO-spec. competition exhausts, 241bhp, 4-wheel disc brakes, rear axle located by Watts linkage, 94.4in short-wheelbase multi-tubular chassis, long-distance 100 litre fuel tank, quick-release filler cap, Marchal spotlamps, 150mph top speed, restored, finished in metallic grey, red leather interior, 70,000km recorded, original.
£500,000+ COYS

1962 Ferrari 250 GTO Berlinetta Reproduction, coachwork by Favre, chassis no. 03839GT, engine no. 03839GT, built on 250 GTE chassis 1987–91, 3 litre, dry-sumped Colombo engine, GTO-type Weber 40DCN carburettors, GTO-type exhaust system, ribbed 5-speed gearbox, correct metric wiring loom, electrical components and instruments, GTO-type fuel tank with safety cell, Borrani wire wheels, all-aluminium body, Plexiglas side and rear windows, finished in Rosso Corsa, competition seats trimmed in correct blue Nomex cloth, racing harnesses, excellent condition.
£100,000–115,000 BKS

Ferrari built only 39 GTOs, which were used almost exclusively for competition, although the car was perfectly tractable on the road.

1964 Ferrari 250 GT Lusso Berlinetta, coachwork by Pininfarina, chassis no. 5953, engine no. 5953, completely restored early 1980s, engine rebuilt and fitted with 6 Weber carburettors, gearbox, suspension, steering, and brakes rebuilt, new front grille, bare-metal respray in red, black leather upholstery, 82,000km recorded, 1 of the last Lussos produced.
£90,000–105,000 BKS

The 250 GT Lusso (Luxury) Berlinetta appeared in late 1962. Styled by Pininfarina and built by Scaglietti, it combined race-track looks with high standards of passenger comfort.

1965 Ferrari 275 GTB Berlinetta, coachwork by Pininfarina, chassis no. 06703, engine no. 06703, rear-mounted 5-speed transaxle, independent rear suspension, Borrani wire wheels, left-hand drive.
£100,000–115,000 BKS

Ferrari's successful 250 series was superseded in 1964 by the 275. The model's designation reflected the cubic capacity of an individual cylinder, so the newcomer displaced 3.3 litres. In standard form, the 60-degree V12 engine delivered 280bhp. A higher – 300bhp – state of tune, employing six Weber carburettors was available and was used for the handful of 275 GTB/C (Competition) models built. Introduced at the same time, the 275 GTS convertible made do with 260bhp.

◀ **1967 Ferrari 275 GTB/4 Berlinetta,** 3286cc, double-overhead-camshaft V12, 300bhp, 5-speed manual gearbox, all-independent suspension, 4-wheel disc brakes, tubular-steel chassis, finished in metallic dark green, excellent condition.
£275,000+ RM

1965 Ferrari 275 GTS Spyder, coachwork by Pininfarina, chassis no. 07189, engine no. 07189, 3286cc V12, 144mph top speed, 0–60mph in 6 seconds, finished in Rosso Corsa, black upholstery, excellent original condition.
£70,000–80,000 COYS

The 275 GTS was styled by Pininfarina and bore little resemblance to its sister, the GTB. Production, which began in the final weeks of 1964, continued until 1966, a total of only 200 cars being built.

1964 Ferrari 330 GT 2+2, coachwork by Pininfarina, chassis no. 6551, 4 litre V12 engine, 300bhp, 4-speed manual gearbox with overdrive, 150mph top speed, 0–60mph in 8 seconds, finished in red, black leather interior, unrestored, 49,512 miles recorded, good condition.
£20,000–25,000 BKS

The first production Ferrari with 2+2 seating was the GTE of 1960. In essence, it was a 250 GT with a slightly longer wheelbase. The extra two seats made it eligible as a police car, at least in the eyes of one Italian official who ordered two for the Italian police. One was written off early in its career, while the other seems to have been largely used by the official who placed the order. The 330 GT 2+2 was the definitive version and was more luxurious than its predecessors.

▶ **1967 Ferrari 330 GT 2+2 Mk II,** coachwork by Pininfarina, chassis no. 9385GT, engine no. 9385GT, 3967cc V12, 300+bhp, 5-speed gearbox, Borrani wire wheels, mechanics restored 1999, finished in Amaranto, black leather interior, 1 of 455 Mk II models built.
£18,000–22,000 BKS

1964 Ferrari 330 GTO Berlinetta Replica, chassis no. 6293, built on a disc-braked 330 GT chassis, 4 litre V12 engine, 320bhp, finished in Rosso Corsa, upholstered in black, quilted transmission tunnel.
£50,000–60,000 BKS

Only three 4 litre 330 GTOs were built.

◀ **1967 Ferrari 330 GTC Coupé,** coachwork by Pininfarina, chassis no. 09197, engine no. 09197, 4 litre, overhead-camshaft V12 engine, 300bhp, 5-speed rear transaxle, all-independent suspension, spaceframe chassis, 150+mph top speed, left-hand drive, restored cosmetically 1997, finished in metallic silver, black leather upholstery, 81,000km recorded.
£50,000–60,000 BKS

▶ **1967 Ferrari 330 GTS Spyder,** coachwork by Pininfarina, 3967cc V12, 300bhp, 5-speed manual gearbox, all-independent suspension, tubular chassis, 13,000 miles recorded, 1 owner, excellent condition.
£160,000–180,000 RM

◀ **1968 Ferrari 365 GT 2+2,** coachwork by Pininfarina, chassis no. 11821, engine no. 11821, 4.4 litre V12, 5-speed gearbox, all-independent suspension incorporating Koni hydro-pneumatic self-levelling system at the rear, power steering, 4-wheel ventilated disc brakes, left-hand drive, finished in silver, red leather interior, air conditioning, 80,000km recorded, noisy 2nd gear synchromesh, otherwise good condition.
£20,000–25,000 BKS

1969 Ferrari 365 GTS Spyder, coachwork by Pininfarina, chassis no. 12307, engine no. 12307, V12 engine, 320bhp, Borrani wire wheels, 150+mph top speed, finished in Rosso Corsa, original black leather interior, period 8-track tape player, 63,780km recorded, 1 of 20 cars built, unrestored, very good original condition throughout.
£160,000–180,000 BKS

A rarity that was built only during the 1969 season, the 365 GTS evolved from the 330 GTS, its engine being enlarged to 4.4 litres.

1970 Ferrari 365 GTB/4 Daytona, chassis no. 13837, 4390cc, double-overhead-camshaft V12, dry-sump lubrication, 352bhp, 5-speed rear transaxle, all-independent wishbone-and-coil spring suspension, 4-wheel servo-assisted disc brakes, 170+mph top speed, restored 1980s, resprayed in red, new chrome and leather upholstery.
£60,000–70,000 BKS

Successor to the 275 GTB/4, the 365 GTB/4 debuted in 1968, soon gaining the unofficial name 'Daytona' in honour of Ferrari's 1–2–3 finish at that circuit in 1967. Aggressively styled by Pininfarina, Ferrari's new supercar boldly restated the traditional sports car 'long bonnet, small cabin, short tail' look while retaining all the elegance associated with the Italian coachbuilder's work. An unusual feature was a full-width transparent front panel, behind which sat the headlamps. However, this was replaced by electrically-operated, pop-up lights, to meet US requirements, shortly after production began in 1969.

1970 Ferrari 365 GTB/4 Daytona, chassis no. 13791GT, clear plastic front panel, resprayed and mechanics overhauled 1984/5 at a cost of £15,000, fitted with air conditioning, finished in Blue Scuro, beige hide trim, fewer than 21,000 miles recorded, excellent condition throughout.
£58,000–65,000 COYS

Most Ferrari model numbers represent the approximate cubic capacity in cc of one cylinder of the car's engine. Thus the Ferrari 365 GTB/4 was so called because the capacity of each of its 12 cylinders was approximately 365cc; the overall capacity was 4390cc. One obvious exception to this rule is the Ferrari F40, introduced in 1987 and so named to celebrate 40 years of the famous prancing horse marque from Maranello.

Miller's is a price GUIDE not a price LIST

1970 Ferrari 365 GTB/4 Daytona Spyder (Conversion), coachwork by Pininfarina, 4390cc, double-overhead-camshaft V12, 352bhp, 5-speed transaxle, all-independent suspension, Borrani wire wheels, left-hand drive, finished in Rosso Corsa, black upholstery with red Daytona inserts, Nardi wooden steering wheel, period radio, c9,000km since conversion.
£75,000–85,000 BKS

A year after the Daytona Berlinetta was launched, it was joined by a sensational Spyder version, the GTS/4. Of approximately 1,300 Daytonas, only 124 were built as Spyders, but with the return of interest in the traditional sports car, a number of Daytona coupés have been converted to Spyders, such as this one.

1971 Ferrari 365 GTB/4 Daytona, 4380cc, double-overhead-camshaft V12, 6 Weber carburettors, 352bhp, 5-speed manual gearbox, all-independent suspension, 4-wheel disc brakes, completely restored, excellent condition.
£95,000–110,000 RM

Shortly after midnight on 15 November 1972, this Ferrari Daytona left the Red Ball Garage in Manhattan and headed west. Thirty-five hours, 54 minutes and one speeding ticket later, it arrived in Redondo Beach, California – the proud winner of the Cannonball Baker Sea-to-Shining-Sea Memorial Trophy Dash. The outrageous race had no entry fees, no prize money and no rules other than to drive a car, any car, from New York to Los Angeles in the shortest possible time. Eight cars, ranging from an almost-new Cadillac Sedan deVille to a five-year-old motorhome, began the race, six finishing it in well under 48 hours.

◀ **1972 Ferrari 365 GTB/4 Daytona Spyder (Conversion),** original coachwork by Pininfarina, converted by Autokraft, chassis no. 14413GT, engine no. 14413, stainless steel exhaust system, suspension rebuilt, resprayed, interior retrimmed, 18,000 miles recorded.
£100,000–110,000 BKS

1977 Ferrari 512 BB, coachwork by Pininfarina, engine top-end overhauled 1997, battery cut-off switch, finished in light metallic grey, original black leather upholstery, 48,700km recorded, very good condition.
£33,000–38,000 BKS

Ferrari announced the 365 GT4/BB in 1973. It had a new multi-tube chassis fitted with a 380bhp, 4.4 litre flat-12 engine. The suspension followed Ferrari's contemporary practice, while Pininfarina created a stylish body. In 1976, the model received a 5 litre engine together with some cosmetic improvements, becoming the 512 BB. Ferrari claimed a top speed 300km/h, and even today there are few cars that can match its performance.

▶ **1978 Ferrari 512 BB,**
5 litre, flat-12, rear-mounted engine, multi-tubular chassis, finished in red, good condition.
£37,000–44,000 KHP

◀ **1994 Ferrari 512 TR,** 5 litre, flat-12 engine, fitted with 512 M wheels, finished in red, 24,000 miles recorded.
£65,000–72,000 KHP

1968 Ferrari Dino 206 GT Berlinetta, coachwork by Pininfarina, 2 litre, double-overhead-camshaft V6 engine, 180bhp, 5-speed transaxle, all-independent suspension, 142mph top speed, 0–60mph in 7.1 seconds, new engine, all other mechanical components overhauled, bare-metal respray in original Rosso Dino, interior retrimmed to original specification in black imitation leather, unused since 1988, excellent condition.
£40,000–45,000 BKS

The Dino 206 GT was the first and rarest mid-engined Ferrari, a mere 100 or so having been made. It was intended as the first of a separate marque established in memory of Alfredino, Enzo Ferrari's only legitimate son, who died at an early age. The name 'Dino' had long been applied to Ferrari's V6 engines, since Dino himself, a gifted engineer, had worked on the prototypes, first with Aurelio Lampredi, then with Vittorio Jano.

1970 Ferrari Dino 246 GT, 2418cc, double-overhead-camshaft V6 engine, all-independent coil-spring suspension, 4-wheel disc brakes, multi-tubular chassis, left-hand drive, restored, finished in red, interior trimmed in black, recently recommissioned, very good condition throughout.
£30,000–35,000 H&H

1971 Ferrari Dino 246 GT, 2418cc, double-overhead-camshaft V6, 190bhp, all-independent suspension, new exhaust, bodywork refurbished, resprayed in Giallo Fly, black interior, history file, good condition.
£30,000–35,000 COYS

1972 Ferrari Dino 246 GT, 2418cc V6 engine, 3 Weber 40DCNF/7 carburettors, 195bhp, Ferrari immobiliser, finished in red, 3 owners, good condition throughout.
£45,000–50,000 BRIT

▶ **1972 Ferrari Dino 246 GT,** 2418cc, double-overhead-camshaft V6, 5-speed gearbox, finished in red, good condition throughout.
£28,000–33,000 H&H

Ferrari Dino 246 GT (1969–74)

Engine: Transverse-mounted, double-overhead-camshaft V6, 2418cc.
Power output: 195bhp at 7,600rpm.
Transmission: Five-speed manual.
Brakes: Discs all-round.
Top speed: 142–148mph.
0–60mph: 7.1 seconds.
Production: Dino 246 GT, 2,732; Dino 246 GTS (Spyder), 1,180.
In its day, the pretty little Dino was the cheapest Ferrari ever marketed, in Ferrari terms at least a budget supercar that was pitched directly at the Porsche 911. It rang changes in other ways, too,

for in place of Ferrari's traditional V12 lump up front, the Dino had a V6 transversely-mounted amidships. In fact, it seems that the Dino was intended as a cheaper companion marque in its own right, as the 246 Dino was initially completely bare of Ferrari script and any prancing horse insignia. Even so, despite a mere 2.4 litres, its near 150mph performance was very Ferrari-like, with brilliant handling to match. As for the Pininfarina shape, many rate it as one of the prettiest and purest of all Ferraris: lithe, lean, and free of the steroid strakes and brutal Rambo garnish that infected Ferraris in the 1980s and beyond.

1972 Ferrari Dino 246 GTS Spyder, coachwork by
Pininfarina, 2418cc, double-overhead-camshaft V6,
195bhp, 5-speed transaxle, Targa-top, restored 1994–95
at a cost of £50,000, 2,200km covered since,
new brakes, finished in Rosso Corsa, black leather
interior, concours condition.
£43,000–48,000 BKS

1973 Ferrari Dino 246 GTS Spyder, 2418cc,
double-overhead-camshaft V6, 5-speed transaxle,
finished in red, good condition.
£44,000–49,000 FOS

1974 Ferrari Dino 308 GT4, air conditioning, electric mirrors, Panasonic car telephone, braking system overhauled,
bodywork restored, resprayed in white, beige leather interior, 43,472 miles recorded.
£13,000–16,000 BKS

Ferrari's family of successful V8-engined road cars began with the 308 GT4 of 1973. Badged until 1977 as a
Dino, thereafter as a Ferrari, the Bertone-styled 308 was Ferrari's first mid-engined 2+2. By placing the front
seats well forward, room was made for two occasional rear seats. The wedge-shaped styling was certainly
distinctive, and the 3 litre quad-cam V8's performance was impressive, its 236bhp proving sufficient for a
150+mph top speed, with 0–60mph in under 7 seconds.

1974 Ferrari Dino 308 GT4, restored, finished in red,
fitted with 16in Compomotive alloy wheels.
£18,000–22,000 KHP

1977 Ferrari 308 GTB Berlinetta, coachwork by
Pininfarina, 3 litre V8, dry-sump lubrication, 205bhp,
finished in original Rosso Dino, light tan leather interior,
84,000km recorded, very good original condition.
£19,000–23,000 BKS

◀ **1979 Ferrari 308 GTB,** 3 litre V8, finished in red,
good condition.
£21,000–24,000 H&H

1981 Ferrari 308 GTSi Spyder, coachwork by Pininfarina, 3 litre V8, fuel injection, 205bhp, wider-than-standard front wheels, finished in white, black leather interior, 48,000km recorded, good condition throughout.
£12,000–15,000 BKS

This car is to 1982 specification, but it was registered in 1981.

1984 Ferrari 308 GTS QV, finished in red, good condition.
£33,000–37,000 TALA

1985 Ferrari Mondial QV Cabriolet, coachwork by Pininfarina, finished in Rosso Corsa, black hood, beige leather interior, c31,000km recorded, good condition throughout.
£13,000–16,000 BKS

Ferrari's first full convertible since the disappearance of the Daytona Spyder in 1973, the Mondial 8 had the 308's 3 litre, quad-cam V8 engine in a lengthened version of the latter's chassis. Transmission and running gear remained much the same, with a five-speed transaxle and independent suspension all-round. Although less sporting than other Ferraris, the Mondial was good for 225+km/h, while its ride quality and comfort scored over long distances. Developments included a Cabriolet and a more-powerful (260bhp) *quattrovalvole* (four-valves-per-cylinder) engine in 1982.

1986 Ferrari 328 GTS Spyder, 3.2 litre V8 engine, Targa top, recently restored, finished in red, interior retrimmed in cream leather, new red carpets, good condition throughout.
£28,000–33,000 BKS

▶ **1989 Ferrari 328 GTS,** 3.2 litre V8 engine, ABS, Targa top, finished in red, cream leather interior, c15,000 miles recorded, good condition.
£43,000–48,000 KHP

1991 Ferrari 348 TS, 3.48 litre V8 engine, 300bhp, c16,000 miles recorded, very good condition.
£45,000–49,000 KHP

1985 Ferrari 288 GTO Berlinetta, coachwork by Pininfarina, 3 litre, double-overhead-camshaft V8 engine, twin IHI turbochargers, Weber-Marelli electronic fuel injection, 400bhp, 190mph top speed, 0–60mph in 5 seconds, finished in red, black leather upholstery, 6,875 miles recorded, 1 owner, excellent condition.
£140,000–160,000 BKS

The 288 GTO was built to compete in Group B which, in the early 1980s, inspired the creation of many extraordinary cars. To comply with the regulations, 278 examples were built, which makes the 288 GTO one of the rarest Ferraris of the past 25 years. It was also the car that inspired Ferrari to make the F40 and, subsequently, the F50.

1978 Ferrari 400 GT Coupé, 4823cc, factory-fitted steel sunroof, alloy wheels, air conditioning, finished in metallic blue, beige leather upholstery and headlining, 18,744 miles recorded.
£16,000–18,000 H&H

1978 Ferrari 400 GT Coupé, 4823cc, finished in Rosso, black and red interior trim, 64,000 miles recorded, concours winner, very good condition.
£13,000–16,000 H&H

This particular car was originally owned by the late John Bonham of Led Zepplin fame.

◀ **1982 Ferrari 400i Coupé,** coachwork by Pininfarina, 4.8 litre V12 engine, fuel injection, 340bhp, 5-speed manual gearbox, finished in metallic silver, light tan leather interior, 65,860km recorded, excellent condition throughout.
£14,000–17,000 BKS

1985 Ferrari Testarossa, 4942cc, double-overhead-camshaft, flat-12 engine, 4 valves per cylinder, fuel injection, dry-sump lubrication, 390bhp, all-independent wishbone-and-coil spring suspension, 4-wheel ventilated disc brakes, steel-tub chassis, 180mph top speed, 0–60mph in 5.4 seconds, finished in Rosso Corsa, tan leather interior, very good condition. **£30,000–35,000 COYS**

The Testarossa was developed by Ferrari as a rival to the Lamborghini Countach. Its striking aluminium coachwork, the work of Pininfarina, cleverly integrated aerodynamics with aesthetic appeal.

◀ **1990 Ferrari Testarossa,** 4942cc, flat-12 engine, finished in silver, good condition. **£47,000–52,000 TALA**

1991 Ferrari Testarossa, coachwork by Pininfarina, 5 litre, mid-mounted flat-12 engine, 4-valve cylinder heads, Koenig SS sports exhaust, 390bhp, 512 TR wheels, left-hand drive, air conditioning, finished in red, tan interior, electrically-adjustable seats, tilt steering wheel, 2 owners, excellent condition throughout. **£38,000–43,000 BKS**

1991 Ferrari F40, coachwork by Pininfarina, catalytic convertors, adjustable suspension, 201mph top speed, 0–60mph in under 4 seconds, finished in red, red seats, 12,803km recorded, 'as new' condition. **£140,000–160,000 BKS**

When Ferrari reached the 40th anniversary of its first car, it celebrated by creating a car that was fabulous even by Ferrari standards. The brief for the F40 was that it had to be the world's fastest production car. It was based on the Ferrari 288 GTO, with a longitudinal engine, five-speed transaxle and all-independent suspension by coil springs and unequal-length wishbones. The bodywork was stripped of carpets and interior door panels – the first cars even had sliding Plexiglas windows to save weight. The engine was a short-stroke variant of the 3 litre QV V8 which, with twin IHI turbochargers and Weber-Marelli electronic fuel injection, produced almost 478bhp and 426lb/ft torque.

1995 Ferrari F355 Berlinetta, finished in red, 7,300 miles recorded, very good condition. **£75,000–83,000 KHP**

▶ **1995 Ferrari F355 Challenge Berlinetta,** coachwork by Pininfarina, winner of the 1995 European Challenge Championship, reconverted for road use, new engine, type 2.7 engine management system, sports exhaust, transmission overhauled, F40 brakes, roll cage, sports seats, resprayed in Rosso Corsa, matching original interior, very good condition throughout. **£60,000–70,000 BKS**

Fiat

Founded in 1899 by Giovanni Agnelli, whose family still controls the company, Fiat has grown into an Italian industrial colossus. The company's initials originally stood for *Societa Anonimo Fabbrica Italiana di Automili Torini*. Cars are only one area of Fiat's wide-ranging interests, and in the motoring field alone, Fiat controls Ferrari, Lancia, Abarth and Alfa Romeo. In its early days, Fiat devoted considerable effort to racing, winning the Targa Florio and French Grand Prix in 1907. Some of the early cars had monstrous engines, up to 11 litres. The first model built in quantity was the 1912 Tipo Zero, of which about 200 were completed. In 1919, with the 1.5 litre 501, the company became a mass producer, and in 1936, the little 500 Topolino revolutionised personal transport, a feat repeated in 1957 with the 500 Nuova. From the 1960s, Fiat's model range broadened considerably. Two models that stand out and have a strong following today are the long-running 124 Spyder, which makes an interesting alternative to an MGB roadster, and the very pretty and slightly exotic Dino Spyder.

1914 Fiat Tipo 2B Seven-Seat Open Tourer, 2813cc, 4-cylinder engine, electric lighting, 70km/h top speed, right-hand drive, older restoration, finished in black and green, black leather upholstery, original specification, excellent condition.
£17,500–20,500 BKS

Fiat's Tipo 2B was introduced in 1912 and remained in production until 1920. Powered by a four-cylinder sidevalve engine of 2813cc, which developed 28bhp, it featured pressure lubrication, high-tension magneto ignition, a multiple-disc clutch, water-pump cooling, a four-speed gearbox, shaft drive and bevel-pinion final drive.

1937 Fiat 500A Topolino, 570cc, 4-cylinder engine, optional rear seats, opening rear window, right-hand drive, completely restored, finished in maroon and black, bodywork fair, otherwise good condition.
£3,750–4,500 BKS

Better equipped than many cars twice its size, the Fiat 500 – soon nicknamed *Topolino* (mouse) – brought a degree of refinement hitherto unknown to small cars when launched in 1936. Lockheed hydraulic brakes, independent front suspension and 12-volt electrics were all part of the package, while an engine mounted ahead of the front axle line helped maximise cabin space. The 570cc, four-cylinder sidevalve engine produced a modest 13bhp, but the lightweight Topolino could manage a respectable 50+mph under favourable conditions. For most buyers, though, the 42–50mpg fuel consumption would have been the major attraction.

FIAT Model	ENGINE cc/cyl	DATES	CONDITION 1	2	3
500B Topolino	569/4	1945–55	£5,000	£2,000	£750
500C	569/4	1948–54	£4,000	£1,700	£1,000
500 Nuova	479,499/2	1957–75	£3,000	£1,500	£750
600/600D	633, 767/4	1955–70	£3,000	£2,000	£1,000
500F Giardiniera	479, 499/2	1957–75	£3,000	£1,500	£1,000
2300S	2280/6	1961–68	£3,000	£1,700	£1,000
850	843/4	1964–71	£1,000	£750	-
850 Coupé	843, 903/4	1965–73	£1,500	£1,000	-
850 Spyder	843, 903/4	1965–73	£3,000	£2,000	£1,000
128 Sport Coupé 3P	1116/ 1290/4	1971–78	£2,500	£1,800	£1,000
130 Coupé	3235/6	1971–77	£5,500	£4,000	£2,000
131 Mirafiori Sport	1995/4	1974–84	£1,500	£1,000	£500
124 Sport Coupé	1438/ 1608/4	1966–72	£3,000	£2,000	£1,000
124 Sport Spyder	1438/ 1608/4	1966–72	£5,500	£2,500	£1,500
Dino Coupé	1987/ 2418/6	1967–73	£8,000	£5,500	£2,500
Dino Spyder	1987/ 2418/6	1967–73	£10,000	£7,000	£5,000
X1/9	1290/ 1498/4	1972–89	£4,000	£2,000	£1,500

Miller's
Starter Marque

Starter Fiats: *Fiat 500, 1957 onward; Fiat 600; Fiat 850 Coupé; Fiat X1/9; Fiat 124 Coupé and Spyder.*

- **500:** When the Fiat 500 Nuova appeared in 1957, long-time Fiat designer Dante Giacosa defended his frugal flyweight by saying, 'However small it might be, an automobile will always be more comfortable than a motor scooter.' Today, though, the diminutive scoot-about needs no defence, for time has justified his faith with production of more than four million 500s and derivatives up to the demise of the Giardiniera estate in 1977. In some senses, the Fiat was a 'mini' before the British Mini, for the baby Fiat not only appeared two years ahead of its British counterpart, but it was also 3in shorter. The original 500 Nuova was rather frantic, with its 479cc tiddler of a two-pot motor, but in 1960, it grew to maturity with the launch of the 500D, which was pushed along by an enlarged 499.5cc engine. Now at last the baby Fiat could almost touch 60mph without being pushed over the edge of a cliff.
- Many Fiat 500 proponents commend the car as a usable every-day commuter classic, and fitting of larger Fiat engines, up to 650cc, is a common and acceptable practice. The engines are generally robust and long-lasting, but the monocoque chassis and body are fairly rust-prone. Unless you enjoy DIY restoration, it's advisable to go for the most solid car you can find, as relatively low values mean your friends will appreciate the results of your restoration more than your bank manager.
- **850 Coupé:** The Fiat 850 Coupé is a delectable little package combining up to 45mpg economy, peppy performance (90+mph for the 903cc versions), front disc brakes, super handling and delightfully neat styling. Again, on these Fiats, rust is the main enemy. Even though around 380,000 were built between 1965 and 1973, they have never been a common sight in the UK. If you take your time to find a good one, you'll discover a tremendously rewarding little car.
- **X1/9:** The merits of the sharp-edged Bertone design are a matter of divided opinion, but it has a few very important things going for it. The X1/9 is just about the only truly affordable and practical, volume-produced, mid-engined sports car, and it also offers exceptional handling. These days, it's undergoing something of a renaissance as an expression of 1970s design. The engine is a little jewel, reliable and generally long-lasting, too. Unfortunately, the same can't be said of the body, so the best buy will usually be a later model that's had less time to rust.
- **124 Spyder:** Elegant Pininfarina styling, all-round disc brakes, twin-cam power and an excellent five-speed gearbox add up to a very appealing and fine-handling, fresh-air sporting package. The model was produced by Fiat from 1966 to 1982; from then until 1985, Pininfarina took over production and built it as the Spyder Europe. Once again, rust can strike hard, with front suspension struts, inner sills and the front and rear edges of the floorpan particularly susceptible. Right-hand-drive versions are very few and far between, but left-right conversion is viable. Of the 200,000 built, a large number went to the USA, so there's every chance of picking up a car that's spent most of its life in a rust-free climate. The best all-round model is the 2 litre carburettor version.

A known continuous history can add value to and enhance the enjoyment of a car.

1939 Fiat 500 Topolino, 570cc, 4-cylinder sidevalve engine, 13bhp, independent front suspension, hydraulic brakes, restored early 1980s, little use since, finished in red, new interior, spare engine block and heads, very good condition throughout.
£7,000–8,000 BKS

1958 Fiat 1100 Saloon, finished in blue, blue upholstery, unrestored.
£800–950 BKS

Fiat has made many cars under the designation 1100 (Millecento), but this particular model, introduced in 1953, was the first with unitary construction. Standard Millecento saloons won their class in the Mille Miglia during 1954–57, and they were equally successful in rallies. Italian specialist makers like Stanguellini, Ermini and Bandini fell on the Millecento and used it as a basis for their sports racers.

1963 Fiat 2300 Coupé, 2279cc, 6-cylinder engine, 4-speed manual gearbox, right-hand drive, finished in original red, cream interior, dry stored for many years, in need of refurbishment.
£1,500–1,800 H&H

1966 Fiat 500D, 500cc, 4-cylinder engine, finished in navy blue, black interior.
£2,000–2,500 COYS

◀ **1969 Fiat 500,** 499cc, twin-cylinder engine, recently restored, new doors and bonnet panel, finished in red, unused for some time, c57,000 miles recorded, good mechanical condition.
£1,500–1,800 BRIT

The minimalist 500 will transport four persons at a squeeze and, given a long stretch of road and a following wind, will achieve a heady 60mph.

1971 Fiat 500 Gamine Roadster, right-hand drive, partially restored, finished in red and yellow, black interior, good condition throughout.
£3,750–4,500 BKS

The closest any major manufacturer has come to building a replica 'Noddy Car', Fiat's Gamine enlivened the motoring scene during the late 1960s and early 1970s. Based on the contemporary Fiat 500F, it was the work of Vignale.

1968 Fiat Samantha Coupé, coachwork by Vignale, 1.6 litre engine, right-hand drive, body and engine restored late 1980s, finished in red with matching interior, coachwork and interior in good condition, engine and running gear in need of recommissioning.
£2,400–2,800 BKS

Based on the contemporary Fiat 124 and 125 models, the Samantha was made in small numbers during the late 1960s. Only six of the 25 cars built are thought to survive.

▶ **1974 Fiat 124 Spyder,** 1765cc, 4-cylinder engine, completely restored 1995, finished in metallic blue, new hood and beige interior trim, excellent condition.
£5,750–6,500 BRIT

The Pininfarina-styled 124 Spyder was produced from 1966 to 1985. Built on a shortened 124 floorpan, it began life with a 1300cc twin-cam engine and evolved through several series, the final examples having a 2 litre unit. The bulk of production went to the USA, although a small number were sold in the UK.

◀ **1979 Fiat 124 Spyder,** 2 litre engine, fuel-injection, automatic transmission, left-hand drive, mechanics refurbished, sump guard, stainless steel exhaust and brake hoses, period Cibié lamps, Dinitrol chassis and body treatment, resprayed in original metallic blue, new hood, 22,500 miles recorded, concours condition.
£6,000–7,000 BKS

▶ **1987 Fiat X1/9,** 1500cc, removable targa top with sunroof, restored to original specification, reconditioned gearbox, finished in red, excellent condition throughout.
£1,750–2,100 BARO

Styled by Bertone, the X1/9 was introduced in 1972 with mid-mounted, transverse engine. Among its features were a removable targa top and pop-up headlamps.

Ford

Henry Ford's incredible motoring career got under way in 1893, when he built an internal-combustion engine on the kitchen table of his Detroit home. In 1896, his first motorised vehicle took to the streets, and in 1903 the Ford Motor Company was established and began producing the Model A Runabout. It was the launch of that car's replacement, the Model T, in 1908 that really brought the company to prominence. The story of Ford in Britain also began with the Model T, when Henry Ford set up his first overseas assembly plant at Trafford Park, Manchester in 1911, and from the 1930s Fords became as much a part of Britain's motoring landscape as our own domestic makes like Austin and Morris. From the enthusiast's point of view, British-built Fords offer a wide variety of affordable classic options, both from before and after the war. American Fords from the 1950s onward offer a touch of transatlantic glamour, while the later Mustang is firmly established as a motoring icon, coveted the world over.

1911 Ford Model T Torpedo Runabout, authentic Runabout coachwork, correct carbide lights, brass fixtures, 16 gallon fuel tank, white tyres, finished in blue, black leather upholstery, museum displayed for many years.
£13,000–16,000 BKS

The Model T put the world on wheels. It came with bodies of all descriptions, and early customers also had the choice of colour. Henry Ford only standardised on black when he discovered that black paint dried significantly faster than any other colour, which reduced the amount of time that cars had to be stored under cover while the paint dried.

1912 Ford Model T, 2890cc, 4-cylinder engine, largely original, engine overhauled, 500 miles covered since, alloy pistons, later 4-blade cooling fan, resprayed, new hood, 1 owner since 1935, VCC dating certificate.
£15,000–18,000 BRIT

During 1907, Ford decided to pursue a one-model policy, that model being the Model T. It was an entirely new design, employing a four-cylinder engine with cylinders cast en-block and, unusually for the period, a detachable cylinder head. The Model T made its debut in 1908, billed as 'The Universal Car'. By October 1911, Ford had decided to establish an assembly plant outside North America and chose Trafford Park in Manchester. So successful was the Model T that, by 1913, Manchester was producing 29 per cent of the cars registered in Great Britain.

◀ **1917 Ford Model T Four-Seat Tourer,** 2900cc, 20bhp, Ruckstell axle, 4-wheel hydraulic disc brakes, wooden spoked wheels, electric headlights, modern amber indicators, folding top.
£14,000–17,000 KOLN

FORD Model	ENGINE cc/cyl	DATES	CONDITION 1	2	3
Model T	2892/4	1908–27	£12,000	£7,000	£4,000
Model A	3285/4	1928–32	£8,500	£6,000	£3,500
Models Y and 7Y	933/4	1932–40	£5,000	£3,000	£1,500
Model C, CX & 7W	1172/4	1934–40	£4,000	£2,000	£1,000
Model AB	3285/4	1933–34	£10,000	£8,000	£4,500
Model ABF	2043/4	1933–34	£9,000	£6,000	£4,000
Model V8	3622/8	1932–40	£8,500	£6,000	£4,500
Model V8–60	2227/8	1936–40	£7,000	£5,000	£2,000
Model AF (UK only)	2033/4	1928–32	£9,000	£6,000	£3,500

A right-hand-drive vehicle will always command more interest than a left-hand-drive model. Coachbuilt vehicles, and in particular tourers, achieve a premium at auction. Veteran cars (i.e. manufactured before 1919) will often achieve a 20% premium.

1918 Ford Model T Two-Seat Roadster, 3222cc, 4-cylinder engine, restored, finished in black, beige hood, red interior, very good condition.
£5,000–6,000 H&H

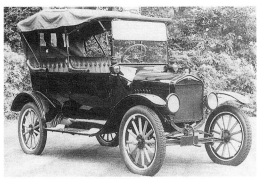

1921 Ford Model T, 2890cc, 4-cylinder engine, transverse springing front and rear, older restoration, original specification throughout, finished in black, trimmed with black leathercloth.
£7,000–8,500 BRIT

1924 Ford Model T Four-Seat Tourer, finished in white and black, stored for many years, good condition throughout.
£3,500–4,000 H&H

Restored values

The cost of a professional restoration will have an influence on, but no direct relation to, a car's market value. A restored car can have a market value lower than the cost of its restoration.

1926 Ford Model T Doctor's Coupé, Canadian-built, recently restored, little use since, finished in black.
£10,000–11,000 BKS

1925 Ford Model T Doctor's Coupé, 2900cc, 3-speed gearbox, left-hand drive, finished in red, tan interior, history file.
£4,750–5,250 H&H

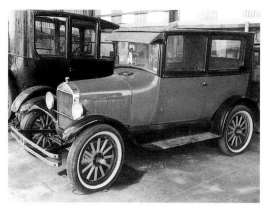

1926 Ford Model T Tudor Saloon, 2892cc,
4-cylinder engine, wooden-spoked wheels,
finished in red and black.
£7,500–8,500 TUC

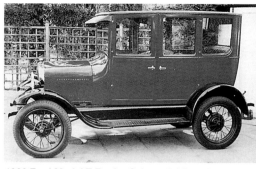

1926 Ford Model T Fordor Saloon, 2.9 litre, 4-cylinder
sidevalve engine, 22bhp, 2-speed epicyclic gearbox,
beam front axle, transverse leaf springs front and rear,
mechanical rear drum brakes, completely restored,
finished in red with black wings, interior trimmed in
period-style grey fabric, very good condition.
£13,750–15,250 C

◄ **1928 Ford Model A Phaeton,** 3285cc, 4-cylinder engine,
right-hand-mounted handbrake, internal door handles,
finished in maroon with black wings, serviceable black vinyl
weather equipment, tan interior, good condition throughout.
£10,000–11,500 BRIT

The Model T's successor, the Model A, was introduced
in 1928 and was modern in styling and specification.
It was powered by a 3.3 litre, 24hp engine (a Model
AF was available in the UK, rated at 14.9hp and
displacing 2033cc). Available in Saloon, Roadster
and Phaeton (tourer) forms, the Model A achieved
success in many parts of the world. It was produced
for four years before yielding place to the Model B.

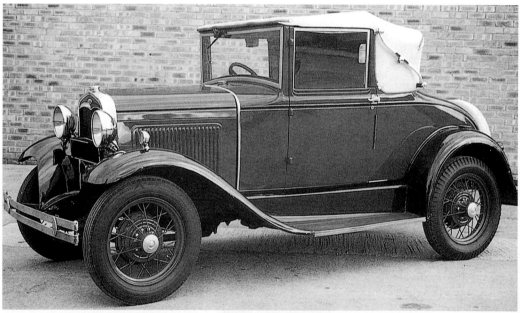

1929 Ford Model A Doctor's Coupé, 4-cylinder
sidevalve engine, 40bhp, 3-speed sliding-gear
gearbox, 4-wheel drum brakes, left-hand drive,
older restoration, finished in grey, matching
interior, very good condition throughout.
£8,000–10,000 BKS

► **1933 Ford Eight Model Y,** 933cc,
4-cylinder sidevalve engine, restored early
1980s, finished in maroon and black, beige
interior, 86,000 miles recorded, very good
condition throughout.
£2,500–3,000 BRIT

1933 Ford Eight Model Y Tudor, 933cc, 4-cylinder sidevalve engine, recently refurbished, new radiator finished in black, yellow wheels, green interior.
£2,750–3,250 BRIT

Introduced in 1932, the Ford Eight Model Y represented remarkable value for money with its £100 price tag for the basic two-door model. As with earlier, larger models, saloons were designated Tudor and Fordor depending on the number of doors.

1934 Ford Eight Model Y Tudor, completely restored to original specification.
£2,800–3,500 WeR

1935 Ford Model C 10hp Fordor De Luxe, restored, finished in beige and black, mechanics and bodywork in very good condition.
£3,000–3,500 WeR

1936 Ford Eight Model Y Tudor, completely restored, concours condition.
£6,000–7,000 WeR

FORD (British built) Model	ENGINE cc/cyl	DATES	CONDITION 1	2	3
Anglia E494A	993/4	1948–53	£2,000	£850	£250
Prefect E93A	1172/4	1940–49	£3,500	£1,250	£900
Prefect E493A	1172/4	1948–53	£2,500	£1,000	£300
Popular 103E	1172/4	1953–59	£1,875	£825	£300
Anglia/Prefect 100E	1172/4	1953–59	£1,350	£625	£250
Prefect 107E	997/4	1959–62	£1,150	£600	£200
Escort/Squire 100E	1172/4	1955–61	£1,000	£850	£275
Popular 100E	1172/4	1959–62	£1,250	£600	£180
Anglia 105E	997/4	1959–67	£1,400	£500	£75
Anglia 123E	1198/4	1962–67	£1,550	£575	£150
V8 Pilot	3622/8	1947–51	£7,500	£5,000	£1,500
Consul Mk I	1508/4	1951–56	£2,250	£950	£400
Consul Mk I DHC	1508/4	1953–56	£6,000	£3,500	£1,250
Zephyr Mk I	2262/6	1951–56	£3,000	£1,250	£600
Zephyr Mk I DHC	2262/6	1953–56	£7,000	£4,000	£1,300
Zodiac Mk I	2262/6	1953–56	£3,300	£1,500	£700
Consul Mk II/Deluxe	1703/4	1956–62	£2,900	£1,500	£650
Consul Mk II DHC	1703/4	1956–62	£5,000	£3,300	£1,250
Zephyr Mk II	2553/6	1956–62	£3,800	£1,800	£750
Zephyr Mk II DHC	2553/6	1956–62	£8,000	£4,000	£1,500
Zodiac Mk II	2553/6	1956–62	£4,000	£2,250	£750
Zodiac Mk II DHC	2553/6	1956–62	£8,500	£4,250	£1,800
Zephyr 4 Mk III	1703/4	1962–66	£2,100	£1,200	£400
Zephyr 6 Mk III	2552/6	1962–66	£2,300	£1,300	£450
Zodiac Mk II	2553/6	1962–66	£2,500	£1,500	£500
Zephyr 4 Mk IV	1994/4	1966–72	£1,750	£600	£300
Zephyr 6 Mk IV	2553/6	1966–72	£1,800	£700	£300
Zodiac Mk IV	2994/6	1966–72	£2,000	£800	£300
Zodiac Mk IV Est.	2994/6	1966–72	£2,800	£1,200	£300
Zodiac Mk IV Exec.	2994/6	1966–72	£2,300	£950	£300
Classic 315	1340/ 1498/4	1961–63	£1,400	£800	£500
Consul Capri	1340/ 1498/4	1961–64	£2,100	£1,350	£400
Consul Capri GT	1498/4	1961–64	£2,600	£1,600	£800

► **1956 Ford Consul Mk I Saloon,** 1508cc, 3-speed gearbox, column-change, finished in black, red interior, 63,083 miles recorded, 1 owner, excellent original condition throughout.
£2,750–3,250 H&H

1960 Ford Zodiac Mk II Farnham Estate, coachwork by Abbott, recently restored, 6-branch manifold and straight-through exhaust, finished in red, cream and black.
£5,500–6,500 BKS

Edward Abbott formed his coachbuilding company in Farnham in 1929. Various bodies were applied to Austin 7 chassis, followed by work for Daimler, Lanchester and Talbot. After WWII, Abbott was one of the few coachbuilders to start in business again, bodying Sunbeam Talbot dropheads and Bentleys. There was also a Healey Abbott. These were followed by Ford saloons, which were converted into estates – approximately 500 Consuls, 75 Zephyrs and 36 Zodiacs received this treatment.

1959 Ford Popular, 1172cc sidevalve engine, 36bhp, restored, good condition.
£1,200–1,400 HMM

1961 Ford Popular Two-Door Saloon, finished in blue with matching interior, 18,200 miles recorded, 1 owner, good condition throughout.
£2,400–2,800 BKS

Ford's small saloon range remained essentially pre-war in concept until 1953, when the introduction of the Anglia and Prefect in 100E guise ushered in a new era. The newcomers were a curious mixture of new and established technology, featuring unitary-construction bodies and MacPherson-strut independent front suspension, yet retaining the existing 1172cc sidevalve engine and three-speed gearbox. Eventually, Ford bestowed the Popular name on its entry-level 100E saloon in 1959, and the model continued in production alongside the new 105E Anglia until 1962.

1964 Ford Anglia 1200 Super, 1198cc, 4-cylinder, overhead-valve engine, finished in grey and white, original red interior in good condition, good mechanical condition, new exhaust system, showroom displayed for some years, fewer than 42,000 miles recorded.
£2,000–2,500 BRIT

The Ford 105E Anglia was introduced in September 1959. Its styling was modern, the reverse-rake rear window being a particularly distinctive feature. The engine was an entirely new overhead-valve unit with over-square dimensions of 1 litre capacity. A 1200cc option followed in 1962. The Anglia continued in production until 1968, when it was replaced by the Escort.

Ford Anglia (1959–67)

In 1959, Ford's new Anglia represented the shape of fins to come, a pretty, compact little saloon that was an instant hit with buyers who might otherwise have opted for something drearily and domestically familiar, like an Austin A40, Morris Minor or Triumph Herald. Although overshadowed by the launch of the top-selling Cortina a couple of years later, the Anglia 105E was a stylish little device with a miniature, full-width version of the 'dollar-grin' grille up front and voguish US-hand-me-down rear fins. Under the skin, there was a little innovation too,

with the first overhead-valve engine for a small Ford and – wonder of wonder – four gears for the first time in a British Ford. The little Anglia was a worthy and peppy little workhorse that went on to sell more than a million before making way for the Escort in 1967.

Pick of the bunch: The Anglia Super 123E, which has an 1198cc engine compared with the 997cc of the 105E, so you'll get to 60mph in 22 seconds rather than 29, and eventually you'll nudge 85mph instead of running out of puff at 75mph.

1965 Ford 105E Anglia Estate, 997cc, 4-cylinder engine, in need of minor cosmetic attention, otherwise good condition.
£1,300–1,600 FORD

A known continuous history can add value to and enhance the enjoyment of a car.

1967 Ford 105E Anglia Saloon, 997cc, restored 1998, brakes overhauled, new exhaust, finished in Ermine white, red interior, 23,000 miles recorded, 'as new' condition.
£2,500–3,000 H&H

Miller's Starter Marque

Starter Fords: *Anglia, Prefect, Popular models from 1948 onward; Mk I, II, III Consul, Zephyr and Zodiac, Mk IV Zephyr/Zodiac; Consul Classic 315/Consul Capri; Cortina Mk I, II, III; Corsair; Capri; Escort.*

- Whatever your tastes, there's a Ford you can afford – in fact more than we have space to mention. Their list of virtues as starter classics is almost as long as the list of models to choose from. Importantly, many were made in their millions, which means that generally there's a ready stock of cars and spares, backed by a healthy network of clubs and specialists. Better still, Fords rarely employ exotic materials or obscure, hard-to-grasp technologies, and that makes them a joy for the DIY enthusiast.
- **Consul, Zephyr, Zodiac (Mk I–III):** These are what you might term lifestyle Fords – there's one to match your taste in clothes and music. The Mk I and II models are favoured as Brit-sized chunks of Americana by the retro crowd. For Mk I models, read early Elvis, rockabilly rather than rock 'n' roll. They are also ideal for post-war swing spivs with Cesar Romero pencil moustaches, double-breasted suits and nylons to sell. The Mk II is mainstream Elvis, structurally reinforced quiffs, pedal-pushers, bowling shirts and Levi 501s. As for the Mk III, that's Elvis at Vegas, teddyboy drape-coats, long sideburns and a tub of Swarfega in the hair. All models are eminently viable for the DIY enthusiast. While performance is hardly shattering by today's standards, they are fast enough to go with the flow of modern traffic without causing a tail-back.

FORD (British built) Model	ENGINE cc/cyl	DATES	CONDITION 1	2	3
Cortina Mk I	1198/4	1963–66	£1,550	£600	£150
Cortina Crayford Mk I	1198/4	1963–66	£3,500	£1,800	£950
Cortina GT	1498/4	1963–66	£1,800	£1,000	£650
Cortina Lotus Mk I	1558/4	1963–66	£10,000	£7,500	£4,500
Cortina Mk II	1599/4	1966–70	£1,000	£500	£100
Cortina GT Mk II	1599/4	1966–70	£1,200	£650	£150
Cortina Crayford Mk II DHC	1599/4	1966–70	£4,000	£2,000	£1,500
Cortina Lotus Mk II	1558/4	1966–70	£6,000	£3,500	£1,800
Cortina 1600E	1599/4	1967–70	£4,000	£2,000	£900
Consul Corsair	1500/4	1963–65	£1,100	£500	£250
Consul Corsair GT	1500/4	1963–65	£1,200	£600	£250
Corsair V4	1664/4	1965–70	£1,150	£600	£250
Corsair V4 Est.	1664/4	1965–70	£1,400	£600	£250
Corsair V4GT	1994/4	1965–67	£1,300	£700	£250
CorsairV4GT Est.	1994/4	1965–67	£1,400	£700	£350
Corsair Convertible	1664/ 1994/4	1965–70	£4,300	£2,500	£1,000
Corsair 2000	1994/4	1967–70	£1,350	£500	£250
Corsair 2000E	1994/4	1967–70	£1,500	£800	£350
Escort 1300E	1298/4	1973–74	£1,900	£1,000	£250
Escort Twin Cam	1558/4	1968–71	£8,000	£5,000	£2,000
Escort GT	1298/4	1968–73	£3,000	£1,500	£350
Escort Sport	1298/4	1971–75	£1,750	£925	£250
Escort Mexico	1601/4	1970–74	£4,000	£2,000	£750
RS1600	1601/4	1970–74	£5,000	£2,500	£1,500
RS2000	1998/4	1973–74	£4,500	£2,200	£1,000
Escort RS Mexico	1593/4	1976–78	£3,500	£2,000	£850
Escort RS2000 Mk II	1993/4	1976–80	£6,000	£3,500	£2,000
Capri Mk I 1300/ 1600	1298/ 1599/4	1969–72	£1,500	£1,000	£550
Capri 2000/ 3000GT	1996/4 2994/6	1969–72	£2,000	£1,000	£500
Capri 3000E	2994/6	1970–72	£4,000	£2,000	£1,000
Capri RS3100	3093/6	1973–74	£6,500	£3,500	£2,000
Cortina 2000E	1993/4	1973–76	£2,500	£550	£225
Granada Ghia	1993/4 2994/6	1974–77	£3,000	£900	£350

1975 Ford Escort RS2000 Mk I, restored, finished in yellow with orange stripes, quarter-bumpers, concours condition. £4,500–5,250 **FORD**

1962 Ford Consul Classic, 1340cc, overhead-valve, 4-cylinder engine, finished in grey and white, blue and silver interior, 78,000 miles recorded, retained by Ford for many years, award winner, excellent condition. £2,700–3,250 **H&H**

◀ **1965 Ford Cortina 1500 De-Luxe Four-Door Saloon,** finished in dark green, good condition. £1,900–2,250 **H&H**

Ford Cortina Mk I (1962–66)

The Ford Cortina appeared late in 1962, and soon you couldn't miss it on Britain's roads as sales soared. With a mean price-tag of just £639, it undercut rivals and in many cases offered a lot more. Overall, it added up to the anatomy of a best-seller, in fact the best-selling British car of its time.
Pick of the bunch: 1500GT and Cortina Lotus

(see Lotus). The 1500GT gave a creditable 13 second 0–60mph time and a 95mph top speed; the Cortina Lotus, with 1558cc, 105bhp Lotus twin-cam engine and uprated suspension, scorched its way to 108mph. There were only 4,012 genuine Mk I Cortina Lotuses; they're highly prized, so watch out for fakes – there are plenty.

1967 Ford Cortina Mk II GT Convertible, Crayford conversion, 1500cc, engine rebuilt 1993, fitted with new front wings and resprayed in white 1987, black interior, original push-button radio, original except for new hood fitted 1972, 63,000 miles recorded, 1 owner, very good condition.
£2,200–2,600 H&H

1969 Ford Cortina Mk II 1600E Saloon, restored at a cost of c£8,000, new steering rack, refurbished Rostyle wheels, new front grille and brightwork where needed, electric windscreen washers, bodywork Waxoyled and cavity waxed, finished in Blue Mink, new black interior trim, all wooden veneers repolished, higher than average oil consumption, some spares including Rostyle wheels.
£2,000–2,500 BKS

The Mk II Cortina 1600E first appeared in 1967. It was intended as a fast, executive-style vehicle, utilizing the 88bhp GT engine, Lotus suspension and Rostyle wheels. The interior was luxurious, having a wooden dashboard, leather-rimmed steering wheel and comprehensive instrumentation. Top speed was in the region of 100mph. By the time production ended in 1970, a total of 55,000 had been built.

◄ **1969 Ford Cortina Mk II 1600E Saloon,** finished in gold, Rostyle wheels, original interior, concours condition.
£4,250–4,750 FORD

Ford Cortina Mk II (1966–70)

Body styles: Two- and four-door saloon, estate, Crayford convertible.
Engine: Four-cylinder, 1297cc, 1498cc, 1599cc (Lotus, 1558cc).
Power output: 53.5–88bhp (Lotus, 106bhp).
Transmission: Four-speed manual, optional automatic.
Brakes: Front discs, rear drums.
Top speed: 80–98mph (Lotus, 105mph).
0–60mph: 12.5–24 seconds (Lotus, 9 seconds).
Production: 1,010,580.
Prices in 1968: Two-door 1300, £792; 1600GT, £939; 1600E, £1,073; Lotus, £1,163.
The Mk I Cortina was a hard act to follow: not only had it been Britain's best-selling car in its day, but also it had been the first British car to top a million sales in four years. As fins faded from automotive fashion, Ford remodelled the Mk I into the square-cut Mk II, which continued the company's domination of middle-market family and

professional motoring. As with the Mk I, there was nothing tricksy or revolutionary about either the styling or engineering of the Mk II, yet once more its mean price undercut rivals and made it difficult to resist. What's more, the Cortina was not so much a single model, but rather a whole model range. There were versions to match your wallet, aspirations and need for speed, from the plain Standard and DeLuxe versions to the sporty 95–100mph, two-door GT or, for £130 more, the 1600E. The 'E' stood for Executive, the car being based on the 1600GT with added luxury trimming, fancy wheels and two extra doors. Fastest and most expensive variant was the rare Cortina Lotus Mk II (see Lotus).
Cortina fact: In 1970, the millionth export Cortina was helicoptered from Ford's Dagenham plant to its buyer in Belgium, achieving a record for the fastest million in overseas sales and the fastest delivery to an export customer.

► **1976 Ford Cortina Mk III 2000E Saloon,** engine completely rebuilt 1997, all mechanics renewed or overhauled, new front wings, doors reskinned, resprayed in red 1981, good condition.
£1,750–2,500 FEO

1977 Ford Granada 3.0 Ghia Coupé, 2994cc, factory-fitted steel sunroof, alloy wheels, finished in metallic red, cream and beige leather interior trim, good condition throughout. **£1,000–1,200 H&H**

1975 Ford Capri 2.0S Mk II, alloy wheels, finished in white with brown vinyl roof, 36,000 miles recorded, original, 'as new' condition. **£2,500–3,000 FORD**

1986 Ford Sierra RS Cosworth Saloon, 1993cc, double-overhead-camshaft, 4-cylinder engine, 4 valves per cylinder, Garrett AiResearch turbocharger, 'first stage' chip to give 280bhp, 64,250 miles recorded, 1 owner, good condition throughout. **£8,000–9,000 BKS**

▶ **1986 Ford Capri 1.6 Laser,** 1593cc, 4-cylinder engine, 5-speed manual gearbox, original factory sliding sunroof, alloy wheels, finished in white, grey interior and trim, 1 owner, 16,948 miles recorded. **£2,750–3,250 H&H**

Ford Capri

Making the transatlantic crossing from Detroit to Dagenham, and with a mediterranean name thrown in, the theme of Ford's hot-selling Mustang fastback resurfaced in Europe in 1969 as the Capri.

The Mustang, with an options list longer than the Golden Gate bridge, was promoted as Ford's 'personal car', while on this side of the pond, the advertising scribes reckoned that the Capri was 'the car you always promised yourself'. And for those medallion men who favoured curved-collared suits tailored from static-sparking, petro-chemical by-products and who splashed on Old Spice to mask the odour, a Ford Capri was the next best thing to sex – and a lot more achievable. Like its American cousin, the Capri offered kaleidoscopic customer choice, from the sheep-in-wolf's clothing, 89mph 1300 to rorty, V6-engined RS, GT and fuel-injected models, some with 130+mph performance. Essentially, if you added the right stick-on goodies, you could make your Dagenham donkey mimic a road-burning RS – in fact, over the years there were an astonishing 900 variants on the Capri theme. Today, with the rediscovery of the dubious styles and values of the 1970s, the Capri is emerging as a New Lad's icon.

Pick of the bunch: V6-engined models, including RS, GT and E designations; troublesome V4 engines best avoided; ordinary 1300 and 1600 models are pretty lame; 1600GT an option in the go-less-slowly stakes.

Ford – USA

◀ **1934 Ford Woody Wagon,** 3621cc, sidevalve V8, 3-speed manual gearbox, transverse-leaf springing front and rear, left-hand drive, very good condition. **£18,000–20,000 PALM**

1951 Ford Country Squire Woody, sidevalve V8, 100bhp, automatic transmission, room for 8 passengers, restored, engine and transmission rebuilt, 4,000 miles covered since, carburettor and dynamo rebuilt, braking system overhauled, finished in correct metallic blue, original factory linoleum on rear floor and lower tailgate, 44,000 miles recorded. **£19,000–22,000 BKS**

1957 Ford Thunderbird, 312cu.in, overhead-valve V8, 245bhp, automatic transmission, soft top, air conditioning, finished in Dusk Rose, 23,000 miles recorded, original unrestored condition. **£18,000–20,000 RM**

Ford introduced the Thunderbird as a response to Chevrolet's Corvette, but in reality, the two cars were quite different. The Thunderbird staked its claim as a personal luxury car, while the Corvette was trying to make a reputation as a sports car. The Thunderbird outsold the Corvette by more than three to one, due to its power and comfort, and its air of sophistication. In 1957, the third and last year of production for the classic two-seater styling, Ford brought out what is thought to be the best Thunderbird. It had a more powerful engine, making it the fastest Thunderbird as well.

▶ **1959 Ford Thunderbird,** 352cu.in V8, 300bhp, 4-seater bodywork, restored, good condition. **£21,500–24,000 HMM**

The four-seat Thunderbird arrived in 1958, having been completely redesigned, with unitary construction, all-coil suspension and a 113in wheelbase. Only one engine was available: a 352cu.in V8 developing 300bhp.

Ford Mustang (1964–68)

Body styles: Two-door, four-seat hardtop, fastback coupé, convertible.
Engine: Six-cylinder, 2781–4100cc; V8, 4262–7012cc.
Power output: 101–155bhp (six); 164–335bhp (V8).
Transmission: Three- or four-speed manual, three-speed automatic.
Brakes: Hydraulic drums; optional front discs.
Top speed: 110–127mph (4727cc).
0–60mph: 15.0 seconds (six); 6.1 seconds (4727cc with options).
Production: 2,077,826.

This one hit the ground running – galloping in fact, for the Mustang rewrote the sales record books soon after it burst on to the market in April 1964 and spawned the term 'pony car' to describe a new breed of sporty 'compacts'. The concept behind the Mustang was to create an inexpensive sports car for the masses, and in realisation it was more than classless, almost universal in appeal. It had an options list longer than the Golden Gate bridge, which meant that there was a flavour to suit every

taste and pocket. At one end, it was a pretty shopping-mall mule, at the other a muscular thoroughbred stallion and race winner. There were Mustangs for mums, sons, daughters, husbands, even young-at-heart grandparents. Why, this car was a four-wheeled democrat. For many, the beginning of the end of the classic era of the Mustang came about in 1969. By then, the Mustang was getting bigger and heavier, and although the hot Boss and Mach I models preserved the performance image, it wouldn't be long before the pony became hobbled by emissions regulations.

Mustang miscellany: The Mustang was such an immediate hit that a Michigan baker advertised his wares with the claim, 'Our hotcakes are selling like Mustangs'. As well as producing the 350 and 500GTs in his Californian workshops, racing legend Carroll Shelby also created 1,000 of his hot Mustangs for the Hertz car rental company. However, the company withdrew these black and gold roadburners from service when it was found that customers were using them for drag racing.

◀ **1964 Ford Mustang Convertible,** Challenger V8 option, 4-barrel carburettor, 220bhp, automatic transmission, optional power hood, restored, 12,000 miles covered since, finished in red, white and red interior.
£10,750–13,000 BKS

▶ **1969 Ford Mustang Convertible,** 351cu.in V8 engine, 290bhp, automatic transmission, disc front brakes, rear drums, left-hand drive, completely restored, finished in red, white hood and interior.
£7,000–8,000 Pou

FORD (American built) Model	ENGINE cu.in/cyl	DATES	CONDITION 1	2	3
Thunderbird	292/				
	312/8	1955–57	£18,500	£13,500	£9,000
Edsel Citation	410/8	1958	£9,000	£4,500	£2,500
Edsel Ranger	223/6–				
	361/8	1959	£6,000	£3,500	£2,000
Edsel Citation convertible	410/8	1958	£12,000	£6,000	£4,000
Edsel Corsair convertible	332/				
	361/8	1959	£10,500	£7,000	£4,500
Fairlane 2-door	223/6–				
	352/8	1957–59	£8,000	£4,500	£3,000
Fairlane 500 Sunliner	223/6– 352/8	1957–59	£12,000	£8,000	£6,500
Fairlane 500 Skyliner	223/6– 352/8	1957–59	£14,000	£10,000	£8,000
Mustang 4.7 V8 FHC/Conv.		1964–66	£9,000	£4,000	£2,000
Mustang GT 350		1966–67	£15,000	£10,000	£6,000
Mustang Hardtop	260/6– 428/8	1967–68	£6,000	£4,000	£3,000
Mustang GT 500		1966–67	£20,000	£14,000	£6,000

Healey

Donald Mitchell Healey's name is usually associated with Austin-Healey sports cars, but the Cornishman's career weaved a meandering path through the British motor industry. As a driver, he had considerable talent, and in 1931 he drove an Invicta to outright victory in the Monte Carlo Rally. In 1933, he joined the Riley experimental team, and in 1935 he moved across Coventry to become experimental manager and technical director at Triumph, where he remained until the company collapsed in 1939. From 1946 until 1954, he produced his own

Healeys at Warwick, using proprietary engines from Riley, then Nash and Alvis. All Healeys were sporting in character, particularly the early Riley-powered models, which were among the first post-war British high-performance cars. In fact, in 1948, a 2.4 litre Riley-engined Healey Elliot recorded 110mph on the Jabbeke autoroute in Belgium, setting a saloon benchmark. The styling was always individual and not universally admired, yet with total Healey production at under 1,200, these fine sporting machines remain very collectable.

c1950 **Healey Westland Roadster,** 2.5 litre, Riley 4-cylinder engine, finished in white, red interior, very good condition.
£14,000–17,000 AHE

c1950 **Healey Silverstone,** 2.5 litre Riley engine, retractable windscreen, aluminium bodywork, very good condition.
£20,000–25,000 AHE

Hillman

William Hillman made his early fortune from bicycles, roller skates and sewing machines. He turned to car manufacture in 1907, initially producing elegant tourers and a few surprisingly large-engined cars before settling down to make quality middle-market cars. He died in 1926, and in 1928 the company came under the control of Humber and the Rootes Group. In the early 1930s, the Minx model name was used for the first time on a range of smart and refined small cars. By 1939, Hillman was ranked fourth in Britain, and by the 1960s it was the

mainstream marque in the Rootes Group. Building the promising, but complex, rear-engined Imp in a new Scottish factory was an ill-fated venture that led to financial troubles, and in 1964 Chrysler stepped in to take a major share of Rootes. Underfunded, neglected and misunderstood by its new parent, the Hillman marque plodded along until 1976, when the name was dropped. A curious footnote came in the form of the Peykan models, which were assembled in Iran into the mid-1980s. These were no more than last-generation Hillman Hunters.

◀ c1934 **Hillman Minx 10/30 Two-Seat Sports,** coachwork probably by Carbodies, partially restored, coachwork and interior in good condition, engine, electrics and gearbox in need of attention.
£2,000–2,500 BKS

Hillman offered a range of models in the early 1930s, from the 1185cc Minx, through the 2110cc and 2810cc Wizards, to the short-lived 2620cc Straight 8. The 10hp Minx was Hillman's answer to the Morris and Austin 10s, and in 1932 the company introduced the sporting Aero Minx, with underslung rear frame, high-compression head, remote gear-change and wire wheels.

Miller's Starter Marque

Starter Hillmans: *Californian; Minx models and variants from 1956; Imp; Avenger.*

- One of the most attractive traits of post-war Hillmans is their price. They're affordable and generally reliable, and if you're into budget, top-down motoring, there's a wide choice from a company that persisted with convertibles when lots of other makers didn't bother.
- The 1950s Hillman Californian offers a suggestion of transatlantic glamour with straightforward Rootes underpinnnings. The problem lies in finding one because, as with later Hillmans, their low values have lured many a salvageable car into the scrapyard. The Super Minx convertible of 1962–66 makes an interesting four-seat, fresh-air alternative to cars like the Triumph Herald. The Super Minx is more substantially bodied and bigger engined.
- The Imp was a real might-have-been – if only the Mini hadn't appeared three years before, and if only it had been built better. It's redeemed, though, by a lovely engine, super gearbox and sheer entertainment value when behind the wheel.
- In the 1970s, the Avenger tilted against Morris Marinas, Ford Escorts and Vauxhall Vivas. The GT was surprisingly nimble and offered 100mph performance. The very rare Tiger tipped 110mph and enjoyed a successful rallying career.

1937 Hillman Hawk, 3181cc, 6-cylinder sidevalve engine, transverse-leaf independent front suspension, box-girder chassis, c68,000 miles recorded, largely original, good mechanical condition.
£4,750–5,500 BRIT

1955 Hillman Minx Convertible, 1265cc, finished in maroon, tan interior, 37,000 miles recorded, 3 owners, excellent condition throughout.
£5,500–6,600 H&H

Miller's is a price GUIDE not a price LIST

◀ **1964 Hillman Super Minx Convertible,** 1600cc, finished in dark red, red interior, recently reupholstered to the rear, 80,000 miles recorded, history file, good condition throughout.
£2,250–2,700 H&H

HILLMAN Model	ENGINE cc/cyl	DATES	CONDITION 1	2	3
Minx Mk I–II	1184/4	1946–48	£1,750	£800	£250
Minx Mk I–II DHC	1184/4	1946–48	£3,500	£1,500	£250
Minx Mk III–VIIIA	1184/4	1948–56	£1,750	£700	£350
Minx Mk III–VIIIA DHC	1184/4	1948–56	£3,750	£1,500	£350
Californian	1390/4	1953–56	£2,000	£750	£200
Minx SI/II	1390/4	1956–58	£1,250	£450	£200
Minx SI/II DHC	1390/4	1956–58	£3,500	£1,500	£500
Minx Ser III	1494/4	1958–59	£1,000	£500	£200
Minx Ser III DHC	1494/4	1958–59	£3,750	£1,500	£400
Minx Ser IIIA/B	1494/4	1959–61	£1,250	£500	£200
Minx Ser IIIA/B DHC	1494/4	1959–61	£3,750	£1,250	£500
Minx Ser IIIC	1592/4	1961–62	£900	£500	£200
Minx Ser IIIC DHC	1592/4	1961–62	£3,000	£1,500	£500
Minx Ser V	1592/4	1962–63	£1,250	£350	£150
Minx Ser VI	1725/4	1964–67	£1,500	£375	£100
Husky Mk I	1265/4	1954–57	£1,000	£600	£200
Husky SI/II/III	1390/4	1958–65	£1,000	£550	£150
Super Minx	1592/4	1961–66	£1,500	£500	£100
Super Minx DHC	1592/4	1962–64	£3,500	£1,250	£450
Imp	875/4	1963–73	£800	£300	£70
Husky	875/4	1966–71	£800	£450	£100
Avenger	var/4	1970–76	£550	£250	£60
Avenger GT	1500/4	1971–76	£950	£500	£100
Avenger Tiger	1600/4	1972–73	£2,000	£1,000	£500

Hispano-Suiza

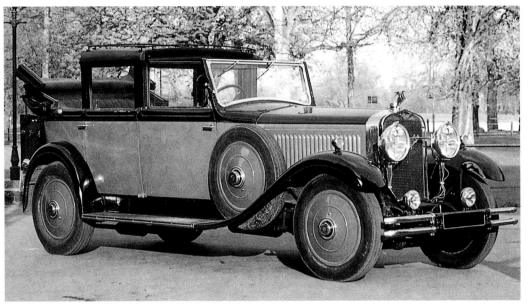

1929 Hispano-Suiza H6B Sedanca Landaulette, coachwork by Kellner, 6.6 litre, 6-cylinder engine, stainless steel exhaust system, stork mascot, Marchal triple-bulb headlamps, RAF wheels, twin side-mounted spares, inwardly-folding front door window frames, rear trunk with four fitted cases, occasional rear seats, rear and overhead luggage carriers, finished in green over black, original black leather to front seats, original light grey cord upholstery to rear, 2 owners in last 33 years, largely original.
£65,000–75,000 BKS

Reflecting aero engineering technology, Hispano-Suiza's H6, introduced in 1919, provided serious competition for Rolls-Royce, Isotta-Fraschini and Pierce-Arrow. For the first time, the radiator bore the *Cigogne Volante* mascot, the insignia of Captain Guynemer's Stork Squadron, whose Spad fighter planes had been powered by Hispano-Suiza engines. The H6 was the mainstay of Hispano-Suiza production for some 15 years.

Honda

▶ **1971 Honda N 600AT,** 4-stroke, overhead-camshaft, parallel twin-cylinder engine, 45bhp, 80mph top speed, restored, good condition.
£2,250–2,750 HMM

The world's largest and most successful motorcycle manufacturer turned to light cars and vans in 1962. This Japanese answer to the Mini was very successful, production running from 1966 until 1974.

HRG

◀ **1949 HRG 1100 Roadster,** tuned Singer 9 engine, tubular front axle, ladder-type chassis, ash-framed alloy coachwork, older restoration, finished in red with matching interior, 1 of 49 built.
£11,000–13,000 BKS

In 1935, ten years after the dissolution of the GN cyclecar company, the 'G' – H.R. Godfrey – was back in business with new partners E.A. Halford and G.H. Robins, the trio's new firm adopting the name HRG. Their aim was to build a lightweight, vintage-style sporting car endowed with the virtues of brisk acceleration and positive steering, and in this they succeeded admirably.

Hudson

1946 Hudson Commodore Eight Series 54 Convertible Brougham, 254cu.in, 8-cylinder sidevalve engine, 121in wheelbase, door-step courtesy lights, older restoration, finished in Sky blue, very good condition throughout. **£22,000–27,000 BKS**

Of the 95,000 Hudsons produced for the 1946 season, only 140 were Convertible Broughams.

Humber

This once-distinguished British make was brought low in its later days by an epidemic of badge-engineering, when the Humber name was little more than a dubious emblem of suburban rank on upmarket Hillmans and Singers. Humber, like so many early British makers, had graduated to cars from bicycles during the early years of the century. In 1928, the company took over Hillman, and both were absorbed into the growing Rootes empire in 1931. Humber's role in these years was to furnish cars for the sober, upper-middle-class market. In the 1930s, the marque's imposing six-cylinder Pullmans and Super Snipes enjoyed official patronage; they also provided stout service as staff cars during WWII. The Super Snipe of the late 1940s continued the tradition as a superior bank manager's carriage. By the 1960s, however, the Humber marque was beginning to lose its individual identity, hastened by Chrysler's take-over of the Rootes Group in 1964. In 1976, the Humber name died for ever.

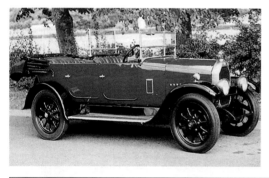

◄ **1926 Humber 12/25 Tourer,** 1795cc, 4-cylinder engine, many period features including rear Auster-type screen and Barker mechanical headlamp dipping system, finished in maroon with black wings, interior trimmed in correct brown Rexene, good condition. **£9,500–11,500 BRIT**

The earliest Humbers were produced in Beeston, but by 1908 production had moved entirely to Coventry. After WWI, the company launched a 15hp model, which was soon joined by a particularly fine light car, the 8/18. As the post-war range expanded, a new model of larger proportions was introduced – the 11.4. This car became highly regarded for its strength and reliability; it evolved into the 12/25 in 1925.

HUMBER Model	ENGINE cc/cyl	DATES	CONDITION 1	2	3
Hawk Mk I–IV	1944/4	1945–52	£3,700	£1,500	£600
Hawk Mk V–VII	2267/4	1952–57	£3,000	£1,500	£400
Hawk Ser I–IVA	2267/4	1957–67	£3,000	£850	£325
Snipe	2731/6	1945–48	£5,000	£2,600	£850
Super Snipe Mk I–III	4086/6	1948–52	£4,700	£2,400	£600
Super Snipe Mk IV–IVA	4138/6	1952–56	£5,500	£2,300	£550
Super Snipe Ser I–II	2651/6	1958–60	£3,800	£1,800	£475
Super Snipe SIII VA	2965/6	1961–67	£3,500	£1,800	£400
Super Snipe S.III–VA Est.	2965/6	1961–67	£3,950	£1,850	£525
Pullman	4086/6	1946–51	£4,500	£2,350	£800
Pullman Mk IV	4086/6	1952–54	£6,000	£2,850	£1,200
Imperial	2965/6	1965–67	£3,900	£1,600	£450
Sceptre Mk I–II	1592/4	1963–67	£2,200	£1,000	£300
Sceptre Mk III	1725/4	1967–76	£2,000	£900	£200

Starter Humbers: *Hawk and Super Snipe from 1957 onward; Imperial, 1965–67; Sceptre, 1963–76.*

- The 1959 Super Snipe and later Imperial were the last of the true Humbers. The Super Snipe was a larger, six-cylinder-engined, more luxurious version of the four-cylinder Hawk of 1957, while the short-lived Imperial topped out the range with even more luxury trimmings. The interiors were the usual British drawing-room mix of leather, wood and quietly ticking clock, and by all accounts these last big Humbers handled pretty much like a drawing-room, too. Then again, Humber owners weren't really inclined to hustle a car along like those flashy types in tyre-squealing Mk II Jags. And that's why, if you're lucky, you might just be able to find one that hasn't been caned into the ground by a succession of lead-footed owners.
- **Pick of the bunch:** Snipe II onward offers better 3 litre performance and front disc brakes; Imperial is the fully-loaded luxury version.
- **What to watch:** Structural rot in unitary shell; prices are low, but all the leather, wood and other luxury fittings are just as expensive to restore as in a more valuable car. Many body panels and trim items are unavailable, so you want a car that's all there.
- **Humber facts:** In 1960, the revised Super Snipe became the first British car to have twin headlamps.

1929 Humber 9/28 Saloon, 885cc, coil ignition, 4-wheel brakes, ribbon radiator shell, finished in maroon, red interior, barn-stored 1977–94, recently recommissioned, good condition.
£5,250–6,500 H&H

The 9/28 Humber was produced during 1929 and 1930. It was the final development of the 8.18 luxury light car of 1923.

A known continuous history can add value to and enhance the enjoyment of a car.

▶ **1961 Humber Hawk Saloon,** 2267cc, 4-cylinder engine, 4-speed gearbox with overdrive, finished in green, green interior, original radio, 1 owner, good original condition throughout.
£1,900–2,300 H&H

Hupmobile

1918 Hupmobile 35hp Series R Tourer, 4-cylinder sidevalve engine, Splitdorf magneto, Stromberg carburettor, electric starting and lighting, centre-change gearbox, period autovac, detachable wire wheels, 2-piece opening windscreen, weather equipment in good condition, built with right-hand drive, finished in brown, black interior, wooden steering wheel, original.
£7,500–8,500 H&H

The Series R Hupmobiles appeared toward the end of 1917. They were comparatively lively and light, and very competitively priced.

Invicta

Invicta's life was short and turbulent. The company was founded in Surrey in 1925 by Lance Macklin and Oliver Lyle, who set out to combine in one car the American virtues of power and flexibility with British standards of roadholding and craftsmanship. Invictas were what was known as 'assembled cars'. For reasons of expediency and the quest for quality, the company gathered together the best proprietary components to create a car of singular quality and performance. The zenith of Invicta's short life came with the lovely and potent 4 litre, low-chassis S-Type. Initially, its Meadows engine produced about 115bhp, giving a top speed of about 95mph, so near the magic century that the car became known colloquially as the '100mph Invicta'. By the end of production, in 1935, output was up to around 140bhp and the 100mph appellation was no longer an exaggeration. Yet those qualities that make Invictas so prized today were also factors in the company's downfall, producing an extravagant, expensive machine – with a near Rolls-Royce price tag – as Britain plunged into depression in the early 1930s. Although Invicta production ceased in 1935, there were two attempted and failed revivals: first in 1937/38, then with the Black Prince, which was built between 1946 and 1950. What was left was a legacy of a mere 1,000 cars, most of them exquisite and none more revered than the rare 4 litre S-Type low-chassis tourer.

◄ **1934 Invicta 4½ Litre S-Type Low-Chassis Tourer,** coachwork by Carbodies, 4467cc Meadows engine, twin SU carburettors, dual ignition by magneto and coil, 140bhp, 4-speed gearbox, semi-floating hypoid rear axle, fold-flat windscreen, aero screens, radiator stone guard, restored, finished in British Racing green, red leather upholstery, 1 of 77 built. **£145,000–165,000 BKS**

Iso

Founded in 1939 by Renzo Rivolta, the Italian company's automotive products represented two extremes. In 1953, Iso began production of the Isetta bubble-car, which later was built under licence and in prodigious numbers by BMW. Then, in the 1960s, Renzo Rivolta turned his attention to producing high-performance sports and GT cars. Chief designer was Giotto Bizzarrini, whose achievements include the Ferrari 250 GTO and Lamborghini's V12 engine. The first offering was the four-seat Rivolta, powered by a Chevrolet Corvette V8; then came the mighty Grifo two-seat coupé. Certainly its name declared its intentions, for *grifo* is Italian for griffin, the mythical bird that preys on horses, an obvious allusion to Ferrari's proud emblem. It didn't quite turn out that way. Successive models, the Fidia and Lele, although excellent performers, didn't have quite the panache of their predecessors. Production slowed to a dribble, and by 1978 there were no more Iso cars.

◄ **1972 Iso Rivolta Lele,** 351cu.in Ford V8 engine, 300bhp, 4-speed manual gearbox, 4-wheel disc brakes, alloy wheels, finished in metallic blue, blue interior, 80,000km recorded. **£9,500–11,000 Pou**

Jaguar

If ever one man's vision guided the fortunes of a motor company, it must surely be that of William Lyons, for the guiding spirit of Jaguar's creator lives on in the lithe, athletic shapes that have characterised the Coventry cats for nearly 70 years. William Lyons was born in Blackpool in 1901. Before dabbling with cars, the young Lyons was an enthusiastic motorcyclist who, on his 21st birthday, formed the Swallow Sidecar Company with partner William Walmsley. In 1927, the company made the transition to four wheels, clothing a strengthened Austin 7 chassis with a stylish, two-toned sports body. In 1931, the rakish SS1 appeared, and in 1935, with William Lyons now sole proprietor of the company, the Jaguar name was used for the first time. Most prized among the pre-war models is the beautifully rakish and fast SS100. In 1948, at the first post-war Motor Show at Earl's Court, William Lyons stole the show with perhaps the most cat-like of all Jaguars, the XK120. Since then, virtually all Jaguars, whether sports cars or sporting saloons, have become an object of desire, perhaps none more so than the 1961 E-Type. Even so, a number of models remain a little overlooked and are worth considering by the Jaguar enthusiast on a budget. The S-Type saloon was, in effect, a Mk II with a stretched boot and better handling through its independent rear suspension, which made it a gangland favourite as a get-away car. Another option is the 420, an S-Type with Mk X-style frontal treatment and a 4.2 litre engine. Other models to consider are the 'thrift' late-model Jaguar Mk II variants, namely the 240 and 340, and Daimler 250 V8 saloon, a Mk II with Daimler grille and a lovely compact V8 engine.

1935 Jaguar SSII Two-Door Saloon, 1052cc, restored 1991, finished in black, red leather interior, bodywork and chrome in very good condition.
£12,750–14,750 H&H

> A known continuous history can add value to and enhance the enjoyment of a car.

1939 Jaguar SS 2½ Litre Saloon, 2663cc, 6-cylinder engine, stored for 27 years, original dark olive leather interior in good condition, complete in almost every respect, in need of restoration.
£5,000–6,000 BKS

William Lyons had not put a foot wrong since he had joined William Walmsley in founding the Swallow Sidecar Company in 1922, progressing swiftly from sidecar manufacture to coachbuilding for car manufacturers such as Austin, Morris, Fiat, Wolseley and Standard, and ultimately setting up SS as a marque in its own right. 'Styled like a Bentley and priced like a Ford' could easily have been the advertising slogan for his new 'Jaguar', announced in 1935. At a price of £385, the 100bhp, 2½ litre saloon offered elegance, quality and economy. Inside, it was trimmed in leather set off by polished walnut fittings, while the sliding roof made summer motoring a delight.

◄ **1947 Jaguar Mk IV Drophead Coupé,** 3485cc, overhead-valve, 6-cylinder inline engine, twin SU carburettors, 125bhp, 4-speed gearbox, Girling mechanical drum brakes, P100 headlights, interior accented with bookmatched walnut veneers, rear-seat picnic tables, completely restored, 1 of 376 left-hand drive examples built.
£40,000–45,000 RM

JAGUAR Model	ENGINE cc/cyl	DATES	CONDITION 1	2	3
SSI	2054/6	1932–33	£26,000	£18,000	£12,000
SSI	2252/6	1932–33	£22,000	£17,000	£13,500
SSII	1052/4	1932–33	£18,000	£15,000	£11,000
SSI	2663/6	1934	£26,000	£22,000	£15,000
SSII	1608/4	1934	£18,000	£15,000	£12,000
SS90	2663/6	1935	£60,000+	-	-
SS100 (3.4)	3485/6	1938–39	£90,000+	-	-
SS100 (2.6)	2663/6	1936–39	£90,000+	-	-

Very dependent on body styles, completeness and originality, particularly original chassis to body.

1952 Jaguar Mk V Drophead Coupé, 3485cc, 6-cylinder engine, older restoration, reconditioned gearbox, original radio adapted for FM reception, finished in silver, serviceable 3-position, black-lined hood, interior trimmed in grey hide, in need of new valve-stem oil seals.
£27,500–32,500 BRIT

Continuing the theme established with the pre-war 2½ and 3½ litre series, the Mk V was a transitional model that retained the pushrod engine, but featured torsion-bar independent front suspension and hydraulic brakes. Further concessions to modernity were the spatted rear wings and faired-in headlamps. The Mk V met with success in the USA as well as at home, the preference for the larger-engined car on the export market being evident by the fact that 8,791 were produced, compared to 1,675 of the 2½ litre version. The larger engine developed 125bhp, sufficient to endow the car with a top speed of almost 95mph.

XK120

The '120' in the XK120's name really did stand for 120mph, thanks to the fabulous double-overhead-camshaft, six-cylinder engine that went on to power E-Types and Jaguar saloons until 1986. At the time, cynical motoring scribes were sceptical, so in 1949 William Lyons, by then an accomplished publicist, flew a band of hacks to Belgium to witness the XK120 perform a 132mph run on the unrestricted Jabbeke autoroute. That Jag had received a little aerodynamic tweaking, but he'd proved his point: the XK120 was the fastest series-production car in the world, no question. In fact, the 3.4 litre XK engine pumped out as much power as the contemporary 5.4 litre Cadillac engine.

One of the earliest XK120 customers was car connoisseur and actor Clark Gable, who reckoned that the XK120 was 'a masterpiece of design and construction'.

1953 Jaguar XK120SE, bodywork recently restored, resprayed in red, low mileage, 1 of only 195 right-hand-drive cars built.
£30,000–33,000 TWY

1954 Jaguar XK120 Drophead Coupé, steel disc wheels, rear spats, left-hand drive, restored, finished in Midnight blue, tan interior, minor blemishes, otherwise very good condition.
£18,000–21,500 BKS

Delays in the gestation of its Mk VII saloon led to Jaguar exploring an alternative method of bringing the new XK 3.4 litre six-cylinder engine to public attention. The result was the XK120 sports car. Launched in 1948, the stunning roadster caused a sensation, setting new standards of comfort, roadholding and performance for British sports cars. Coupé and drophead coupé versions followed, and for customers who found the standard car too slow, there was a Special Equipment package, which boosted power from the standard 160bhp to 180bhp. With either engine and regardless of the type of bodywork, the XK120 was a genuine 120mph car capable of sustained high-speed cruising.

JAGUAR Model	ENGINE cc/cyl	DATES	CONDITION 1	2	3
XK120 Roadster aluminium	3442/6	1948–49	£65,000	£30,000	£20,000
XK120 Roadster	3442/6	1949–54	£30,000+	£20,000+	£15,000
XK120 DHC	3442/6	1953–54	£25,000+	£17,000+	£12,000
XK120 Coupé	3442/6	1951–55	£16,000+	£12,000+	£10,000
C-Type	3442/6	1951	£150,000+	-	-
D-Type	3442/6	1955–56	£500,000+	-	-
XKSS (original)	3442/6	1955–57	£400,000+	-	-
XK140 Roadster	3442/6	1955–58	£32,000+	£23,000	£16,000
XK140 DHC	3442/6	1955–58	£28,000	£22,000	£15,000
XK140 Coupé	3442/6	1955–58	£18,000	£12,000	£7,500
XK150 Roadster	3442/6	1958–60	£35,000	£22,000	£15,000
XK150 DHC	3442/6	1957–61	£28,000	£18,000	£10,000
XK150 Coupé	3442/6	1957–60	£16,000	£10,000	£6,000
XK150S Roadster	3442/ 3781/6	1958–60	£40,000+	£26,000	£20,000
XK150S DHC	3442/ 3781/6	1958–60	£36,000+	£22,000	£18,000
XK150S Coupé	3442/ 3781/6	1958–61	£22,000	£18,000	£10,000

D-Type with competition history considerably more.
Watch out for left- to right-hand-drive conversions in the XK series.

Jaguar XK150 (1957–61)

Engine: Double-overhead-camshaft, six-cylinder, 3442 or 3781cc.
Power output: 190–265bhp (XK150S, 3.8 litre).
Top speed: 136mph (XK150S, 3.8 litre).
0–60mph: 7.2 seconds (XK150S, 3.8 litre).

Take the lithe athleticism and sensational performance of the 1948 XK120, add nine years of road-car evolution, a beefier body, technological spin-offs from five Le Mans victories and you end up with the Jaguar XK150. Yet the sports car remains a slightly overlooked, in-betweeny in the Jaguar canon: to some, it looks a little bloated and lacks the primal, pure, raw magnetism of the leaner XK120 and XK140; others prefer the few more mph and the instant and obvious statement of the later E-Type. However, the XK150 is a consummate cat. At its heart is that fabulous twin-cam six that first appeared in the XK120, powered the fifties Le Mans winners and endured until 1986; it will outrun XK120s and XK140s, and in top XK150S spec. won't trail too far behind an E-Type. It's also more civilised and luxurious than its XK forebears, and technically superior too, having better steering and 4-wheel disc brakes that were more than man enough to match the sizzling supercar performance.
Pick of the bunch: The XK150S, with 265bhp, triple-carb 3.8S engine, is the most potent and most pricey model in both fixed-head and open versions; best all-round value are the 3.4 and 3.8 drophead coupés, which can be slightly cheaper than roadsters, yet have more luxurious furnishings, better weather equipment and the addition of rear seats – albeit small ones. One reason they're cheaper is that, although the retracting hood gives better weather protection, it makes a considerable bustle when folded.

1955 Jaguar XK140 Coupé, 3442cc, 6-cylinder engine, restored c1991, finished in dark green, Suede green interior trim, good mechanical condition, rear wings in need of attention.
£9,500–11,000 BRIT

In the wake of the legendary XK120 came the XK140, introduced in October 1954. Readily identifiable by wider bumpers and a heavier grille with fewer slats, the XK140 retained basically the same attractive styling. The 3.4 litre engine developed 190bhp in standard trim, 210bhp being available from Special Equipment models. Between 1954 and 1957, 2,797 XK140 coupés were produced, a large proportion being exported.

Restored values

The cost of a professional restoration will have an influence on, but no direct relation to, a car's market value. A restored car can have a market value lower than the cost of its restoration.

1957 Jaguar XK150 Coupé, 3442cc, 6-cylinder engine, older restoration, finished in red, good condition.
£14,000–16,000 WILM

1957 Jaguar XK150, Special Equipment package, wire wheels, fog lamps, finished in black, red leather interior, very good condition.
£14,000–16,500 COYS

1958 Jaguar XK150 Coupé, manual gearbox with overdrive, converted to right-hand drive, engine rebuilt, c2,150 miles covered since, silver painted wire wheels, resprayed in Cotswold blue, minor paintwork blemishes, original red leather interior in good condition, stored since 1990.
£11,000–13,000 BKS

1959 Jaguar XK150 Coupé, 3781cc, 6-cylinder engine, manual gearbox with overdrive, left-hand drive, restored, stainless steel twin-box exhaust system, wire wheels rebuilt and powder-coated in silver, bare-metal respray in Indigo blue 1995, refurbished original light grey leather upholstery, excellent condition.
£14,000–16,500 BRIT

1959 Jaguar XK150S Coupé, restored, stored for 6 years, finished in red, unmarked magnolia leather upholstery, good condition.
£15,500–18,500 COYS

1959 Jaguar XK150SE Coupé, 3442cc, manual gearbox, new exhaust and clutch, wire wheels, finished in red, tan interior, 4,400 miles recorded, overdrive not working, otherwise very good condition.
£15,000–18,000 H&H

◄ **1959 Jaguar XK150 Drophead Coupé,** 3442cc, completely restored 1994, 300 miles covered since, engine rebuilt, new exhaust, gearbox reconditioned, new clutch, rewired, new wheels, new lights and chrome, resprayed in red, new beige hood and interior, very good condition throughout.
£15,000–18,000 H&H

1959 Jaguar XK150SE Drophead Coupé, Special Equipment package, overdrive, completely restored, finished in Cornish grey, red leather upholstery, very good condition throughout.
£25,000–28,000 BKS

Introduced in 1957, the XK150 represented the final flowering of Jaguar's immensely successful XK range. Although it had softer lines, under the skin the XK150 retained the spirit of the XK120: the chassis was similar, while power had increased from 160bhp to a minimum of 210bhp with improved torque. The XK150 was good for 132mph and 0–60mph in 7.5 seconds. It was the world's first road car to have four-wheel disc brakes.

1961 Jaguar Mk II 3.8 Saloon, 3781cc, 6-cylinder engine, 4-speed manual gearbox with overdrive, independent front suspension, leaf-sprung live rear axle, 4-wheel servo-assisted disc brakes, wire wheels, left-hand drive, restored 1990, little use since, finished in red, matching retrimmed interior, excellent condition.
£14,000–16,000 BKS

A progressive development of the Mk I, Jaguar's first unitary-construction saloon, the Mk II debuted in 1959. Slimmer windscreen pillars and deeper side windows enlarged the glass area, while the deletion of its predecessor's wheel spats allowed the rear track to be widened, a move that increased roll resistance and stability. Otherwise, the running gear remained much the same as before. With the launch of the Mk II, the 3.8 litre version of the XK six became available for the first time in the company's medium-sized saloon.

1961 Jaguar Mk II 3.8 Saloon, 3781cc, 6-cylinder engine, manual gearbox, 4-wheel disc brakes, power steering, chrome wire wheels, finished in Carmen red, retrimmed red hide interior.
£11,000–12,500 S

1961 Jaguar Mk II 3.4 Saloon, automatic transmission, independent front suspension by wishbones and coil springs, leaf-sprung live rear axle, 4-wheel servo-assisted disc brakes, engine rebuilt 1992, finished in grey with red leather interior, very good condition throughout.
£5,000–6,000 BKS

◀ **1961 Jaguar Mk II 3.4 Saloon,** 3442cc, 6-cylinder engine, 4-speed manual gearbox, restored, very good condition.
£14,000–16,000 BC

JAGUAR Model	ENGINE cc/cyl	DATES	CONDITION 1	2	3
1½ Litre	1775/4	1945–49	£8,500	£5,500	£2,000
2½ Litre	2663/6	1946–49	£10,000	£7,500	£2,000
2½ Litre DHC	2663/6	1947–48	£17,000	£11,000	£8,000
3½ Litre	3485/6	1947–49	£12,000	£6,000	£4,000
3½ Litre DHC	3485/6	1947–49	£19,000	£13,500	£5,500
Mk V 2½ Litre	2663/6	1949–51	£8,000	£5,000	£1,500
Mk V 3½ Litre	3485/6	1949–51	£13,000	£8,000	£3,000
Mk V 3½ Litre DHC	3485/6	1949–51	£22,000+	£17,000+	£8,500
Mk VII	3442/6	1951–57	£10,000	£7,500	£2,500
Mk VIIM	3442/6	1951–57	£12,000	£8,500	£2,500
Mk VIII	3442/6	1956–59	£8,500	£5,500	£2,000
Mk IX	3781/6	1958–61	£9,000	£7,000	£2,500
Mk X 3.8/4.2	3781/6	1961–64	£7,500	£3,500	£1,500
Mk X 420G	4235/6	1964–70	£6,000	£3,000	£1,200
Mk I 2.4	2438/6	1955–59	£7,000+	£5,500	£2,000
Mk I 3.4	3442/6	1957–59	£10,000	£6,000	£2,500
Mk II 2.4	2483/6	1959–67	£8,000	£6,000	£3,000
Mk II 3.4	3442/6	1959–67	£12,000	£8,000	£4,000
Mk II 3.8	3781/6	1959–67	£16,000	£9,000	£5,000
S-Type 3.4	3442/6	1963–68	£9,000	£6,500	£2,000
S-Type 3.8	3781/6	1963–68	£10,000	£6,500	£2,000
240	2438/6	1967–68	£9,000	£6,000	£2,500
340	3442/6	1967–68	£8,000	£7,000	£3,000
420	4235/6	1966–68	£6,000	£3,000	£2,000

Manual gearboxes with overdrive are at a premium.
Some concours examples make as much as 50% over Condition I.

Jaguar Mk II (1960–68)

In one respect at least, 1960s cops owe a debt of gratitude to their villainous counterparts. If the crooks hadn't cottoned on to the get-away capabilities of the Mk II and Mk II-based S-Type, the police probably wouldn't have been given Mk IIs as the tool to catch them. This Jag is a true sports saloon – especially in bigger-engined forms – a rare blend of grace, pace and plenty of space in the boot for loot.
Original 1960 prices: 2.4 litre, £1,534; 3.4 litre, £1,669; 3.8 litre, £1,779.
Pick of the bunch: Post-1965 cars with much smoother, all-synchro box. Most-prized is the 3.8 litre, but the extra 400cc costs a lot more than the 3.4, which runs it close in performance.
What to watch: Late-1980s price-hikes encouraged pretty cosmetic bodges that are now losing their sheen. Any Mk II is a potential wallet-wilting welder's wonderland.
Marque fact: Guildford dealer and saloon car racer John Coombs created his own highly-tuned Coombs Mk II, which could match an E-Type on the 0–60mph sprint. Coombs Jags are identifiable by louvred vents on the bonnet, which were taken from changing-room locker doors and welded in. Cynics say that of the 28 or so Coombs Mk IIs built, there are only 40 or 50 survivors.

◄ **1962 Jaguar Mk II 3.8 Saloon,** manual gearbox with overdrive, restored, engine converted to unleaded fuel, power steering, chrome wire wheels, resprayed in light burgundy, light biscuit-coloured leather upholstery, Mota-Lita steering wheel, 66,133 miles recorded, concours winner.
£16,000–18,000 S

1964 Jaguar Mk II 3.8 Saloon, 3781cc, manual gearbox with overdrive, wire wheels, completely restored, finished in white, red interior trim, excellent condition.
£7,500–9,000 H&H

1967 Jaguar Mk II 2.4 Saloon, 2483cc, 6-cylinder engine, new radiator, new clutch master and slave cylinders, new Koni rear shock absorbers, chrome wire wheels, new fuel tank, resprayed 1988, finished in red, 9,900 miles recorded, body, paintwork and original leather-trimmed interior in good condition.
£5,000–6,000 H&H

Cross Reference
See Colour Review

1966 Jaguar S-Type 3.4 Saloon, manual gearbox with overdrive, completely restored 1994, resprayed original Carmen red, slight gearbox whine, otherwise good condition.
£14,000–16,000 BKS

Introduced in 1964, the S-Type was intended as an intermediate model to fill the gap between the compact Mk II and the much larger Mk X. It shared the former's wheelbase, but was 7in longer, allowing greater interior and luggage space. Featuring independent rear suspension, the latest Dunlop Mk III disc brakes and a choice of 3.4 or 3.8 litre power unit, the new model was well received. This particular car's first owner was the actor Robert Morley.

1967 Jaguar S-Type 3.8 Saloon, 3781cc, 6-cylinder engine, manual gearbox with overdrive, power steering, chrome wire wheels, new exhaust system, suspension and braking systems overhauled, finished in white, red leather interior, good mechanical condition.
£6,000–7,000 BRIT

1961 Jaguar E-Type 'Flat-Floor' Roadster, 3781cc, double-overhead-camshaft 6-cylinder engine, triple carburettors, 265bhp, 4-speed manual gearbox, independent torsion-bar front suspension with anti-roll bar, independent rear suspension by wishbones, radius arms and coil springs, 4-wheel disc brakes, inboard at the rear, left-hand drive, finished in red, black leather interior, 85,000 miles recorded, very good condition.
£28,200–31,100 C

Of all versions of Jaguar's long-lived sports car, the earliest 'flat-floor' 3.8 litre cars, built before February 1962, are considered the most desirable by many enthusiasts. About 170 are thought to survive.

◀ **1961 Jaguar E-Type 'Flat-Floor' Roadster,** 3.8 litres, left-hand drive, external bonnet locks, finished in black, interior and original Series I competition-style bucket seats in light tan, 2 family owners, good unrestored condition.
£16,000–18,000 COYS

▶ **1961 Jaguar E-Type 'Flat-Floor' Roadster,** 3781cc, 6-cylinder engine, completely restored 1989–92, finished in red, retrimmed in correct biscuit leather, concours winner.
£25,000–28,000 BRIT

Jaguar E-Type (1961–74)

Engine: Double-overhead-camshaft, six-cylinder, 3781 and 4235cc; V12, 5343cc.
Power output: 265–272bhp.
0–60mph: 7–7.2 seconds.
Top speed: 143–150mph.
Production: 72,520.
Price when new: £2,097.19s.2d (roadster).
A sensational show-stopper at the 1961 Geneva motor show. British motoring magazines had published road tests of pre-production models to coincide with the launch – and yes, the fixed-head coupé really could do 150.4mph (149.1mph for the roadster), although most owners found 145mph a more realistic maximum. What's more, its shattering

performance came relatively cheaply. In fact, to match it, you would have had to pay at least £1,000 more, while Aston Martins and Ferraris were more than double the money. E-Types took off again in the late 1980s, as grasping speculators drove prices into orbit, nudging a stratospheric £100,000 before the gravitational tug of the market pulled them back down to earth in a big way. That's good news for today's buyer, who stands a chance of owning an E-Type for less than has been lavished on its restoration.
E-Type facts: Of every three E-Types built, two were exported. Originally, the fixed-head coupé cost £100 more than the roadster; today, roadsters are far more highly prized.

JAGUAR Model	ENGINE cc/cyl	DATES	CONDITION 1	2	3
E-type 3.8 'flat-floor' Roadster (RHD)		1961	£40,000	£30,000	£22,000
E-Type SI 3.8 Roadster	3781/6	1961–64	£30,000	£19,000	£15,000
E-Type 3.8 FHC	3781/6	1961–64	£20,000	£13,000	£10,000
E-Type SI 4.2 Roadster	4235/6	1964–67	£28,000	£18,000	£14,000
E-Type 2+2 manual FHC	4235/6	1966–67	£16,000	£11,000	£9,000
E-Type SI 2+2 auto FHC	4235/6	1966–68	£14,000	£10,000	£9,000
E-Type SII Roadster	4235/6	1968–70	£30,000	£21,000	£14,000
E-Type SII FHC	4235/6	1968–70	£18,000	£12,000	£10,000
E-Type SII 2+2 manual FHC	4235/6	1968–70	£15,000	£10,000	£8,000
E-Type SIII Roadster	5343/12	1971–75	£40,000+	£26,000	£17,000
E-Type SIII 2+2 manual FHC	5343/12	1971–75	£19,000	£14,000	£10,000
E-Type SIII 2+2 auto FHC	5343/12	1971–75	£17,000	£12,000	£9,000
XJ6 2.8 Ser I	2793/6	1968–73	£3,000	£1,500	£1,000
XJ6 4.2 Ser I	4235/6	1968–73	£3,500	£2,000	£1,000
XJ6 Coupé	4235/6	1974–78	£8,000	£5,000	£3,500
XJ6 Ser II	4235/6	1973–79	£3,500	£2,000	£750
XJ12 Ser I	5343/12	1972–73	£3,500	£2,250	£1,500
XJ12 Coupé	5343/12	1973–77	£9,000	£5,000	£3,000
XJ12 Ser II	5343/12	1973–79	£3,000	£2,000	£1,000
XJS manual	5343/12	1975–78	£6,000	£4,500	£2,500
XJS auto	5343/12	1975–81	£4,500	£3,000	£2,000

Jaguar E-Type Series III Commemorative Roadster fetches more than SIII Roadster – 50 limited editions only.

1968 Jaguar E-Type Coupé, 4.2 litres, left-hand drive, completely restored 1998, 6,500 miles covered since, factory reconditioned engine, converted to unleaded fuel, new gearbox, new differential, finished in yellow, new green leather interior trim and upholstery, excellent condition throughout.
£9,500–11,000 H&H

1969 Jaguar E-Type Series 1½ Roadster, 4.2 litres, restored c1997, new engine and front subframe, Series I headlight covers, finished in British Racing green, tan leather interior.
£14,500–17,000 BKS

Proposed changes in US automobile legislation would result in the Series II E-Type in October 1968. From late 1967, the sports car began to embody some of the forthcoming modifications. These interim cars are known as Series 1½ models.

1968 Jaguar E-Type Series 1½ Roadster, converted to right-hand drive, restored, all mechanical components overhauled, bodywork, interior trim and hood refurbished, finished in dark red, tan hood and interior.
£23,000–25,500 COYS

1969 Jaguar E-Type Series II Coupé, 4.2 litres, manual gearbox, completely restored, engine rebuilt, new chrome wire wheels, finished in red, beige leather interior, history file, 56,200 miles recorded, very good condition.
£12,000–14,000 BKS

The 4.2 litre version of the E-Type debuted in 1965. Along with the bigger, torquier engine came a more user-friendly gearbox with synchromesh on first gear. Changes to US safety and emissions legislation prompted the revised Series II of 1968. The headlight fairings were deleted, and enlarged side and rear lights adopted, while a thicker front bumper centre section bridged a larger radiator intake. Interior changes included a collapsible steering column and rocker switches in place of the earlier toggles.

1970 Jaguar E-Type Series II 2+2 Coupé, automatic transmission, US export model converted to right-hand drive, finished in light blue, dark blue leather upholstery, excellent condition.
£5,000–6,000 BKS

1972 Jaguar E-Type Series III 2+2 Coupé, 5343cc V12 engine, restored, finished in carmine red with magnolia leather trim, 23,000 miles recorded, concours condition throughout.
£19,000–21,000 BRIT

By 1966, when the 4.2 litre E-Type was introduced, Jaguar had identified the need for a coupé capable of accommodating more than one passenger – a 2+2, enabling three adults to travel on short journeys, and two adults and two children on longer outings. To provide the extra room, the coupé's wheelbase was extended by 9in, the roof line was raised to increase headroom and the doors were lengthened. A lower axle ratio provided better acceleration than the lighter standard coupé, 100mph being reached in less than 20 seconds.

Auction prices

Miller's only includes cars declared sold. Our guide prices take into account the buyer's premium, VAT on the premium, and the extent of any published catalogue information relating to condition and provenance. To identify cars sold at auction, cross-refer the source codes at the ends of photo captions with the Key to Illustrations on page 330.

1972 Jaguar E-Type Series III 2+2 Coupé, 5343cc, overhead-camshaft V12 engine, 250bhp, 4-speed manual gearbox, all-independent suspension, servo-assisted 4-wheel disc brakes, power steering, original chrome wheels and hub caps, finished in primrose yellow, black leather interior, well maintained.
£11,000–13,000 RM

◀ **1972 Jaguar E-Type Series III Roadster,** 5343cc V12 engine, 272bhp, manual gearbox, ventilated front disc brakes, chrome wire wheels, 140+mph top speed, left-hand drive, restored 1998, emissions air pump removed, European-spec. bumpers, finished in British Racing green, tan leather interior, 52,000 miles recorded, excellent condition throughout.
£19,000–22,000 BKS

▶ **1972 Jaguar E-Type Series III 2+2 Coupé,** 5343cc V12 engine, 4-speed manual gearbox, full Webasto sliding sunroof, chrome steel wheels, finished in white, black leather interior, 61,668 miles recorded, very good condition.
£12,000–14,000 H&H

1974 Jaguar E-Type Series III 'Johnnie Walker Black Label' Roadster, 5343cc, double-overhead-camshaft V12 engine, 272bhp, all-synchromesh gearbox, anti-dive front suspension, ventilated front disc brakes, 18 gallon fuel tank, left-hand drive, finished in black with matching upholstery.
£20,000–23,000 COYS

This particular E-Type was the feature prize in a Johnnie Walker Black Label whisky competition promoted in duty-free shops at the world's major airports.

1974 Jaguar E-Type Series III Roadster, 5343cc, double-overhead-camshaft V12 engine, 250bhp, 4-speed manual gearbox, all-independent suspension, 4-wheel disc brakes, power steering, wire wheels, air conditioning, recently resprayed in red, beige interior.
£18,000–21,000 RM

1977 Jaguar XJ6C Coupé, 4235cc, automatic transmission, restored 1990, engine and transmission overhauled, converted to unleaded fuel, resprayed, original leather upholstery refurbished, new carpets and headlining, 79,900 miles recorded.
£3,750–4,500 H&H

1978 Jaguar XJ12C Coupé, 5343cc V12 engine, automatic transmission, finished in white, black interior, 2 owners, 53,000 miles recorded, 1 of 2,270 cars built, excellent condition throughout.
£3,500–4,000 H&H

1978 Jaguar XJS, 5343cc V12 engine, finished in black, air conditioning overhauled, 29,000 miles recorded, good condition throughout.
£4,000–5,000 BRIT

1983 Jaguar XJS HE Coupé, 5343cc, double-overhead-camshaft V12, finished in metallic blue, good condition.
£1,500–1,750 H&H

1991 Jaguar/Chasseur XJS Coupé, 4 litres, 310bhp, engine rebuilt with Weber Alpha engine management system, Weber throttle bodies, gas-flowed head, uprated camshafts, big-bore stainless steel exhaust and 6-branch manifold, uprated and lowered suspension, racing-spec. brakes, uprated power steering, Power Track traction control, low-profile tyres on 17in alloy wheels, 155+mph top speed, 0–60mph in less than 6 seconds, Chasseur front and rear body styling panels, finished in red.
£13,000–15,000 BARO

Chasseur Design purchased this vehicle in 1993 to use as a demonstrator for the company's XJS performance enhancement modifications. Well-known for its twin-turbo Jaguar XJ40 saloons, Chasseur was about to begin marketing similar modifications for the XJS.

◄ **1986 Jaguar XJS Cabriolet,** 3.6 litres, 5-speed manual gearbox, full TWR body conversion with rear seats, finished in red, grey trim, 86,000 miles recorded.
£4,000–5,000 H&H

1991 Jaguar XJR–15, 6 litre, fuel-injected V12 engine, 400+bhp, carbon-composite chassis structure, moulded composite and fibreglass bodywork, stored 8 years, restored 1999, resprayed in metallic British Racing green, grey leather interior, 496 miles recorded.
£130,000–145,000 BKS

When Jaguar produced the limited-edition, road-going XJ220 series of twin-turbocharged V6-engined coupés in the early 1990s, the company set new performance standards for the charismatic Coventry marque. However, many Jaguar enthusiasts considered then – and believe even more fervently today – that the XJ220s would not become the most desirable of all Jaguars in future decades, but rather the Jaguar V12-engined XJR–15. Tom Walkinshaw Racing manufactured a batch of only 50 of these outstandingly beautiful high-performance cars during 1990–92, of which fewer than 25 were prepared for racing in what proved to be a very spectacular, one-model international race series.

Jeep

Today, the word 'jeep' has become part of the universal motoring lexicon, a debased generic covering all manner of pearlescent disco vehicles. The original, though, had a more serious intent, conceived from desperate wartime necessity and ingenuity to fulfil the US Army's brief for a 'light reconnaissance vehicle' to replace the traditional motorcycle and sidecar. Of all the designs tendered, those produced by the tiny Bantam company impressed most, but the Army doubted Bantam's ability to produce enough vehicles and passed blueprints on to Willys and Ford, who developed the theme independently. In the end, the Army selected the Willys version for production, not least because of its torquey Go-Devil engine, which was the only one to exceed the power requirement. Consequently, Willys won the all-or-nothing

contract for 16,000 vehicles at the rate of 125 a day. But later that year, as demand increased, the Army requested that Willys turn over the vehicle's designs to Ford. During WWII, Willys and Ford produced more than 600,000 Jeeps, with Willys accounting for more than half at 368,000. Beleaguered Bantam supplied only 2,675 units. Ford versions were festooned with 'F's on virtually every bolt-head, along with a bigger 'F' on the rear. Apparently, even in wartime, Henry Ford wanted people to know that they were being towed by a Ford. The late General George C. Marshall described the Jeep as 'America's greatest contribution to modern warfare.' In other ways, though, the end of the war was only the beginning of a new career for the Jeep, one that would combine, military, civilian, industrial, agricultural and recreational use.

> **Cross Reference**
> See Military Vehicles

◄ **1967 Jeep Jeepster Commando,** 3687cc, 6-cylinder engine, automatic transmission, power hood, heater, restored, finished in blue and white, very good condition.
£5,000–6,000 BRIT

Jensen

With American V8 muscle, Italian styling and British engineering, the 1967 Interceptor could so easily have been a mongrel; instead its mixed bloodlines created a new pedigree, brought the small West Bromwich firm into the automotive mainstream and became the most prolific of all Jensen models. Jensen had adopted a Chrysler V8 for its domestically styled, fibreglass-bodied CV8 in 1962, but with the addition of Touring's crisp styling, Jensen at last mated all that prodigious poke with truly handsome, lantern-jawed good looks to create a formidable high-performance GT. The Interceptor was one of the brightest stars of the 1966 Earls Court Motor Show, but even more sensational was the much more pricey FF model, which pioneered saloon-car four-wheel drive and anti-lock brakes – 14 years ahead of the Audi Quattro. For a few carefree years, the Interceptor was the preferred road-wear of a certain type of very well-heeled, polo-necked swinger. But with its epic fuel consumption, this joyride of thick-waisted executive excess bogged down through two oil crises and a worldwide recession that saw sales slide nearly as fast as an Interceptor's fuel gauge. Although Jensen closed its doors in 1976, the Interceptor wasn't quite dead and buried. Out of receivership a faltering revival produced a dozen Series IV Interceptors between 1983 and 1993, priced at an outrageous £100,000 each. But the story of Jensen isn't just about the chisel-chinned Interceptor. In fact, the name was first used by Jensen long before that. Brothers Richard and Allen Jensen started out as coachbuilders before producing their own cars from 1936 onward. The original Interceptor of 1950–57 had a 4 litre Austin engine, which was also employed in the dramatic fibreglass-bodied 541 of 1954. From 1962, with the launch of the CV8, Jensen adopted Chrysler V8 power. Both the 541 and CV8 enjoy an enthusiastic following, although the cars were produced in far fewer numbers than the later Interceptor.

1961 Jensen 541S, 3993cc V8 engine, triple carburettors, 3-speed automatic transmission, mechanics overhauled, resprayed in dark blue, red hide trim, 58,000 miles recorded, 2 owners, 1 of only 127 built.
£8,000–9,000 H&H

1971 Jensen Interceptor Mk II, 6276cc, Chrysler V8 engine, over £7,000 spent on refurbishment, new front and rear wings, finished in metallic burgundy, magnolia hide trim, good mechanical condition.
£6,000–7,000 BRIT

▶ **1972 Jensen Interceptor Mk III,** 7.2 litre, Chrysler V8 engine, automatic transmission, finished in California Sage, excellent condition throughout.
£4,500–5,400 BARO

The Interceptor offered very high levels of performance and typically British interior appointments. With quite generous 2+2 seating and a huge luggage area, this hand-built super touring car offered Italian styling, reliable American muscle and enough room for the average family.

JENSEN Model	ENGINE cc/cyl	DATES	CONDITION		
			1	2	3
541/541R/541S	3993/6	1954–63	£13,000	£7,000	£4,500
CV8 Mk I–III	5916/				
	6276/8	1962–66	£14,000	£7,000	£6,000
Interceptor SI–SIII	6276/8	1967–76	£11,000	£8,000	£6,000
Interceptor DHC	6276/8	1973–76	£25,000	£16,000	£10,000
Interceptor SP	7212/8	1971–76	£13,000	£9,000	£5,000
FF	6766/8	1967–71	£17,000	£11,000	£7,000
Healey	1973/4	1972–76	£5,000	£3,000	£1,500
Healey GT	1973/4	1975–76	£6,000	£3,000	£2,000

The Jensen CV8 and 541 are particularly sought after.

1973 Jensen Interceptor Mk III, 7212cc, Chrysler V8 engine, automatic transmission, alloy wheels, 135mph top speed, restored, good condition. £7,000–8,000 HMM

1974 Jensen Interceptor Mk III, 7212cc, Chrysler V8 engine, 3-speed automatic transmission, electric sunroof, electric windows, air conditioning, finished in copper, black hide trim, 38,200 miles recorded, excellent condition throughout. £8,000–9,000 H&H

1974 Jensen Interceptor III Convertible, 7212cc, Chrysler V8 engine, 385bhp, 3-speed automatic transmission, 4-wheel servo-assisted disc brakes, finished in red, cream Connolly leather upholstery, walnut dashboard, original AM/FM 8-track stereo, 42,000 miles recorded. £15,000–17,000 RM

Jensen-Healey

1973 Jensen-Healey, 1973cc, 4-cylinder engine, hard and soft tops, new wings and sills, resprayed in orange 1997, good mechanical condition. £2,000–2,400 BRIT

Launched in 1972, the Jensen-Healey was the direct result of the take-over of Jensen Cars by Kjell Qvale in 1970 and his associaton with Donald Healey. After concentrating initially on Vauxhall components, it was decided to use the new Lotus twin-cam engine. The Jensen-Healey sold steadily and production continued until 1976, when Jensen Motors ceased trading.

Jowett

The Bradford company founded by Benjamin and William Jowett began series car production shortly after 1910, offering a string of commendable small cars powered by flat-twin engines, followed by flat-four engines in 1936. The company's most exciting period was after 1945 with the advent of the advanced Javelin saloon and Jupiter sports model, but the company ceased car manufacture in 1954, shortly after announcing the fibreglass-bodied R4 sports model, of which only three are thought to have been produced.

1952 Jowett Jupiter Tourer, 1486cc 4-cylinder engine, completely restored, 2,000 miles covered since, finished in red, beige hood and interior trim, good condition. **£11,000–13,000 H&H**

Jowett Javelin (1947–53)

The Jowett Javelin outshone many dreary mainstream offerings in styling, engineering and performance. Its unitary construction, efficient flat-four engine, four-speed gearbox, sophisticated suspension and precise rack-and-pinion steering were combined with an up-to-the-minute, wind-cheating shape and clever packaging to create a compact five-seater saloon with refined road manners, superb passenger comfort and an impressive turn of speed. Sporting successes included a class win in the 1949 Monte Carlo Rally and race-track victories over more powerful machines, certainly justification enough for Jowett to adopt the slogan, 'Take a good look when it passes you.' Unfortunately, the Javelin's reputation had been tarnished early on by weaknesses in the engine and gearbox that were rectified later. That, combined with the Javelin's high price – considerably more than an Austin A40 or Morris Oxford – helped end the brave Bradford company's car making activities in 1954.

Lagonda

Lagonda's distinctions are many, and some of them rather unusual. For example, how many car manufacturers do you know that were founded by opera singers? That's what Wilbur Gunn was when he came to the UK. Not only that, but the founder of one of Britain's quintessential sporting marques was also an American. In the last years of the 19th century, Gunn set up Lagonda Engineering not far from London, naming the company after the local Indian name for one of the rivers in his native Ohio. Initially, Gunn's company produced motorcycles, but quickly progressed from two-wheels to three, and then four. As early as 1909, a Lagonda 16/18hp raced at Brooklands, and most early Lagondas went for export, before becoming readily available in the UK in 1912. Gunn died in 1920, and in the mid-1920s the company moved away from production of light cars to concentrate on the fast sporting cars and tourers that came to characterise the marque. A Le Mans victory was gained in 1935 and, with W.O. Bentley as technical director, the company produced the magnificent V12. David Brown, owner of Aston Martin, acquired Lagonda in 1947, gaining access to Bentley's last engine design, the 2580cc twin-cam six, employed in the Aston Martin DB2. Since then, the Lagonda name has been used intermittently on larger, luxury express versions of Astons.

◄ **1927 Lagonda 14/60 Tourer,** 2 litres, older restoration, finished in red over black, new black duck weather equipment and tonneau, bench front seat with adjustable backrest, tan leather upholstery, unused since 1995, 1 owner since 1965. **£13,000–15,000 BKS**

Lagonda's 14/60 was announced in 1925, originally for production alongside the somewhat dated 12/24 model, but it soon replaced the earlier model. The14/60 featured a new 2 litre, four-cylinder engine, which proved a landmark in Lagonda history. It featured twin high camshafts operating overhead valves. The chassis design was new, and the car was the first Lagonda to have four-wheel brakes.

1934 Lagonda M45 Sports Saloon, 4½ litre Meadows engine, finished in dark green, original condition throughout. £28,000–32,000 **COYS**

'Swift silence, safety and perfect comfort at high speeds, and performance that is attained only by high class cars – that is the Lagonda!' Such was the company's description of its 4.5 litre M45 model and, with the factory's own open T7 coachwork, it was the archetypal 1930s British sports car. Handsome, rugged and fast, these brisk and expensive motor cars caught the rich sporting fraternity's imagination. While only in production for two years, the cars won a tremendous following. If other vehicles offered more creature comforts and sophistication, the M45 was aimed at the sporting owner-driver, whose idea of transport was not to sit behind a chauffeur, but rather to thunder at speed behind his own wheel.

1939 Lagonda 4½ Litre V12 Saloon, engine rebuilt and chassis and brakes overhauled 1990 at a cost of £14,000, rewired, period radio, original paint, chrome, leather and woodwork in good condition, further £12,000 spent on recommissioning, 12,015 miles recorded. £30,000–33,000 **BKS**

Two of the greatest names in British motoring history, Lagonda and Bentley, combined to produce a masterpiece of engineering that was to power the finest of pre-war luxury saloons. Walter Owen Bentley had never been comfortable at Rolls-Royce following its take-over of his old company and, unwilling to let his talents be stifled, he welcomed the opportunity to join Lagonda to develop an all-new V12 engine. He was joined by Stuart Tresillian, who had played a major role in the development of the Rolls-Royce V12 Phantom III. Together, they developed a 100mph motor car with an engine that revved to 5,500rpm and produced a quoted 180bhp.

◄ **1950 Lagonda 2.6 Drophead Coupé,** 2600cc, finished in metallic grey, dark plum leather interior trim and burr walnut cappings, 34,000 miles recorded, excellent original condition. £22,000–25,000 **H&H**

A very small number of drophead coupés were built in 1950. This particular car was ordered at the 1949 Motor Show to a similar specification as that displayed and presented to HRH The Duke of Edinburgh.

1955 Lagonda 3 Litre Mk I, restored, engine rebuilt and converted to run on unleaded fuel, brakes overhauled, rewired, bare-metal respray in British Racing green, new weather equipment, interior retrimmed in tan leather with matching carpets, excellent in all aspects. £31,000–34,500 **COYS**

The 3 Litre was introduced in 1953 and retained the 1.6 litre Mk II's chassis, albeit altered to carry handsome new coachwork from Tickford and with a specially balanced propshaft and flexibly-mounted final drive. Initially, only a two-door saloon was offered, but it was soon followed by a drophead coupé, then a four-door saloon. A Mk II saloon with floor-mounted gearchange appeared in 1956, but the problems of making two ranges of cars led to Aston Martin Lagonda terminating production early in 1958.

LAGONDA Model	ENGINE cc/cyl	DATES	CONDITION		
			1	2	3
12/24	1421/4	1923–26	£14,000	£10,000	£8,000
2 Litre	1954/4	1928–32	£28,000	£25,000	£19,000
3 Litre	2931/6	1928–34	£40,000	£30,000	£22,000
Rapier	1104/4	1934–35	£15,000	£9,000	£5,000
M45	4429/6	1934–36	£50,000+	£30,000	£20,000
LG45	4429/6	1936–37	£45,000	£32,000	£22,000
LG6	4453/6	1937–39	£40,000	£28,000	£20,000
V12	4480/V12	1937–39	£75,000+	£50,000	£25,000
Prices are very dependent upon body type, dhc or saloon, originality and competition history.					

Lamborghini

Having owned a number of Ferraris, wealthy industrialist Ferruccio Lamborghini became convinced that he could build a better supercar and pursued his goal by recruiting some of the best design and engineering talent for his fledgling supercar concern, names likes Giotto Bizzarrini, Giampaolo Dallara, Franco Scaglione, Touring of Milan and Bertone. His first car, the 350 GT of 1964, certainly looked the part and was powered by a magnificent V12, but it was the launch of the staggering Miura at the 1966 Geneva motor show that many commentators count as the motoring sensation of the decade. When the Miura's lease of life came to an end, the brutal-looking Countach debuted in 1974 and became the company's flagship model to the end of the 1980s. By then, Ferruccio Lamborghini had long since lost interest and the company passed through several changes of ownership.

1967 Lamborghini 400 GT 2+2, 3929cc, double-overhead-camshaft V12 engine, 6 Weber 40DCOE carburettors, 320bhp, 5-speed gearbox, all-independent suspension, 4-wheel disc brakes, finished in metallic blue, biscuit leather interior trim in excellent condition, fewer than 35,000 miles recorded.
£23,000–27,000 RM

Flushed with the success of the 350 GT two-seater, Lamborghini debuted a more refined GT in 1966. In addition to the 3929cc version of the V12 engine, the company began to produce its own gearboxes (replacing ZF boxes in the two-seaters) and differentials (replacing Salisbury units). Most importantly, however, subtle reshaping of the body by Touring increased interior room to permit 2+2 seating while maintaining the distinctive shape of the two-seater. Bodies were steel rather than aluminium, making the 400 GT 2+2 400lb heavier than previous models.

1971 Lamborghini Espada Series II Coupé, coachwork by Bertone, finished in metallic dark green, tan leather interior, 43,000km recorded, original.
£7,500–9,000 BKS

Five years after introducing its first car, and three years after launching the sensational Miura, Lamborghini upstaged Ferrari again by announcing a full four-seater – the Espada – at the 1968 Geneva show. The Espada was styled along similar lines to the stillborn Marzal, but carried its 4 litre, quad-cam V12 up front. The engine produced 325bhp, sufficient to propel the distinctive Bertone-styled coupé to 150mph. Introduced in 1970, the Series II cars offered an extra 25bhp, 155mph top speed and an improved dashboard layout.

Lamborghini Miura (1966–72)

Engine: Transverse-mounted V12, double-overhead-camshaft, 24-valve, quadruple triple-choke Weber carburettors, 3929cc.
Power output: 350–385bhp.
Transmission: Five-speed manual.
Brakes: Ventilated discs all-round.
Top speed: 165–175+mph.
0–60mph: 6–6.7 seconds.
Production: 763 (some say 764).

LAMBORGHINI Model	ENGINE cc/cyl	DATES	CONDITION 1	2	3
350 GT FHC	3500/12	1964–67	£55,000	£45,000	£25,000
400 GT	4000/12	1966–68	£45,000	£40,000	£25,000
Miura LP400	4000/12	1966–69	£60,000	£50,000	£30,000
Miura S	4000/12	1969–71	£75,000	£60,000+	£40,000
Miura SV	4000/12	1971–72	£90,000+	£75,000	£60,000
Espada	4000/12	1969–78	£18,000	£14,000	£10,000
Jarama	4000/12	1970–78	£22,000	£15,000	£11,000
Urraco	2500/8	1972–76	£18,000	£11,000	£8,000
Countach	4000/12	1974–82	£60,000+	£40,000	£30,000

Countach limited editions are sought after as well as Miura SV.

◀ **1973 Lamborghini Espada III,** 4 litre, double-overhead-camshaft V12, 350bhp, ventilated disc brakes, 150+mph, well maintained, good condition.
£6,000–7,000 BARO

▶ **1973 Lamborghini Urraco P250 Coupé,** coachwork by Bertone, 2.5 litre, overhead-camshaft, transverse-mounted V8 engine, 220bhp, 143km/h top speed, finished in white, original red cloth upholstery, 66,000km recorded, good condition throughout.
£5,000–6,000 BKS

Intended to compete with rivals such as Ferrari's Dino and Porsche's 911, the Urraco was announced in 1970. The P250 was superseded in 1974 by the P300, after 520 cars had been built.

1984 Lamborghini Countach LP500S, completely restored 1988/89, engine rebuilt, Ansa sports exhaust system, rear wing not fitted but supplied with car, resprayed in original Acapulco blue, interior retrimmed in magnolia and dark blue leather, 42,827 miles recorded.
£30,000–35,000 BKS

The sensation of the 1971 Geneva Salon, the Countach was styled by Bertone and retained the quad-cam V12 of its predecessor, albeit installed longitudinally. To achieve optimum weight distribution, the five-speed gearbox was placed ahead of the engine, between the seats, and the differential – driven by a shaft passing through the sump – at the rear. When production began in 1974, the Countach sported an improved chassis and the standard 4 litre engine. The aerodynamically efficient Countach could attain 170mph and came with race-track roadholding to match. The car's largest potential market, the USA, remained closed to it until the arrival of the emissions-friendly LP500S in 1982. Although no more powerful than before, the newcomer's 4754cc engine brought with it a useful increase in torque.

◀ **1986 Lamborghini LM 002 Cabriolet,** configured for 2-wheel drive, all necessary 4-wheel-drive components, electric winch, air conditioning, electric windows, black mohair hood and tonneau, finished in red, beige Connolly leather interior, 18,500km recorded, 1 of 241 built, only example with a cabriolet top, original.
£35,000–40,000 BKS

One of the most exciting off-road vehicles ever conceived, the LM 002 resulted from the marriage of the Countach QV's 5.2 litre V12 to a functionally styled 4x4, the union resulting in scintillating performance and a top speed in excess of 200km/h.

Lanchester

Today, the name is almost forgotten, but without doubt Frederick Lanchester was one of the most important early pioneers and original thinkers of Britain's fledgling automobile industry. In fact, it was in 1895 that Fred, with his brother George, produced the very first, all-British, four-wheeled petrol car, a year before the formation of the Daimler company, which is generally credited with giving birth to the British motor industry. The cars produced under the Lanchester name were a curious blend of innovation and caution; for example, while early Lanchester cars were noted for many advanced features, they persisted with tiller steering as late as 1911, when most firms had long since adopted steering wheels. By 1909, Lanchester was also a consultant to the British Daimler company, and in 1914 he resigned altogether from the company that bore his name. Ironically, in 1931, Lanchester was acquired by BSA, which also owned Daimler. Thereafter, Lanchester models began to lose much of their distinction, and although the name survived WWII, the Lanchester marque faded away in 1956.

1933 Lanchester Drophead Coupé, coachwork by Charlesworth, 6-cylinder engine, unrestored, history file.
£3,000–3,500 TEN

1934 Lanchester Ten Two-Door Saloon, completely restored 1989, finished in blue and black, blue leather interior trim.
£4,750–5,500 BKS

In the main, post-WWI Lanchesters were large, well-appointed, high-speed conveyances aimed at the luxury car market. The company's 1930 merger with Daimler brought with it a change of policy, subsequent Lanchesters being smaller and cheaper cars. Introduced in 1932, the Ten was unique in its class at the time, having a Daimler fluid flywheel and a Wilson pre-selector gearbox. The engine was a 1.2 litre (later 1.3 litre), four-cylinder, overhead-valve unit producing 34bhp.

1935 Lanchester II Saloon, coachwork by Mulliner, 1344cc, 4-cylinder engine, 4-speed pre-selector gearbox, restored, many new parts, brightwork rechromed, some ash body framing replaced, finished in red and black, new red leather interior trim, 98,527 miles recorded.
£5,000–6,000 H&H

▶ **1938 Lanchester 14,** post-WWII 1809cc, 6-cylinder engine, pre-selector gearbox with fluid flywheel, finished in red and black.
£3,000–3,500 BRIT

◀ **1930 Lagonda 3 Litre Tourer,** 2931cc, 6-cylinder, overhead-valve engine, c80bhp, completely restored early 1990s, original engine, body, wings, headlamps, instruments, flat-profiled radiator and surround.
£50,000–55,000 COYS

A descendant of the 16/65, the 3 Litre was introduced as an upmarket companion to the better-known 2 Litre. To accommodate roomier touring and saloon coachwork, it was offered with high and low chassis options. By the 1930s, the model had grown into a handsome touring car with a 10ft 9in wheelbase and a choice of fabric or fully-panelled, painted bodies, characterised by sleek, rounded radiators and P100 headlamps.

1970 Lamborghini Miura S, coachwork by Bertone, 3929cc, double-overhead-camshaft V12 engine, 370bhp, electric windows, finished in red, black interior, 1 of 140 built, excellent condition throughout.
£45,000–55,000 COYS

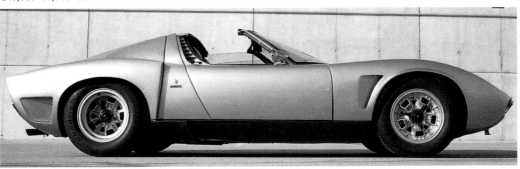

1971 Lamborghini Miura P400S Jota Spyder, coachwork by Bertone/Lambomotor, 4 litre, double-overhead-camshaft V12 engine, restored late 1980s, engine rebuilt 1991, resprayed silver over grey, black and grey leather interior, excellent condition throughout.
£85,000–95,000 BKS

Lamborghini's sole competition version of the Miura S was known as the Jota and featured lightweight alloy bodywork, Plexiglas side windows, racing suspension, magnesium wheels and a 440bhp engine. Inspired by Bertone's one-off open-top Miura Roadster, this car features Jota-style bodywork and special suspension. Although not an 'official' Jota replica, it was constructed as a Jota Spyder by the Swiss company Lambomotor. There were rumours of the factory putting it into production, but it remains unique.

1971 Lamborghini Jarama, partially restored early 1990s, finished in blue, beige leather upholstery, 80,000km recorded, good mechanical condition.
£10,000–12,000 BKS

Launched in 1970, the Jarama was the last of Lamborghini's front-engined road cars. The 160mph 2+2 had a platform-type chassis based on the Espada's, but shorter wheelbase. An unusual feature was the nose with its headlamps partially obscured by electrically raised covers. The Jarama continued in production until 1978, by which time 327 cars had been built.

1992 Lancia Delta HF Integrale Club Italia, Abarth boost kit, aluminium fuel filler, push-button starting, competition gear lever, red leather Recaro seats, original blue paintwork, 1 owner, 5,000km recorded, excellent condition throughout.
£28,000–34,000 BKS

Capitalising on the Integrale's run of competition successes, Lancia introduced a number of limited-edition models aimed at connoisseurs and collectors. Only 15 examples of the Club Italia model were produced, exclusively for members of that group of Italian car collectors.

1937 Lincoln Zephyr Coupé, 267cu.in, sidevalve V12 engine, 110bhp, 3-speed manual gearbox, 125in wheelbase, Art-Deco-style instrument panel, completely restored, well maintained, concours condition.
£42,000–47,000 RM

Introduced as a more affordable alternative to the coachbuilt K-series cars, the Zephyr was a sleek, striking design, and it sold in numbers unprecedented at Lincoln. Technically, it was advanced, too, its body being the first unibody designed as a stressed structure. The result was lighter and far stronger than the conventional body/separate chassis arrangement. The engine was also new, being a V12 based on Ford's proven sidevalve V8.

1928 Mercedes-Benz 27/170/225 Modell SSK Sport Tourer, assembled in 1966 using many genuine SSK parts, including axles, radiator, instruments, lamps and 20in wheels, reproduction chassis and 2-seater coachwork, in need of correct 7.1 litre engine and associated gearbox.
£60,000–70,000 BKS

The rakish and aggressive Modell SSK (*Super Sport Kurz*) was powered by a 7067cc, overhead-camshaft, supercharged engine. It had an ultra-short wheelbase and compact cockpit that left little room for the passenger as the driver heaved on the massive steering wheel. Without the supercharger engaged, the SSK developed 170bhp, but at full throttle with the blower activated, a massive 225bhp was available, giving a top speed of 200km/h.

◄ **1953 Mercedes-Benz 300S Cabriolet,** coachwork by Sindelfingen, 3 litre, 6-cylinder engine, 150bhp, all-synchromesh 4-speed gearbox, floor-mounted gearchange, cosmetically and mechanically restored early 1990s, finished in black, black hood and interior, dark wood cappings, very good condition.
£105,000–120,000 BKS

In its day, the 300S was one of the most expensive cars in the world. It was built on a shortened 300 chassis, and employed the 300's basic running gear and suspension layout. As the latter was similar to that of the Gullwing, the 300S Cabriolet was light on its feet for an opulent 2+2 Grand Tourer. Only 760 examples of the 300S (all variants) were made between 1952 and 1958.

1957 Mercedes-Benz 300SL Gullwing, Rudge knock-off wheels, Becker Le Mans radio, 1 owner since 1959, museum displayed since 1976, 42,991km recorded, recommissioned, original.
£95,000–105,000 BKS

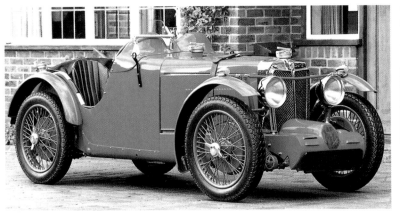

1931 MG Supercharged C-Type Midget, rebuilt using an original C-Type body late 1980s, recent engine overhaul, EN40B crankshaft, Cosworth conrods, 1 of only 5 running C-types in the UK, road legal, ex-Hugh Hamilton and Norman Black Brooklands car.
£80,000–90,000 BKS

This ex-works team C-Type has an impressive history, having been driven by 'Hammy' Hamilton to third place in the 1931 Brooklands Double Twelve endurance race. Later that year, it took the class course record in the Ulster TT. In 1932, Norman Black used it to take third and pick up the JCC Trophy in the Brooklands 1000, while in the Brooklands 500, he drove it to sixth place. More recently, it set five British land speed records at Millbrook in 1994 and has been active in sprints and hill climbs.

1934 MG K3 Magnette, 1097cc, 6-cylinder engine, supercharged, 74bhp, manual gearbox, 4-wheel drum brakes, restored, finished in dark blue, very good condition.
£53,000–59,000 RM

The K3 Magnette first appeared at the Mille Miglia in 1933. In the hands of George Eyston and Johnny Lurani, it won its class outright. Later that year, Tazio Nuvolari won the Tourist Trophy in a K3. Excellent power-to-weight ratio combined with agile handling made the car a formidable competitor on the race circuits of Europe.

▶ **1954 MG TF Midget,** 1250cc, 4-cylinder engine, substantially restored mid-1990s, finished in dark blue, new black mohair hood, grey leather trim, 3 owners from new, excellent condition throughout.
£12,500–15,000 BRIT

1947 MG TC Midget, 1250cc, overhead-valve, 4-cylinder engine, twin SU carburettors, 54bhp, 4-speed manual gearbox, semi-elliptic leaf spring suspension, older restoration, finished in green.
£10,000–12,000 COYS

◀ **1959 MG Twin Cam Roadster,** 1588cc, 4-cylinder engine, 4-speed manual gearbox, centre-lock wheels, restored, finished in red, boot rack, black interior, excellent condition throughout.
£16,000–18,000 WCL

1982 Mini Mayfair Flag Special, 1000cc engine, automatic transmission, good condition.
£1,800–2,200 MINI

1917 Morris Cowley 11.9hp Coupé De Luxe, 4-cylinder Continental engine, older restoration, fitted with coil ignition, cooling system improved, finished in maroon, beige upholstery, good condition.
£11,500–14,000 TEN

◄ **1928 Morris Cowley Flatnose Saloon,** 1200cc, 4-cylinder Hotchkiss engine, front-wheel brakes, restored, finished in maroon with black wings, brown interior, well maintained.
£5,000–6,000 COYS

This car previously belonged to the TV gardening expert Alan Titchmarsh.

1929 Packard Custom Eight 640 Tourer, 6.3 litre, 8-cylinder inline engine, 105bhp, hypoid final-drive gears, Bijur chassis lubrication system, parabolic headlamps, 4-door, 7-seater coachwork, restored early 1990s, finished in white and grey, orange chassis, axles and suspension, black leather upholstery, noisy 2nd gear, otherwise good condition throughout.
£49,000–55,000 BKS

With the introduction of the Custom models in 1926, Packard's Eight range increased dramatically. New for 1929 was the base-model 5.2 litre Standard Eight, the larger 6.3 litre engine continuing to power the Custom and DeLuxe Eights. The latter models featured coachwork by Dietrich, LeBaron and Rollston.

1934 Packard Twelve Coupé Roadster, 445cu.in V12 engine, 160bhp, 3-speed synchromesh gearbox, 4-wheel vacuum-assisted brakes, dickey, restored, 1 of 50 built, excellent condition.
£200,000+ RM

The eleventh series is considered by many to be the ultimate Packard Twelve. It was the last with classic swept wings, before the advent of the streamlined look. Although many body styles were offered, the rarest is the striking Coupé Roadster, of which fewer than 20 are known to have survived.

1913 Peugeot Bébé 6hp Two-Seater, 856cc, twin concentric propshafts, quarter-elliptic leaf-spring rear suspension, folding windscreen, hood, klaxon horn, Mondia fork-mounted acetylene headlamps, rampant lion mascot, restored, engine rebuilt, very good condition throughout.
£7,000–9,000 BKS

Ettore Bugatti was responsible for the design of the Peugeot Bébé at a time when production of Bugatti cars was slowly getting off the ground. The sale of the T-head, lateral-valve engine design to Peugeot generated useful capital for Bugatti's operation. It also put Peugeot at the forefront of French light-car design.

1958 Porsche 356A Speedster, 1600cc, rear-mounted, air-cooled engine, synchromesh gearbox, all-independent torsion-bar suspension, left-hand drive, restored, engine rebuilt mid-1990s, new correct floor panels, custom front and rear bumpers, finished in silver, black leather interior piped in white, 40,130 miles recorded.
£25,000–30,000 BB(S)

1988 Porsche 959, 2.9 litre, flat-6 engine, water-cooled 4-valve heads, twin turbochargers, 450bhp, 6-speed transaxle, permanent 4-wheel drive with ABS and electronic torque-split to the wheels, computer-adjusted ride height, electronic monitoring of tyre pressures, rear seats, sound insulation, air conditioning, 197mph top speed, 0–62mph in 3.7 seconds, finished in silver, black leather upholstery, 7,800km recorded.
£100,000–120,000 BKS

1931 Riley Nine Two-Seat Tourer, 1087cc, 4-cylinder engine, refurbished mechanically, engine rebuilt, hardened valve-seat inserts for unleaded fuel, new exhaust system, rewired, tonneau cover, finished in British Racing green, coachwork and red interior trim in excellent condition.
£8,500–10,000 BRIT

The Riley Nine was far ahead of its contemporaries in terms of performance and handling. Initially introduced as the Monaco fabric saloon, it was soon joined by an enlarged model range and rapidly attained many sporting successes. The reason for the Nine's success was its advanced engine, which featured double high-set camshafts and hemispherical combustion chambers. This car began life as a Monaco saloon, but was rebodied with sporting tourer coachwork.

▶ **1932 Rolls-Royce 20/25hp Three-Position Sedanca Coupé,** 4-seater Mulliner Sedanca-style coachwork by Wildae Restorations, fitted with later overdrive gearbox, otherwise to original mechanical specification, P100 headlights, rear-mounted spare, finished in two-tone blue, 3-position duck hood, powder blue hide upholstery, interior wood cappings inlaid with silver.
£75,000–83,000 BKS

1926 Rolls-Royce 20hp Drophead Coupé, uprated to 20/25 specification, fitted with Ranalah coachwork, Ace wheel discs, finished in cream over beige.
£22,000–25,000 COYS

From 1906 to 1922, Rolls-Royce had kept to a one-model policy, that being the 40/50hp Silver Ghost, but after WWI inflation resulted in a drop in sales and it was decided to produce a smaller car. This was the 20hp model, originally identifiable by its horizontal radiator shutters. The 20hp featured a six-cylinder, overhead-valve engine of just over 3 litres, giving about 50bhp.

◀ **1947 Rolls-Royce Silver Wraith Sedanca De Ville,** coachwork by H.J. Mulliner, finished in black and silver, interior retrimmed in grey cloth, rear compartment with picnic tables and occasional seats, original radio, good condition throughout.
£27,000–32,000 RCC

1952 Sunbeam Alpine Prototype, older restoration, in road-going trim, accompanied by its Jabbeke undertray, alloy tonneau and wooden bucks, finished in Alpine silver, red leather interior, history file, good condition throughout, ex-Stirling Moss and Sheila van Damm.
£19,000–23,000 BKS

Aimed squarely at the North American market, the Alpine was based on the Sunbeam Talbot 90 saloon. Its 2267cc, overhead-valve, four-cylinder engine received a power boost courtesy of a revised cylinder head and special carburation. The new model's launch was enhanced by a blaze of publicity following this car's record-breaking runs at Jabbeke in Belgium and Montlhéry, France. The prototype was prepared for the record attempts in March 1953. Modifications included a 105bhp engine, an undertray, passenger-seat cockpit cover, Laycock overdrive and removal of the windscreen. The car was driven on the Jabbeke-Aeltre highway by Stirling Moss and rally driver Sheila van Damm. Moss was timed at 120.459mph, while van Damm clocked 120.135mph over the flying kilometre and 119.402 over the flying mile. The following day, Leslie Johnson covered 111.2 miles in one hour at Montlhéry, and Stirling Moss lapped the banked circuit at 116mph.

◄ **1947 Triumph 1800 Roadster,** 1776cc, overhead-valve, 4-cylinder engine, 63bhp, 4-speed manual gearbox, transverse-leaf independent front suspension, 4-wheel drum brakes, new interior trim and Wilton carpets, concours condition.
£13,000–15,000 RM

The Triumph 1800 Roadster combined saloon components with flowing, 1930s-style aluminium coachwork that featured the world's last production dickey seat – complete with its own pop-up windscreen. It was intended to compete with Jaguar, but although a more powerful 2 litre model was introduced in 1949, it was no match for the new XK120. As a result, production was discontinued to make way for an all-new sports car – the well-known TR series.

1922 Vauxhall OD 23/60 Kington Tourer, older restoration, new radiator, steering box rebuilt, reproduction Kington touring body, original wings and bonnet, finished in red with black wings and polished aluminium bonnet, beige leather upholstery, excellent weather equipment, very good condition.
£32,000–36,000 BKS

This car was discovered abandoned behind a hedge near Edinburgh in 1982. It was in chassis form, but complete with wings, running boards and bonnet.

1925 Vauxhall 14/40 Princeton Tourer, 2297cc, 4-cylinder engine, restored 1980, little use since, finished in British Racing green, serviceable hood and sidescreens, tan leatherette interior trim in good condition, good mechanical condition.
£15,000–18,000 BRIT

The 14/40 was introduced in the autumn of 1921. The earlier M-series was superseded in 1924 by the improved LM, which benefited from a more powerful engine, four-speed gearbox, wire wheels and four-wheel braking.

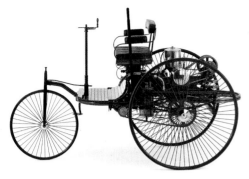

1886 Benz Motorwagen Replica, built in 1986, 984cc, single-cylinder, water-cooled engine, vertical crankshaft, surface carburettor which also acts as a fuel tank, electric ignition, single-speed belt drive, lever-actuated fast-and-loose pulley to give free engine facility, tubular chassis, large-diameter spoked wheels.
£22,000–26,000 BKS

The 1886 Benz Motorwagen was the world's first successful, purpose-built motor car.

1914 Pierce-Arrow 48–B–3 Vestibule Brougham,
8.6 litre, 6-cylinder engine, T-head cylinders cast in pairs, dual ignition, triple spark plugs, aluminium-panelled body, external opera lamps, original interior with crystal flower vases, period fittings, in need of total restoration.
£17,000–20,000 BKS

Chosen transport of American presidents for many years and instantly recognisable thanks to its unique wing-mounted headlamps, the Pierce-Arrow was superb in every respect. Vestibule Brougham coachwork was favoured by the White House and had an enclosed chauffeur's compartment.

1926 Rolls-Royce Silver Ghost Coupé,
2-seater coachwork by Willoughby, Springfield model with enclosed valve springs, left-hand drive and 3-speed centre-change gearbox, barn discovery, roof fabric deteriorated, original dark chocolate interior trim dilapidated, smoky engine, drivable.
£50,000–60,000 BKS

1962 Messerschmitt KR 200 Roadster, completely restored 1989, finished in Marine blue, dark blue hood, fitted with factory-issued Tiger nose section.
£5,750–7,500 S

1961 Messerschmitt KR 200 Sport, single-cylinder, 2-stroke Fichtel & Sachs engine, 4-speed manual gearbox with reverse, restored, engine and transmission rebuilt, finished in Old English white, black canvas tonneau, chrome luggage rack, imitation spoke wheel covers, unused since 1997, good condition.
£20,000–23,000 BKS

The KR 200 Sport's roadster styling gave it a very sleek and sporting look compared to the bubble-top 'cabin scooter'. Approximately 12 sport models were manufactured, and there are no other known survivors.

Lancia

The world of book-keeping's loss was certainly the automobile enthusiast's gain, for that's how Vincenzo Lancia started out, as a humble clerk. In 1899, he got his break when he became chief inspector at Fiat after its take-over of the company for which he worked. In 1900, he began an eight-year racing career as a Fiat works driver, even though he left the company in 1906 to form Lancia. His first model, the Alpha, began the trend of naming Lancia cars after letters of the Greek alphabet. Early on, Lancia gained a reputation for innovation and advanced engineering. The Theta of 1913 was the first European car with full electrics, and the Lambda of 1923 not only pioneered unitary construction, but also possessed independent front suspension and a compact V4 engine. Vincenzo Lancia's final design was the Aprilia, a little gem with unitary construction, all-independent suspension, four-wheel hydraulic brakes and a 1352cc V4 that gave a commendable top speed of 80mph. The Aprilia appeared in 1937, the same year in which Vicenzo Lancia died. From the post-war era, the Aurelia coupés have often been heralded as the first of the modern GTs. In the 1950s, Lancia made some able and beautiful machines, but could never offer a line-up that was comprehensive enough to compete with Alfa Romeo and Fiat. In 1969, mounting debts forced a sell-out to Fiat.

1951 Lancia Aurelia B20GT Coupé, 2000cc, 6-cylinder engine, restored, engine mildly tuned, larger twin-choke carburettor, external fuel filler, Perspex side and rear windows, rev-counter, water temperature gauge, period-type competition bucket seats, full harnesses.
£22,000–25,000 COYS

Lancia's Aurelia, the first car ever to employ a V6 engine, was launched in 1950. The basic saloon was joined in 1951 by the Pininfarina-styled B20 Coupé, a fastback 2+2 GT which, with its sports car performance and saloon car practicality, effectively introduced the Gran Turismo concept to the world. The early-series cars are a popular choice for historic rally competitors, since their independent rear suspension imparts an oversteering tendency; later examples have a de Dion set-up that causes understeer. The 2 litre first- and second-series cars are also much lighter and, with lower gearing, acceleration is surprisingly impressive.

1954 Lancia Aurelia B20 3rd Series Coupé, 2451cc, pushrod V6, 118bhp, c115mph top speed, older restoration, Nardi floor-change conversion, finished in blue, tan interior, good condition.
£14,500–17,000 BKS

1960 Lancia Appia GTZ Coupé, coachwork by Zagato, 1089cc V4, 60bhp, 4-speed gearbox, restored late 1980s, finished in red, black interior, very good condition.
£15,000–18,000 BKS

The Appia was offered in special editions, built in open and closed coupé styles by Pininfarina, Viotti, Vignale and Zagato. Zagato's slippery coupé, known as the GTZ, was a popular competition car, which achieved success in the Mille Miglia and also won the Italian GT Championship.

1961 Lancia Flaminia Sport 3C, coachwork by Zagato, 2458cc V6 engine, triple carburettors, 140bhp, 4-speed manual gearbox, 4-wheel disc brakes, 196km/h top speed, restored, finished in metallic grey, very good condition.
£17,000–20,000 Pou

1965 Lancia Flaminia SS Coupé, coachwork by Zagato, 2.8 litre V6 engine, 175bhp, 5-speed transaxle, limited-slip differential, 4-wheel disc brakes, finished in metallic grey, red interior, wooden dashboard, unrestored, good original specification.
£70,000–80,000 BKS

Between 1957 and 1967, Lancia made about 1,000 Flaminias a year. The car was aimed at the discerning buyer, who could choose from a menu of engines and body styles created by Zagato, Pininfarina and Touring. The rarest and most desirable models, however, were the Sport and Super Sport two-seat coupés, which accounted for a total of 525 cars, only 150 of which wore Zagato coachwork.
This particular car was ordered by Amedeo di Savoia, the Duke of Aosta, who later commissioned the ultimate road car, the mid-engined Bizzarrini P538.

Miller's Starter Marque

Starter Lancias: *Beta Coupé and Spyder, Beta HPE, 1972–84.*

- There are lots of lovely Lancias, and many models are affordable. However, in many cases, they only came to the UK in penny numbers, and this relative rarity makes them more difficult to keep on the road than other more populous, late-era classics. In other cases, their innovative engineering, which is one of their joys, can also stretch the resources and patience of a DIY enthusiast.
- A good all-round introduction to classic Lancia ownership is the lively Beta Coupé, Spyder or HPE – the high-performance estate. For a start, they've had less time to rust than older models, and unfortunately that's an important consideration with many Lancias. The Beta saloon, introduced in 1972, was the first 'Fiat-Lancia' and one of its chief virtues was the Fiat-derived, double-overhead-camshaft engine, which had proved so successful in the Fiat 124. Over the model's lifetime, customers were offered a choice that ran from 1300cc to 2000cc, and all of them, even when inserted in the humblest saloon, were good for a genuine 100+mph.
- The model you'll encounter most frequently is the Beta Coupé, which was made in far greater numbers than the HPE and Spyder, and that makes the Coupé the easiest to buy and live with.

1966 Lancia Flaminia 3C Supersport 'Double Bubble' Coupé, partially restored, stainless steel exhaust system, radiator overhauled, original, concours winner.
£33,000–37,000 COYS

◀ **1965 Lancia Flavia Coupé,** coachwork by Zagato, 1488cc flat-4 engine, 78bhp, front-wheel drive, 4-wheel disc brakes, 100mph top speed, finished in silver, blue interior, stored since late 1980s, good general condition.
£4,000–4,800 BKS

LANCIA Model	ENGINE cc/cyl	DATES	CONDITION 1	2	3
Theta	4940/4	1913–19	£24,000	£16,500	£8,000
Kappa	4940/4	1919–22	£24,000	£16,000	£8,000
Dikappa	4940/4	1921–22	£24,000	£16,000	£8,000
Trikappa	4590/4	1922–26	£25,000	£18,000	£10,000
Lambda	2120/4	1923–28	£40,000	£20,000	£12,000
Dilambda	3960/8	1928–32	£35,000	£16,000	£10,000
Astura	2604/8	1931–39	£30,000	£20,000	£10,000
Artena	1925/4	1931–36	£9,000	£5,000	£2,000
Augusta	1196/4	1933–36	£9,000	£4,000	£2,000
Aprilia 238	1352/4	1937–39	£10,000	£5,000	£3,000

Coachbuilt bodywork is more desirable and can increase prices.

LANCIA Model	ENGINE cc/cyl	DATES	CONDITION 1	2	3
Aprilia 438	1486/4	1939–50	£11,000	£6,000	£3,000
Ardea	903/4	1939–53	£10,000	£5,000	£3,000
Aurelia B10	1754/6	1950–53	£9,000	£6,000	£3,000
Aurelia B15–20–22	1991/6	1951–53	£15,000+	£10,000	£8,000
Aurelia B24–B24 Spyder	2451/6	1955–58	£40,000+	£17,000	£12,000
Aurelia GT	2451/6	1953–59	£18,000+	£11,000	£9,000
Appia C10–C105	1090/4	1953–62	£6,000	£3,000	£2,000
Aurelia Ser II/IV	2266/6	1954–59	£11,000	£6,000	£4,000
Flaminia Zagato	2458/6	1957–63	£18,000+	£10,000	£7,000
Flaminia Ser	2458/6	1957–63	£18,000	£10,000	£5,000
Flavia 1500	1500/4	1960–75	£6,000	£4,000	£2,000
Fulvia	1091/4	1963–70	£3,000	£2,000	£1,000
Fulvia S	1216/4	1964–70	£5,000	£4,000	£1,500
Fulvia 1.3	1298/4	1967–75	£6,000	£4,000	£2,000
Stratos	2418/6	1969–71	£45,000	£20,000	£10,000
Flavia 2000	1991/4	1969–75	£3,000	£2,000	£1,000
Fulvia HF/1.6	1584/4	1969–75	£9,000	£5,000	£2,000
Beta HPE	1585/4	1976–82	£3,000	£1,500	£500
Beta Spyder	1995/4	1977–82	£4,000	£1,500	£800
Monte Carlo	1995/4	1976–81	£6,000	£3,000	£1,000
Gamma Coupé	2484/4	1977–84	£2,500	£1,500	£500
Gamma Berlina	2484/4	1977–84	£2,500	£1,200	£300

Competition history and convertible coachwork could cause prices to vary.

◄ **1973 Lancia Flavia 2000 Coupé,** 1991cc, transverse-mounted, overhead-valve, flat-4 engine, 5-speed ZF gearbox, power steering, mechanics completely overhauled, 89,000 miles recorded, excellent condition throughout.
£3,000–3,500 H&H

1972 Lancia Fulvia Coupé, coachwork by Zagato, V4 engine, 5-speed gearbox, 4-wheel disc brakes, partially restored 1994/95, 3,000km covered since, finished in blue, black upholstery.
£5,250–6,750 BKS

The Fulvia has been described as the last of the true Lancias because it was designed before the company was sold to Fiat in 1969. Actually, it demonstrates why Lancia hit difficulties – it was designed to meet the exacting standards of some of the best engineers in the business, not to please corporate accountants. The most desirable and rarest of the Fulvia variants is Zagato's short-wheelbase, lightweight coupé.

1988 Lancia Delta Integrale, 1930cc, turbocharger, 4-wheel drive, refurbished at a cost of over £3,500, Terox brakes, Koni adjustable suspension, new suspension bushes, 17in alloy wheels, finished in red, grey suede interior, 96,000km recorded, excellent condition.
£7,000–8,000 H&H

◄ **1988 Lancia Thema 8.32 Saloon,** 5-speed manual gearbox, factory sunroof, finished in metallic grey, tan interior, good condition.
£5,000–6,000 BKS

The ultimate Thema, and a real 'Q' car, the 8.32 came with Ferrari's 308 32-valve V8 mounted transversely beneath the bonnet and, with 215bhp on tap, was capable of giving more exotic rivals a severe fright. Electronically-controlled damping matched suspension characteristics to driving conditions, while the luxuriously appointed interior went some way toward justifying the £43,200 price tag. Only 2,370 8.32s – all left-hand drive – were built.

Land Rover

The genesis of the remarkable success story of the Land Rover began just after WWII, when Maurice Wilks, then Rover's technical chief, wanted something to replace the clapped-out Willys Jeep on his Anglesey estate. Rover also needed a stop-gap model for its Solihull factory to produce while the new post-war models were readied for production. The original Land Rover, with its galvanised chassis, permanent four-wheel drive and simple aluminium bodywork, went on sale in 1948 and has since become a powerful, world-recognised brand in its own right, setting the standard for working, go-anywhere vehicles. In fact, at times, the unstoppable utility vehicle has been more important to the company's success than its cars. By 1977, Land Rover production topped a million, and of course it's still going strong, having recently been taken over by Ford.

◄ **1950 Land Rover Series 1,** 2 litre sidevalve engine, permanent 4-wheel drive, finished in deep bronze green, khaki hood, full weather gear, correct green vinyl interior, good condition throughout.
£2,000–2,500 CGC

LAND ROVER Model	ENGINE cc/cyl	DATES	CONDITION 1	2	3
Ser 1	1595/4	1948–51	£6,000	£3,000	£1,500
Ser 1	1995/4	1951–53	£4,500	£2,500	£1,000
Ser 1	1995/4	1953–58	£4,000	£2,000	£500
Ser 1	1995/4	1953–58	£3,000	£1,800	£800
Ser 2	1995/4	1958–59	£2,000	£950	£500
Ser 2	1995/4	1958–59	£2,800	£1,200	£500
Ser 2	2286/4	1959–71	£2,000	£950	£500
Ser 2	2286/4	1959–71	£2,500	£1,200	£500
Range Rover	3528/V8	1970–	£5,000	£1,200	£600

Series 1 Land Rovers are very sought after.

Lea-Francis

1946 Lea Francis Mk IV 14hp Saloon, 1767cc, double-overhead-camshaft engine, 4-speed gearbox, aluminium bodywork, framing and interior restored, finished in brown and cream, good condition.
£5,500–6,500 Mot

1948 Lea Francis 14hp Sports Tourer, 1767cc, restored using original parts where possible, engine rebuilt, finished in original cream, dark green interior, used as the works demonstrator, 26th example built, originally used as factory demonstrator.
£11,500–13,000 H&H

LEA-FRANCIS Model	ENGINE cc/cyl	DATES	CONDITION 1	2	3
12hp	1944/4	1923–24	£10,000	£5,000	£3,000
14hp	2297/4	1923–24	£10,000	£5,000	£3,000
9hp	1074/4	1923–24	£7,000	£4,000	£2,000
10hp	1247/4	1947–54	£10,000	£5,500	£3,000
12hp	1496/4	1926–34	£12,000	£6,000	£4,000
Various 6-cylinder models	1696/6	1927–29	£13,500	£9,500	£5,000
Various 6-cylinder models	1991/6	1928–36	£10,500	£8,750	£5,000
14hp	1767/4	1946–54	£10,000	£6,000	£4,000
1.5 Litre	1499/4	1949–51	£11,000	£6,000	£3,000
2.5 Litre	2496/4	1950–52	£14,000	£8,000	£4,000

Lincoln

Henry Leland, founder of Cadillac, formed Lincoln in 1917, and the company's first car appeared in 1919. Two years later, Ford stepped in to rescue the young and ailing concern. With Henry Ford's son, Edsel, at the reins, Lincoln went on to build some of the world's finest luxury cars. Perhaps it would have given Henry Leland some pleasure to have seen the marque he named after Abraham Lincoln go on to enjoy enduring Presidential patronage to this day.

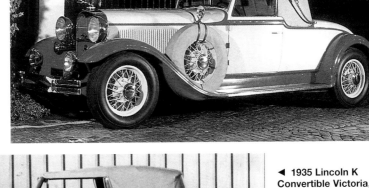

◀ **1931 Lincoln Model K Dual-Cowl Phaeton,** 120bhp, synchromesh on top 2 gears, completely restored, 200 miles covered since, finished in silver and black, red wheels, fawn top and side curtains, red interior, 1 of 12 built with dual-cowl phaeton coachwork. **£55,000–60,500 BKS**

The Model K was a turning point in Lincoln's history. It added excitement and glamour to the company's well-founded reputation for sound engineering.

1931 Lincoln Model K Covertible Coupé, coachwork by Le Baron, 384cu.in, sidevalve V8 engine, 120bhp, 3-speed manual gearbox with free-wheel device, semi-elliptic leaf-spring suspension front and rear, 4-wheel drum brakes, left-hand drive, finished in yellow with red wings, brown leather interior. **£40,000–44,000 C**

◀ **1935 Lincoln K Convertible Victoria,** coachwork by Brunn, 414cu.in V12 engine, automatic spark control, 150bhp, 3-speed manual gearbox, servo-assisted mechanical drum brakes, wire wheels, completely restored, engine rebuilt, new folding top, 1 of 15 Convertible Victorias built. **£50,000–55,000 RM**

▶ **1964 Lincoln Continental Convertible,** 7 litre V8 engine, 300bhp, automatic transmission, power steering, servo-assisted brakes, electric windows, restored 1985, finished in ivory, blue leather interior, excellent condition. **£8,000–9,500 BKS**

LINCOLN Model	ENGINE cu.in/cyl	DATES	CONDITION 1	2	3
Première Coupé	368/8	1956–57	£6,000	£4,000	£2,000
Première Convertible	368/8	1956–57	£14,000	£8,000	£5,000
Continental Mk II	368/8	1956–57	£10,000	£6,000	£4,000
Continental 2-door	430/8	1958–60	£6,000	£4,000	£2,000
Continental Convertible	430/8	1958–60	£18,000+	£10,000+	£7,000+

Lotus

From selling used cars just after the end of WWII, Colin Chapman took Lotus from its birthplace in a lock-up garage to top place on the podium at the pinnacle of motor sport. The remarkable story began when he was studying at London University and selling used cars during the brief post-war boom. In 1948, he took an unsold Austin 7 and created a lightweight trials car. Other competition cars followed, and in 1952 the first production Lotus emerged from the stables behind the north London pub run by Chapman's father. The Mk 6 was based on a multi-tubular frame with stressed aluminium panels and was sold in kit form. The theme developed into the legendary Lotus 7, remaining in kit-car production as a Lotus until 1973, then being taken up by Caterham (see page 78), which still produces a much evolved version of this pulse-quickening pocket rocket. Meanwhile,

back in the 1950s, the tiny Lotus company was a frenzy of activity: its first single-seater appeared in 1956; then in 1958, the firm produced the lovely Elite, not only the first closed Lotus, but also the world's first road-going fibreglass monocoque and the first true Lotus road car. In 1960, another major milestone was reached when Stirling Moss won the Monaco Grand Prix in a privately-entered Lotus 18. Colin Chapman died in 1982, but the latest generation of Lotus cars – the Elise and the 340R – still bear the hallmarks of a Chapman Lotus, full of innovation with power-to-weight ratios that guarantee driving excitement and handling finesse to embarrass many a rival. Moreover, Lotus Engineering is a leading automotive consultancy, whose technical expertise is called upon by car makers the world over.

1969 Lotus 7, 1600cc engine, completely restored, c1,500 miles covered since, engine and gearbox rebuilt, new brakes and wheels, steering rack refurbished, rewired, chassis refurbished, new aluminium bodywork, resprayed in green and yellow, correct dashboard, interior retrimmed to original spec. using correct black 'basketweave' material, finished in green and yellow.
£14,000–16,000 H&H

1972 Lotus 7 S4, 1599cc, spaceframe chassis with steel side panels, all-fibreglass body, fitted with reconditioned engine, c600 miles covered since, finished in red, black interior, in need of tidying.
£3,750–4,500 H&H

▶ **1960 Lotus Elite S1,** 1216cc, overhead-camshaft Coventry-Climax engine, twin SU carburettors, reworked cylinder head, multi-branch stainless steel exhaust, remote brake servo, Koni dampers, completely restored 1990, finished in red.
£23,000–27,500 BKS

The pretty Elite won its class at Le Mans every year from 1959 to 1964.

Lotus Elite (1957–63)

Body style: Two-door, two-seat sports coupé.
Construction: Fibreglass monocoque.
Engine: Four-cylinder, overhead-camshaft Coventry Climax, 1216cc.
Power output: 75–105bhp at 6,100–6,800rpm.
Transmission: Four-speed manual MG or ZF gearbox.
Suspension: All-independent by wishbones and coil springs at front and MacPherson-type 'Chapman struts' at rear.
Brakes: Discs all-round (inboard at rear).
Top speed: 118mph.
0–60mph: 11.1 seconds.
Average fuel consumption: 35mpg.
Production: Approximately 988.
If ever a car was a marque landmark this is it.

The Elite was the first Lotus designed for road use rather than out-and-out racing, paving the way for a string of stunning sports and GT cars that, at the least, were always innovative. But the first Elite was much more than that. Its all-fibreglass construction – chassis as well as body – was a bold departure which, coupled with many other innovations, marked out the Elite as truly exceptional, and all the more so considering the small-scale operation that created it. What's more, its built-in Lotus race-breeding gave it phenomenal handling which, together with an unparallelled power-to-weight ratio, brought an almost unbroken run of racing successes. It also happens to be one of the prettiest cars of its era, in short, a superb GT in miniature.

Lotus Elan (1962–73)

Engine: Four-cylinder, double-overhead-camshaft Ford, 1588cc.
Power output: Up to 126bhp (Elan Sprint).
Transmission: Four- or five-speed manual.
Brakes: Discs all-round.
Top speed: 121mph (Elan Sprint).
0–60mph: 6.7 seconds (Elan Sprint).
Production: 12,224.

Colin Chapman's original Lotus Elite was an exquisite delicacy enjoyed by a very lucky few, but its successor, the Elan, was the small company's first really practical road-going package.

Little larger than a half-sucked boiled sweet and just as sticky when it came to gripping the road, the lithe fibreglass-bodied Elan could embarrass and bait much bigger-engined sports rivals on the road and track, thanks to its superb dynamics and inbuilt race-breeding. Over the years from 1962 to 1973, the little Lotus evolved into a very accelerative machine, culminating in the Elan Sprint, a 126bhp banshee. In the 1980s, there was much talk of how the Mazda MX-5 recreated the spirit of the original Elan. Well, the Elan – any Elan, in fact – had stronger acceleration than the latter-day pastiche.

1967 Lotus Elan S3, 1558cc, double-overhead-camshaft engine, fibreglass body, steel box-section backbone chassis, all-independent suspension, 112mph top speed, restored, good condition.
£8,500–9,500 HMM

1971 Lotus Elan Sprint, big-valve head, 1 family owner, 47,000 miles recorded, original condition.
£10,000–11,000 UMC

▶ **1973 Lotus Elan Sprint,** double-overhead-camshaft, 4-cylinder engine, 126bhp, 4-speed all-synchromesh gearbox, completely restored, new chassis, finished in red and white Gold Leaf Team Lotus colours, new black leather interior trim and upholstery, 35,600 miles recorded, excellent condition.
£10,500–12,000 H&H

LOTUS Model	ENGINE cc/cyl	DATES	CONDITION 1	2	3
Six		1953–56	£13,000+	£7,000+	£5,000+
Seven S1 Sports	1172/4	1957–64	£12,000+	£9,000+	£5,000+
Seven S2 Sports	1498/4	1961–66	£10,000+	£8,000+	£5,000+
Seven S3 Sports	1558/4	1961–66	£10,000+	£8,000+	£5,000+
Seven S4	1598/4	1969–72	£8,000	£5,000	£3,000
Elan S1 Convertible	1558/4	1962–64	£12,000+	£8,000	£4,500
Elan S2 Convertible	1558/4	1964–66	£12,000+	£7,000	£4,000
Elan S3 Convertible	1558/4	1966–69	£12,000+	£8,000	£5,000
Elan S3 FHC	1558/4	1966–69	£13,000	£7,000	£5,000
Elan S4 Convertible	1558/4	1968–71	£14,000+	£9,500	£7,000
Elan S4 FHC	1558/4	1968–71	£10,000+	£7,500	£5,000
Elan Sprint Convertible	1558/4	1971–73	£15,000+	£8,500+	£7,000
Elan Sprint FHC	1558/4	1971–73	£10,000+	£7,000	£6,000
Europa S1 FHC	1470/4	1966–69	£4,000+	£3,500	£2,000
Europa S2 FHC	1470/4	1969–71	£5,500+	£3,000	£2,000
Europa Twin Cam	1558/4	1971–75	£8,000	£6,000	£4,000
Elan +2S 130	1558/4	1971–74	£8,000	£5,000	£4,000
Elite S1 FHC	1261/4	1974–80	£3,500	£2,500	£1,500
Eclat S1	1973/4	1975–82	£3,500	£3,000	£1,500
Esprit 1	1973/4	1977–81	£6,500	£5,000	£3,000
Esprit 2	1973/4	1976–81	£7,000	£4,000	£2,500
Esprit S2.2	2174/4	1980–81	£7,000	£5,500	£3,000
Esprit Turbo	2174/4	1980–88	£10,000	£7,000	£4,000
Excel	2174/4	1983–85	£5,000	£3,000	£2,500

Prices vary with some limited-edition models and with competition history.

Lotus Elan +2 (1967–74)

Engine: Four-cylinder, double-overhead-camshaft, cast-iron block, aluminium head, 1558cc.
Power output: 118–126bhp.
Transmission: Four-speed manual; five-speed on 130-5 model.
Brakes: Discs all-round.
Top speed: 115+mph; 120+mph (+2S 130).
0–60mph: 8.5 seconds; 7.5 seconds (+2S 130).
Production: 3,300.

Patrick McGoohan drove a Lotus 7 in *The Prisoner*; Diana Rigg, as Emma Peel, drove a Lotus Elan in *The Avengers*; and Roger Moore was all at sea in an Esprit in *The Spy Who Loved Me* Bond caper. But there was one Lotus whose star never shone quite as brightly, the Elan for the family man. The '+2' stood for the two extra close-coupled seats in the rear, and if the original hedonistic baby two-seater Elan shouted that you were young, free and single, the Elan +2 meekly apologised for you – for being married and responsible, for having kids, and for not being sure that's what you wanted. With the Elan +2, Colin Chapman was aiming to spread the appeal of Lotus up market, on to the driveways of the posher

commuter belts. It was more refined and better trimmed than the baby Elan, but the +2 scarely approached the annoying and smug self-satisfaction of the Jaguar E-Type 2+2, the car for the married man who still swung like a bachelor. The other drawback of the Elan +2 was that it was only available as a fixed-head coupé. In truth, though, this elongated Elan possessed most of the pace, sizzling acceleration and race-bred handling of its smaller brother, but at nearly 2ft longer wasn't quite as agile. In 1969, it also became the first Lotus not to be available for home assembly, so the build quality of later versions was generally higher. Without doubt, the best of the bunch is the awkwardly named +2S 130-5 with the 126bhp, big-valve engine from the Elan Sprint and five-speed gearbox. The Elan +2 was built in far fewer numbers than the baby Elan, but the married-with-children stigma means that, car for car, they are considerably cheaper.
Elan fact: On cars supplied to the Press, the rev-limiter was adjusted from 6,500 to 6,850rpm to allow the Elan to reach 120mph and sometimes a bit more.

◄ **1973 Lotus Elan +2S 130,** 1558cc, double-overhead-camshaft, big-valve engine, 126bhp, restored at a cost of £20,000, new chassis, later 5-speed gearbox, finished in dark metallic blue and silver, Oatmeal interior.
£7,000–8,000 BKS

Launched in 1966 and based on the successful Elan, the +2 retained the former's backbone chassis, but had a longer wheelbase to make room for two occasional rear seats. Aimed at the enthusiast with a young family, the car featured an improved interior, electric windows, radio and alarm as standard. Build quality was improved with the +2S of 1968 – the first Lotus not offered in kit form – and then in 1971 came the +2S 130 with increased performance.

▶ **1972 Lotus Europa Twin Cam,** 1558cc, double-overhead-camshaft engine, completely restored, 25 miles covered since, Waxoyled, resprayed in red, black interior, 3 owners, 61,000 miles recorded.
£5,500–6,500 H&H

Lotus Europa (1966–75)

Colin Chapman's original intention with the Europa had been to produce a mid-engined car that would compete on price with the MG Midget. Well, he didn't quite pull it off. Instead, the price pitched it pretty much against the Lotus Elan, but it still bore the hallmarks of Chapman's genius, combining fabled finesse with stunning, almost outrageous looks. Handling was sensational and the steering, if well-sorted, razor sharp. That low-profile Kamm-tailed body was honed in the wind tunnel to produce a remarkably low drag co-efficient of 0.29. In short, it's an uncompromised sports car – but, of course, that means compromises. The ridiculous ventilation system and sliver of rear window were

hardly practical, and the flying buttresses all but obliterated what little rear vision there was. If you travel with more than a squash racket as luggage, you're in trouble. The Europa really came of age when the tad-underpowered Renault engine was replaced in 1971 with the Lotus-Ford twin-cam. Then, in 1972, came the Europa Special, fitted with a big-valve version of the Elan's twin-cam engine. Its 0–60mph time of 6.6 seconds and top speed of 123mph make it the number-one performance choice.
Europa fact: A limited edition of 100 John Player Special Europas was built by Lotus in the same black and gold colours as the F1 racing team.

1963 Ford Cortina Lotus Mk I, restored 1992, original aluminium bellhousing and differential, rear-suspension A-frame changed to later leaf-spring set-up, finished in white with green side flashes, black interior, in need of recommissioning following period of storage.
£5,750–7,000 BKS

Launched in 1963, the Cortina Lotus featured the Elan's 1.6 litre, Ford-based, twin-cam engine in the two-door bodyshell. The standard McPherson-strut independent front suspension was retained, with revised spring and damper rates, but the rear leaf springs were replaced by coil-spring/damper units, axle location being handled by twin trailing arms and an A-frame. The use of an aluminium differential casing proved a mixed blessing, the lightweight component proving far less oil-tight than the original. Reversion to Ford's standard leaf-sprung axle in 1964 cured the problem. Production ceased in 1966 with the introduction of the Mk II.

1963 Lotus 23B Sports Racer, engine uprated to full race spec., not raced since 1991, new bodywork, finished in dark green, red interior, correct historic papers, race-ready condition.
£28,000–32,000 BKS

Lotus made its reputation with small-capacity sports-racing cars, but after 1959 directed most of its energy into single-seaters and production cars. However, the company returned to sports racers in 1962 with the Mk 23, essentially a two-seat version of its highly successful Formula Junior cars which, in turn, were closely related to the F1 machines. From the start, the Lotus 23 was in a class of its own and was, beyond argument, the best small-capacity sports car in the world. The 23B had a stiffer and stronger spaceframe chassis. It was also the last sports racer that Lotus made in significant numbers.

1969 Lotus 61M Formula Ford, 1600cc engine, restored 1996, race-ready condition.
£13,000–14,500 Car

1967 Ford Cortina Lotus Mk II, 1558cc, double-overhead-camshaft, 4-cylinder engine, 106bhp, 108+mph top speed, new front wings, finished in white with green side flashes, very good mechanical condition.
£2,500–3,000 BRIT

The Mk II Cortina Lotus utilised the two-door bodyshell of the standard Ford saloon. It was built at Dagenham, whereas the earlier car had been assembled by Lotus at Cheshunt.

1956 Lotus 11 Le Mans, Coventry Climax engine, de Dion rear axle, 4-wheel disc brakes, lightweight aluminium bodywork, completely restored using all original parts, ex-Team Lotus car.
£45,000–55,000 HRL

1964 Lotus 11 Westfield, built by Westfield Sports Cars, 1275cc engine, fibreglass body, multi-tube spaceframe chassis.
£11,000–12,250 HMM

A model of a 1972 Lotus 72D, finished in the colours of Emerson Fittipaldi's 1972 World Championship-winning car.
£175–200 PC

Marcos

1969 Marcos 3 Litre, 2997cc, Ford V6 engine, spaceframe chassis, alloy wheels, fibreglass bodywork, good condition.
£6,500–7,500 HMM

1970 Marcos 3 Litre, 2997cc, Ford V6 engine, manual gearbox, heated windscreen, restored 1987 at a cost of £7,000, reconditioned engine, finished in red, grey leather interior.
£5,000–6,000 BKS

Maserati

When the five Maserati brothers formed a company to build cars under their own name, in 1926, they had already amassed an impressive collective track record in the automobile and engineering industries – manufacturing spark plugs, constructing race cars for Isotta-Fraschini and Diatto, working on aero engines, and racing cars and motorcycles. The impetus that caused them to become a manufacturer in their own right was a supercharged Grand Prix car designed for Diatto. When the latter went bankrupt, the car reverted to the Maserati brothers and led to the formation of the Maserati marque, which took as its insignia Neptune's trident, the symbol of Bologna where the brothers were based. The Maserati competition cars were a major force from the late 1920s through to the mid-1950s, even though the brothers had sold their interest in the firm in 1937. In 1957, Juan Manuel Fangio won the World Championship in a Maserati 250F, but that proved to be Maserati's mainstream competition swansong. A series of accidents at the Venezuelan Grand Prix destroyed all four Maserati cars entered in that race, and with top-flight competition becoming increasingly expensive, Maserati withdrew and concentrated its limited resources on sports racers and GTs. The first Maserati road car, the A6, had appeared a decade before at the 1947 Geneva show, but it was produced in very small numbers and was, in effect, a spin-off from the competition machines. With the withdrawal from competition, the firm could concentrate for the first time on true series-production road cars. The first of these 'Masers' was the 3500GT, and lots of memorable cars have followed, but for many enthusiasts the ultimate Maserati is the gorgeous Ghibli, rated by many as the most beautiful car in the world.

1955 Maserati A6G/54 Berlinetta, coachwork by Zagato, restored 1980s, fitted with electric fan, finished in red, grey interior, good condition throughout.
£170,000–190,000 BKS

1961 Maserati 3500GT Coupé, coachwork by Touring, 4-speed manual gearbox, wishbone-and-coil-spring independent front suspension, leaf-sprung live rear axle, 4-wheel disc brakes, Borrani wire wheels, tubular chassis frame, completely restored 1993, 300–400 miles covered since, new stainless steel exhaust, finished in blue with matching leather interior, very good to excellent condition throughout.
£23,000–26,000 BKS

1961 Maserati 3500GT Coupé, coachwork by Touring, 5-speed manual gearbox, wishbone-and-coil-spring independent front suspension, leaf-sprung live rear axle, tubular chassis frame, left-hand drive, partially restored 1989, uprated alternator electrics, finished in red, good condition.
£12,000–15,000 BKS

1963 Maserati 5000GT Coupé, 4935cc, double-overhead-camshaft V8 engine, 350bhp, 5-speed manual gearbox, 4-wheel disc brakes, finished in Azure blue, 1 of 33 built, mostly original, very good mechanical condition.
£65,000–75,000 RM

The 5000GT's engine was based on the quad-cam V8 of the 450S sports racer, but enlarged to 5 litres. Early cars used the engine virtually in race trim, with gear-driven cams and four Weber 451DM carburettors. Later, Lucas fuel injection, a five-speed gearbox and four-wheel disc brakes were added (early cars had drums at the rear). The last few cars had engines with chain-driven cams, marking the engine's transition from an out-and-out competition powerplant to one for fast road use, which appeared later in the Quattroporte, then the GT models of the 1960s and 1970s.

◄ **1967 Maserati Quattroporte,** coachwork by Frua, 4.2 litre, double-overhead-camshaft V8 engine, 260bhp, engine rebuilt, finished in dark metallic silver, Cognac leather upholstery, good condition.
£4,000–4,500 BKS

Introduced in 1964, the Quattroporte was Maserati's first high-performance saloon rather than a GT with four seats. When launched, it was the world's fastest four-door production saloon, having a top speed of 130mph.

► **1983 Maserati Quattroporte III,** coachwork by Italdesign, 4.9 litre, double-overhead-camshaft V8 engine, automatic transmission, finished in green, tan leather upholstery, 80,000 miles recorded, excellent condition throughout
£5,000–5,500 BKS

The first owner of this car was the late King Hassan II of Morocco, descendant of the prophet Mohammed and 17th sovereign of the Alaouite dynasty.

1966 Maserati Mistral Coupé, coachwork by Frua,
3.7 litre engine, 5-speed manual gearbox, Borrani wire
wheels, partially restored 1989/90, c2,000km covered since,
fitted with Weber carburettors, new radiator and exhaust
system, bare-metal respray, good condition throughout.
£11,500–13,000 BKS

The last of the classic straight-six Maseratis, the
Mistral was introduced in 1963. It was built in two-
seat coupé and spyder versions, with 3.5, 3.7 and
4 litre engines. A five-speed gearbox, disc brakes and
fuel injection were standard equipment; automatic
transmission and air conditioning were options.
Production ceased in 1970, by which time a total of
828 coupés and 120 spyders had been built.

1972 Maserati Mexico Coupé, coachwork by Vignale,
4.7 litre, double-overhead-camshaft V8 engine, 5-speed
ZF gearbox, Borrani wire wheels, electric windows,
completely restored late 1980s, finished in metallic
Sable, mustard Connolly hide interior, well maintained.
£9,000–10,000 BKS

1969 Maserati Mistral Spyder, 4 litre engine,
fuel injection, hard and soft tops, finished in red,
black interior, 1 of 120 built, minor paintwork blemishes,
otherwise very good condition.
£28,000–32,000 CGC

1967 Maserati Mexico Coupé, coachwork by Vignale,
5-speed ZF gearbox, 4-wheel disc brakes, Borrani wire
wheels, finished in silver, burgundy leather interior,
original Blaupunkt radio, good condition throughout.
£7,000–8,000 BKS

Effectively the replacement for the six-cylinder
3500GT and Sebring models, Maserati's four-seat
Mexico debuted in 1966. It was named in honour of
Cooper-Maserati's victory in the 1966 Mexican Grand
Prix and sported elegant Vignale coachwork.
The company's quad-cam V8 was employed for the
newcomer which, with 260bhp on tap, was good for
around 220km/h. Production ceased in 1973 after 250
cars had been built.

1968 Maserati Ghibli Coupé, coachwork by Ghia, 4.7 litre, double-overhead-camshaft V8 engine, tubular chassis
frame, completely restored at a cost of c£44,000, new windscreen, bare-metal respray in turquoise, brightwork
rechromed, interior renovated with new carpets and dashboard covering, original blue leather seats, side and back
cushions in good condition, 1st right-hand-drive car to leave the factory, excellent condition.
£20,000–25,000 BKS

The Ghibli debuted in late 1966. Named after a Sahara Desert wind, it rivalled the Ferrari Daytona for straight-
line performance – top speed was close to 170mph – while beating it on price and, arguably, looks.

▶ **1969 Maserati Ghibli Coupé,** coachwork by Ghia,
4.7 litre, double-overhead-camshaft V8 engine, 330bhp,
manual gearbox, partially restored, finished in silver,
retrimmed black leather interior, good condition throughout.
£15,000–18,000 BKS

Ghibli production ceased in 1973 after 1,149 coupé
and 125 spyder models had been built.

1972 Maserati Ghibli SS Spyder, coachwork by Ghia, 4.9 litre, double-overhead-camshaft V8 engine, 5-speed ZF manual gearbox, power steering, wire wheels, completely restored over 6 years, finished in black, matching Connolly hide interior, 'as new' condition.
£60,000–70,000 BKS

1972 Maserati Indy America, coachwork by Vignale, 4.9 litre, double-overhead-camshaft V8 engine, 335bhp, automatic transmission, 150+mph top speed, restored 1990, finished in red, light tan leather upholstery, good condition throughout.
£8,000–9,500 BKS

Maserati launched the Indy in 1968 and, with the Ghibli, it formed the backbone of the company's production into the early 1970s. While the Ghibli was a two-seater, and a rival to the Ferrari Daytona, the Indy was a generous 2+2 GT coupé and a natural competitor of the Aston Martin DBS and Ferrari 365 GT 2+2. The Indy, however, outsold both. It was built on a similar chassis to the Quattroporte, but was slightly shorter with a wider track.

1975 Maserati Merak, completely restored 1985–90, engine and gearbox rebuilt, bare-metal respray in red, black leather upholstery, 1 of only 50 right-hand-drive models built, original condition.
£8,500–10,000 BKS

Maserati followed its first mid-engined Bora supercar with the similar Merak. Launched in 1972, it had a 3 litre, 190bhp version of the quad-cam V6 designed for the Citroën SM. The French firm owned Maserati at the time, so the Merak also made use of the SM's transmission and excellent servo-assisted 4-wheel disc brakes. The unitary construction, all-independent suspension and impeccable handling mirrored those of the V8-engined Bora. The most successful Maserati of its day, the Merak remained in production until 1983.

1973 Maserati Indy America, coachwork by Vignale, 31,000km recorded, well maintained, 2 owners, excellent original condition.
£17,000–20,000 COYS

1974 Maserati Bora , coachwork by Italdesign, 4.9 litre, double-overhead-camshaft V8, 5-speed transaxle, all-independent double-wishbone suspension, engine rebuilt 1997, finished in red, black leather interior, well maintained.
£11,000–13,000 BKS

The mid-engined Bora was introduced in 1971 with Maserati's familiar 4.7 litre quad-cam V8, which was enlarged to 4.9 litres in 1973. It remained in production until 1978, by which time 571 had been built.

1988 Maserati Bi-Turbo SE Spyder, 2491cc, 18-valve, aluminium V6 engine, dual water-cooled turbochargers, sports exhaust, 5-speed ZF gearbox, power steering, split rims, full body kit, air conditioning, remote central locking, electric seats, windows, aerial and headrest adjustment, finished in black, beige leather interior, 36,000 miles recorded.
£8,000–9,000 H&H

Mercedes-Benz

In truth, Mercedes-Benz motor cars have only existed since 1926, following the merger of the separate Daimler (Mercedes) and Benz companies, although both can claim to have fathered the motor car. Working independently, both Karl Benz and Gottlieb Daimler produced petrol-engined road vehicles in 1886. In 1894, Benz's Velo became the world's first true production automobile. The name Mercedes was first used on a Daimler in 1899. When Benz, an early pace-setter in volume production, merged with the dynamic Daimler, the combination proved formidable. In the 1930s, the range of road cars was thoroughly comprehensive, and from 1934 to the outbreak of WWII, Mercedes-Benz dominated the Grand Prix scene along with its compatriot Auto Union. Following post-war reconstruction, Mercedes-Benz signalled to the world that it was back on top with the gorgeous 300SL Gullwing, the forerunner of modern supercars. Since then, the company has concentrated on producing upmarket executive saloons, sporting coupés and cabriolets, all formidably engineered. In most cases, Mercedes-Benz has shunned the merely voguish to produce some long-lived models, the designs of which have remained modern, while other manufacturers have adopted and dropped the latest styling fads. A prime example is the so-called 'pagoda-roof' SL-series cars produced from 1963 to 1971, never the absolute zenith of high fashion, but all the better for it. Although other contemporary sporting rivals aged quickly and soon looked outmoded, the design of these SLs is so crisp and fresh that it's difficult to believe that the youngest is now 30 years old.

 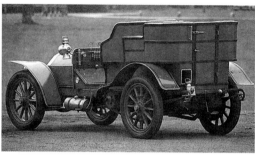

1904 Mercedes Simplex 28/32hp Four/Five-Seat Rear-Entrance Tonneau, 5.3 litres, gate-change gearbox, pressed-steel chassis, honeycomb radiator, restored, fitted with replica rear-entrance tonneau coachwork, unused since 1997, VCC dating certificate.
£260,000–290,000 BKS

This car was owned originally by a Plymouth timber merchant who donated it to the War Department for military use in 1914. Subsequently, it was sent to France, possibly bodied as a truck. Following the Armistice, the Mercedes was sold by the War Disposals Board to a farmer and butcher near Tavistock. He used it to transport pig swill from Gunnislake to his farm, but it was already in a badly neglected state and it completed only one trip before damaging its gearbox. It was relegated to a barn, where it was used to drive farm machinery. In the early 1970s, it was discovered in a sorry state, with a 6in-diameter sapling growing through it.

1934 Mercedes-Benz 500 Nürburg Tourer, 4.9 litre, sidevalve V8 engine, all-independent suspension by semi-elliptic leaf springs, unrestored, mostly original, engine completely overhauled, new hood, resprayed in black, black leather interior, excellent mechanical condition.
£125,000–140,000 BKS

Introduced in 1928, the Nürburg remained in production until 1939, which made it the most long-lived Mercedes-Benz model until then. Most examples received formal bodywork, but this car features rare and attractive open touring coachwork reminiscent of that seen on the Grosser 770K model.

◄ **1954 Mercedes-Benz 300B Saloon,** 2996cc, overhead-camshaft, 6-cylinder inline engine, twin Solex carburettors, 125bhp, 4-speed manual gearbox with column-change, all-independent coil-spring suspension with supplementary rear torsion bars, 4-wheel servo-assisted drum brakes, tubular cruciform chassis, recently refurbished at a cost of over £20,000, engine, steering and wiring overhauled, new clutch, fuel pump, fuel tank and stainless steel exhaust system, finished in black, red leather interior, original, excellent mechanical condition.
£8,500–10,000 COYS

1954 Mercedes-Benz 300S Coupé, 3 litre, 6-cylinder inline engine, 100bhp, 4-speed manual gearbox, tubular chassis, all-independent coil-spring suspension, 4-wheel servo-assisted drum brakes, sunroof, finished in Bordeaux red, cream interior, 1 of only 216 coupés built, good condition throughout.
£58,000–68,000 COYS

Aimed at the sports and grand touring market, the 300S was produced in low numbers, some 560 being manufactured between 1951 and 1955. Nevertheless, they were sought after, despite being three times more expensive than contemporary Cadillacs.

► **1957 Mercedes-Benz 300Sc Cabriolet,** 2996cc, overhead-camshaft, 6-cylinder engine, fuel injection, 175bhp, 4-speed manual gearbox with column-change, independent coil-spring front suspension, single-pivot rear swing-axle on coil springs, servo-assisted 4-wheel hydraulic drum brakes, left-hand drive, finished in black, red leather interior.
£224,000–248,000 C

MERCEDES-BENZ Model	ENGINE cc/cyl	DATES	CONDITION 1	2	3
300ABCD	2996/6	1951–62	£15,000	£10,000	£8,000
220A/S/SE Ponton	2195/6	1952–60	£10,000	£5,000	£3,000
220S/SEB Coupé	2915/6	1956–59	£11,000	£7,000	£5,000
220S/SEB Cabriolet	2195/6	1958–59	£28,000+	£18,000	£7,000
190SL	1897/4	1955–63	£20,000+	£15,000+	£10,000
300SL 'Gullwing'	2996/6	1954–57	£120,000+	£100,000	£70,000
300SL Roadster	2996/6	1957–63	£110,000+	£90,000	£70,000
230/250SL	2306/ 2496/6	1963–68	£14,000+	£10,000+	£7,000
280SL	2778/6	1961–71	£16,000	£12,000	£9,000
220/250SE	2195/ 2496/6	1960–68	£10,000	£7,000	£4,000
300SE	2996/6	1961–65	£11,000	£8,000	£6,000
280SE Convertible	2778/6	1965–69	£25,000	£18,000	£12,000
280SE V8 Convertible	3499/8	1969–71	£30,000+	£20,000	£15,000
280SE Coupé	2496/6	1965–72	£12,000	£8,000	£5,000
300SEL 6.3	6330/8	1968–72	£12,000	£7,000	£3,500
600 & 600 Pullman	6332/8	1964–81	£40,000+	£15,000	£8,000

1959 Mercedes-Benz 300D Four-Door Cabriolet, 3 litre, overhead-camshaft, 6-cylinder engine, fuel injection, 160bhp, hypoid-bevel final drive, electrically-controlled rear suspension ride height, oval-tube chassis, c106mph top speed, bodywork completely restored 1991, resprayed in Rolls-Royce ivory, interior trimmed in red leather with matching carpets, original radio, 71,715 miles recorded, very original, 1 of 65 cabriolets built, formerly owned by Jimmy Page, excellent condition.
£60,000–70,000 BKS

1959 Mercedes-Benz 300D Four-Door Cabriolet, 3 litre, overhead-camshaft, 6-cylinder engine, fuel injection, 160bhp, all-independent suspension, hypoid-bevel final drive, electrically-controlled rear suspension ride height, power steering, oval-tube chassis, restored 1999, finished in silver, blue leather interior, 1 of 65 cabriolets built.
£90,000–100,000 BKS

1960 Mercedes 190B Ponton Saloon, 1897cc, 65bhp, completely restored 1993, c3,700 miles since, finished in correct Mercedes off-white, original light grey interior, period Blaupunkt radio.
£3,750–4,500 BKS

The 190, introduced in 1956, was the first saloon powered by the new-generation overhead-camshaft, four-cylinder engine that had been shown in the 190SL of 1954.

◄ **1956 Mercedes-Benz 220S Saloon,** manual gearbox, stored for 20 years, clutch, brakes and steering overhauled, finished in grey, red interior, very good condition throughout.
£5,000–6,000 BKS

Along with the 190 and 219, the 220S saloon debuted in 1956. Like the contemporary 180, the trio featured unitary construction, all-independent suspension and 4-wheel drum brakes. Powered by a 100bhp version of the 219's 2195cc, overhead-camshaft, six-cylinder engine, the 220S was good for a top speed of around 160km/h. Apart from a power increase to 106bhp in 1957, it changed little during its comparatively short life, production ceasing in late 1959.

► **1959 Mercedes-Benz 220SE Cabriolet,** 2195cc, overhead-camshaft, 6-cylinder engine, Bosch mechanical fuel injection, 115bhp, 4-speed gearbox, all-independent suspension, recently restored, bare-metal respray, concours winner, excellent condition.
£60,000–70,000 RM

Mercedes-Benz 300SL Gullwing (1954–57)

Body style: Two-door, two-seat coupé.
Construction: Multi-tubular spaceframe with steel and alloy body.
Engine: Inline six-cylinder, overhead-camshaft, 2996cc.
Power output: 240bhp at 6,100rpm.
Transmission: Four-speed, all-synchromesh manual gearbox.
Suspension: All-independent by coil-springs; double wishbones at front, swing-axles at rear.
Brakes: Finned alloy drums.
Top speed: 135–165mph, depending on gearing.
0–60mph: 8.8 seconds.
0–100mph: 21.0 seconds.
Average fuel consumption: 18mpg.
Production: 1,400.

In 1952, Mercedes had stormed back into motorsport with a spaceframe-chassised car that didn't allow for conventional doors. Its engine was a development of the 3 litre engine of the 300-series saloons. This aluminium-bodied car was called the 300SL – 'SL' stood for *Super Leight* – and it was right straight out of the box. In its first race, the 1952 Mille Miglia, it finished second, snatched outright victory at the Berne Grand Prix, took a 1-2 at Le Mans, won at the Nürburgring, and finished the year with a 1-2 in the ultra-gruelling Carrera Panamericana Mexican road race. Mercedes had proved its point, and in 1954 turned its attention once more to Grand Prix goals. But the 300SL Gullwing was about to enter a new life, and New York sports car importer Max Hoffman was instrumental in Mercedes' decision to unleash the 300SL Gullwing as undoubtedly the fastest and most glamorous production car of its era. Hoffman was so convinced of the 300SL's appeal that he was willing to back his word with a large firm order – up to 1,000 – if Mercedes would build them. The road-going 300SL was still clearly based on the racer, although it was kitted out with a host of luxury refinements and its suspension was derived from the 330 saloons. Most importantly, it shared the spaceframe chassis of the racer, and that meant it retained its gullwing doors.

1955 Mercedes-Benz 300SL Gullwing, completely restored, 400km covered since, finished in silver, interior trimmed in red leather with matching carpets.
£110,000–125,000 BKS

▶ **1955 Mercedes-Benz 300SL Gullwing,** 2996cc, 6-cylinder engine, Bosch mechanical fuel injection, dry-sump lubrication, completely restored late 1980s, finished in dark grey, burgundy leather upholstery.
£145,000–160,000 COYS

1957 Mercedes-Benz 300SL Roadster, 2996cc, 6-cylinder engine, fuel injection, dry-sump lubrication, finished in Gunmetal grey, original red leather interior, correct Blaupunkt self-seeking radio, c40,000 miles recorded, superb condition.
£90,000–100,000 COYS

In 1957, Mercedes-Benz introduced the 300SL Roadster to meet the demand for a convertible version of the sports car and overcome the problem of the admittedly claustrophobic Gullwing cabin. It was to prove just as glamorous and even more successful than its sibling. The hood folded down to disappear beneath a deck lid behind the seats. With redesigned rear suspension that made handling safer and more predictable, and more luggage space, the roadster soon became the sports car of the emerging 'jet set'.

◀ **1957 Mercedes-Benz 190SL Roadster,** completely restored, 1,500 miles covered since, engine, gearbox and all other mechanical components rebuilt, new chrome, exhaust and mohair hood, bare-metal respray in silver, black leather upholstery, original clock and Becker Mexico radio, 'as new' condition throughout. **£28,000–32,000 BKS**

With a top speed of 105mph, a well-appointed cockpit, a smooth 105bhp engine and sensible luggage space, the 190SL was perfect for its market. It also had the kudos of sharing overall styling cues with its fabulous big sister, the 300SL Gullwing.

1959 Mercedes-Benz 190SL Roadster, 1897cc, 4-cylinder engine, twin Solex carburettors, 4-speed manual gearbox, hardtop, left-hand drive, finished in grey, red leather interior with matching carpets.
£19,000–22,000 Pou

A Mercedes-Benz dealer's domed enamel sign, 12in (30.5cm) diam.
£100–120 BLM

1960 Mercedes-Benz 190SL Roadster, 1897cc, 4-cylinder engine, twin Solex carburettors, 120bhp, 4-speed manual gearbox, all-independent coil-spring suspension, servo-assisted drum brakes, 115mph top speed, 0–60mph in 13 seconds, complete mechanical restoration, little use since, finished in red, cream interior.
£16,000–18,000 COYS

1961 Mercedes 190SL Roadster, 1897cc, 4-cylinder engine, 120bhp, restored, good condition.
£19,000–21,000 HMM

Mercedes-Benz 190SL (1955–63)

Engine: Four-cylinder, overhead-camshaft, 1897cc.
Power output: 105bhp at 5,700rpm.
Transmission: Four-speed, all-synchromesh manual gearbox.
Brakes: Hydraulic drums.
Top speed: 108mph.
0–60mph: 13.3 seconds.
Production: 25,881.
Price in 1956: £2,776.7s (including purchase tax).
No one doubts that the gorgeous Mercedes-Benz 300SL was quite simply the world's first genuine supercar, with its tricksy multi-tubular spaceframe chassis, scorching performance, sublime impracticality and drop-dead looks. Well, the 190SL roadster shared most of the 300SL's good looks – albeit diluted for modesty – but that's where any similarity ended. The 190SL could just about match

the performance of the MGA, was no match at all for the Austin-Healey 100/6 and couldn't hold a candle anywhere near the Jaguar XK140. Yet for the price of 'the poor man's 300SL', you could have bought three MGAs or a Jaguar XK140 and an Austin-Healey to go with it. It doesn't seem to make any sense at all, yet for its price the 190SL sold well, particularly in the USA. And that's where it *did* make sense. As a promenade sports car with a soft boulevard ride, it was just the thing for the well-heeled folk of the Hollywood Hills, who cared more about caché than mere cash. The fact that Grace Kelly drove a 190SL in the 1956 movie *High Society* was surely a perfect piece of automotive casting.
190SL fact: Ringo Starr owned a 190SL from 1972 to 1987. Subsequently, it sold at auction in 1997 for just over £28,000.

Mercedes-Benz Fin-tail Saloons (1959–68)

Body style/construction: Four-door monocoque.
Engines: Four- or six-cylinder, 1897–2996cc.
Power output: 55bhp (1897cc, diesel) to 185bhp (2996cc, six-cylinder).
Transmission: Four-speed manual or four-speed automatic; both column-change.
Brakes: Four-wheel drums on early models; front discs/rear drums from late 1963.
Top speed: 107mph (220SE, 2195cc, six-cylinder).
0–60mph: 12.8 seconds (220SE, 2195cc, six-cylinder).
Production: 1,001,796.
Price in 1959: £2,689.19s.2d (220SE).

The boffins at Bletchley Park may have broken the Enigma code, but it's doubtful whether they'd have been able to unravel the key to this most cryptic of Mercedes model ranges. In-house at Mercedes, but not the world at large, the four-door saloons were known as the W110, W111 and W112; on the road, they were ascribed model numbers from 190 to 300, to which were tagged an alphabet soup of letter suffixes. The result: as no one other than the most ardent aficionado would know that a W111 220SE was a car rather than a post code, they've

become known to their large flock of fans as 'fin-tails'. True, their modest rear wings seem almost guilty and possibly even ashamed that German engineering should be compromised by pandering to an American fad, but those fins are just about the one common element throughout this extended family. Now forget all that and recall the 1960s Austin Cambridge and Peugeot 404. There's an undeniable resemblance, and what those models were in Britain and France, the Mercedes fin-tails were in Germany, straightforward and largely unglamorous family saloons. Where BMC's models ran the gamut from humdrum Austin and Morris, through MG, Riley and Wolseley, up to the plush Vanden Plas 4 Litre R, the Mercedes range rose from Teutonic taxis chugging on diesel to a bechromed crescendo with a 3 litre autobahn armchair, the 300SE. Any further comparison is unfair, because although the Mercedes models were certainly superior, they were correspondingly much more expensive. And today, preferably in sinister diplomatic black, these fin-tail Mercs offer an undeniable touch of elegant cold-war chic.

1964 Mercedes-Benz 220SE Coupé, 2195cc, 6-cylinder engine, factory sunroof, air conditioning, finished in blue, tan interior, original Becker radio, well maintained, original condition.
£6,500–8,000 BRIT

1964 Mercedes-Benz 220S Saloon, 2195cc, 6-cylinder engine, all-independent suspension, front disc and rear drum brakes, 165km/h top speed, finished in black, brown leather interior.
£3,000–3,500 Pou

1965 Mercedes-Benz 220SEb Coupé, 2195cc, overhead-camshaft, 6-cylinder engine, fuel injection, 124bhp, automatic transmission with floor-change, independent front suspension, swing axle rear, front disc/rear drum brakes, 107mph top speed, sunroof, air conditioning, Parchment leather interior, burled chestnut dash, 1,874 miles recorded, original, excellent mechanical condition.
£20,000–23,000 RM

1967 Mercedes-Benz 300SE Cabriolet, US export model, left-hand drive, restored 1992, 1,200 miles covered since, finished in black, tan leather interior, new seat covers, 60,000 miles recorded, 1 of 253 coupé/cabriolet models built in 1967, good condition throughout.
£18,000–22,000 BKS

The 300SE saloon entered production in 1961, with coupé and cabriolet models arriving in the following year. It featured 600-type self-levelling air suspension, four-wheel disc brakes and, from August 1963, dual-circuit braking. From 1964, the 2996cc, Bosch fuel-injected, M189 six-cylinder engine produced 170bhp, an output sufficient to propel the luxuriously equipped 300SE to around 195km/h.

◄ **1966 Mercedes-Benz 250SE Coupé,** 2496cc, 6-cylinder engine, electronic ignition, electric sunroof, heated rear window, electric aerial, finished in metallic blue, cream leather interior, excellent condition throughout.
£11,000–13,000 BRIT

1970 Mercedes-Benz 600 Limousine,
air conditioning, picnic tables, refrigerator,
restored 1986, finished in metallic Sand, brown leather
interior, very good condition throughout.
£25,000–30,000 BKS

1975 Mercedes-Benz 600 Pullman Limousine, finished
in black, rear sunroof, interior trimmed in cream leather,
division, cocktail bar, intercom, single rear seats,
completely original, 16,500km recorded, some wear to
interior, otherwise very good condition throughout.
£55,000–60,500 BKS

◀ **1965 Mercedes-Benz 230SL,** 2308cc, overhead-
camshaft, 6-cylinder engine, fuel injection, 170bhp,
4-speed automatic transmission, independent front
suspension by coil springs and double wishbones,
swing-axle rear, 120mph top speed, 0–60mph in
10.7 seconds, finished in blue, grey leather interior,
excellent condition throughout.
£22,000–25,000 BKS

The Mercedes-Benz *Super Leicht* series was
the successor to the fabulous 300SL, but was
deliberately less exotic. The latter had been a
flagship on which the company had made little profit;
its replacement had to earn its keep. This particular
car was delivered new to John Lennon.

▶ **1966 Mercedes-Benz
230SL,** 2308cc, engine
rebuilt, resprayed in red
1995, new hood,
brightwork rechromed,
new external trims,
black interior trim, unused
for 2 years, very good
condition throughout.
£8,500–10,000 H&H

1967 Mercedes-Benz 250SL, automatic transmission, factory hardtop, partially restored 1997, resprayed in Old
English white, black interior, c38,500 miles recorded, good condition.
£11,000–13,000 BKS

First produced in 1966, the 250SL had the same bodyshell as the 230SL, which it replaced. Minor
improvements were made to the interior, but the major differences were the new 2.5 litre, six-cylinder engine
and disc brakes instead of drums at the rear. The larger engine improved flexibility and responsiveness,
although the car's 120mph top speed remained the same. It was built for just one production year before
being superseded by the 280SL. Christened 'pagoda roof' after the distinctive hardtop shape, the SL models
were among the best-loved sports-tourers of their day.

1969 Mercedes-Benz 280SL, manual gearbox, hardtop, left-hand drive, older bodywork restoration, resprayed in silver, original red leather interior, very good condition throughout.
£11,000–13,000 BKS

The last of a popular and very successful line that began with the 230SL of 1963, the 280SL was introduced in 1967. Although similar to that of the preceding 250SL, the 280's overhead-camshaft, six-cylinder engine was entirely new. Maximum power of the fuel-injected unit was up from 150 to 180bhp, and while the 280's 190+km/h top speed was no greater, it was significantly quicker off the mark than the 250. Otherwise the 280 was virtually identical mechanically to its predecessor.

◄ **1984 Mercedes 280SL,** finished in red, beige interior, rear seats, 59,000 miles recorded, 2 owners, good condition.
£15,000–16,500 SJR

1970 Mercedes-Benz 280SE Cabriolet, 3.5 litre, overhead-camshaft V8 engine, 200bhp, automatic transmission with column-change, air conditioning, electric windows, 127mph top speed, 0–60mph in 9.5 seconds, resprayed 1986 in Anthracite, dark grey interior, 64,505 miles recorded, good condition.
£45,000–50,000 BKS

1970 Mercedes-Benz 280SE Cabriolet, 3.5 litre V8 engine, automatic transmission, air conditioning, electric windows, new hood, finished in metallic silver, original Bordeaux leather interior, 53,500km recorded, very good condition.
£30,000–35,000 BKS

Mercedes-Benz's 3.5 litre V8 engine debuted in 1969 in the 280SE coupé/cabriolet and the 300SEL saloon. An over-square design featuring a cast-iron block and aluminium cylinder heads – each equipped with an overhead camshaft – the all-new power unit produced 200bhp courtesy of Bosch electronic fuel injection and transistorised ignition. Thus equipped, the 280SE was good for 200km/h, with 100km/h attainable in 9.5 seconds.

► **1971 Mercedes-Benz 280SE Cabriolet,** 3.5 litre V8 engine, fuel injection, transistorised ignition, 200bhp, 4-speed automatic transmission, independent coil-spring front suspension, swing-axle rear, 4-wheel disc brakes, air conditioning left-hand drive, finished in dark brown with matching hood, Cognac leather interior, 2 owners.
£43,000–47,500 C

1971 Mercedes-Benz 280SE Coupé, 3.5 litre, overhead-camshaft V8 engine, electronic fuel injection, transistorised ignition, 200bhp, air conditioning, electric windows, restored 1991, finished in metallic red, beige leather interior, good condition throughout.
£17,000–20,000 BKS

◄ **1972 Mercedes-Benz 280SEL Saloon,** 4500cc V8 engine, finished in brown, brown leather interior, 1 owner, excellent condition.
£9,000–11,000 BRIT

1985 Mercedes-Benz 230CE Coupé, 2299cc, electric sunroof, electric windows, central locking, cruise control, finished in blue with matching interior trim, 47,000 miles recorded, excellent condition throughout.
£5,000–6,000 H&H

1986 Mercedes-Benz 280CE Coupé, 2746cc, automatic transmission, factory sunroof, alloy wheels, finished in Thistle green, green interior trim, 92,000 miles recorded, 2 owners.
£4,250–5,000 H&H

▶ **1972 Mercedes-Benz 350SL,** all-independent suspension, 4-wheel disc brakes, 130mph top speed, factory hardtop, new water pump, front brakes overhauled, resprayed in green, beige upholstery.
£5,000–6,000 BKS

Introduced in 1971 as a replacement for the popular 230/250/280SL family, the 350SL was larger and heavier than its predecessors, although its 200bhp, 3.5 litre V8 more than offset the increase in bulk. Production of the 350 ceased in 1980, but the SL line continued in the form of the similar 380SL.

1978 Mercedes-Benz 350SL, 3499cc V8 engine, automatic transmission, alloy wheels, hard and soft tops, finished in red, tan interior trim, 64,000 miles recorded, paintwork in excellent condition.
£8,500–10,000 H&H

◀ **1973 Mercedes-Benz 350SLC,** 3.5 litre V8, automatic transmission, left-hand drive, good condition.
£1,000–1,200 BARO

▶ **1986 Mercedes-Benz 420SL,** 4196cc V8 engine, 218bhp, hard and soft tops, finished in Anthracite, black leathercloth interior with check cloth inserts, 3 owners, good condition.
£13,000–14,500 BRIT

A continuation of the line of SL sports models, the 420SL replaced the 380SL during 1985.

1981 Mercedes-Benz 450SL, 4520cc, alloy wheels, recent engine overhaul, new exhaust and new chrome at a cost of c£5,000, finished in cream, black interior trim, very good condition throughout.
£8,000–9,000 H&H

1978 Mercedes-Benz 450SLC, restored over 5 years, new gearbox, resprayed in Cypress green, new Moss green velour upholstery.
£3,000–3,500 BKS

1979 Mercedes-Benz 450SLC, 4520cc V8 engine, finished in Inca red, cream leather interior trim, bodywork in good condition.
£3,000–3,500 BRIT

1979 Mercedes-Benz 450SEL Saloon, 6.9 litre V8 engine, hydro-pneumatic self-levelling suspension, 140mph top speed, 0–60mph in 7 seconds, left-hand drive, finished in metallic gold, tan leather interior, original Becker Mexico radio, climate control, cruise control.
£3,000–3,500 BKS

First shown in 1974, the 450SEL filled a gap at the top of the Mercedes-Benz range left by the departure of the 300SEL. The newcomer employed the long-wheelbase bodyshell of the larger S-class, which was fitted with an enlarged version of the overhead-camshaft V8 engine found in its predecessor and the 600 models.

◄ **1979 Mercedes-Benz 450SEL,** 6834cc V8 engine, self-levelling suspension, air conditioning, heat-absorbing glass, finished in silver, black leather upholstery, good condition throughout.
£4,000–5,000 BRIT

► **1983 Mercedes-Benz 500SEC Convertible,** 5 litres, automatic transmission, chromed alloy wheels, power-assisted hood, air conditioning, left-hand drive, finished in metallic blue, grey leather interior trim, electric seats, 83,000 miles recorded, excellent condition throughout.
£7,000–8,000 H&H

Originally a coupé, this 500SEC was turned into a convertible in the USA.

◄ **1984 Mercedes-Benz 500SEC Coupé,** 5 litre, overhead-camshaft V8, uprated engine management system, automatic transmission, refurbished, resprayed in black.
£11,500–13,000 S

The first owner of this car was F1 World Champion Ayrton Senna.

Mercer

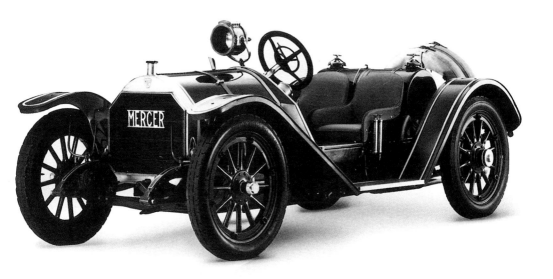

1912/13 Mercer Model 35J Raceabout, restored 1996, Rayfield racing carburettor, single wet-plate clutch with racing spider taper cone, new wings, bonnet, dashboard and seats to the original style, original radiator, Jasco fuel tank with quick-release fillers, original instruments, pedals, foot-rests, exhaust cut-out and brass fittings, Rushmore swivel spotlamp, finished in dark burgundy, chestnut and tan Connolly hide upholstery.
£105,000–120,000 BKS

The Mercer Raceabout was the first mass-produced sports car to be equally at home on road and track. Powered by a 300cu.in T-head engine, it featured high-lift camshafts and a relatively high compression ratio. Despite a modest 30–35bhp rating, the engine combined with other design features to create a car of outstanding performance. Not an ounce was wasted in the car's construction, giving a power-to-weight ratio second to none, while the low-slung chassis contributed to superb handling. Racing successes became almost a matter of course between 1911 and 1915, and included the 1911 AAA Stock Car Championship, second place in the 1912 Vanderbilt Cup, third place in the 1912 Indy 500, second place in the 1913 Indy 500 and victory in the 1914 American Grand Prix.

MG

The origins of MG date back to 1923, when Cecil Kimber, general manager of Morris Garages in Oxford, attached a stylish two-seat sporting body to a standard Morris chassis to create the first MG (the initials being taken from 'Morris Garages'). Until the outbreak of WWII, MG remained a specialist marque, rather than a real volume producer, creating a string of cars that offered the sporting driver affordable performance.

In 1935, the company was incorporated into Morris, later to become part of BMC and British Leyland, with an ever increasing influence on MG products. Nevertheless, for many years MG managed to keep its distinct sporting identity with memorable cars like the T-series Midgets, the pretty MGA, world-beating MGB and the Midget. The low point was the 1980s, when the MG octagon badge was debased by being tacked on to Montegos and Maestros, and for a while it looked as though the marque would fade away. Yet in 1992, the marque's renaissance began with the RV8, an update of the original MGB, and has now gathered real momentum with the capable little MGF.

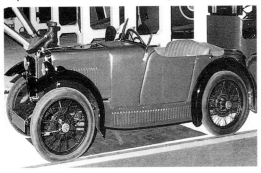

◄ **1929 MG M-Type Midget,** completely restored, finless brake drums, correct rear-hinged doors, early-pattern hood frame, double-duck hood, finished in brown, tan fabric upholstery, white-faced instruments, stored since 1996, 1 of the first 100 cars built, excellent condition throughout.
£8,000–10,000 BKS

With the introduction of the M-Type Midget in 1929, Cecil Kimber single-handedly created the market for small, cheap sports cars. His new baby was based on the contemporary Morris Minor and featured pretty, boat-tailed coachwork by Carbodies. The 847cc, overhead-camshaft, four-cylinder engine was derived from that of the Wolseley Ten and was mated to a three-speed crash gearbox.

1933 MG J2 Midget, 847cc, recently restored, 1,175 miles covered since, all mechanical components rebuilt, new ash framing and body tub, brightwork and interior trim refurbished, finished in correct Ulster and Dublin green, green interior trim.
£16,000–18,000 H&H

▶ **1936 MG TA Midget,** 1250cc, finished in red, black interior trim, good condition throughout.
£7,500–9,000 H&H

1946 MG TC Midget, 1250cc, 4-cylinder engine, restored c1988, 3,500 miles covered since, finished in red, original specification with matching numbers, very good condition.
£14,000–16,000 BRIT

In 1936, the T-series Midget was introduced to replace the overhead-camshaft P-Type. The new model was altogether larger, while the engine was a 1292cc unit of Morris Ten origin. The TA, as the model was known, was produced until 1939, when the TB took its place. The latter was similar in appearance, but its engine displaced 1250cc. This engine, the immortal XPAG, was destined to power all subsequent MGs until 1955. The TC was hastily put into production in October 1945, only months after the cessation of hostilities, and was very similar to the short lived pre-war TB. In the austere post-war times, 'export or die' was the order of the day, and the TC won the hearts of many enthusiasts in the USA, achieving phenomenal success in competition. The TC remained in production until 1949, by which time 10,000 had been built.

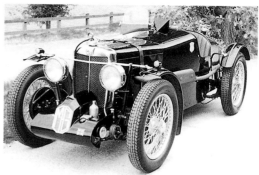

1934 MG Q-Type Competition Replica, 850cc engine, new counterbalanced Phoenix crankshaft with 83mm stroke, Carillo conrods, original Marshall J100 supercharger, pre-selector gearbox, correct instruments including large Jaeger rev-counter, accurate replica Q-type bodywork.
£30,000–33,000 BKS

Only eight Q-Types were built between May and September 1934. With 113bhp and a best Brooklands outer-circuit lap of 122mph, the Q-Type represents an exciting club racing car today. Equally at home on the open road, it is one of the more practical of the prized competition MGs, being capable of transporting two people in reasonable comfort and providing the option of pump or racing fuel.

◀ **1935 MG PB,** 847cc, restored over 20 years, 145 miles covered since, engine rebuilt, new water manifold and SU fuel pump, new running gear and braking systems, chassis refurbished, new bodywork and ash framing, new hood, sidescreens, tonneau cover and hood bag, new steering wheel, instruments reconditioned, finished in red, light tan interior, excellent condition.
£17,500–20,000 H&H

MG Milestones

1923	Cecil Kimber, the general manager of Morris Garages in Oxford, introduces his first special bodies on standard Morris chassis.
1928	MG Car Company formed.
1935	Lord Nuffield sells his privately held shares in the MG Car Company to Morris Motors Limited.
1955	MGA roadster launched.
1961	MGA production tops 100,000.
1962	MGB roadster launched.
1967	MGB GT fixed-head coupé launched.
1968	MG, with the rest of BMC, becomes part of British Leyland.
1980	BL discontinues MG sports cars; badge applied to saloons.
1992	Return of MG sports cars with RV8.
1995	MGF launched at Geneva motor show in March, first deliveries in August.
1996	10,000th MGF built in July.

MG TC/TD/TF Midgets (1945–55)

Engine: Four-cylinder, 1250cc (1466cc, TF 1500).
Power output: 54–57bhp (63bhp, TF 1500).
Top speed: 75–80+mph (85+mph, TF 1500)
0–60mph: 19–22 seconds (18+ seconds, TF 1500).
Even at the launch of the TC in September 1945, MG's Midget theme was pretty well mature, if not pushing middle age. The two-seat TC was a make-over of the pre-war TB, itself an update of the 1935 TA, which carried genes dating back to the original M-Type Midget of 1929. In effect, the post-war TC Midget was a brand-new vintage sports car. Yet it took off, spearheading MG's export trail around the world and particularly to the USA. I suppose that makes the TC the first branded product in the Britain-as-Heritage-Theme-Park souvenir shop. In any case, the TC sold in greater numbers than any previous MG, and two-thirds of the 10,000 built

went abroad, even though they were only produced in right-hand drive. In 1950, the winning formula was warmed over slightly to create the TD, with rack-and-pinion steering, a few extra bhp from the 1250cc engine and independent front suspension. The TD, the first MG available in left-hand drive, sold 29,664, again most going abroad. The final fling was the restyled TF, which paid passing lip service to modernity with a lower bonnet line, raked grille and headlamps blended into the wings. In its last year, the TF received a 1500cc engine, but with falling demand – 9,600 TFs were built – the theme was played out in terms of volume sales. Looked at differently, if they'd kept making it, the T-series could have become another Morgan – but then we would never have had the pretty MGA or world-beating MGB.

1947 MG TC Midget, 1250cc, overhead-valve, 4-cylinder engine, 54bhp, c80mph top speed, completely restored to original specification 1990, finished in cream, cream and brown interior, excellent condition throughout.
£11,500–13,000 BKS

1951 MG TD Midget, 1250cc, finished in red, original specification in all major respects.
£7,500–9,000 BKS

The TD Midget of 1949 was the penultimate model in the T-series cars. It combined features from the previous TC Midget and the Y-Type saloon, having a coachbuilt body on a wooden frame in the best vintage tradition, but coil-spring independent front suspension instead of the traditional leaf springs. Smaller pressed-steel wheels were the most obvious distinguishing feature, but there was no mistaking its MG pedigree, which was reflected in its performance, handling and value for money. Top speed was in the region of 80mph, 30mpg was possible, and the car would cruise comfortably at around 60mph.

1951 MG TD Midget, 1250cc, 4-cylinder engine, 4-speed manual gearbox, restored 1992–93, 3,000 miles covered since, engine reconditioned, MGA differential, new electrical equipment, new ash body frame, resprayed in black, new beige interior trim.
£11,500–13,000 H&H

Auction prices

Miller's only includes cars declared sold. Our guide prices take into account the buyer's premium, VAT on the premium, and the extent of any published catalogue information relating to condition and provenance. To identify cars sold at auction, cross-refer the source codes at the ends of photo captions with the Key to Illustrations on page 330.

1951 MG TD Midget, 1250cc engine, independent front suspension, rack-and-pinion steering, restored 1988, unused since, finished in red, black interior.
£9,500–11,000 BKS

1953 MG TD II Midget, 1250cc engine, independent front suspension, rack-and-pinion steering, resprayed in green, tonneau and sidescreens, unused since 1968, in need of recommissioning, bodywork in very good condition.
£9,500–11,000 BKS

1954 MG TF Midget, 1250cc, finished to special order when new in Riley metallic green, hood, tonneau and sidescreens, fewer than 48,000 miles from new, 3 owners, completely original, paintwork in good condition apart from minor cosmetic blemishes.
£11,500–13,000 BKS

1954 MG TF Midget, 1250cc, 4-cylinder engine, stainless steel exhaust system, extensively refurbished, bare-metal respray in red, new hood and sidescreens, interior retrimmed in red, very good mechanical condition.
£12,500–14,000 BRIT

Originally conceived as a stop-gap while the MGA was being developed, the TF was effectively a facelifted TD. Despite a cool reception at its launch (the TF was considered far too old-fashioned in the face of sleek newcomers, such as the Triumph TR2 and Austin-Healey 100), it went on to become one of the most revered of all MGs. In all, 9,600 were produced, most going overseas.

1954 MG TF Midget, 1250cc, 4-cylinder engine, left-hand drive, finished in silver, black leather upholstery.
£10,000–12,000 COYS

► **1955 MG TF 1500 Midget,** 63bhp, restored late 1980s, finished in red, unused for 12 months.
£17,000–19,000 BKS

Initially, BMC exported the TF 1500 to the USA in the summer of 1954, the UK market having to wait until November for the first deliveries. Registered in January 1955, this TF 1500 is therefore one of the first home-market right-hand-drive cars to be produced.

MG Model	ENGINE cc/cyl	DATES	CONDITION 1	2	3
14/28	1802/4	1924–27	£26,000	£18,000	£10,000
14/40	1802/4	1927–29	£25,000	£18,000	£10,000
18/80 Mk I/Mk II/Mk III	2468/6	1927–33	£40,000	£28,000	£20,000
M-Type Midget	847/4	1928–32	£11,000	£9,000	£7,000
J-Type Midget	847/4	1932–34	£15,000	£12,000	£10,000
J3 Midget	847/4	1932–33	£18,000	£14,000	£12,000
PA Midget	847/4	1934–36	£13,000+	£10,000	£8,000
PB Midget	936/4	1935–36	£15,000	£10,000	£8,000
F-Type Magna	1271/6	1931–33	£22,000	£18,000	£12,000
L-Type Magna	1087/6	1933–34	£26,000	£18,000	£12,000
K1/K2 Magnette	1087/6	1932–33	£35,000	£30,000	£20,000
N-Series Magnette	1271/6	1934–36	£30,000	£28,000	£20,000
TA Midget	1292/4	1936–39	£13,000+	£12,000	£9,000
SA 2 litre	2288/6	1936–39	£22,000+	£18,000	£15,000
VA	1548/4	1936–39	£12,000	£8,000	£5,000
TB	1250/4	1939–40	£15,000	£11,000	£9,000

Value will depend on body style, history, completeness, racing history, the addition of a supercharger and originality.

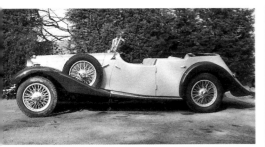

1939 MG SA Tourer, coachwork by Charlesworth, 2322cc, finished in two-tone blue, beige trim, paintwork in need of refurbishment, otherwise good condition.
£13,500–15,000 H&H

Approximately 90 SA tourers were made, with a variety of body styles. About ten are known to survive.

1950 MG YA Saloon, 1250cc, 4-cylinder engine, finished in green, original green leather interior, 53,282 miles recorded, very good mechanical condition.
£3,750–4,500 BRIT

Originally, MG had intended launching the YA saloon in 1940 as the MG Ten, powered by the 1250cc XPAG engine, which had debuted in 1939 in the TB Midget. However, the outbreak of war curtailed production, and it was not until the spring of 1947 that the model was introduced. It was the first production MG to utilise independent front suspension, and it shared many components with the Series E Morris Eight. It was particularly well finished and offered high quality in a compact package. In 1951, the model evolved into the YB which, although outwardly virtually identical, had such modifications as a front anti-roll bar and smaller-diameter wheels to improve handling. By 1953, however, the model had begun to look particularly dated and yielded place to the ZA Magnette.

1948 MG YT Tourer, 1250cc, original right-hand drive, restored early 1990s, 500 miles covered since, finished in red, new red Connolly hide interior at a cost of £3,500, excellent condition throughout.
£10,500–12,000 H&H

The YT tourer was derived from the YA saloon and TD Midget – it had the former's chassis, the latter's engine and four-seat open bodywork. Only 877 were produced, and although all of them were exported, a considerable number went to Commonwealth countries in right-hand-drive configuration. About 170 YTs are known still to exist.

1957 MGA Roadster, 1489cc, 4-cylinder engine, completely restored 1991, stainless steel exhaust system, new chassis, finished in red, serviceable red vinyl hood and sidescreens, red leatherette interior trim, good mechanical condition.
£7,500–9,000 BRIT

Introduced in late 1955 to replace the TF Midget, the MGA was the first modern MG sports car. It featured the BMC B-series engine within its curvaceous and aerodynamic bodywork. The MGA was to remain in production until 1962 and undergo two upgrades of engine, while a twin-cam version was also produced between 1958 and 1960.

MGA (1955–62)

Body styles: Two-seat roadster and fixed-head coupé.
Engine: Four-cylinder, overhead-valve, 1489, 1588 and 1622cc.
Power output: 72–108bhp.
Transmission: Four-speed manual.
Steering: Rack-and-pinion.
0–60mph: 13–15.5 seconds.
Top speed: 95–114mph.
With its simple, smooth lines, the MGA seems the epitome of a 1950s traditional British sports car, just the thing to complement the cravat, corduroys and sports jacket. But back in 1955, it seemed unsportingly civilised to those MG die-hards who thought MGs should have separate wings, running boards and fewer creature comforts than an Outward Bound course. Apart from pert looks – a little like a scaled-down Jaguar XK120 – and lively handling, the MGA had another thing going for it: it was cheaper than either the rival Austin-Healey 100 or Triumph TR3. The original 1955 MGA was

fitted with BMC's rugged B-series 1489cc engine, which eventually grew to 1622cc. The MGA 1600 of 1959 also introduced front disc brakes to the standard models, but most exotic of all was the short-lived Twin Cam, which offered 114mph and 4-wheel disc brakes to stop it. Only 2,111 of these fast, but temperamental, machines were built. Of the 101,000 MGAs built between 1956 and 1962, a staggering 81,000 were exported to America. Although that makes it rare compared with the MGB, the MGA is still eminently practical and usable. Its separate-chassis structure is a simpler proposition than the monocoque MGB, and another bonus is that so many parts – including the unburstable B-series engine – were shared with other vehicles under the Morris-BMC-Nuffield banner.
Pick of the bunch: For more go and whoa, and extra refinement, go for later 1600 models; the fast and fragile Twin Cam is strictly for enthusiasts whose fingers have mutated into socket sets.

► **1958 MGA Roadster,** 1489cc, 4-cylinder engine, 72bhp, c100mph top speed, restored, finished in blue, black interior trim.
£8,000–9,000 BRIT

1959 MGA Roadster, uprated with later 1600cc 4-cylinder engine, new clutch, wire wheels, finished in white, red interior trim, excellent condition throughout.
£8,500–10,000 S

1958 MG Magnette ZB Varitone, completely restored, stainless steel exhaust system, Minilite alloy wheels, bare-metal respray in original burgundy and cream, new interior trim and carpets.
£2,750–3,250 BARO

The Varitone offered a little individual styling to the Wolseley 4/44-based Magnette, its two-tone paint finish and waistline chrome strip making the car look far lower and sleeker than the monotone standard model. The ZB was said to be the best handling sports saloon of its day, and even now it is capable of quite reasonable performance.

1960 MGA Roadster, 1600cc, 4-cylinder engine, 80bhp, coil-spring independent front suspension, disc wheels, finished in Dove grey, black hood, red interior, stored for some years, in need of refurbishment.
£3,500–4,000 BKS

MG Model	ENGINE cc/cyl	DATES	CONDITION 1	2	3
TC Midget	1250/4	1946–49	£13,000	£11,000	£7,000
TD Midget	1250/4	1950–52	£13,000	£9,000	£5,000
TF Midget	1250/4	1953–55	£15,000	£13,000	£8,000
TF 1500 Midget	1466/4	1954–55	£16,000	£14,000	£9,000
YA/YB	1250/4	1947–53	£5,500+	£2,750	£1,500
Magnette ZA/ZB	1489/4	1953–58	£3,500	£2,000	£500
Magnette Mk III/IV	1489/4	1958–68	£3,500	£1,200	£350
MGA 1500 Roadster	1489/4	1955–59	£12,000+	£7,000	£4,000
MGA 1500 FHC	1489/4	1956–59	£8,000	£6,000	£3,000
MGA 1600 Roadster	1588/4	1959–61	£13,000	£9,000	£4,500
MGA 1600 FHC	1588/4	1959–61	£7,000	£5,000	£3,000
MGA Twin Cam Roadster	1588/4	1958–60	£18,000	£12,000	£9,000
MGA Twin Cam FHC	1588/4	1958–60	£14,000	£9,000	£7,000
MGA 1600 Mk II Roadster	1622/4	1961–62	£13,000	£10,000	£4,000
MGA 1600 Mk II FHC	1622/4	1961–62	£9,000	£7,000	£3,000
MGB Mk I	1798/4	1962–67	£7,000	£4,000	£1,200
MGB GT Mk I	1798/4	1965–67	£5,000	£3,500	£1,000
MGB Mk II	1798/4	1967–69	£7,500	£4,000	£1,500
MGB GT Mk II	1798/4	1969	£4,500	£2,500	£850
MGB Mk III	1798/4	1969–74	£6,500	£4,000	£1,100
MGB GT Mk III	1798/4	1969–74	£4,500	£2,500	£1,000
MGB Roadster (rubber bumper)	1798/4	1975–80	£6,000	£4,500	£1,200
MGB GT	1798/4	1975–80	£5,000	£3,000	£1,000
MGB Jubilee	1798/4	1975	£5,000	£3,000	£1,200
MGB LE	1798/4	1980	£8,500	£4,750	£2,250
MGB GT LE	1798/4	1980	£6,000	£3,750	£2,000
MGC	2912/6	1967–69	£8,000	£6,500	£4,000
MGC GT	2912/6	1967–69	£7,000	£5,000	£2,000
MGB GT V8	3528/8	1973–76	£9,000	£6,000	£3,000
Midget Mk I	948/4	1961–62	£4,000	£2,000	£850
Midget Mk II	1098/4	1962–66	£3,000	£2,000	£850
Midget Mk III	1275/4	1966–74	£3,200	£2,000	£850
Midget 1500	1491/4	1975–79	£3,000	£2,000	£850

All prices are for British right-hand-drive cars. Deduct 10–15% for left-hand-drive versions, even if converted to right-hand drive.

MG Midget (1961–79)

Construction: Unitary, all-steel.
Engine: Four-cylinder, overhead-valve, 948, 1098, 1275 and 1493cc.
Power output: 47–65bhp.
Transmission: Four-speed manual.
Top speed: 85–100+mph.
0–60mph: 12–20 seconds.
Production: 222,526 (plus 80,363 Austin-Healey Sprite versions).
Price in 1961: £679.

When it comes to breezy budget motoring, about the only thing that matches the MG Midget is the Austin-Healey Sprite, for apart from badging, trim and instruments, they're the same thing (the Mk I 'Frogeye' Sprite, though, was only produced as an Austin-Healey). The Midget is a compelling classic cocktail for the cost conscious – in fact, about the only cheaper way of enjoying fresh-air on four wheels is probably to buy a skateboard. Midgets have a massive following, with more than 200,000 built up to 1979, and that means there's tremendous club support, a well-established and competitive spares and remanufacturing industry, and a mature network of established marque specialists and restorers. Better still, the 'Spridget', as the Midget/Sprite models are often called, is a

BMC parts-bin special based on the mechanicals and running gear from the likes of the million-selling Morris Minor and Austin A35. If the body's riddled with rust, you can also get a complete new bodyshell from Rover's subsidiary, British Motor Heritage.
What to watch: Particular points include the inner and outer sills. Be wary of ill-fitted replacement sills and check the closing action of the doors. If they bind or snag, someone may have welded on new sills without supporting the car in the middle to ensure that the frame maintains its correct shape. Another trouble spot is the door pillar. Shake each door firmly in this area to reveal any flexing. The engines are generally reliable and long-lasting, but check for fluid leaks. Gearboxes can be noisy, but are similarly robust, while the rear axle – similar to the Morris Minor's – rarely gives trouble.
Pick of the bunch: For classic credibility, the Sprite Mk IV and Midget Mk III (1966–70) are probably the best bet, offering better performance from the 1275cc engine than earlier cars. They are still chrome-era classics, however, with all the visual appeal of the older versions. If performance matters more, the 1500cc Triumph Spitfire-engined Midgets from 1974 will touch 100mph, but they have those vast black plastic bumpers that some people loathe.

1973 MG Midget, 1275cc, 4-cylinder engine, resprayed in red, beige interior trim, good condition throughout.
£2,400–2,800 LF

1978 MG Midget 1500, 1491cc, 4-cylinder engine, rebuilt and converted to earlier chrome-bumpered spec. c1993.
£3,250–3,750 BRIT

From October 1974, the Midget underwent major changes. To comply with American safety regulations, large urethane rubber bumpers were fitted, while the ride height was increased. In addition, the car received the 1500cc engine from the contemporary Triumph Spitfire. The bigger engine meant that the top speed was now in the region of 100mph.

◄ **1978 MG Midget 1500,** 1491cc, hard and soft tops, tonneau, refurbished over 6 years at a cost of over £11,700, engine reconditioned, carburettor overhauled, gearbox rebuilt, new clutch, radiator and hood, bodywork repaired, resprayed in British Racing green, Biscuit and black interior, excellent condition.
£2,000–2,500 BKS

▶ **1979 MG Midget 1500,** 1491cc, 4-cylinder engine, restored, new front wings, front panels, bonnet, doors, sills and hood, finished in red, 76,550 miles recorded, excellent condition throughout.
£3,250–3,750 H&H

MGB (1962–80)

Original 1962 specification
Engine: Four-cylinder, twin SU carburettors, 1798cc.
Transmission: Four-speed manual, optional two-speed overdrive.
Brakes: Front discs, rear drums.
0–60mph: 12.2 seconds.
Top speed: 105mph.
Price: £834.6s.3d (including purchase tax).
The MGB has to be one of the most practical, affordable and enjoyable classic sporting packages around. For a start, it's the most popular British sports car ever made, a winning formula based on rugged reliability, simple clean lines, fine road manners and adequate performance. For sheer classic credentials, models before the 1974 introduction of rubber-bumper cars with higher ride height are favoured, but later models can be even more affordable. There is also a superb parts and specialist network, even down to brand-new bodyshells made using original tooling. The fixed-head MGB GT is cheaper than the open roadster, yet offers additional practicality and comfort.
What to watch: Few worries with engines and mechanicals, but MGBs can rot, so it is essential to pay particular attention to sills and other structural aspects.

1962 MGB Roadster, 1978cc, original 3-bearing, 4-cylinder engine, wire wheels, new black hood and interior trim, 1 owner, good condition.
£6,000–7,000 BRIT

1967 MGB Roadster, manual gearbox with overdrive, left-hand drive, restored 1995, engine overhauled and uprated, twin Weber carburettors, high-performance pistons, converted to unleaded fuel, new dynamo, regulator and chrome wire wheels, finished in ivory, red leather interior, very good condition.
£5,750–6,750 BKS

Conceived in the late 1950s, the MGB dispensed with the preceding MGA's separate chassis in favour of unitary construction. The existing B-series engine was stretched to its practical limit of 1798cc, and the car's smooth, aerodynamically-efficient lines made the most of the 95bhp available to achieve a top speed of over 100mph. One of the most successful sports cars of the post-war era, the MGB enjoyed an 18-year production life. World-wide sales totalled in excess of 500,000 cars, and the 'B' was the last MG to leave Abingdon.

1963 MGB Roadster, 1798cc, recently refurbished, little use since, wire wheels, new exhaust, chrome luggage rack, finished in Iris blue, black interior trim.
£8,000–9,000 H&H

1967 MGB Roadster, completely restored 1992, new Heritage body shell, finished in Flame red, black upholstery.
£7,500–8,500 COYS

1967 MGB Roadster, 1798cc, 4-cylinder engine, overdrive, refurbished, bare-metal respray in British Racing green, new hood, original black interior trim and mechanics in excellent condition.
£5,750–6,750 BRIT

◄ **1969 MGB Roadster,** 1798cc, 4-cylinder engine, 4-speed manual gearbox, recently restored, mechanics overhauled, new Heritage bodyshell, finished in black, new black and red leather interior trim, 56,100 miles recorded, excellent condition.
£7,500–8,500 H&H

◄ **1970 MGB Roadster,** 2 litre, double-overhead-camshaft, Rover 4-cylinder engine, 4 valves per cylinder, fuel injection, electronic ignition, catalytic converter, 5-speed manual gearbox, Heritage bodyshell, conversion completed 1994, finished in Nordic blue, matching leather interior, excellent condition throughout.
£10,000–11,000 BKS

An MGB admirer, motoring journalist Eric Dymock set about producing this updated version in 1989, starting with a wreck, a new British Motor Heritage bodyshell and a Rover M16 engine. Designed for transverse installation, the engine was adapted to fit 'north-south' by means of a Sherpa van bellhousing, which was mated to a Rover SD1 gearbox and shortened propshaft.

1970 MGB Roadster, 1798cc, 4-cylinder engine, automatic transmission, new hood, finished in burgundy, good mechanical condition.
£3,500–4,200 BRIT

1972 MGB Roadster, US-export model, restored at a cost of c£17,000, fewer than 1,000 miles covered since, engine bored to 1950cc and tuned, overdrive gearbox, converted to right-hand drive, Minilite wheels, MGC bonnet, finished in metallic blue, Parchment leather upholstery with blue piping, Motolita steering wheel, excellent condition throughout.
£10,000–11,500 BKS

1973 MGB GT, left-hand drive, finished in dark green, black interior, little use since 1995, 49,000km recorded.
£4,000–5,000 BKS

The MGB GT coupé, which arrived in 1965, was styled with assistance from Pininfarina. Its performance figures were only fractionally down on the Roadster; most of what it lost by being slightly heavier, it clawed back by being more efficient aerodynamically.

1973 MGB GT, 1798cc, overdrive gearbox, finished in white, blue interior trim, very good condition throughout.
£3,250–3,750 H&H

1974 MGB GT, 1798cc, overdrive, restored, all panels replaced, resprayed in red, new black and red interior trim, 1 of the last chrome-bumper cars built, 70,000 miles recorded, 3 owners, excellent condition throughout.
£5,500–6,500 H&H

◄ **1974 MGB GT,** 1798cc, refurbished, Gold Seal replacement engine, new nearside front wing, doors and front bumper, Webasto sunroof re-covered, resprayed in Glacier white, 63,000 miles recorded, 2 owners, good structural condition.
£2,750–3,250 BRIT

1978 MGB Roadster, 1798cc, tonneau cover, chrome luggage rack, finished in brown, black interior trim, 61,000 miles recorded, very good condition throughout.
£3,500–4,250 H&H

1978 MGB GT, 1798cc, 4-cylinder engine, recent bodywork restoration, new panels and sills, finished in green.
£2,750–3,250 BRIT

1979 MGB Roadster, 1798cc, 4-cylinder engine, recent engine overhaul, finished in vermilion, c68,000 miles recorded, very good condition throughout.
£3,500–4,250 BRIT

1979 MGB GT, 1798cc, 4-cylinder engine, wire wheels, finished in black, good condition.
£6,300–7,000 BKS

1980 MGB Roadster, 1798cc, 4-cylinder engine, Minilite-style wheels, finished in vermilion, new double-duck hood, original striped upholstery replaced with black cloth, 65,400 miles recorded, good mechanical condition.
£4,750–5,500 BRIT

1980 MGB Limited-Edition Roadster, overdrive gearbox, wire wheels, not registered until 1996, c1,600 miles recorded, BMIHT certificate, excellent condition.
£7,000–8,000 BKS

1981 MGB Limited-Edition GT, overdrive gearbox, alloy wheels, new engine and clutch, finished in pewter, in need of some cosmetic attention.
£2,500–3,000 BKS

Introduced in 1979 to celebrate 50 years of MG production at Abingdon, the Limited-Edition Roadster and GT were the last models built before the factory's closure in October 1980. With a bronze metallic finish for the Roadster and pewter metallic finish for the GT, they featured chin spoilers and Triumph 1500S-type alloy wheels, wire wheels being optional for the Roadster. Only 1,000 cars were built: 480 Roadsters and 520 GTs.

1981 MGB Limited-Edition Roadster, new exhaust, alloy wheels, finished in metallic bronze, original hood and cover, tonneau, 765 miles recorded.
£9,500–10,500 BKS

◄ **1968 MGC GT,** 2912cc, 6-cylinder engine, overdrive gearbox, disc-type wheels, new rear spring hangers, bodywork restored, resprayed in Old English white, interior in good original condition, carburettor in need of tuning, rev-counter in need of attention.
£3,500–4,500 BKS

► **1968 MGC Roadster,** 2912cc, 6-cylinder engine, 4-speed manual gearbox with overdrive, completely restored, finished in red, black interior trim and upholstery, excellent condition throughout.
£10,000–11,500 H&H

◄ **1969 MGC Roadster,** 2912cc, 6-cylinder engine, overdrive gearbox, stainless steel exhaust system, Kenlowe fan, new hood, finished in green, good condition.
£6,000–7,000 BRIT

The MGC was intended as a replacement for the ageing Austin-Healey 3000, which was fighting a losing battle with ever-stricter safety regulations in the USA. In terms of appearance, it differed from the 'B' by having 15in wheels and 'power' bulges on the bonnet, which were needed to clear its tuned 3 litre Austin engine. Because of the size of this engine, torsion-bar front suspension was employed.
The MGC was built in GT and Roadster form between October 1967 and August 1969, a large number being intended for export. With its effortless, long-legged cruising gait, it was more of a fast tourer than an outright sports car.

1973 MGB GT V8, restored at a cost of c£21,000, stainless steel exhausts and manifolds, Ron Hopkinson handling kit, copper brake piping, Waxoyl treatment, finished in Aconite blue, grey leather interior trim and seats, walnut-veneered dashboard, grey Wilton carpets, Heritage certificate, previous concours winner.
£11,500–12,750 BKS

In 1971, tuning specialist Ken Costello converted his MGB to V8 power, then went on to sell similar specials for a couple of years. This prompted British Leyland to produce the MGB GT V8, using the 137bhp, 3.5 litre, light-alloy Rover V8 engine. The result was a 125mph top speed and a 0–60mph time of 8.6 seconds. Moreover, the American-born V8 was capable of running on unleaded fuel from the outset. However, the project's success was limited and only 2,591 cars were sold over the three-year production run.

1989 MG Maestro Turbo, alloy wheels, driving lights, electric front windows and mirrors, central locking, Motorola car phone, finished in Flame red, 86,000 miles recorded, MG 'M' certificate and engraved limited-edition plaque, 2 owners, completely original.
£2,750–3,250 BARO

1970 MG 1300 Mk 2 Saloon, 1275cc, recently restored, many new parts including clutch, brake pipes and big-bore exhaust system, finished in British Racing green, black interior.
£550–660 H&H

The MG 1300 was a tuned version of the Pininfarina-styled Austin 1100.

1995 MG RV8, 3946cc V8 engine, air conditioning, finished in pearlescent Woodcote green, beige leather interior, fewer than 9,000 miles recorded, excellent condition throughout.
£16,000–17,750 BRIT

Launched in 1992, the MG RV8 was an entirely new car, yet still an evolution of the MGB/C, having revised suspension and a most effective and tastefully restyled body. It proved beyond doubt that there was still a market for a product bearing the famous octagon logo, despite an absence of 12 years. By the time production ceased in 1995, 2,000 examples had been built, 75 per cent of them having been exported to Japan, where they were eagerly received. The 3946cc Rover V8 engine produced 190bhp, giving masses of torque, together with a 0–60mph acceleration time of 5.9 seconds and a top speed of over 135mph.

1995 MG RV8, 3946cc, Rover V8 engine, 190bhp, air conditioning, finished in pearlescent Woodcote green, beige leather interior excellent condition.
£17,000–18,000 BRIT

Mini

A commuter runabout, a racing and rallying giant-killer and a living legend, the Mini is all of these things. Alec Arnold Constantine Issigonis, creator of the Morris Minor and Mini, would have made a great end-of-pier gypsy clairvoyant. For this Greek-born son of an itinerant marine engineer once showed an uncanny prophetic talent when he quipped to Italian automobile couturier Sergio Farina, 'Look at your cars, they're like women's clothes – they're out of date in two years. My cars will still be in fashion after I've gone.' Sir Alec Issigonis died in 1988, yet the Mini is still here, just. The revolutionary, front-wheel-drive car with its east-west engine layout and brilliant compact packaging, was launched in 1959. Offered originally as an Austin 7 Mini (badged Se7en at first) or Morris Mini Minor, this pocket-sized wonder car had achieved its own identity by 1970, becoming simply the Mini. The Austin Metro of 1980 was supposed to replace the Mini, but wasn't up to the task. The Mini was so right at its launch that it's actually benefited from being left pretty much alone. Five-million-plus customers can't be wrong. It really is going to be a hard act to follow.

1961 Austin Mini Saloon, finished in red, original, very good condition.
£3,500–4,200 MINI

1963 Morris Mini Saloon, 848cc, 4-speed manual gearbox, all chromework original, finished in green, beige trim, 27,000 miles recorded, 2 owners, excellent original condition.
£2,000–2,400 H&H

◄ **1965 Britax Mini Cooper S,** 998cc, 4-cylinder engine, Minilite-type wheels, finished in yellow and black, good condition.
£7,000–8,000 MINI

1966 Austin Mini Cooper, 998cc, restored 1994–96, finished in Tweed grey with Old English white roof, Dove grey interior, 88,000 miles recorded, BMIHT certificate, concours condition.
£6,000–7,000 BKS

1967 Austin Mini Moke, hard and soft tops, finished in dark green with white roof, green upholstery, c40,000 miles recorded, in need of recommissioning.
£3,800–4,600 BKS

The Mini Moke combined standard Mini mechanics with Jeep-inspired bodywork.

Dealer prices

Miller's guide prices for dealer cars take into account the value of any guarantees or warranties that may be included in the purchase. Dealers must also observe additional statutory consumer regulations, which do not apply to private sellers. This is factored into our dealer guide prices. To identify dealer cars cross-refer the source codes at the ends of photo captions with the Key to Illustrations on page 330.

Miller's
Starter Marque

Starter Minis: *All models.*

- Whether yours is a 1959 car with sliding windows, cord door-pulls and external hinges, or a 1995 model, all Minis are classics. Even though modern Minis are still closely related to the 1959 original, the early cars have an extra, subtle charm. Parts are rarely a problem, but the Mini's major enemy is rust.
- Before looking underneath, inspect the roof panel, guttering and pillars supporting the roof. If they are rusted or show signs of filler, the rest of the structure may be in similar, or worse, shape.
- Examine floorpans from above and below, joints with the inner sill, front and rear bulkheads, crossmember and jacking points. If the subframe has welded plates, check that they've been properly attached. Look inside the parcel compartment on each side of the rear seat, beneath the rear seat, all corners of the boot, spare-wheel well and battery container. These are all common rust spots.
- Clicking from beneath the front of the car indicates wear in the driveshaft constant-velocity joints – not easy or cheap to rectify.
- Rear radius-arm support bearings deteriorate rapidly unless regularly lubricated; check the grease points ahead of each rear wheel for signs of recent attention.
- The A-series engine is generally reliable and long-lived. However, expect timing-chain rattle on older units; exhaust-valve burning may be evident on high-mileage examples, also exhaust smoke under hard acceleration, indicating cylinder/piston wear.
- A Mini Cooper can be worth more than double the price of an ordinary classic Mini. Consequently, fakes abound. It's not only a question of checking the uprated specification – twin carbs, disc brakes, badges and the like – but also of unravelling engine and chassis numbers, and the subtle tell-tale signs that you'll only learn about from club and professional experts. First join the club, then go shopping.

1967 Mini Cooper Innocenti Mk I, 998cc, big-valve cylinder head, competition camshaft, Janspeed exhaust manifold, Cooper S big-bore tail pipe, all mechanical components overhauled, finished in Almond green with Old English white roof, 37,500km recorded, well maintained.
£6,500–7,500 BKS

Innocenti in Italy was an independent company that built Minis under licence, incorporating a number of Cooper S components, including wheels, brakes and competition-bred hydrolastic suspension.

1968 Morris Mini Cooper S, 1275cc, 4-cylinder engine, 4-speed manual gearbox, finished in green and white, black interior trim, very good condition.
£4,500–5,500 H&H

1969 Austin Mini Cooper S Mk II, 1275cc, finished in Almond green with white roof, very good condition.
£6,500–7,500 MINI

What did John Cooper get from the original Mini Cooper? A £2 royalty for each one built. But he's not complaining. He recalls, 'Harriman [then BMC chairman George Harriman] said we had to make 1,000 – but we eventually made 150,000.' That translates into £300,000 commission.

1969 Mini Wood & Pickett, 998cc, 4-cylinder engine, hatchback conversion, completely rebuilt, finished in silver over Velvet green.
£6,000–7,000 COYS

A number of companies made special variants of the Mini. Apart from engine tuners, Broadspeed offered a cut-down version and Crayford built a convertible, while firms such as Harold Radford and Wood & Pickett created miniature luxury cars. By the mid-1970s, a top-specification Wood & Pickett car could cost as much as £26,000 – at the time, you could buy a Ferrari 250 GTO for that and have enough change for a couple of MGs.

MINI Model	ENGINE cc/cyl	DATES	CONDITION 1	2	3
Mini	848/4	1959–67	£3,500	£1,200	-
Mini Countryman	848/4	1961–67	£2,500	£1,200	-
Cooper Mk I	997/4	1961–67	£8,000	£5,000	£2,500
Cooper Mk II	998/4	1967–69	£6,000	£4,000	£1,500
Cooper S Mk I	var/4	1963–67	£7,000	£5,000	£2,000
Cooper S Mk II	1275/4	1967–71	£6,000	£5,000	£2,000
Innocenti Mini Cooper	998/4	1966–75	£4,500	£2,000	£1,000

1971 Austin Mini Cooper S, 1275cc, 4-cylinder engine, completely restored early 1980s at a cost of c£8,000, 5,000 miles covered since, new bodyshell, rewired, Minilite wheels, rally seats, rev-counter, finished in white with Ecurie Ecosse blue roof.
£4,500–5,500 BRIT

Miller's is a price GUIDE not a price LIST

1972 Austin Mini Cooper S Mk III, 1275cc, Downton-tuned engine, Minilite wheels, sunroof, finished in dark blue, 1 of the last Mk III Cooper S models built in 1971, unrestored, original.
£9,500–10,500 MINI

1974 Innocenti Mini Cooper 1300, new 71bhp A-type engine and gearbox, 4,600km covered since, rebuilt original engine supplied, fully rustproofed, resprayed 1981 in red with black roof, 2 owners, excellent original condition.
£3,000–3,500 BKS

Mini designer Alec Issigonis didn't approve when John Cooper approached him with plans for a hot Mini. The creator of the miniature marvel car stuck steadfastly to his vision of a car that would provide 'everyman transport'. But Cooper went over his head, got the go-ahead to breathe magic on the Mini and created an unlikely sporting legend. The Mini's engine was bored out to 997cc and fitted with twin SU carburettors, gear ratios were altered, a remote gear-change was installed in place of the waggly wand, and to stop this pocket rocket he challenged Lockheed to produce 7in front disc brakes. The result was a rallying world-beater, which was so invincible that when Coopers came home 1-2-3 in the infamous 1966 Monte Carlo Rally, the miffed organisers disqualified them on trumped up technicalities.

1975 Morris Mini 1000, 998cc, 4-cylinder engine, 4-speed manual gearbox, finished in yellow, blue interior trim and upholstery, 65,502 miles recorded, 2 owners, very good condition throughout.
£2,400–2,800 H&H

1975 Innocenti Mini Cooper, 1300cc, left-hand drive, finished in red, black interior trim, 74,000 miles recorded, excellent condition throughout.
£3,000–3,500 H&H

1980 Mini Clubman Estate, 998cc, automatic transmission, finished in Blaze orange, black cloth upholstery, c18,000 miles recorded, excellent condition.
£2,000–2,500 BKS

The 1970s saw Austin and Morris dropped as marque names for the Mini, and the introduction of a new top-of-the-range variant, the Mini Clubman. The latter featured an extended nose and, together with the rest of the Mk III Minis, had a revised bodyshell with internal door hinges and wind-up windows.

1989 Mini Moke, finished in metallic blue, white upholstery piped in red, 30,000km recorded, last example built, commemorative plaque.
£7,000–8,000 BKS

This Moke was the last to be built by the Austin-Rover Group. It has a number of unique features and was bought new by the head of Austin Rover's Portuguese production facility, being used exclusively by his wife in Lisbon.

1980 Mini 1275GT, 4-cylinder engine, Dunlop Denovo wheels, finished in red, 42,000 miles recorded, excellent condition throughout.
£3,000–3,500 BRIT

1991 ERA Mini Turbo, 1275cc turbocharged engine, alloy wheels, front air dam, side skirts, wheel-arch kit, sunroof, additional driving lights, finished in Flame red, grey leathercloth interior, 5,784 miles recorded, excellent condition throughout.
£6,000–7,000 BKS

Not so much a conversion, more a completely re-engineered package, this Mini Turbo is the product of ERA, a division of the Jack Knight Group. It boasts a specification to rival that of many current range-topping models twice its size and was used by ERA as a demonstrator.

1993 Wood & Pickett Mini De Ville, 1275cc engine, fuel injection, automatic transmission, Minilite wheels, deseamed bodywork, raised roof line, electric sunroof and tinted windows, central locking, air conditioning, finished in metallic grey, burgundy leather interior, walnut dashboard, wood-rimmed steering wheel, 150 miles covered since 1996.
£14,000–16,000 BKS

When delivered new in 1993, this car had a price tag of £28,400.

1910 Benz 'Prince Henry' Works Racing Car,
partially restored 1990s, original 2-seater body,
bolster fuel tank, chassis, axles, engine, radiator and
gearbox, further work required to complete restoration,
substantial quantity of archival material.
£150,000–170,000 BKS

This car was bought new by Australian businessman
A. T. Craig and raced by him at Brooklands in 1911,
where he achieved a trio of wins. Craig's chauffeur,
George Wilkinson, drove it in a 100 mile race, on
which occasion the hand throttle vibrated full open
on the finishing straight at almost 100mph, sending
the car over the Members' Banking and damaging it
extensively. It was shipped to the Benz factory and
repaired at a cost of £1,100, while Wilkinson was
patched up in hospital. Both drivers and car returned
to Melbourne, where the race-bred Benz proved
unsuitable for regular transport, oiling its plugs in
traffic. It was sold shortly after.

▶ **1930 Chrysler Carrera Indy-type Race Car,**
268cu.in, 6-cylinder inline engine, wire wheels,
restored, very good condition.
£18,000–20,000 KI

**1929 Alfa Romeo 6C-1500 Supercharged Super Sport
Third Series Racing Two-Seater,** original racing
Zagato coachwork replaced by Freestone & Webb
2-seater bodywork, restored, retaining all original
mechanical features.
£145,000–170,00 BKS

The superbly engineered and very quick Tipo 6C twin-
cam, supercharged Alfa Romeos were unequalled in
their class during 1928–30. In total, 1,059 6C–1500s
were built, the rarest being the ten supercharged,
short-chassis Super Sports. This car was one of three
works cars entered by Alfa Romeo's British agent,
Fred Stiles, for the 1929 Brooklands Double Twelve race.

1934 Alfa Romeo Tipo B (P3), 2992cc, double-overhead-camshaft, 8-cylinder engine, twin superchargers,
255bhp, Dubonnet-type front suspension, live rear axle with semi-elliptic springs, rod-operated 4-wheel drum
brakes, 104in wheelbase, restored, original engine, later telescopic dampers fitted to the rear, fully race prepared.
£1,200,000+ RM

A design from the pen of the great Vittorio Jano, the Alfa Romeo Tipo B debuted for the factory team at the
Tenth Grand Prix of Italy in 1932. Driven by the likes of Nuvolari and Caracciola, the car won outright on home
turf and continued to dominate the remainder of the season. The factory lent the cars to Scuderia Ferrari for
the 1934 season. With the engines bored out to 2.9 litres and producing 255bhp, the Tipo B proved yet again
that its advanced design was second to none, its 1934 race victories being unmatched by competitors.
This car is an ex-Scuderia Ferrari car and is known to have raced many times in 1935, for which season
Scuderia Ferrari installed the later, Dubonnet-type independent front suspension.

◀ **1953 Connaught A-Type,** restored to 1953 spec.,
using all original components, race-ready condition.
£95,000–110,000 COYS

This car was the last A-Type to be built on the 7ft 1in
chassis, and one of only two A-Types to be fitted with
fuel injection in place of the more conventional Amal
carburettors. It ran during the 1953 season as one of
the works cars, being driven by John Coombs,
Prince Bira and Stirling Moss. Bira gave the car its
best result, finishing seventh in the British Grand Prix
at Silverstone. That season it was also entered in the
French, German and Italian Grands Prix.

1964 2 Litre BRM P261, first full monocoque BRM, ex-works and Graham Hill, restored, fitted with 2 litre Tasman Formula version of original double-overhead-camshaft BRM V8 engine, 1 of only 6 built.
£300,000+ BKS

This BRM was the prototype P61 Mk 2 car, a type name reversed by BRM to coin the P261 nomenclature. It made its test debut at Silverstone early in 1964, in the hands of 1962 World Champion Graham Hill. It was fitted with 15in wheels and Dunlop racing tyres, and Hill was very complimentary about its handling. The car made its public debut at Snetterton in March that year. Race day was marred by heavy rain, but Hill made the best start and tore away into the lead, only to strike deep standing water approaching the Esses on his eighth lap. He lost control of the BRM, which aquaplaned off line, struck an earth bank and became airborne. The car crashed back to earth with its left front wheel torn off and the monocoque's forward structure distorted, but fortunately Hill escaped unhurt. The car was set aside while BRM concentrated upon completing two sister chassis. These later cars adopted the latest generation of 13in wheels and Dunlop 'doughnut' tyres, but Hill spent much of the following season bemoaning the fate of the prototype, claiming that none of its successors 'handled as well as that 15in wheel car.'

1962/63 Ferrari Dino 196SP Endurance-Racing Sports Prototype, completely restored, rear bodywork revised to duplicate Fantuzzi's 1961 high tail-decked Dino 246SP.
£800,000+ BKS

The original Dino 246SP made its debut in early 1961 and employed the Dino 246 four-cam V6 engine that had just been made redundant by the ending of the 2.5 litre F1 Grand Prix class at the end of the 1960 season. The styling of the new car created a sensation, having a high tail-decked body, in which the windscreen and door glasshouse were fared back into an abrupt Kamm-type tail with a clear Perspex carburettor clearance blister above the engine. Only two of these cars were built and run by the factory during the 1961 season, and both lost their original Fantuzzi bodywork after that season. The bodywork was recreated on this Dino 196SP, an ex-works/North American Racing Team entry in the 1962 Endurance World Championship series.

1963 Elva Porsche Mk VII, 1679cc, rear-mounted, double-overhead-camshaft, 4-cylinder Porsche 547 engine, 183bhp, 5-speed transaxle, 4-wheel independent suspension, tubular spaceframe chassis, only left-hand-drive example built.
£22,000–25,000 RM

The Elva Porsche hybrid was conceived by American Porsche distributor Oliver Schmidt and his race team. For the lightweight chassis, they chose the Elva Mk 7, widening and reinforcing the rear to accept the 180+bhp Porsche Type 547 engine.

1970 Abarth SE018 1000 Cuneo Spyder, 982cc, double-overhead-camshaft engine, 2 twin-choke Weber carburettors, 120bhp, 5-speed gearbox, independent suspension all-round, 4-wheel disc brakes, spaceframe chassis, 150mph top speed, restored early 1990s, only testing mileage since, finished in red, original black cloth seats.
£25,000–28,000 BKS

The 1000 Cuneo was one of the last cars that Abarth built while still under the control of Karl Abarth.

1970 3 Litre Alfa Romeo Tipo 33/3 Sports Prototype, 3 litre, double-overhead-camshaft V8, 4 valves per cylinder, fuel injected, 440bhp, aluminium monocoque, completely restored, in need of race preparation.
£110,000–121,000 BKS

◄ **1985 Jaguar XJR-6 Group C Racing Coupé,** 6.5 litre, overhead-camshaft V12, 700bhp, carbon-composite monocoque, full ground-effects aerodynamics, ex-TWR Racing, finished in 1985-style Jaguar Racing livery, concours condition.
£110,000–121,000 BKS

► **1954 Tojeiro-Jaguar Sports-Racing Car,** coachwork by Gray & Rich, 3.4 litre Jaguar engine, front suspension by coil springs and wishbones, de Dion back axle, multi-tubular spaceframe, aluminium body, removable roll-bar, restored, used sparingly since.
£80,000–100,000 BKS

1955 HWM-Jaguar Series II Sports-Racing Two-Seater, 3.8 litre, double-overhead-camshaft, 6-cylinder engine, coil-spring de Dion rear suspension, Alfin drum brakes, completely restored.
£225,000+ BKS

HWM was a well-known name in Continental F2 and Grand Prix racing during 1950–51. However, after the demise of F2 at the end of the 1953 season, it became more difficult to make single-seater racing pay, so the company turned to sports-racing car development, using modified single-seater type chassis, Jaguar engines and all-enveloping roadster bodywork. The original slab-sided HWM-Jaguars did well, but for 1955–56, a second series of two works cars was laid down, of which this car was the first and most successful.

1956 Kurtis 500S, Chevrolet V8 engine, suspension by trailing arms and torsion bars front and rear, double-channel chassis with tubular crossmembers, light aluminium bodywork, restored.
£50,000–60,000 COYS

By the early 1950s, to be successful in Midget, Sprint or Indy racing, you had to use a Frank Kurtis chassis. At around this time, Kurtis borrowed an Allard sports car, which he liked sufficiently to build a car along similar lines. The first Kurtis, the 500K, was based on a ladder frame with torsion-bar suspension and solid axles, front and rear. It evolved into the 500KK, the first sports car to be offered as a bare chassis in kit form. It was designed to accept any type of body style currently in vogue and a selection of power units. However, there were few takers, so Kurtis developed the 500S, which was marketed as a complete sports car. The purchaser was able to choose and supply the power unit, and Kurtis provided kits to fit Cadillac, Chrysler and Ford V8 and Hudson straight-six engines.

1956 Jaguar D-Type 'Shortnose' Sports-Racing Two-Seater, restored, original engine, gearbox, chassis, bonnet, centre-section monocoque and tail section, very good condition.
£600,000+ BKS

No sports-racing car of the mid-1950s has greater historic significance and charisma than the immortal D-Type Jaguar, examples of which won the Le Mans 24-hour endurance race on no fewer than three consecutive occasions. D-Types were built in three different forms: the original experimental integral-frame 1954 'shortnose' works cars; the rare 'longnose' works team cars of 1955–56; and the mainstream series of detachable-front-frame 'shortnose' production cars. This example is from the last group.

1959 Ferrari 250 Testarossa Reproduction, coachwork by Giordanengo/Fantuzzi, completed 1996, 250GT engine rebuilt to original TR specification, Weber carburettors, 250TR megaphone exhausts, 300bhp, tubular-steel chassis, aluminium body, Borrani wire wheels, finished in Giallo Fly, black leather interior, road legal, 1,000km recorded, 1 of 7 built, excellent condition.
£125,000–138,000 BKS

1957 Porsche 356A, 1750cc, air-cooled flat-4 engine, 120bhp, completely rebuilt, new intake manifolds, Weber carburettors, gearbox and differential, electronic ignition, 12 volt electrics, rev limiter, suspension fitted with 22mm (front) and 19mm (rear) anti-roll bars, rear camber corrector, carbon-fibre brake drums, 5.5in wheels, belly pan, full rollcage, Corbeau competition seat, 5-point safety harness, quick-release steering wheel, finished in German Racing silver, black interior, excellent condition.
£17,000–20,000 BKS

1959 MGA Twin Cam, 1903cc, B-series block, highly modified double-camshaft head, twin 48DCOE Weber carburettors, 180bhp, MGA gearbox with straight-cut gears.
£24,000–28,000 PC

◀ **1957 Ferrari 250 GT Competizione LWB 'Double-Bubble' Berlinetta,** coachwork by Zagato, chassis no. 0665GT, engine no. 0665GT, mechanics wiring and braking system recently overhauled, 1 of only 5 built, original.
£1,000,000+ BKS

1961 Jaguar E-Type Competition Roadster, aluminium bonnet, boot and doors, factory competition hardtop, 16th right-hand-drive roadster built.
£165,000–182,000 COYS

▶ **1965 Alfa Romeo TZI Competizione Berlinetta,** coachwork by Zagato, 1570cc double-overhead-camshaft, 4-cylinder engine, tubular chassis, completely restored, only road use since.
£80,000–90,000 BKS

1966 Ferrari 275 GTB/C Competizione, coachwork by Scaglietti, 3285cc, overhead-camshaft V12, dry-sump oil system, 190bhp, 5-speed manual transmission, all-independent suspension, Koni telescopic dampers, Dunlop disc brakes, lightweight tubular-steel ladder frame, Borrani wire wheels, Plexiglas side and rear windows.
£1,000,000+ RM

Tony Smith, Pescara 1957, depicting Stirling Moss in a Vanwall, oil on board, signed, framed, 11¾ x 23⅜in (30 x 60cm).
£475–575 S

Michael Wright, 1958 Targa Florio, depicting Peter Collins in the TR58 Testarossa Ferrari ahead of Stirling Moss in his DBRI Aston Martin, mixed media, signed and inscribed, mounted, framed and glazed, 17¼ x 26in (44 x 66cm).
£800–900 BKS

Helen Taylor, Fangio in the BRM V16, Formula Litre Race, Silverstone, 1953, mixed media on white textured paper, framed and glazed, 30¾ x 24in (78 x 61cm).
£700–800 BKS

Tony Upson, Monza 1948, acrylic on board, framed, 48 x 96in (122 x 244cm).
£200–250 BKS

After The Tout, a caricature view of the paddock at Brooklands, showing various personalities, their names printed below, mounted, 15 x 12in (38 x 30.5cm).
£150–180 BKS

After F. Gordon Crosby, MG 18/100 Tigress racing on the banking at Brooklands, limited-edition print of 251, issued by MG Car Club in the 1980s, slight fading, framed and glazed, 22 x 28in (56 x 71cm).
£140–170 BKS

Oval and Kosteradvertising lithographic poster, advertising the Calcium Light and Film Company's film display of the World International Auto Races, Indianapolis, May 30, 1914, fine condition, good colour and images, 84 x 45in (213.5 x 114.5cm).
£6,000–7,000 BKS

Poster advertising the 1901 Salon de l'Automobile, held in the Champs Elysées Grand Palais, framed and glazed, 53 x 39in (134.5 x 99cm).
£1,100–1,300 BKS

◄ Lithographic poster advertising the Grosser Preis von Deutschland, Nürburgring, 1934, excellent condition.
£2,250–2,750 BKS

A pair of CIJ clockwork models of Alfa Romeo P2 racing cars, 1 painted in Italian Racing red, the other in French Racing blue, both retaining original paint and markings, treaded tyres, Andre brake drums, fully operational steering, opening petrol, oil and radiator cap, faux rusted exhaust and faux cracked leather seats, c1926.
l. £2,500–2,750
r. £3,500–3,850 BKS

A Meccano tinplate racing car, pressed steel wheels with Firestone rubber tyres, painted driver figure, steering mechanism, detailed dashboard, windscreen missing, clean condition, c1932.
£300–350 BKS

A scratch-built Ferrari 553 Squalo F1 by Michael Conti, finished in Ferrari red, opening bonnet, chromed faux wire wheels, disc brakes, sprung suspension, detailed copper exhaust pipe and radiator grille, aero screen, detailed cockpit, good condition.
£1,700–2,000 BKS

A cold-painted bronze depicting a Ferrari Testarossa, with a flurry of road dust and exhaust giving the impression of speed and acting as a base, 13in (33cm) long.
£1,250–1,500 BKS

▶ A scratch-built 1:14 scale model of a 1967 Ferrari P3/4 by Precision Model Workshop, painted resin body, faux gold cast-alloy wheels retained by aluminium wheel nuts, treaded tyres, detailed 12-cylinder engine and cockpit, with Perspex base and lid.
£1,500–1,700 BKS

A Sparco race suit worn by Nelson Piquet during his 1985 season with Brabham, together with a pair of blue and grey Sparco gloves and a pair of Adidas Monza driving boots.
£2,000–2,300 S

A BAR pit-crew suit, worn during the team's 1999 debut season.
£300–350 GPT

An Advanced Wear & Safety Pioneer 1 race suit worn by Gerhard Berger during the 1990 season, driver's name and national flag on embroidered patches.
£1,500–1,800 S

This particular suit has extra layers of flame-retardant material and is elasticated above the ankle. These modifications were ordered by Berger after his horrific, fiery crash at the 1989 San Marino Grand Prix.

◀ A Formula One Raceware race suit worn by Stirling Moss, embroidered name and blood group, BRDC and sponsors' badges, early 1980s.
£500–600 P(E)

A leather driver's helmet worn by Guiseppe Farina during the 1934 and 1935 Grand Prix seasons, together with period goggles, display-mounted in a glass case.
£1,800–2,200 S

A set of 5 racing-team peaked caps, signed by various drivers.
£75–90 each GPT

A Shoei crash helmet worn by Ayrton Senna during the 1992 F1 season, sponsors' logos, blue lining, microphone and lead, tinted visor, together with Shoei helmet bag and large colour photograph showing Senna in 1992 wearing a similar helmet.
£23,000–27,000 S

◀ A set of 4 original racing-team shirts.
£75–90 each GPT

Morgan

Early in 2000, Morgan unveiled the new Aero 8 at the Geneva motor show. It was a momentous occasion in more ways than one for the small British company, for the Aero 8 is Morgan's first wholly new car for 64 years (barring the short-lived and unsuccessful fibreglass-bodied Plus Four Plus of 1964–66). The Aero 8 bristles with technology, yet in one sense remains very traditional, for underneath the muscular body, there is still an ash frame in time-honoured Morgan tradition. At the launch of the Aero 8, Charles Morgan made something of an understatement when he said, 'Morgan does not adopt passing fashions in the motor industry.' Indeed, for most of its life, Morgan has spurned fashion and modern practices to produce time-warp machines that somehow have remained enduringly fashionable. Founded in 1910 by HFS Morgan, the Malvern company initially produced motorcycle-engined three-wheelers, which remained the mainstay until the first four-wheeler, the 4/4, was introduced in 1935. By then, the three-wheelers were on their last legs and no longer able to challenge more conventional cars on performance and price. The 4/4 soon earned a fine reputation and today's products still display a direct lineage back to that original pre-war model. Whether the Aero 8 will herald a new era remains to be seen.

▶ **1933 Morgan Sports,** restored, finished in dark green, red upholstery, unused for some years, very good condition. **£13,000–14,500 BKS**

The forerunner of the economy light car, the three-wheel Morgan was remarkably successful as a runabout, but in Aero and Grand Prix form, it soon proved a formidable competitor in race meetings, trials and speed events. The Sports two-seater was introduced in 1933 to replace the Aero. It featured a Matchless sidevalve, twin-cylinder, air-cooled engine, a spare wheel mounted in the tail and a downswept exhaust that ran along the bottom edge of the body.

1969 Morgan 4/4, 1599cc, 4-cylinder engine, finished in red, hood in good condition, black leather trim, very good condition. **£9,500–11,000 BRIT**

By 1936, Morgan had introduced the four-wheel sports car, with a choice of Ford 10 or Coventry Climax engines. Later models had Triumph and Ford engines, while the powerful Plus 8, introduced in 1969, utilised the 3.5 litre Rover V8 unit.

1980 Morgan Plus 8, 3528cc, Rover V8 engine, 161bhp, 5-speed manual gearbox, limited-slip differential, 125mph top speed, 0–100mph in 19 seconds, full weather equipment, finished in silver and blue, black interior trim, 29,000 miles recorded, excellent condition throughout. **£13,500–15,000 H&H**

1982 Morgan 4/4, 1600cc CVH engine, 96bhp, 4-speed gearbox, chrome wire wheels, 103mph top speed, 0–60mph in 10 seconds, stainless steel exhaust, Plus 8 spotlamps, luggage rack, wind deflectors, finished in Royal ivory, black leather upholstery, c21,000 miles recorded, 1 owner.
£10,500–13,000 BKS

1985 Morgan Plus 8, 3528cc, Rover V8 engine, 5-speed manual gearbox, Koni shock absorbers, stainless steel exhaust system, alloy wheels, 125mph top speed, finished in British Racing green, stone leather interior, walnut dash, 12,900 miles recorded.
£18,000–20,000 PC

◀ **1990 Morgan Plus 8,** 3528cc, Rover V8 engine, alloy wheels, finished in red, 7,000 miles recorded.
£20,000–22,000 PORT

1991 Morgan Plus 8, 3528cc, Rover V8 engine, 5-speed manual gearbox, finished in Rosso red, stone leather interior, walnut dash, 35,000 miles recorded.
£21,000–23,250 FHD

◀ **1986 Morgan 4/4,** 1597cc, 4-cylinder engine, 5-speed manual gearbox, stainless steel exhaust, chrome wire wheels, stainless steel luggage rack, spotlamps, bonnet stay kit, wind deflectors, finished in British Racing green, black leather trim, mahogany dashboard, Motalita steering wheel, 27,000 miles recorded, 'as new' condition.
£14,000–16,000 H&H

Morris

Morris may be no more – the name disappeared from the Austin-Rover inventory in 1984 – but for 70 years the marque, founded by William Morris in 1913, stood out as a byword for stout middle-class motoring. The firm's early reputation was built on the sturdy and reliable 'bullnose' Morris Oxford and Cowley models. In fact, in 1924, Morris was Britain's number-one car manufacturer, ahead of Ford, and in 1929 Morris produced 51 per cent of all new cars built in Britain that year. Through the 1930s, Morris's market share dwindled, and in 1952 William Morris, by now Viscount Nuffield, agreed to merge with Austin to form the British Motor Corporation. Thereafter, the Morris marque struggled for prominence, but one car that was conceived before the merger, the miraculous Morris Minor, went on to become Britain's first million-selling car. In the 1960s and 1970s, other Morris offerings were little more than rebadged Austins.

1925 Morris Cowley Bullnose 11.9hp Two-Seater with Dickey, sound and original, in need of restoration.
£3,750–4,500 BKS

Such was the success of William Morris's outstanding bullnose models that over 154,000 chassis were built between 1913 and 1926. From 1923, the robust Hotchkiss engine, adopted in 1919, was built by Morris Engines at Coventry, and the finished car was assembled at Cowley. RAC rated at 11.9hp, the Cowley engine displaced 1548cc and was of a conventional sidevalve design, with a cork clutch and three-speed centre-change gearbox. Six different body styles were offered, as well as a commercial traveller's car with a samples box-van body to the rear.

▶ 1930 Morris Cowley Two-Seater with Dickey, 1500cc, 3-speed and reverse gearbox, older restoration, new hood and sidescreens, very good mechanical condition.
£7,800–8,750 Mot

1929 Morris Cowley Colonial Two-Seater with Dickey, completely restored, finished in maroon, red interior, excellent condition throughout.
£8,000–9,000 H&H

The Colonial model was built with a stronger, wider chassis and various other modifications thought necessary for the likely harder working life in the Colonies.

MORRIS Model	ENGINE cc/cyl	DATES	CONDITION		
			1	2	3
Minor Series MM	918/4	1948–52	£3,000	£1,600	£800
Minor Series MM Conv	918/4	1948–52	£4,500	£2,200	£1,200
Minor Series II	803/4	1953–56	£2,000	£1,000	£500
Minor Series II Conv	803/4	1953–56	£5,500	£3,500	£1,500
Minor Series II Est	803/4	1953–56	£3,000	£1,250	£800
Minor 1000	948/4	1956–63	£1,750	£925	£250
Minor 1000 Conv	948/4	1956–63	£4,000+	£2,000	£750
Minor 1000 Est	948/4	1956–63	£4,000	£2,200	£1,200
Minor 1000	1098/4	1963–71	£2,000	£950	£250
Minor 1000 Conv	1098/4	1963–71	£4,500	£3,000	£1,500
Minor 1000 Est	1098/4	1963–71	£4,000	£3,000	£1,500
Cowley 1200	1200/4	1954–56	£1,675	£1,000	£300
Cowley 1500	1489/4	1956–59	£1,750	£950	£350
Oxford MO	1476/4	1948–54	£2,000	£850	£250
Oxford MO Est	1476/4	1952–54	£3,000	£1,500	£350
Series II/III	1489/4	1954–59	£2,000	£1,200	£300
Series II/III/IV Est	1489/4	1954–60	£2,250	£1,350	£250
Oxford Series V Farina	1489/4	1959–61	£1,800	£800	£250
Oxford Series VI Farina	1622/4	1961–71	£1,750	£750	£200
Six Series MS	2215/6	1948–54	£2,500	£1,500	£500
Isis Series I/II	2639/6	1955–58	£2,500	£1,300	£450
Isis Series I/II Est	2639/6	1956–57	£2,600	£1,350	£500

1934 Morris 10/4 Four-Door Saloon, 1292cc, 4-cylinder engine, finished in correct green and black, green leather interior, original apart from flashing indicators, good mechanical condition.
£4,750–5,500 BRIT

1934 Morris Minor Four-Door Saloon, 847cc, 4-cylinder engine, new carburettor and kingpins, brakes overhauled, finished in black, in need of cosmetic attention, otherwise good condition.
£1,900–2,250 BRIT

Introduced in 1928, the Morris Minor was intended to compete with the very successful Austin 7. Originally, it was powered by an overhead-camshaft, Wolseley-designed engine, but in an effort to reduce production costs, a sidevalve engine was used from 1931. For 1934, the model's last season, a long-wheelbase four-door version was available.

1936 Morris Eight Series I Two-Door Saloon, sliding roof, luggage rack, fitted trunk, finished in green and black, green interior, 4 owners, excellent condition.
£4,750–5,500 UMC

1937 Morris Eight Series I Two-Door Saloon, 918cc, 4-cylinder engine, Pytchley sliding roof, cane picnic basket, restored 1994, finished in two-tone blue over black, blue leather upholstery, very good condition throughout.
£3,000–3,500 BKS

Introduced in 1934 to replace the well-proven Minor, the Morris Eight had an engine with a slightly longer stroke to give a capacity of 918cc. Available in two- and four-door saloon versions, and in open tourer form, it catered well for the first-time car buyer and proved popular.

◀ **1938 Morris Eight Two-Seat Tourer,** 918cc, 4-cylinder sidevalve engine, 'barn discovery', complete, in need of restoration.
£1,750–2,100 BRIT

Morris Oxford Series II, III & IV (1954–59)

Body styles: Saloon and estate.
Engine: Four-cylinder, overhead-valve, 1489cc.
Power output: 50–53bhp.
Transmission: Four-speed manual, column-change; optional Manumatic two-pedal drive from 1956.
Brakes: Hydraulic drums all-round.
Top speed: 74.2–80mph.
0–60mph: 27–29 seconds.
Production: 145,458.
Price in 1954: £744.7s.6d.
The most remarkable thing about this Morris is that it's still being built. When UK production wound down in 1959, to make way for the new square-rigged, Farina-designed Morris Oxford, the tooling for the old model was sold off to India where, to this day, it's produced as the Hindustan Ambassador. In fact, Indian production has passed one-and-a-half

million, and the sturdy plodder has even earned the affectionate nickname 'fatted duck'. During its production life in the UK, it inspired little affection, although it earned a reputation of a sort as a generally competent, but unexciting, family hack with decent enough ride and handling. The trouble was, as Britain emerged from the strictures of rationing, cars like Ford's glamorous Consul, Zephyr and Zodiac, and Vauxhall's glitzy Wyvern and Cresta seemed to deliver the long-awaited rewards of victory. By comparison, the mediocre Morris Oxford still smacked of austerity and must hardly have seemed worth winning the war for. Today, the 1954–59 Oxford has a limited period appeal among those who still consider Camp coffee, tinned peaches and condensed milk exotic delicacies.

1938 Morris Eight Series II Four-Door Saloon, 918cc, -cylinder engine, restored 1995, finished in black and green, green interior trim, new carpeting and headlining, good condition.
£4,000–5,000 BRIT

During late 1937, the Morris Eight underwent several cosmetic changes, subsequently being designated Series II. The model's appearance was modernised by fitting Easiclene wheels and a painted radiator surround with chromed vertical slats rather than honeycomb mesh.

1955 Morris Minor Series II Saloon, 803cc, restored, finished in Sandy beige, maroon interior trim, concours condition.
£4,750–5,500 H&H

1960 Morris Minor 1000 Two-Door Saloon, restored, underside replaced or repaired as necessary, undersealed, fitted with flashing indicators, but retaining original trafficators (disconnected), finished in Trafalgar grey, red leather-faced upholstery, well maintained.
£1,500–1,800 BKS

The Alec Issigonis-designed Morris Minor was launched in 1948. The first post-war Morris design, it boasted unitary-construction, torsion-bar independent front suspension, rack-and-pinion steering and a four-speed synchromesh gearbox. Initially, it was powered by the company's existing 918cc sidevalve four, but it received an 803cc overhead-valve engine in 1953. Two-door saloon and convertible models were offered at first, a four-door saloon appearing in 1950, followed by an estate and commercials. In 1956, the Minor 1000, with 948cc A-series engine, was introduced; the model received a further capacity boost, to 1098cc, in 1962.

1962 Morris Minor 1000 Traveller, 1147cc, original woodwork in good condition, resprayed in light blue-grey, blue-grey interior trim, new driver's seat and carpets, 77,800 miles recorded, well maintained.
£1,500–1,800 H&H

1962 Morris Minor 1000 Traveller, later 1098cc engine, woodwork in good condition, finished in Clarendon grey, interior retrimmed in dark red vinyl, good mechanical condition.
£2,100–2,600 BRIT

1964 Morris Minor 1000 Convertible, 1098cc, 4-cylinder engine, genuine convertible, recently restored, finished in Smoke grey with matching interior trim, dark blue hood.
£3,500–4,000 BRIT

1967 Morris Minor 1000 Traveller, restored 1992 at a cost of over £17,000, finished in dark blue, blue and cream leather interior, excellent condition.
£5,000–6,000 BKS

▶ **1970 Morris Minor 1000 Four-Door Saloon,** 1098cc, 4-cylinder engine, finished in maroon, red interior trim, very original and complete car, 34,000 miles recorded, last used 1993, in need of recommissioning.
£400–600 H&H

1964 Morris Minor 1000 Convertible, 1098cc, 4-cylinder engine, finished in off-white, red hood and interior, very good condition throughout.
£2,750–3,250 H&H

1965 Morris Minor 1000 Traveller, 1098cc, 4-cylinder engine, converted to unleaded fuel, floors and chassis rails replaced, finished in blue, blue interior, very good condition throughout.
£1,700–2,000 H&H

Nissan

◀ **1991 Nissan Figaro Convertible,** 1000cc turbocharged engine, automatic transmission, full cabriolet roof, electric windows, air conditioning, finished in pale blue, Stone leather interior, small rear bench seat, 23,646km recorded, limited-edition model, very good condition throughout.
£8,000–9,000 H&H

Oldsmobile

The company takes its name from Ransom Eli Olds, who formed the Olds Motor Vehicle Company in Michigan in 1897 and quickly enjoyed considerable success. The Curved Dash Olds led the way in 1901 as America's first series-produced car and also its most popular.

By 1905, Ransom Eli Olds had left the company to form REO (named after his initials). Meanwhile, in 1908, Oldsmobile was bought by William Durant's fledgling General Motors and since then has spent most of its life as a middle-market mainstay of the US giant.

1953 Oldsmobile Fiesta Convertible, 4978cc V8 engine, automatic transmission, restored 1990, finished in pearlescent white over turquoise with matching upholstery.
£25,000–28,000 COYS

Oldsmobile built only 458 Fiestas in 1953. The model came with a specially tuned version of the Rocket V8, leather upholstery and just about every option as standard, including Hydramatic transmission, power steering and brakes, electric windows, power seats and hood, and Autronic-eye automatic headlight dipping.

1937 Oldsmobile L-37 Saloon, 6-cylinder inline engine, good condition.
£11,000–12,250 HMM

1958 Oldsmobile Super 88 J-2 Hardtop, 371cu.in., overhead-valve V8 engine, automatic transmission, servo-assisted drum brakes, largely original, factory skirts, continental kit, spotlamps, finished in red with matching interior, unrestored, 42,000 miles recorded, excellent, condition throughout.
£18,000–20,000 RM

The Rocket V8 engine, with its single Rochester four-barrel carburettor, gave Oldsmobile a reputation for high performance. In J-2 guise, however, the 371cu.in engine was fitted with three two-barrel carburettors and produced a healthy 312bhp; impressive even by today's standards. Fewer than 12 cars were equipped with the J-2 option, making it extremely rare and very desirable.

▶ **1966 Oldsmobile Toronado,** 6966cc V8 engine, 130mph top speed, automatic transmission, front-wheel drive, restored 1993, finished in black, black interior, very good condition.
£3,500–4,200 COYS

The Toronado had an unusual 'two-piece' transmission arrangement in which the torque converter was mounted behind the engine, while the gearbox was located remotely under the left-hand cylinder bank. The two were joined by a chain drive and sprocket arrangement.

OLDSMOBILE Model	ENGINE cc/cyl	DATES	CONDITION 1	2	3
Curved Dash	1600/1	1901–04	£16,000	£14,000	£12,000
30	2771/6	1925–26	£9,000	£7,000	£4,000
Straight Eight	4213/8	1937–38	£14,000	£9,000	£5,000

Opel

The German Opel company, named after Adam Opel, produced sewing machines and bicycles before building its first car in 1898. By 1913, the company was ranked sixth in Europe, and by 1928 was also Germany's largest car producer. If you've ever wondered why from the 1960s Opel and Vauxhall models converged, it is because General Motors acquired both companies in the 1920s: Vauxhall in 1925, followed by Opel in 1929.

◄ **1972 Opel GT Coupé,** rotating-pod headlamps, finished in metallic blue, black interior, good condition. **£2,000–2,500 BKS**

Although sold in the UK, the pretty two-seat Opel GT was really produced for mainland Europe and was only available in left-hand-drive form. It employed the same platform and suspension as the contemporary Kadett. While there was a choice of engines in Europe, UK models were restricted to the 90bhp 1897cc Rekord unit.

Packard

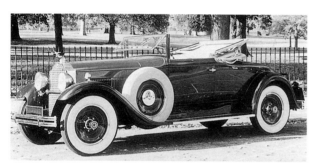

1930 Packard Type 840 Doctor's Coupé, sidevalve, 8-cylinder inline engine, completely restored, finished in maroon, tan leather upholstery, concours condition. **£57,000–64,000 COYS**

Packard's philosophy was similar to that of Rolls-Royce, in that the company built conservative cars that combined effortless and silent performance with reliability and longevity. In 1923, the first straight-eight was announced, being of 5.7 litres capacity, which was increased to 6.3 litres in 1927. The engine developed 106bhp at a modest 3,200rpm and was not highly stressed; when fitted to the Speedster model, it developed 145bhp at 3,400rpm, which was impressive for a sidevalve unit. Contemporary writers considered it to be smoother than the V8 engines used by other makers.

1932 Packard 900 Coupé Roadster, 310cu.in, sidevalve 8-cylinder inline engine, 3-speed synchromesh gearbox, 4-wheel mechanical drum brakes, dual side-mounted spare wheels with metal covers, wheel trim rings, heater, restored, finished in black, tan Stayfast convertible top, brown leather upholstery, excellent condition. **£60,000–70,000 RM**

The Depression had an enormous impact on fine car makers, reducing sales to a fraction of what they had been in the 1920s. The 900 was Packard's attempt at offering a more affordable car to aid the company's survival. At $1,795, it was well equipped and technically advanced for the time. Chassis features included ride-control adjustable suspension, vacuum-assisted brakes and an automatic clutch. Unfortunately, the 900 was built to the same exacting standards as other Packards and, while very much a sales success, it lost the company money. Production was discontinued after a year.

| PACKARD | ENGINE | DATES | CONDITION | | |
Model	cc/cyl		1	2	3
Twin Six	6946/12	1916–23	£30,000	£20,000	£15,000
6	3973/6	1921–24	£20,000	£15,000	£12,000
6, 7, 8 Series	5231/8	1929–39	£35,000+	£25,000+	£14,000+
12	7300/12	1936–39	£50,000+	£30,000+	£18,000+

Auction prices

Miller's only includes cars declared sold. Our guide prices take into account the buyer's premium, VAT on the premium, and the extent of any published catalogue information relating to condition and provenance. To identify cars sold at auction, cross-refer the source codes at the ends of photo captions with the Key to Illustrations on page 330.

◀ **1937 Packard 115-C Six Sedan,** left-hand drive, completely restored, finished in cream, very good condition.
£12,000–14,000 PALM

Palmer-Singer

1910 Palmer-Singer Model 6-40 Five-Seat Tourer, sidevalve 6-cylinder engine, 4-speed manual gearbox, shaft final drive, brass oil side lamps, acetylene headlamps, 2-piece folding windscreen, spare wheel rims and tyres, folding hood with 'chapel' rear window, finished in Brunswick green, Apple green chassis detail and wheels, upholstered in deep-buttoned brown leather.
£36,000–42,000 BKS

Charles Singer, whose family had made a fortune from making sewing machines, joined forces with Henry Palmer, a Brooklyn barrel maker, to produce the Palmer-Singer car at a purpose-built factory in Long Island City. The quality of their products was undoubted, and production soon concentrated on large, comfortable, fast touring cars rather than the smaller four-cylinder Skimabout, which was the company's first offering.

Panhard

◀ **1966 Panhard 24CT Coupé,** 850cc, air-cooled, flat-twin engine, 60bhp, 4-speed manual gearbox, front-wheel drive, 4-wheel disc brakes, restored, finished in red, concours condition.
£4,000–5,000 Pou

Peugeot

Peugeot's history dates back to the dawn of motoring, for not long after the earliest Daimler and Benz vehicles had taken to the road, the French company was also in contention. In 1889, Peugeot turned out four vehicles and is also credited with being the first manufacturer to sell a car to a private owner. Since 1974, Peugeot has also been in control of Citroën, and in 1978 acquired Chrysler's European interests, annexing the Talbot, Sunbeam and Simca brands.

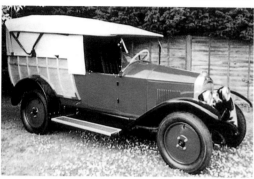

1925 Peugeot 177B Boulangere Normande, 1400cc, 4-cylinder engine, completely restored, fewer than 20 miles covered since, finished in red and black, cream folding hood.
£7,000–8,000 BKS

1938 Peugeot 202, 1133cc, overhead-valve 4-cylinder engine, 3-bearing crankshaft, headlamps concealed behind grille, sunroof, finished in black, red leatherette interior trim, museum displayed for some time, 21,000 miles recorded, very good condition.
£3,500–4,000 BRIT

▶ **1958 Peugeot 403 Four-Door Saloon,** factory sunroof, left-hand drive, finished in black, grey interior, original, good unrestored condition.
£3,500–4,000 BKS

Introduced in 1955, the 403 used an upgraded version of the existing 203's running gear and a 1.5 litre derivative of the latter's 1290cc engine with an all-synchromesh 4-speed gearbox in a larger, more spacious and pleasingly styled unit-construction body. Like the 203, the 403 was solidly built and proved extremely reliable, being ideally suited for the fast, sweeping Continental highways.

◀ **1980 Peugeot 104 ZS,** 1360cc, engine rebuilt 1997, bodywork refurbished, finished in red, 80,000 miles recorded, very good condition throughout.
£2,250–2,500 CPUK

PEUGEOT Model	ENGINE cc/cyl	DATES	CONDITION		
			1	2	3
Bébé	856/4	1912–14	£18,000	£12,000	£8,000
153	2951/4	1913–26	£9,000	£5,000	£3,000
163	1490/4	1920–24	£5,000	£4,000	£2,000
Bébé	676/4	1920–25	£7,000	£6,000	£3,000
156	5700/6	1922–24	£7,000	£5,000	£3,000
174	3828/4	1922–28	£7,500	£5,000	£2,000
172	714/4	1926–28	£4,000	£3,000	£1,500
183	1990/6	1929–30	£5,000	£3,000	£1,500
201	996/4	1930–36	£6,000	£3,000	£1,500
402	2140/4	1938–40	£4,500	£3,000	£1,000

Right-hand-drive cars and tourers will always achieve more interest than left-hand-drive models. Good solid cars.

Plymouth

◀ **1929 Plymouth Four-Door Sedan,** 4-cylinder engine, 48bhp, hydraulic brakes, all-steel construction, completely restored, chassis and running gear overhauled to original specification, finished in black, olive green and brown, very good condition throughout.
£3,500–4,200 BKS

▶ **1931 Plymouth Deluxe Model PA Four-Door Saloon,** 4-cylinder engine, hydraulic brakes, restored, finished in burgundy and black, 51,179 miles recorded, original, very good condition throughout.
£3,750–4,500 BKS

For 1931, the Plymouth PA's engine was mounted on heavy-duty rubber blocks to insulate it from the chassis. Billed as 'Floating Power', this innovation allowed Plymouth to claim, with little exaggeration, that the model had 'the smoothness of an eight and the economy of a four', which helped sales no end.

Pontiac

One of the few subsidiary US marques to have been created rather than acquired, Pontiac emerged as a General Motors brand in 1926, slotting in above Chevrolet and below the flagship Cadillac. In the 1960s, though, Pontiac changed direction dramatically with the tyre-smoking 1964 GTO, the car that started the whole muscle-car movement. The GTO was followed by the joyfully excessive Trans-Am, which reigned in its full glory for just a few years, before the mid-1970s fuel crisis and American emission laws toned down its extravagant behaviour.

◀ **1926 Pontiac Six Saloon,** 3200cc, 6-cylinder engine, 3-speed manual gearbox, original klaxon, front cowl lamps, discrete indicators, left-hand drive, restored, finished in green and black, brown interior trim, 39,000 miles recorded, believed to be the oldest Pontiac outside the USA and the 3rd oldest survivor.
£6,000–7,000 H&H

1969 Pontiac GTO, V8 engine, left-hand drive, finished in metallic blue with blue vinyl roof, very good condition.
£9,000–11,000 PALM

Porsche

Volkswagen Beetle designer Ferdinand Porsche may have given the world the people's car, but it was his son, Ferry, who, with long-time associate Karl Rabe, created a car that people all over the world would prize from the day the first Porsche rolled off the production line. These days, a Porsche – virtually any Porsche – stands for precision, performance, purity and perfection, and the 356 is the first chapter in that story. Well, not quite. The 356 was so named because it was actually the 356th project from the Porsche design office since it had been set up in 1930. It was also the first car to bear the Porsche name. Post-war expediency forced a make-do reliance on VW Beetle underpinnings, but the 356 is much more than a Bug in

butterfly's clothes. Its concept, rear-engined layout and design descended directly from the parent car, but in the handsome athletic offspring, the genes mutated miraculously into a true sporting machine. Some aficionados adore the first-of-breed purity of the earliest 'jelly mould' cars, but with each successive modification, the Porsche detached itself further from its humble roots. A pert, nimble, tail-happy treat, the 356 is still the prettiest production Porsche there's ever been, the foundation stone of a proud sporting tradition. Why, if you squint at more modern Porsches, like the 911 and today's models, you can still identify the genetic inheritance passed down from a true original.

◄ **1958 Porsche 356 Speedster,** 1.6 litres, engine fitted with later 912 barrels and carburettors, resprayed in black, black double-duck weather equipment in good condition, interior with original coupé-style seats as supplied new, upholstered in red leather, original, very good condition. **£34,000–38,000 COYS**

1960 Porsche 356B Roadster, restored 1991, finished in red, beige leather interior, very good condition throughout. **£25,000–28,000 BKS**

Like the immortal Beetle, the Porsche 356 employed a platform-type chassis with rear-mounted, air-cooled engine and all-independent torsion-bar suspension. In 1951, a works car finished first in the 1100cc class at Le Mans, thus beginning the marque's long and illustrious association with La Sarthe. By the time the 356B arrived, in September 1959, the car had gained a one-piece, rounded windscreen and 15in-diameter wheels. The newcomer's introduction also brought with it further styling revisions and a 1600cc engine.

1960 Porsche 356B Roadster, 1582cc, overhead-valve flat-4 engine, 2 Zenith twin-choke carburettors, 70bhp, 4-speed manual gearbox, all-independent suspension, 4-wheel drum brakes, restored, little use since, finished in black, tan interior. **£18,000–20,000 RM**

► **1960 Porsche 356 Super 90,** restored, finished in red, very good condition. **£9,500–11,000 COYS**

► **1963 Porsche 356 1600SC,** 1600cc, 4-cylinder engine, 95bhp, all-synchromesh gearbox, 4-wheel disc brakes, 2 owners, excellent condition throughout.
£12,500–14,000 COYS

1963 Porsche 356C, restored 1996, unused since, finished in red, black interior.
£9,500–11,000 COYS

The 356C was introduced in 1963 as an updated version of the 356B and was the final incarnation of the venerable sports car. The major changes were mechanical: disc brakes were fitted all-round, there were new 15in wheels and the suspension was improved. The engine was revised with changes to the cylinder heads and was offered in 1600C, 1600SC and potent 2000GS guises.

1964 Porsche 356SC, 1600cc, 90bhp, 4-wheel disc brakes, completely restored, engine, brakes and suspension rebuilt, finished in silver, red leather interior, excellent condition.
£18,000–20,000 BKS

► **1973 Porsche 911,** 2341cc, 6-cylinder air-cooled engine, fuel injection, 165bhp, 4-speed manual gearbox, 4-wheel disc brakes, left-hand drive, finished in Bordeaux red, very good condition.
£9,000–10,000 Pou

PORSCHE Model	ENGINE cc/cyl	DATES	CONDITION 1	2	3
356	var/4	1949–53	£15,000	£8,000	£5,000
356 Cabriolet	var/4	1951–53	£20,000	£14,000	£10,000
356A	1582/4	1955–59	£13,000	£9,000	£5,000
356A Cabriolet	1582/4	1956–59	£16,000	£10,000	£7,000
356A Speedster	1582/4	1955–58	£25,000	£19,000	£14,000
356B Carrera	1582/1966/4	1960–65	£40,000+	£30,000+	£18,000
356C	1582/4	1963–65	£15,000	£11,000+	£5,000
356C Cabriolet	1582/4	1963–64	£25,000+	£16,000	£10,000
911/911L/T/E	1991/6	1964–68	£12,000	£7,000	£5,000
912	1582/4	1965–68	£6,500	£5,000	£2,000
911S	1991/6	1966–69	£12,000	£8,000	£5,500
911S	2195/6	1969–71	£13,000	£9,000	£6,000
911T	2341/6	1971–73	£13,000	£8,000	£6,000
911E	2341/6	1971–73	£12,000+	£8,000	£6,000
914/4	1679/4	1969–75	£4,000	£3,000	£1,000
914/6	1991/6	1969–71	£6,000	£3,500	£1,500
911S	2341/6	1971–73	£16,000	£10,000	£8,500
Carrera RS lightweight	2687/6	1973	£40,000	£28,000+	£16,000
Carrera RS Touring	2687/6	1973	£30,000	£26,000	£17,000
Carrera 3	2994/6	1976–77	£14,000	£9,000	£7,000
924 Turbo	1984/4	1978–83	£5,000	£4,000	£2,000
928/928S	4474/4664/V8	1977–86	£10,000	£7,000	£4,000
911SC	2993/6	1977–83	£13,000	£8,000	£6,000

Sportomatic cars are less desirable.

1973 Porsche 911RS, 2687cc, 6-cylinder engine, complete bodywork restoration 1980s, finished in Grand Prix white with blue Carrera scripts, good condition.
£27,000–30,000 COYS

The RS (*Rennsport*) was based on the 911S, but had lightweight bodywork and a revised 2.7 litre, fuel-injected flat-six. With 210+bhp on tap, the RS could achieve a genuine 158mph, with 0–60mph in just over five seconds. It was one of the fastest production cars in the world. The RS was offered in two versions: a stripped-down quasi racing car known as the L (Lightweight) and a more civilised, better-trimmed version called the T (Touring). This particular car is one of the latter.

1979 Porsche 911 Turbo, 3.3 litre engine, gearbox overhauled 1998, modified with stiffer Bilstein shock absorbers all-round, braced front shock-absorber turrets, thicker torsion bars, wider 9in rear wheel rims, finished in Arrow blue, black leather interior, period Blaupunkt radio, well maintained, 77,000km recorded, very good original condition throughout.
£14,000–16,000 BKS

Porsche's top-of-the-range supercar grew to 3.3 litres for 1977, the capacity increase boosting maximum power to 300bhp.

1974 Porsche 914 Targa, 1991cc, 6-cylinder engine, left-hand drive, finished in red, black targa top, black interior and red carpets, 73,000km recorded.
£3,500–4,000 BKS

The histories of Porsche and Volkswagen are intertwined, and in 1969 came the first public expression of that relationship, the mid-engined 914 targa-top sports car. Helped by its mid-engine layout, the 914's roadholding and handling were of a high order. Four-wheel disc brakes and a five-speed gearbox were standard and, with the 100bhp, fuel-injected, 1971cc engine fitted from 1972, top speed was a respectable 120mph, with 0–60mph in 8.7 seconds. The model was phased out in 1975 in favour of the forthcoming 924.

1983 Porsche 911SC Cabriolet, 2993cc, Turbo spoiler, electric windows and mirrors, new hood, finished in metallic red, black leather interior.
£11,000–13,000 BARO

1986 Porsche 911, 3.2 litre, overhead-camshaft flat-6 engine, 200bhp, servo-assisted brakes, 140+mph top speed, electric windows, air conditioning, headlight washers, finished in red, nose recently resprayed to remove stone chips, black leather interior, 59,000 miles recorded, original.
£9,500–11,000 BKS

1987 Porsche 911 Carrera, £5,000 spent in the last year, finished in white, 66,000 miles recorded, very good condition throughout.
£9,500–11,000 BARO

1964 Porsche 904 GTS Carrera, 1996cc, 4-cylinder engine, 5-speed transaxle, all-independent suspension, 4-wheel disc brakes, box-section chassis, fibreglass body, completely restored, little use since, finished in red, black interior trim, excellent condition throughout.
£170,000–190,000 BKS

The 904 GTS was a road/race car built in strictly limited numbers with a chassis and body quite unlike the mainstream production cars. It was also the first series-built Porsche coupé to have a mid-engined layout. This exciting road car was tough enough to take a 1-2 victory in the gruelling Targa Florio race around the Madonie Mountains of Sicily in 1964, and to place second in the 1965 Monte Carlo rally, which was run in heavy snow. There was nothing to touch a 904 in its class in regular GT racing. Of the first 12 finishers at Le Mans in 1964, no fewer than five were 904s. Of eight competing in 1965, all lasted the race and one finished fourth overall. Eight started the Reims 12-hour race and all finished.

Rambler

◄ **1964 Rambler Classic Four-Door Station Wagon,** 2996cc, left-hand drive, finished in gold and white with matching interior trim, recently imported from USA, rust free, converted to unleaded fuel, original working radio, 43,000 miles recorded, 2 owners, very good original condition throughout.
£2,750–3,250 H&H

Rauch & Lang

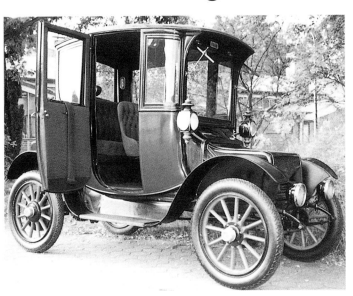

◄ **1914 Rauch & Lang Electric Brougham,** 50 mile range on full charge, new batteries and charger, improved lighting, horn and flashers, finished in maroon, blue upholstery.
£18,000–22,000 BKS

The Rauch & Lang company had been a coachbuilder since the middle of the 19th century, and even in 1914 those skills were very apparent in the design of its Brougham. The electric vehicle allowed the driver to select his driving position – front or rear – according to the number of passengers, by the simple expediency of turning the front seat. This particular example was owned new by the Rockefeller family and has spent much of its life in museums.

Reliant

◄ **1963 Reliant Sabre 4,** 1703cc, 4-cylinder engine, twin SU carburettors, Alexander manifold, Ace Mercury wheel trims, engine rebuilt 1995, little use since, new front brake calipers, resprayed in red, black vinyl hood and interior, original, good condition throughout.
£2,500–3,000 BRIT

Introduced in 1961, the Sabre was a new direction for Reliant, previously well-known for the production of three-wheelers. It had a very strong chassis, while power came from the sturdy 1.7 litre Ford Consul engine. The striking fibreglass body was produced in both open and hardtop GT forms. Approximately 200 Sabre 4s were built, of which it is believed only 55 were sold in the UK.

Reliant Scimitar GTE (1968–86)

Engine: Ford V6, 2994cc (1968–79); 2792cc (1979–86).
Power output: 128–135bhp.
Transmission: Four-speed manual, optional overdrive; automatic.
Brakes: Front discs, rear drums.
Top speed: 116–118mph.
0–60mph: 10.2–10.8 seconds.
Production: Approximately 16,000.
Price when new: £1,759.

Del Boy and Rodders might have suffered delusions of adequacy in their Reliant Regal van, but there was one Reliant that really was regal – the Scimitar. Princess Anne owned no less than eight Scimitar GTE estates over the years, and Prince Edward once owned a Scimitar convertible. Until the 1960s, Reliant was best known for its traders' three-wheelers, but in 1961 turned its attention to four-wheeled sporting products, first with the rather ugly Sabre, then the more harmonious Sabre Six.
The elegant Scimitar coupé of 1964 was certainly

something of a breakthrough for Reliant, but it was the 1968 Scimitar GTE that marked a quiet revolution. Although there was nothing revolutionary in the production of its moulded-fibreglass body, the shape, styling, glass rear hatch and split rear seats created a new class of car – the sports estate, a sporting, four-seat, cross-country carry-all with luggage space increased at a stroke from 19 to 36cu.ft. In Reliant parlance, 'GTE' stood for grand-touring estate and, although the concept seems obvious today, it was years ahead of its time.
The Scimitar GTE appeared three years before Volvo leapt on the sports-wagon band-wagon with the P1800ES. Today, it's still one of the few sports estates that actually looks right as an estate. As a work-a-day classic hack, there's also little to match its blend of sporting style and practicality at the price – with its massive and strong, deep-box-section chassis, no-nonsense mechanicals, Ford V6 engine and rust-free fibreglass body.

► **1974 Reliant Scimitar GTE,** 3 litre Ford V6 engine, 135bhp, all-synchromesh 4-speed manual gearbox, front disc brakes, rear drums, alloy wheels, two-door fibreglass sports estate body, restored, good condition.
£4,000–5,000 HMM

RELIANT Model	ENGINE cc/cyl	DATES	CONDITION 1	2	3
Sabre 4 Coupé & Drophead	1703/4	1961–63	£5,500	£2,750	£1,000
Sabre 6 Coupé & Drophead	2553/6	1962–64	£6,000	£3,500	£1,500
Scimitar GT Coupé SE4	2553/6, 2994 V6	1964–70	£4,500	£2,500	£1,000
Scimitar GTE Sports Estate SE5/5A	2994/V6	1968–75	£6,000	£3,000	£750
Scimitar GTE Sports Estate SE6/6A	2994/V6	1976–80	£6,000+	£3,500+	£1,250
Scimitar GTE Sports Estate SE6B	2792/V6	1980–86	£8,000	£5,000	£2,000
Scimitar GTC Convertible SE8B	2792/V6	1980–86	£9,000	£8,000	£5,500

Renault

For the enthusiast, many of Renault's most engaging post-war cars come in small packages. The 4CV of 1947–61 was an advanced little device with a rear-mounted, overhead-valve engine, rack-and-pinion steering and all-independent suspension. Eventually, over a million were sold, but the Dauphine was even more successful, claiming honours as the first French car to sell over two million. As petite sporting boulevardiers, the Floride and Caravelle made up for their lack of outright performance with plenty of charm. The long-lived Renault 4 was both innovative and versatile. Seemingly 'unstyled', it was an excellent little carry-all that could be readily adapted from family hack to utility vehicle by removing the seats and tailgate if necessary. In production from 1962 to 1986, it sold an astonishing seven million-plus. The Renault 5 carried the theme forward and set a standard in small-car styling that's rarely been matched since.

1919 Renault 15.8hp Type EU Drophead Coupé, coachwork by Hayes and Miller, 2816cc, 4-cylinder engine, dynastart, electric lighting, finished in pale green and black, black and grey interior.
£9,500–11,500 BRIT

1958 Renault Dauphine, 1000cc, 4-cylinder engine, finished in red, good condition.
£1,000–1,200 YEST

1959 Renault 4CV Saloon, 747cc, overhead-valve 4-cylinder engine, 19bhp, 60mph top speed, good condition.
£1,800–2,000 HMM

1959 Renault 8 Saloon, 956cc, rear-mounted engine, unused for 7–8 years, in need of complete refurbishment and recommissioning.
£200–400 LF

Renault Dauphine (1956–67)

Engine: Four-cylinder, 845cc.
Power output: 32bhp at 4,500rpm.
Transmission: Three-speed manual, four-speed from 1961; three-speed automatic with electric clutch.
Brakes: Drums all-round, discs all-round from 1964.
0–60mph: 31.6 seconds.
Top speed: 71mph.
Fuel consumption: 35–45mpg.

Back in 1956, the new Renault Dauphine brought a touch of flair and modernity to budget motoring. This delightfully unorthodox little machine had a water-cooled, but rear-mounted, engine, all-independent suspension and an adventurously streamlined, unitary-construction body. It was also better equipped than many home-grown UK products, with a steering lock as standard, automatic choke, and new-fangled gew-gaws like courtesy lights in the front luggage compartment and rear engine bay. It even

had special concave headlamp lenses that were supposed to build up a pocket of air that prevented insects from committing suicide. Most daring of all was an optional semi-automatic, three-speed transmission. The motor mags waxed lyrical, and discerning British motorists eventually cottoned on to the revolutionary Renault whose production run eventually numbered well over two million.

Pick of the bunch: Amedee Gordini did for the little Renault what John Cooper later did for the Mini. The Dauphine Gordini's 845cc engine produced 37.8bhp and pushed top speed up to 75.6mph; no road burner, but a bit more fun than the base Dauphine.

Dauphine fact: From 1956 to 1958, right-hand-drive Dauphines were assembled in Britain at Acton, west London. In 1958, a basic Dauphine won the Monte Carlo Rally; in that same year, Dauphines took first to fourth in class in the Mille Miglia.

► **1962 Renault Floride Convertible,** 845cc, hard and soft tops, original right-hand drive, finished in red and black, stored since 1989. **£1,750–2,100 BKS**

Introduced to the UK in 1958, the pretty Floride was styled in Italy by Frua.

◄ **1965 Renault Caravelle 2+2 Convertible,** 1108cc, 4-cylinder engine, 4-speed manual gearbox, completely restored, bare-metal respray in red, excellent condition. **£4,500–5,000 Mot**

► **1984 Renault 5 Turbo 2,** 160bhp, completely restored 1994/95, finished in dark metallic blue, beige velour interior, non-standard Sparco rally-type seats, 27,000 miles recorded, never raced or rallied, excellent condition throughout. **£7,500–8,500 BKS**

The Renault 5 Turbo 2 was a homologation special built in limited numbers for Group B rallying between 1983 and 1986. The mid-engined, two-seater had 160bhp at its disposal in road trim, an output sufficient for a top speed of 125mph and a 0–60mph time of under seven seconds.

RENAULT Model	ENGINE cc/cyl	DATES	CONDITION 1	2	3
4CV	747/ 760/4	1947–61	£3,500	£2,000	£850
Fregate	1997/4	1952–60	£3,000	£2,000	£1,000
Dauphine	845/4	1956–66	£1,500	£1,000	£350
Dauphine Gordini	845/4	1961–66	£2,000	£1,000	£450
Floride	845/4	1959–62	£3,000	£2,000	£600
Caravelle	956/ 1108/4	1962–68	£4,500	£2,800	£750
R4	747/ 845/4	1961–86	£2,000	£1,500	£350
R8/R10	1108/4	1962–71	£1,800	£750	£200
R8 Gordini	1108/4	1965–66	£8,000	£5,000	£2,000
R8 Gordini	1255/4	1966–70	£8,000	£5,500	£2,500
R8S	1108/4	1968–71	£2,000	£1,200	£400

Riley

The small firm of Riley was right at the forefront of the early British motor car industry, producing its first car in 1898. In the 1920s and 1930s, the Coventry firm produced some very appealing and highly regarded small sporting cars, with elegant bodies and excellent power units, all of which had twin low-set camshafts operating pushrods and overhead valves. In the later 1930s, the company spread itself too thinly with too many models and not enough capital, and was forced to sell out to Morris in 1938. The immediate post-war products, the RM-series cars, were hallmark Riley sporting saloons, still much appreciated by enthusiasts today for their looks, long-legged cruising ability and assured handling. For many fans, the RMs also rate as the last real Rileys. Sadly, later models were rather ill-served under the BMC banner, which spawned a series of dull, badge-engineered look-alikes. About the only intriguing offspring was the Elf – basically, a Mini with a boot, a fancier grille and a smattering of wood veneer, but it can make a distinctive budget classic. Eventually, the Riley name faded away for good in 1969.

1934 Riley 9hp Monaco, 1087cc, engine overhauled, 50 miles covered since, finished in dark green with black wings, green leather upholstery, stored for some years, original, bodywork and mechanics in good condition.
£4,000–5,000 BRIT

Since its introduction in 1926, the Riley 9hp was favoured by the discerning sporting motorist, and the Monaco saloon proved to be the cornerstone of the range. Initially fabric-bodied, the Monaco adopted a semi-panelled construction late in 1931 with the introduction of the Plus Ultra series. This style of coachwork was superseded late in 1933, and for the last two years of production, the Monaco was of conventional aluminium on ash-frame construction.

1949 Riley RMA Saloon, 1500cc engine, completely restored 1995, all new suspension and bushes, flashing indicators, finished in brown and fawn with matching interior, seats retrimmed, new carpets, heater.
£5,500–6,500 H&H

1948 Riley RMB, 2443cc, 4-cylinder engine, stainless steel exhaust, roof rewooded and recovered, fitted heater, radio, engine in need of attention, ex Sussex police car.
£6,000–7,000 UMC

1950 Riley RMA Saloon, completely restored 1998, engine reconditioned, mechanics overhauled, rewired, chassis zinc-coated, body frame repaired, flashing indicators, finished in maroon, red interior.
£5,000–6,000 BKS

By the end of the 1930s, Riley had lost its battle to remain independent and had become part of the Nuffield Organisation. Nevertheless, Rileys of the immediate post-war years were recognisably products of the 'old firm'. Most popular of these was the 1.5 litre RMA sports saloon, which came with torsion-bar independent front suspension, hydro-mechanical brakes and Percy Riley's classic twin-camshaft, overhead-valve engine in four-cylinder guise. An improved version – the RME, with fully hydraulic brakes – appeared in 1952, and the model continued in production until 1955.

RILEY Model	ENGINE cc/cyl	DATES	CONDITION 1	2	3
9hp	1034/2	1906–07	£9,000	£6,000	£3,000
Speed 10	1390/2	1909–10	£10,000	£6,000	£3,000
11	1498/4	1922–27	£7,000	£4,000	£2,000
9	1075/4	1927–32	£10,000	£7,000	£4,000
9 Gamecock	1098/4	1932–33	£14,000	£10,000	£6,000
Lincock 12hp	1458/6	1933–36	£9,000	£7,000	£5,000
Imp 9hp	1089/4	1934–35	£35,000	£28,000	£20,000
Kestrel 12hp	1496/4	1936–38	£8,000	£5,000	£2,000
Sprite 12hp	1496/4	1936–38	£40,000	£35,000	£20,000
Many Riley 9hp 'Specials' available ideal for VSCC and club events.					

RILEY Model	ENGINE cc/cyl	DATES	CONDITION 1	2	3
1½ litre RMA	1496/4	1945–52	£6,000	£3,500	£1,500
1½ litre RME	1496/4	1952–55	£6,000	£3,500	£1,500
2½ litre RMB/F	2443/4	1946–53	£9,000	£7,000	£3,000
2½ litre Roadster	2443/4	1948–50	£18,000	£11,000	£9,000
2½ litre Drophead	2443/4	1948–51	£18,000	£14,000	£10,000
Pathfinder	2443/4	1953–57	£3,500	£2,000	£750
2.6	2639/6	1957–59	£3,000	£1,800	£750
1.5	1489/4	1957–65	£3,000	£2,000	£850
4/68	1489/4	1959–61	£1,500	£700	£300
4/72	1622/4	1961–69	£1,600	£800	£300
Elf I/II/III	848/4	1961–66	£1,500	£850	£400
Kestrel I/II	1098/4	1965–67	£1,500	£850	£400

1950 Riley 2½ Litre Roadster, 2443cc, 4-cylinder engine, torsion-bar independent front suspension, rack-and-pinion steering, restored 1990, engine rebuilt, 17,000 miles covered since, finished in ivory, new maroon upholstery, original apart from flashing indicators, excellent condition.
£15,000–17,000 BRIT

The third year of RM production saw the appearance of the drophead version of the 2½ Litre, together with an attractive two/three-seat roadster. The latter was a formidable motor car, being capable of the 'magic ton'.

1952 Riley RMB, 2443cc engine, unrestored, finished in maroon, good condition.
£5,000–6,000 RIL

1963 Riley Elf, 848cc, 4-cylinder engine, finished in grey and cream, red interior trim, 44,000 miles recorded, 1 owner, original condition.
£2,250–2,750 UMC

Rochdale

◀ **1958 Rochdale GT Olympic Coupé,** 948cc, Ford 4-cylinder engine, twin SU carburettors, older restoration, finished in red, grey and red interior, some crazing to body, otherwise good condition.
£1,750–2,100 H&H

The Rochdale Olympic Mk I coupé was in production for seven years. Its fibreglass body had excellent aerodynamics, and the car could be fitted with a 1500cc BMC engine or 948cc Ford 100E unit, as is the case with this example.

Rolls-Royce

Henry Royce was a Manchester electrical engineer, who built three experimental 10hp, two-cylinder cars in 1903. The Honourable Charles Rolls was an entrepreneur who sold foreign cars in London. They teamed up in 1904 to form Rolls-Royce, a name that ever since has represented excellence with elegance and supreme luxury. From the beginning of their partnership, they established Rolls-Royce's credentials as an exclusive producer of very expensive and superb motor cars of the highest quality. The 40/50, which became known universally as the Silver Ghost, really could make a plausible claim to being the 'best car in the world', although in the 1930s, for example, such an extravagant claim was more difficult to justify against rival luxury contenders at home and abroad. The Silver Ghost was continually developed through the years until it was replaced in 1925 by the New Phantom, later referred to as the Phantom I. This continued the Rolls-Royce policy of evolution rather than revolution – it was, in essence, a Ghost chassis with a new overhead-valve engine. Earlier in

1922, Rolls-Royce had added the smaller 3127cc 20 model, which evolved in 1929 into the 3669cc 20/25 and later into the 25/30. In 1931, Rolls-Royce bought Bentley – some suggest the main motive was to stifle competition from the magnificent Bentley 8 Litre. In 1949, Rolls-Royce entered a new era with the Silver Dawn, the first Rolls-Royce offered complete by the factory rather than as a chassis to be fitted with bespoke coachwork of the owner's choosing. Rolls-Royce continued to offer chassis to coachbuilders alongside its own factory-bodied cars until 1965 and the launch of the Silver Shadow. This new Rolls-Royce was the first to feature monocoque construction, having an integral body and chassis which, at a stroke, removed the scope for coachbuilt bodies, although the Phantom V Limousine still retained a separate chassis. In 1971, Rolls-Royce became bankrupt after trouble with the RB211 aircraft engine, and the car division was separated out and floated as a public company. These days, of course, the quintessential British luxury brand is owned by BMW.

1919 Rolls-Royce Silver Ghost Alpine Eagle,
7428cc, 6-cylinder engine, completely restored, finished in red with black wings and hood, original.
£95,000–105,000 BLE

Michael Wright, Ghost in the Highlands, depicting a Rolls-Royce Silver Ghost passing Loch Maree, in the heart of the Scottish Highlands, water-colour, signed, mounted, framed and glazed, 18 x 24in (46 x 61cm).
£2,000–2,500 BKS

1925 Rolls-Royce 40/50 Silver Ghost Dual-Cowl Tourer,
Barker-style coachwork by Cassini & Tonolo, chassis no. 62EU, engine no. U155, equipped with nickel fittings throughout, Barker dipping headlamps, scuttle-mounted side lamps, twin side-mounted spares, 2-piece windscreen with side deflectors, Auster-type rear screen, finished in ivory with black wheels, good condition throughout.
£47,000–54,000 BKS

Produced between 1907 and 1925, the Rolls-Royce Silver Ghost was powered by a six-cylinder, bi-block engine with a capacity of 7428cc. This particular car was delivered new with Thrupp & Maberly coachwork, but during restoration in 1968, the bodywork was replaced by the current Barker-style dual-cowl coachwork.

1924 Rolls-Royce 20hp Cabriolet, coachwork by Barker, chassis no. GH38, centre window pillars fold into a recess between the doors, divided windscreen, correct early wheels and lamps, older restoration, finished in pale yellow and black, beige leather upholstery.
£38,000–44,000 RCC

1926 Rolls-Royce 20hp Sedanca Limousine,
chassis no. GYK49, engine no. G1861, Barker dipping
headlights, rear-mounted luggage trunk, side-mounted
spare, windscreen visors, older restoration, recent major
engine overhaul, finished in dark blue with black wings.
£38,000–44,000 BKS

This car was first registered in December 1927
to HRH The Prince of Wales, sporting sedanca
limousine coachwork. It remained with the Royal
household until 1929, when it was acquired by
Lady Cunard, after which it passed through a
succession of owners. In the late 1930s, it was
fitted with a saloon body, then at some later
date the present sedanca limousine coachwork.

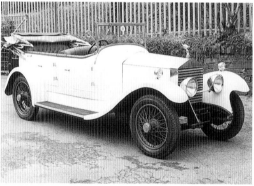

1927 Rolls-Royce 20hp Tourer, coachwork by
Horsfield, chassis no. GMJ56, correct nickel lamps and
fittings, 21in wheels, trunk with fitted suitcases, finished
in ivory, buttoned red leather interior in good condition,
stored for some time, in need of recommissioning.
£26,000–29,000 RCC

▶ **1927 Rolls-Royce 20hp Tourer,** chassis no. GYK28,
originally a Barker limousine, rebodied in recent years,
new exhaust system, correct 21in wheels, nickel lamps,
full wet weather gear, finished in blue with black wings,
polished aluminium bonnet, blue leather upholstery in
good condition.
£24,000–27,000 RCC

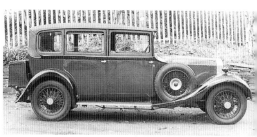

1926 Rolls-Royce 20hp Limousine, coachwork by
Grosvenor, chassis no. GZK37, correct instrumentation
and lamps, rear-mounted trunk, engine overhauled 1991
at a cost of c£10,000, little use since, finished in green,
original brown leather interior, 1 of only 3 20hp models
bodied by Grosvenor, in need of minor cosmetic
attention, otherwise good original condition.
£20,000–23,000 RCC

1926 Rolls-Royce 20hp Tourer, Barker-style coachwork
by Horsfield & Son, chassis no. GCK44, engine no.
61571, 3127cc, 6-cylinder engine, rebodied mid-1960s,
engine recently overhauled, finished in off-white,
red leather upholstery in need of minor attention to
the stitching, otherwise good condition throughout.
£16,000–19,000 BRIT

Joining the 40/50 Ghost in 1922, the Rolls-Royce
20hp was offered to meet the need for a smaller car
suitable for the owner/driver. It was powered by a six-
cylinder, overhead-valve engine displacing 3.1 litres,
and when fitted with touring coachwork, the car was
capable of maintaining comparatively high average
speeds with a surprisingly modest fuel consumption.
Initially, the 'Baby Rolls', as the 20hp has often been
called, was identifiable by its horizontal radiator slats.

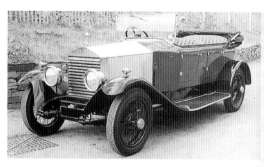

ROLLS-ROYCE Model	ENGINE cc/cyl	DATES	CONDITION 1	2	3
Silver Ghost 40/50	7035/6	pre-WWI	£350,000+	£120,000	£80,000
Silver Ghost 40/50	7428/6	post-WWI	£110,000+	£70,000	£40,000
20hp (3-speed)	3127/6	1922–25	£29,000+	£23,000	£15,000
20hp	3127/6	1925–29	£30,000+	£24,000	£15,000
Phantom I	7668/6	1925–29	£50,000+	£28,000	£22,000
20/25	3669/6	1925–26	£30,000+	£18,000	£13,000
Phantom II	7668/6	1929–35	£40,000+	£30,000	£20,000
Phantom II Continental	7668/6	1930–35	£60,000+	£40,000	£28,000
25/30	4257/6	1936–38	£24,000+	£18,000	£12,000
Phantom III	7340/12	1936–39	£38,000	£28,000	£14,000
Wraith	4257/6	1938–39	£38,000	£32,000	£25,000

Prices will vary considerably depending on heritage, originality, coachbuilder, completeness and body
style. A poor reproduction body can often mean that the value is based only upon that of a rolling
chassis and engine.

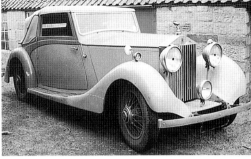

1927 Rolls-Royce 20hp Drophead Coupé, coachwork by Southern Motors, chassis no. GRJ17, engine no. U7G, 3 litre engine, period lighting, correct instrumentation, aluminium coachwork and upholstery in good condition, last used 1987, in need of refurbishment and recommissioning.
£11,000–13,000 BKS

When first registered, this car had Hooper cabriolet coachwork. In the mid-1930s, it was consigned to Southern Motors, where it was clothed in contemporary drophead coupé style.

1927 Rolls-Royce 20hp Weymann Saloon, coachwork by Mulliner, chassis no. GHJ12, engine no. 07L, 3.1 litres, windscreen visor, dummy pram irons, side-mounted spare, original lightweight Weymann saloon coachwork covered in black fabric, original red leather upholstery in very good condition.
£18,000–22,000 BKS

1928 Rolls-Royce 20hp Fabric-Bodied Saloon, Weymann-style coachwork by Mulliner, chassis no. GTM38, side- and rear-mounted spares, nickel lamps, interior in need of attention, original.
£19,000–22,000 RCC

◄ **1929 Rolls-Royce 20hp Tourer,** 3127cc, 6-cylinder engine, 4-speed manual gearbox with right-hand change, reconditioned cylinder head, new tonneau and hood bag, replacement Barker-style aluminium coachwork, finished in ivory, paintwork and nickel fittings in good condition.
£20,000–23,000 Mot

1929 Rolls-Royce 20hp Sedanca Cabriolet, coachwork by Windovers, 3 litres, 4-wheel brakes, finished in ivory and black, brown leather upholstery to the front, West of England cloth to the rear, original mechanical specification.
£22,000–25,000 BKS

It is thought that originally this car had two bodies for winter and summer use, one a Hooper formal landaulette, the other the sedanca cabriolet shown here.

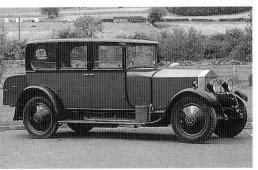

◄ **1929 Rolls-Royce 20hp Limousine,** finished in red and black, well maintained, good condition.
£16,000–18,000 TEN

◀ **1925 Rolls-Royce Phantom I Four-Door Hearse,** coachwork by Startin of Birmingham, chassis no. 50RC, finished in blue, chassis and mechanics correct and complete, stored for some years, sound condition.
£14,000–16,000 RCC

1925 Rolls-Royce 40/50hp Phantom I Convertible Cabriolet, coachwork by Hooper, replacement engine, Barker dipping headlamps, CAV tail lights, fishtail exhaust, twin side-mounted spares, fold-away occasional seats to the rear, finished in black with polished aluminium bonnet, new black mohair hood 1989 to original pattern.
£50,000–55,000 BKS

The 'New Phantom' was developed by Rolls-Royce and announced in 1925 as a successor to the acclaimed Silver Ghost. The chassis detail was similar in many respects to that of the Silver Ghost, and although there was a trend for unit-construction engine/gearbox assemblies, separate units were retained for the new model. The 7668cc engine had a one-piece detachable cast-iron cylinder head and pushrod-operated overhead valves. This particular car was displayed on the Rolls-Royce stand at the Olympia Motor Exhibition of October 1925. It features full seven-seat coachwork. The hood and window arrangement allows the car to be fully enclosed, have an open chauffer's compartment, or be completely open, with windows, division and side pillars folded away and hood fully down.

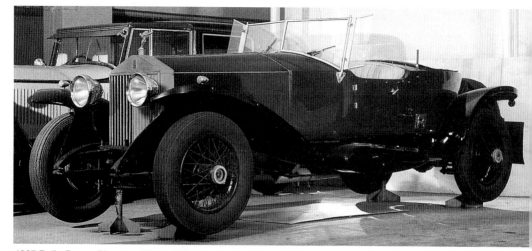

1927 Rolls-Royce Phantom I Boat-Tail Tourer, chassis no. 95EF, 7668cc engine, AT spring gaiters, speedometer with trip, bonnet-side security locks, lightweight tapered wings and aerodynamically styled mounting steps, split windscreen with wind deflectors, rear passenger screen, originally bodied with open tourer coachwork by Barker, finished in burgundy with black wings, tan upholstery.
£33,000–37,000 COYS

1931 Rolls-Royce 40/50hp Phantom I Limousine,
7668cc engine, full wheel discs, left-hand drive, restored, finished in maroon and black, excellent condition.
£48,000–54,000 COHN

1930 Rolls-Royce 20/25 Sedanca De Ville, D-back coachwork by Frederick Wood, chassis no. GWP37, rear-mounted spare, finished in black and maroon, 43,000 miles recorded, original, good mechanical condition.
£30,000–33,000 RCC

1930 Rolls-Royce 20/25hp Close-Coupled Coupé,
coachwork by Park Ward, long-wheelbase chassis, rewired, finished in cream and black, black leather interior, 55,000 miles recorded.
£20,000–23,000 BKS

Introduced in 1929, the 20/25hp had a 3669cc engine and was built alongside the 40/50hp Phantom II. As demand for the big Phantom slowed during the Depression, so sales favoured the 20/25hp, an owner/driver car offering an extra 500cc over the 20hp, together with remarkable flexibility and quietness from the smooth six-cylinder engine. This car is one of 150 coupé models bodied by Park Ward in 1930.

1933 Rolls-Royce 20/25 Landaulette, coachwork by Hooper, chassis no. GHA17, finished in black and maroon, black leather to front compartment, beige cloth to rear, interior woodwork refinished, good mechanical and bodywork condition.
£30,000–33,000 RCC

1931 Rolls-Royce Phantom I Tourer, coachwork by Newmarket, chassis no. S201PR, wind-up windows, removable centre pillars, low windscreen, twin side-mounted spares, left-hand drive, finished in black and yellow, beige leather upholstery, in need of cosmetic attention, good mechanical and structural condition.
£50,000–55,000 RCC

This car was one of the last Phantom Is to be produced in Rolls-Royce's American Springfield factory.

1933 Rolls-Royce 20/25 Limousine, D-back coachwork by Mulliner, chassis no. GMU22, occasional seats, finished in white, beige leather interior in good condition, in need of tidying.
£14,000–17,000 RCC

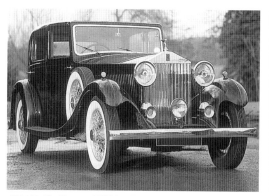

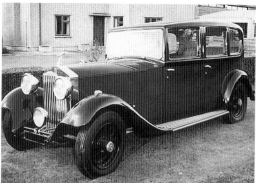

1934 Rolls-Royce 20/25hp Sports Saloon, coachwork by H.J. Mulliner, 3699cc, overhead-valve 6-cylinder inline engine, 4-speed manual gearbox with side-change, synchromesh on top ratios, beam front axle, semi-elliptic leaf springs front and rear, servo-assisted 4-wheel mechanical drum brakes, long-wheelbase chassis, louvred bonnet, twin side-mounted spares, older restoration, complete and correct set of tools in boot lid tray, finished in black, red leather interior, in need of cosmetic attention and recommissioning.
£13,800–15,200 C

1935 Rolls-Royce 20/25 Limousine, coachwork by Barker, chassis no. GWE41, engine no. Q8E, 3669cc, 6-cylinder engine, recently restored, finished in dark green and black, black leather-trimmed chauffer's compartment, beige West of England cloth to rear, interior woodwork in very good condition.
£23,000–26,000 BRIT

By the time production had ceased in 1937, with the introduction of the 25/30, 3,827 20/25hp chassis had been built.

1936 Rolls-Royce 20/25 Sports Saloon, coachwork by Mulliner, 3.7 litre, 6-cylinder engine, second spare wheel, extra sound insulation, sprung steering wheel, completely restored 1997, finished in burgundy and black, burgundy leather interior trim.
£20,000–24,000 BKS

1929 Rolls-Royce Phantom II Boat-Tail Tourer, chassis no. 151XJ, 7668cc, restored, finished in maroon with matching leather interior trim.
£22,000–26,000 H&H

1930 Rolls-Royce Phantom II Close-Coupled Limousine, coachwork by Thrupp & Maberly, louvred bonnet and cowl, semi-elliptic leaf-spring rear suspension, finished in beige over brown with yellow wheels.
£32,000–36,000 COYS

The Phantom II, introduced in 1929, was said to have been the last model that Royce designed himself. Between 1929 and 1935, about 1,770 of these chassis were built, in 144 and 150in wheelbases, the former being used for the Continental models.

1930 Rolls-Royce Phantom II Sports Sedanca De Ville, coachwork by Windovers, chassis no. 64GY, Grebel pillar lamp, rear-mounted spare, helmet wings, side steps in place of running boards, finished in black, polished aluminium bonnet top and waistline ledge, chrome dashboard and door cappings, interior recently retrimmed.
£50,000–60,000 RCC

1933 Rolls-Royce Phantom II Limousine, D-back coachwork by Thrupp & Maberly, chassis no. 78MY, new cylinder head, twin side-mounted spares, luggage trunk, occasional seats, finished in black and maroon, black leather-trimmed chauffer's compartment, fawn cloth to rear.
£22,000–25,000 RCC

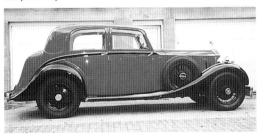

1936 Rolls-Royce 25/30hp Saloon, coachwork by James Young, chassis no. GTL6, engine no. K22R, sliding sunroof, wind-up glass partition, completely restored, finished in burgundy over black, new beige leather interior.
£18,000–20,000 BKS

1937 Rolls-Royce 25/30 Saloon, coachwork by Barker, chassis no. GLP16, sunroof, starter motor, dynamo and water pump overhauled, finished in ivory and black, brown interior trim, very good condition.
£18,500–21,000 H&H

1937 Rolls-Royce 40/50hp Phantom III Razor-Edge Sedanca De Ville, coachwork by Mulliner, original engine with solid-tappet conversion, chassis and suspension replaced 1960s following an accident, twin external trumpet horns, centre spotlamp, wind-down glass division, rear picnic tables, original brown leather upholstery to front compartment, cloth to rear, in need of restoration.
£13,000–15,500 BKS

Calling on the company's vast experience of building V12 aero engines, with such advanced features as skeleton cylinder blocks with wet liners and aluminium cylinder heads, Rolls-Royce launched the radical V12 Phantom III in late 1935. It was a generation ahead of its time, the 7.3 litre engine driving through a four-speed gearbox. Independent front suspension provided additional comfort.

▶ **1937 Rolls-Royce Phantom III Limousine,** coachwork by Hooper, chassis no. 3BUT170, V12 engine, finished in black, deep red leather interior trim, in need of tidying and cosmetic attention, good original condition.
£20,000–24,000 RCC

1937 Rolls-Royce Phantom III Limousine, coachwork by Hooper, chassis no. 3BT115, engine no. L18Q, 7340cc V12 engine, independent front suspension, finished in black and green, leather upholstery to the front compartment, cloth to the rear, 4 owners, chassis in good condition, remainder fair.
£25,000–28,000 BKS

A 1938-design silver-plated Rolls-Royce electric desk lamp, to an original design by Charles Sykes, published in the magazine of the American Rolls-Royce Owners' Club, May 1973.
£650–800 BKS

A known continuous history can add value to and enhance the enjoyment of a car.

▶ **1954 Rolls Royce Silver Dawn Saloon,** 4566cc, 6-cylinder engine, finished in black and silver-grey, good condition.
£20,000–22,000 BLE

1952 Rolls-Royce Silver Wraith Limousine, coachwork by Mulliner, long-wheelbase chassis, P100 headlamps, division, occasional seats, finished in two-tone green, black leather-trimmed front compartment, fawn cloth to rear, unused for some time.
£23,000–26,000 RCC

1956 Rolls-Royce Silver Cloud I Saloon, automatic transmission, picnic tables, 106mph top speed, transmission, brake servo, wheel and master cylinders rebuilt, new stainless steel exhaust system, brightwork rechromed, resprayed in Ebony green, new Connolly hide upholstery, excellent condition.
£22,000–25,000 BKS

The Silver Cloud I was the last Rolls-Royce car to be powered by a six-cylinder engine, adopting the strong and reliable 4887cc power unit it shared with the Silver Wraith.

1963 Rolls-Royce Silver Cloud III Saloon, 6230cc V8 engine, £18,000 recently spent on mechanical work, bodywork restored 1979, including new wings and sills, resprayed in Shell grey over Midnight blue, original interior trim, all interior woodwork in very good condition.
£15,000–17,000 BRIT

At its introduction in 1962, the Silver Cloud III represented the ultimate development of the Cloud series. It was powered by the 6.2 litre V8 engine that had been introduced in 1969 in the Silver Cloud II. Various modifications had been carried out on the engine, including the installation of larger SU carburettors and an increase in compression ratio, producing an extra 15bhp. The Silver Cloud III was the last Rolls-Royce to be built on a separate chassis and remained in production until 1965, when it was replaced by the Silver Shadow.

1964 Rolls-Royce Silver Cloud III Limousine, long-wheelbase chassis, over £40,000 spent in last 10 years, air conditioning, tinted glass, finished in metallic green with gold coachlining, recently retrimmed in red leather to the front, green suede to the rear, dark wood veneers, gold-plated door pulls, 10,225 miles recorded, 2 owners.
£15,000–17,000 S

The S1, 2 and 3 were Bentley's equivalents of the Rolls-Royce Silver Cloud I, II and III. Although virtually identical, apart from the distinctive radiator, Bentley versions can often be cheaper than Rolls-Royce counterparts. This is not a factor of rarity, as with the launch of the Silver Cloud II in 1959, Rolls-Royce versions outnumbered Bentley offerings for the first time.

◄ **1965 Rolls-Royce Silver Cloud III Flying Spur Saloon,** coachwork by Mulliner Park Ward, 6.2 litre, aluminium V8 engine, 4-speed automatic transmission, new stainless steel exhaust system, 48,100 miles recorded, excellent condition throughout.
£40,000–44,000 BKS

This Silver Cloud III features the elegant Mulliner Park Ward Flying Spur four-door coachwork that debuted on the Bentley Continental in 1957, and which became available on the Rolls-Royce chassis shortly after the introduction of the Cloud III. However, virtually all Flying Spur bodywork was built on the Bentley chassis; only 54 were made for Rolls-Royces.

1963 Rolls-Royce Phantom V Seven-Seat Limousine, coachwork by James Young, 4-speed automatic transmission, power steering, left-hand drive, air conditioning, restored, finished in Oxford blue, Dove grey interior, very good condition throughout.
£50,000–55,000 BKS

A limited-production model even for Rolls-Royce, the Phantom V was launched in 1959. With a similar 6.2 litre V8 engine and running gear to the Silver Cloud II, it was the largest Rolls-Royce ever built, having a 145in wheelbase and measuring an impressive 20ft from bumper to bumper. The Phantom V attracted clients from among the rich, the famous and the aristocratic, with a customer list that ranged from Queen Elizabeth to the celebrated Las Vegas entertainer Liberace. Although it came late in the company's coachbuilding history, the James Young Phantom V limousine proved a tremendous success, 195 examples being delivered.

1969 Rolls-Royce Phantom VI Limousine, coachwork by Mulliner Park Ward, original Sony TV to rear compartment, occasional seats, finished in silver, blue leather interior, internal veneers in good condition.
£32,000–36,000 RCC

The first owner of this car was the actor Stanley Baker.

1971 Rolls-Royce Silver Shadow LWB Saloon, 6750cc, pushrod V8 engine, 3-speed automatic transmission, left-hand drive, finished in Bordeaux red, black leather interior trim, very good condition throughout.
£9,000–11,000 BKS

The Silver Shadow marked a major departure for Rolls-Royce, for it was the company's first unitary-construction model. Another major step was the adoption of four-wheel disc brakes and independent rear suspension, the latter incorporating a self-levelling mechanism.

1972 Rolls-Royce Silver Shadow Saloon, 6750cc V8 engine, all-independent suspension, finished in brown, tan leather upholstery, 87,300 miles recorded, in need of cosmetic attention, good condition throughout.
£6,000–7,000 BKS

1974 Rolls-Royce Silver Shadow Saloon, 6750cc V8 engine, all-independent suspension, left-hand drive, original 8-track stereo player, finished in metallic green, dark green vinyl roof, beige Connolly interior, 64,000km recorded, 'as new' condition throughout.
£9,000–11,000 BKS

1976 Rolls-Royce Silver Shadow I, 6750cc, Waxoyled, new carpets, finished in metallic silver-blue, two-tone blue interior trim and upholstery, 89,000 miles recorded, well maintained.
£6,000–7,000 H&H

1979 Rolls-Royce Silver Shadow II, 6750cc, new exhaust system, brakes overhauled, finished in original Champagne yellow, black hide interior, 82,287 miles recorded, good condition.
£8,500–10,000 H&H

1974 Rolls-Royce Corniche Convertible, finished in white, dark blue fully-lined hood, interior recently retrimmed in Biscuit leather, pale satin-finished woodwork, good condition.
£18,000–22,000 RCC

ROLLS-ROYCE Model	ENGINE cc/cyl	DATES	CONDITION		
			1	2	3
Silver Wraith LWB	4566/ 4887/6	1951–59	£25,000	£17,000	£10,000
Silver Wraith SWB	4257/ 4566/6	1947–59	£20,000	£13,000	£10,000
Silver Wraith Drophead	4257/ 4566/6	1947–59	£50,000	£35,000	£25,000
Silver Dawn Std Steel	4257/ 4566/6	1949–52	£25,000	£15,000	£10,000
Silver Dawn Std Steel	4257/ 4566/6	1952–55	£30,000	£20,000	£15,000
Silver Dawn Coachbuilt	4257/ 4566/6	1949–55	£35,000+	£25,000	£18,000
Silver Dawn Drophead	4257/ 4566/6	1949–55	£60,000	£50,000	£30,000
Silver Cloud I	4887/6	1955–59	£18,000	£10,000	£8,000
SCI Coupé Coachbuilt	4887/6	1955–59	£30,000	£20,000	£15,000
SCI Conv (HJM)	4887/6	1955–59	£80,000+	£60,000+	£40,000
Silver Cloud II	6230/8	1959–62	£19,000	£10,000	£8,000
SCII Conv (HJM)	6230/8	1959–62	£80,000	£75,000	£40,000
SCII Conv (MPW)	6230/8	1959–62	£60,000	£40,000	£32,000
Silver Cloud III	6230/8	1962–65	£25,000	£12,000	£10,000
SCIII Conv (MPW)	6230/8	1962–65	£70,000	£45,000	£35,000
Silver Shadow	6230/ 6750/8	1965–76	£14,000	£9,000	£7,000
S Shadow I Coupé (MPW)	6230/ 6750/8	1965–70	£15,000	£10,000	£8,000
SSI Drophead (MPW)	6230/ 6750/8	1965–70	£33,000	£25,000	£18,000
Corniche FHC	6750/8	1971–77	£15,000	£11,000	£8,000
Corniche Convertible	6750/8	1971–77	£28,000	£22,000	£18,000
Camargue	6750/8	1975–85	£35,000	£25,000	£18,000

1976 Rolls-Royce Corniche Convertible, 6750cc, 220bhp, power-operated fully-lined hood, air conditioning, finished in dark blue, grey hide interior, well maintained.
£19,000–23,000 BKS

1980 Rolls-Royce Corniche Convertible, 120mph top speed, 0–60mph in 9.6 seconds, split-level air conditioning, finished in black with black hood, tan Connolly hide upholstery, 65,000 miles recorded, 2 owners, good condition throughout.
£27,000–30,000 BKS

The Rolls-Royce Corniche was made in small numbers, never more than 300 a year. It was not built at Rolls-Royce's main factory in Crewe, but at the Park Ward works in London. It was one of the last cars to be constructed using traditional coachbuilding skills by a diminishing band of craftsmen who were regarded as the best in the world.

1980 Rolls-Royce Silver Wraith Saloon, 6750cc V8 engine, finished in metallic beige and brown, good condition.
£11,500–13,500 BLE

1981 Rolls-Royce Silver Spirit Saloon, 6750cc V8 engine, finished in Ice green, Sand interior trim, 42,556 miles recorded, 3 owners, excellent condition.
£13,000–15,000 H&H

The Rolls Royce Silver Spirit was introduced in October 1980 to replace the ageing Silver Shadow II.

1981 Rolls-Royce Silver Spur LWB Saloon, finished in black, black Everflex roof, beige interior trim, fitted drinks cabinets and picnic tables, telephones to front and rear compartments, 42,000 miles recorded, excellent condition throughout.
£14,000–16,000 TEN

▶ **1982 Rolls-Royce Silver Spur Saloon,** 6750cc V8 engine, finished in Exeter blue, Mushroom hide interior trim, 84,000 miles recorded, very good original condition.
£10,000–12,000 BRIT

Rover

Rover's roots were in the booming bicycle industry of the closing decades of the 19th century. The first Rover car appeared in 1904. In its early years, Rover had never been a high-volume car maker, and during the mid-1920s it concentrated on the solid middle-class territory that, to this day, is Rover's home ground. As Rover emerged from the war, it made do with the P3, an updated pre-war design, until the now much loved and so-called 'Auntie' Rover, the P4, was ready in 1950. Thoroughly modern and at first considered even avant-garde by some more traditionally-minded motorists, it went on to establish Rover's post-war reputation for dependable and robust quality cars. The big P5 saloon, launched in 1959, became a newsreel fixture outside 10 Downing Street as a P5 fleet loyally served ministers and prime ministers from Harold Wilson to Margaret Thatcher. The stylish

P6, especially in V8 form, has also become a favourite, admired and enjoyed in enthusiastic daily use. But while Rover models remained distinguished, Britain's motor industry was in turmoil and suffered from merger mania. No longer could Rover remain independent against this tide, and in 1967 it merged into the Leyland Motor Corporation. In this environment, Rover could have slithered into oblivion, but it managed to produce one great vehicle: the Range Rover of 1970 is, without doubt, a living classic. Somehow, Rover weathered the BL years and emerged on top when the organisation was named Rover Group in 1986. In 1994, it was acquired by BMW. Now, in the year 2000, BMW's troubled ownership is over and a trimmed-down Rover, divested of Land Rover, is owned by a British consortium. It's going to be an interesting few years.

1947 Rover 14 Saloon, 1901cc, fuel pump reconditioned, new kingpins, brakes and chassis refurbished, finished in black, blue upholstery, c1,000 miles in last 8 years, engine and gearbox in excellent condition, otherwise good condition.
£900–1,050 H&H

1947 Rover 14 Saloon, 1901cc, 6-cylinder engine, 4-speed manual gearbox, finished in black, tan interior, unused for some years, recommissioned 1996, 47,900 miles recorded.
£1,100–1,300 H&H

◄ **1948 Rover 12 Tourer,** 1496cc, period centre spotlamp, twin chrome horns, finished in maroon with matching interior, 1 owner for 33 years, in need of refurbishment.
£4,800–5,400 H&H

In all, 150 Rover 12 Tourers were built, and of these it is thought that only 50 survive.

Dealer prices

Miller's guide prices for dealer cars take into account the value of any guarantees or warranties that may be included in the purchase. Dealers must also observe additional statutory consumer regulations, which do not apply to private sellers. This is factored into our dealer guide prices. To identify dealer cars cross-refer the source codes at the ends of photo captions with the Key to Illustrations on page 330.

1952 Rover 75, finished in Sage green, green interior, 36,000 miles recorded, 3 owners, stored for over 30 years, in need of minor restoration, very good condition throughout.
£2,000–2,500 COYS

ROVER Model	ENGINE cc/cyl	DATES	CONDITION		
			1	2	3
10hp	998/2	1920–25	£5,000	£3,000	£1,500
9/20	1074/4	1925–27	£6,000	£4,000	£2,000
10/25	1185/4	1928–33	£7,000	£4,000	£2,500
14hp	1577/6	1933–39	£6,000	£4,250	£2,000
12	1496/4	1934–37	£7,000	£4,000	£1,500
20 Sports	2512/6	1937–39	£7,000	£4,500	£2,500

1954 Rover 90 Drophead Coupé, 2638cc, restored at a cost of £20,000, finished in gold, magnolia interior, 1 of only 2 produced, BMIHT certificate, concours condition.
£17,500–20,000 H&H

The Rover 90 was produced between 1953 and 1959, and approximately 35,000 examples were built. Rover's experimental department decided to investigate the concept of a drophead model and actually built two examples, this car being one of them. It is a Mulliner copy of a Pinin Farina design.

1963 Rover 95, 2625cc, 6-cylinder engine, finished in beige, mostly original, coachwork and chrome good, all mechanical components in excellent condition.
£2,000–2,500 BRIT

1963 Rover 95, 2695cc, finished in blue, grey interior, 81,000 miles recorded, 2 owners, very good condition throughout.
£1,300–1,550 H&H

► **c1960 Rover 100**, 2625cc, 6-cylinder engine, 4-speed manual gearbox, finished in grey, blue interior, stored for some years, 26,769 miles recorded, carpets in need of replacement, otherwise good condition throughout.
£3,500–4,000 H&H

◄ **1970 Rover P5B Coupé,** 3528cc V8 engine, 3-speed automatic transmission, completely restored, bare-metal respray in silver and Pine green, tan interior, 48,500 miles recorded, very good condition throughout.
£4,250–4,750 H&H

► **1971 Rover P5B Saloon,** 3.5 litre V8, bodywork restored, exterior brightwork replated, finished in blue, magnolia interior, good condition throughout.
£2,500–3,000 BKS

The installation of the Buick-derived, light-alloy V8 in the 3 litre P5 model gave Rover's stately flagship a new lease of life. Introduced in 1967, the 3.5 litre P5B was considerably faster than its predecessor, the V8's 160bhp boosting top speed to 110mph and chopping seven seconds from the 0–60mph time. Automatic transmission and power-assisted steering were standard features.

1971 Rover 2000 SC, 1978cc engine, finished in white, red leather interior, 62,000 miles recorded, 3 owners, excellent condition.
£2,000–2,500 H&H

1973 Rover 2000 SC, 1978cc engine, finished in white, brown interior, 32,000 miles recorded, 1 family ownership, excellent condition throughout.
£1,800–2,200 H&H

Rover P6 (1963–76)

Engine: Four-cylinder, 1978cc or 2204cc; V8, 3528cc.
Power output: 90–114bhp (2000); 98–115bhp (2200); 144bhp (3500).
Transmission: Four-speed manual; three-speed automatic.
Brakes: Discs all-round, servo-assisted.
Top speed: 94mph (2000 auto); 102 mph (2000 manual); 122mph (3500 manual).
0–60mph: 18 seconds (2000 auto); 15 seconds (2000 manual); 9.1 seconds (3500 manual).
Production: 327,808.
Price in 1963: £1,265.

In the 1950s, the warm and gentle charms of Rover's P4 had earned it the nickname of the 'Auntie' Rover, cherished affectionately by owners as one of the family. But frankly, by the early 1960s, the dumpy dowager was well past pensionable age and becoming something of a burden. That's where the P6 came in, at the October 1963 Earls Court Motor Show, young, vigorous, strikingly modern, almost avant-garde and all the more surprising for being a Rover, a name then more associated with staid sobriety than with dash and daring. Rover's traditional clientele may have choked into their cravats, but the press raved about it.

Autocar declared it 'one of the outstanding cars of the decade', and in 1964 it was voted Car of the Year. The praise was deserved, because there was no carry-over engineering from previous models. The sleek shape, evolved from an earlier gas-turbine prototype project, doffed its hat a little at the Citroën DS, as did the construction – a skeletal 'base unit' to which the body panels were bolted. Anchors were discs all-round, while suspension geometry was up to the minute. The initial version, the 2000, contributed a large part to Rover's 24 per cent upturn in sales during 1964, and for once the company didn't sit on its laurels. A pokier 2000TC – twin-carb model – followed in 1966, along with an automatic (the only P6 that couldn't top the ton). But the most exciting development came in 1968, when Rover squeezed in the fabulous Buick-derived 3.5 litre V8 to create the 3500. Initially, it was only available as an automatic, but a four-speed manual-gearbox version, the 3500S, became available in 1971, offering serious 120+mph performance, much appreciated by the police. In the final count, the P6 sold more than one-and-a-half times as many as any previous Rover. It should have led to greater things – but then came the SD1. You know the rest of the Rover story.

ROVER Model	ENGINE cc/cyl	DATES	CONDITION 1	2	3
P2 10	1389/4	1946–47	£3,200	£2,500	£1,000
P2 12	1496/4	1946–47	£3,500	£2,800	£1,200
P2 12 Tourer	1496/4	1947	£7,500	£3,500	£1,500
P2 14/16	1901/6	1946–47	£4,200	£3,000	£1,000
P2 14/16 Saloon	1901/6	1946–47	£3,700	£2,500	£700
P3 60	1595/4	1948–49	£5,000	£2,500	£1,000
P3 75	2103/6	1948–49	£4,000	£3,000	£800
P4 75	2103/6	1950–51	£4,000	£2,000	£1,200
P4 75	2103/6	1952–64	£3,500	£1,800	£1,200
P4 60	1997/4	1954–59	£3,200	£1,200	£1,200
P4 90	2638/6	1954–59	£4,000	£1,800	£1,200
P4 75	2230/6	1955–59	£3,800	£1,200	£1,000
P4 105R	2638/6	1957–58	£4,000	£2,000	£1,000
P4 105S	2638/6	1957–59	£4,000	£2,000	£1,000
P4 80	2286/4	1960–62	£3,000	£1,200	£800
P4 95	2625/6	1963–64	£3,000	£1,600	£500
P4 100	2625/6	1960–62	£3,800	£2,000	£1,000
P4 110	2625/6	1963–64	£3,800	£2,000	£1,000
P5 3 litre	2995/6	1959–67	£4,000	£2,500	£1,000
P5 3 litre Coupé	2995/6	1959–67	£5,500	£3,800	£1,000
P5B (V8)	3528/8	1967–74	£6,250	£4,500	£1,500
P5B (V8) Coupé	3528/8	1967–73	£6,250	£4,500	£1,500
P6 2000 SC Series 1	1980/4	1963–65	£2,200	£800	-
P6 2000 SC Series 1	1980/4	1966–70	£2,000	£800	-
P6 2000 SC Auto Series 1	1980/4	1966–70	£1,500	£600	-
P6 2000 TC Series 1	1980/4	1966–70	£2,000	£900	-
P6 2000 SC Series 2	1980/4	1970–73	£2,000	£900	-
P6 2000 SC Auto Series 2	1980/4	1970–73	£1,500	£800	-
P6 2000 TC Series 2	1980/4	1970–73	£2,000	£900	-
P6 3500 Series 1	3500/8	1968–70	£2,500	£1,400	-
P6 2200 SC	2200/4	1974–77	£1,750	£850	-
P6 2200 SC Auto	2200/4	1974–77	£2,500	£1,000	-
P6 2200 TC	2200/4	1974–77	£2,000	£1,000	-
P6 3500 Series 2	3500/8	1971–77	£3,000	£1,700	-
P6 3500 S Series 2	3500/8	1971–77	£2,000	£1,500	-

◀ **1974 Rover 2200 SC,** 2204cc engine, finished in Tobacco Leaf, black interior, new torque converter and drive plate, otherwise completely original, 40,800 miles recorded, 3 owners.
£1,400–1,650 H&H

1972 Rover 3500 S, 3528cc V8 engine, manual gearbox, 4-wheel disc brakes, 125mph top speed, 0–60mph in 9.1 seconds, carburettor overhauled, new alternator, finished in Almond and black, fewer than 40,000 miles recorded, original condition.
£3,600–4,000 BRIT

1975 Rover 2200, 2204cc, 4-cylinder engine, finished in Tobacco Leaf, beige leather interior, well maintained, 3 owners, very good condition.
£1,000–1,200 BRIT

▶ **1977 Rover SDI 3500 Estate,** 3.5 litre V8 engine, restored, 1 of only 2 built, good condition throughout.
£4,250–4,750 HMM

Saab

When Saab made its first foray into four-wheeled transport, it could so easily have come down to earth with a bump. For *Svenska Aeroplan AB* was a Swedish aeroplane manufacturer, and to design its first car it employed a sculptor. Well that's not quite true: Sixten Sason had started out as a sculptor, but had since become a talented engineer. Remarkably, that first production Saab 92 formed the basis of a model series that ran from 1950 to 1979. The aircraft associations and clean slate resulted in a car that tossed convention aside. Its teardrop shape was like no other car of the era, slippery and aerodynamic. Meanwhile, in 1967, Saab augmented its line-up with the new-generation 99, another unconventional looker. In 1978, Saab raised its game to a new plane with the formidable 99 Turbo, a true mould-breaker that transformed the company's image for good and raised its profile to a higher level altogether.

1972 Saab 96 V4, finished in white, 2 owners, 80,000 miles recorded, completely original, unrestored.
£3,000–3,500 SAB

1974 Saab Sonett III, steel structure refurbished, engine and suspension uprated for competition, 3 owners, very good condition.
£5,000–6,000 SAB

Like most Sonetts, this Sonett III was exported originally to the USA.

Siata

1954 Siata 208S Spyder America Special, coachwork by Vignale, 283cu.in. Chevrolet V8 engine, dual 4-barrel carburettors, GM T-10 manual gearbox with Muncie floor-change, rewired, bare-metal respray in indigo blue.
£60,000–70,000 BKS

Siata (*Societa Italiana Applicazione Transformazione Automobilistiche*) was founded in 1926 by Giorgio Ambrosini. Initially, Siata tuned cars, mainly Fiats, and sold performance equipment. In 1948, the company built its first car. Every sports-car maker eyed the American market, and in 1952 Siata began to build cars with American engines, from the 720cc Crosley to the Chrysler V8. At the same time, it became the only specialist to use Fiat's 2 litre V8 engine, mating it to a five-speed gearbox of the company's own design. This set-up was fitted into a tubular chassis with all-independent suspension and Alfin drum brakes. Giovanni Michelotti, then at Vignale, styled the body. Only 35 Siata 208s were made, and this car is believed to be the third off the production line. Subsequently, it was fitted with a Chevrolet engine.

1970 Siata Spring Cabriolet, wire wheels, finished in blue, 62,000km recorded, good original condition.
£2,750–3,300 BKS

A two-seat sports roadster constructed on the rear-engined Fiat 850S floorpan, the Spring lasted until 1970, with a brief revival by Orsa in 1973.

Simca

◄ **1949 Simca 6 Coupé,** 570cc, 4-cylinder engine, 4-speed manual gearbox, disc brakes, left-hand drive, finished in cream and grey, very good condition.
£2,000–2,500 Pou

Singer

Via sewing machines and bicycles, George Singer produced his first motor car in Coventry in 1905. The Singer Nine of the 1930s had a really fine 972cc engine and, in open form, was a serious rival to MG offerings. Both designs endured into the 1950s without radical changes. The other great pre-war Singer was the 1½ Litre Le Mans. Post-war, Singer's products were too expensive to compete with the likes of BMC, and in 1955 the company was acquired by the Rootes empire. There, the marque was reduced to an upmarket badge that faded away for good in 1970.

1934 Singer Nine Le Mans Sports, 972cc, overhead-camshaft 4-cylinder engine, restored, engine and gearbox overhauled, rear axle fitted with modern hub seals, steering and brakes refurbished, new clutch and stainless steel exhaust, finished in British Racing green with red wheels, red leatherette interior, hood and sidescreens in excellent condition.
£10,000–11,000 BRIT

By the late 1920s, Singer had become Britain's third largest manufacturer behind Morris and Austin, sales having benefited from many competition successes. In terms of motor sporting achievements, the company's best years were the 1930s, thanks to the 9hp sports model, which proved its mettle in trials, racing and rallying.

1951 Singer Nine 4AB Roadster, 1074cc, overhead-camshaft 4-cylinder engine, 4-speed gearbox, independent front suspension, hydro-mechanical brakes, aluminium body, steel wings, older restoration, engine and running gear recently overhauled, new tonneau cover, finished in white, original tan interior.
£4,500–5,000 Mot

► **1961 Singer Gazelle Convertible,** finished in green, original, good condition.
£2,250–2,750 UMC

SINGER Model	ENGINE cc/cyl	DATES	CONDITION 1	2	3
10	1097/4	1918–24	£5,000	£2,000	£1,000
15	1991/6	1922–25	£6,000	£3,000	£1,500
14/34	1776/6	1926–27	£7,000	£4,000	£2,000
Junior	848/4	1927–32	£6,000	£3,000	£1,500
Senior	1571/4	1928–29	£7,000	£4,000	£2,000
Super 6	1776/6	1928–31	£7,000	£4,000	£2,000
9 Le Mans	972/4	1932–37	£13,000+	£8,000	£5,000
Twelve	1476/6	1932–34	£10,000	£7,000	£6,000
1½ Litre	1493/6	1934–36	£3,000	£2,000	£1,000
2 Litre	1991/6	1934–37	£4,000	£2,750	£1,000
11	1459/4	1935–36	£3,000	£2,000	£1,000
12	1525/4	1937–39	£3,000	£2,000	£1,000

Standard

From modest beginnings, Standard was marketing Britain's first inexpensive six-cylinder car by 1906. The company specialised in medium-range cars during the 1920s, but it was the Standard Little Nine that carried the company on in the 1930s. In 1945, with Captain John Black at the helm, Standard acquired the defunct Triumph marque as an upmarket badge. Standard-Triumph was merged into Leyland in 1961 and, ironically, it was the Standard name that was dropped almost immediately, while Triumph soldiered on until 1980.

1955 Standard Ten Saloon, 948cc, 4-cylinder engine, finished in black, red interior, little recent use, very good condition throughout.
£800–1,000 H&H

STANDARD Model	ENGINE cc/cyl	DATES	CONDITION 1	2	3
12	1609/4	1945–48	£2,000	£950	£250
12 DHC	1509/4	1945–48	£3,200	£2,000	£500
14	1776/4	1945–48	£3,000	£950	£250
Vanguard I/II	2088/4	1948–55	£2,200	£1,000	£250
Vanguard III	2088/4	1955–61	£1,800	£900	£200
Vanguard III Est	2088/4	1955–61	£2,000	£1,000	£250
Vanguard III Sportsman	2088/4	1955–58	£2,500	£1,200	£400
Vanguard Six	1998/6	1961–63	£2,000	£1,000	£500
Eight	803/4	1952–59	£1,250	£500	-
Ten	948/4	1955–59	£1,400	£800	-
Ensign I/II	1670/4	1957–63	£1,000	£800	-
Ensign I/II Est	1670/4	1962–63	£1,000	£850	-
Pennant Companion	948/4	1955–61	£1,800	£850	£300
Pennant	948/4	1955–59	£1,650	£825	£250

Stoewer

◄ **1912 Stoewer 15/30hp Torpedo Tourer,** acetylene brass headlamps, oil side and rear lamps, detachable wire wheels, side-mounted spare, mahogany-framed windscreen, King of the Road bulb horn, original instruments, finished in dark blue, black hood.
£25,000–28,000 BKS

Stoewer produced cars at Stettin from 1899 to 1939. A brief dalliance with electric cars was short-lived and the company soon began to build an excellent range of well-engineered two-, four- and six-cylinder models. The 15/30hp model of 1912 was powered by a conventional 2.4 litre, four-cylinder monobloc engine, driving through a three-speed, right-hand-change gearbox with conventional shaft drive.

Stutz

Built in just five weeks, Harry C. Stutz's first car did sufficiently well at the 1911 Indianapolis 500 to prompt its creator to commence manufacture, production models being closely based on the successful Indy car. Although the company was small by American standards, its Bearcat sports car's competition successes ensured that Stutz enjoyed a disproportionately high-profile reputation from the very outset, although by 1925 the emphasis had switched from sports to luxury cars. To this end, the company introduced the magnificent Vertical Eight, a model destined to feature some of the finest examples of the contemporary coachbuilders' art and, without question, one of the greatest of American automobiles.

◀ **1932 Stutz DV32 Convertible Sedan,** coachwork by Le Baron, completely restored 1991–92, resprayed in black, tan hood, brown leather upholstery, 'as new' condition. **£60,000–70,000 BKS**

Stutz added the DV32 to its range in 1931. It was truly race-bred, being a development of the Vertical 8, which had been renamed the SV16. The DV32 featured a double-overhead-camshaft engine with four valves per cylinder, displacing 5.3 litres and developing some 156bhp.

Sunbeam

The firm that became Sunbeam was started in 1859 by 23-year-old John Marston, initially to make tin-plate and japanned goods in Wolverhampton. In 1887, he changed the name to Sunbeam Cycles, which soon gained a reputation for turning out fine bicycles. A Sunbeam car appeared in 1901, but it was the arrival of French designer Louis Coatalen, who had worked previously at Humber and Hillman, that propelled the company forward to its glory years in the 1920s with a string of successful GP cars, record breakers and fine sports and touring machines. In the early 1930s, the best Sunbeams rivalled Bentley and Alvis, although they were not quite a match in outright performance. By then, the company was in trouble as part of the unwieldy and inefficient Sunbeam-Talbot-Darracq combine. Subsequently, Rootes bought the company in 1935. After the war, Sunbeam continued its sporting tradition: a Sunbeam Mk III won the 1955 Monte Carlo Rally, while the Sunbeam Rapiers proved useful in rallying and touring-car racing. Eventually, though, most Sunbeams – with the exception of the 1959 Alpine and the fearsome Tiger – were nothing more than slightly peppier and posher Hillmans. Chrysler acquired Rootes in 1964, and the Sunbeam marque faded into the sunset in 1976.

1928 Sunbeam 25hp Four-Seat Tourer, 3.6 litre, overhead-valve engine, period triple SU carburettors, 4-speed manual gearbox, servo-assisted front-wheel brakes, fold-flat windscreen, aero screens, bonnet straps, stone guards, Bentley-like fuel tank, finished in green. **£21,000–25,000 BKS**

Prior to WWI, Sunbeam had developed a range that was race bred, yet offered reliability, which earned the company's products an enviable reputation in arduous military service during the war. The demands of wartime aero-engineering brought new expertise and rapid developments, which enabled Sunbeam to produce a range of refined touring cars in the 1920s.

1962 Sunbeam Alpine Series II, 1592cc, 4-cylinder engine, alloy wheels, hard and soft tops, restored, finished in red, black interior, 2 owners, excellent condition throughout. **£6,000–6,600 BRIT**

Introduced in 1959, the Alpine was based on contemporary Rootes Group components. It proved popular from the outset, with its attractive styling and glamorous image. Initially in 1500cc form, the Alpine was gradually upgraded to 1600cc, and in its final guise had the aluminium-head, 1725cc engine of the contemporary Humber Sceptre.

1963 Sunbeam Alpine Series III GT, 1592cc, 4-cylinder engine, period Lucas fog lamps, correct wing mirrors, finished in Carnival red, black interior, new black leather upholstery, well maintained, 93,500 miles recorded, 3 owners, very good condition.
£5,000–5,500 BRIT

Introduced in 1963, the GT offered increased interior accommodation and a number of minor refinements.

1966 Sunbeam Tiger Mk I, 4261cc, Ford V8 engine, completely restored, alloy wheels, finished in dark green, very good condition.
£7,500–8,500 COYS

The Tiger was originally conceived in early 1963 to meet a demand in the USA for a more powerful sports car than the little 1500cc Alpine. It used the compact Ford V8 engine that gained popularity in the Mustang.

1966 Sunbeam Tiger Mk I, 4261cc, Ford V8 engine, completely restored, 15,000 miles covered since, finished in Forest green, black interior, well maintained, very good condition.
£7,500–8,500 H&H

1981 Sunbeam Lotus, 2200cc, 4-cylinder engine, 150+bhp, completely restored, alloy wheels, finished in black and silver.
£4,000–4,500 IMP

SUNBEAM-TALBOT/ SUNBEAM Model	ENGINE cc/cyl	DATES	CONDITION 1	2	3
Talbot 80	1185/4	1948–50	£3,500	£2,250	£1,000
Talbot 80 DHC	1185/4	1948–50	£6,000	£4,500	£2,000
Talbot 90 Mk I	1944/4	1949–50	£4,000	£2,100	£750
Talbot 90 Mk I DHC	1944/4	1949–50	£7,000	£4,750	£2,000
Talbot 90 II/IIa/III	2267/4	1950–56	£5,000	£3,000	£1,500
Talbot 90 II/IIa/III DHC	2267/4	1950–56	£7,000	£5,000	£2,250
Talbot Alpine I/III	2267/4	1953–55	£11,000	£7,500	£3,750
Talbot Ten	1197/4	1946–48	£3,500	£2,000	£750
Talbot Ten Tourer	1197/4	1946–48	£7,000	£4,000	£2,000
Talbot Ten DHC	1197/4	1946–48	£6,500	£4,000	£2,000
Talbot 2 Litre	1997/4	1946–48	£4,000	£2,500	£1,000
Talbot 2 Litre Tourer	1997/4	1946–48	£7,500	£4,000	£2,250
Rapier I	1392/4	1955–57	£1,200	£700	£300
Rapier II	1494/4	1957–59	£1,800	£900	£300
Rapier II Conv	1494/4	1957–59	£3,000	£1,500	£450
Rapier III	1494/4	1959–61	£2,000	£1,200	£400
Rapier III Conv	1494/4	1959–61	£3,500	£1,600	£600
Rapier IIIA	1592/4	1961–63	£2,000	£1,200	£400
Rapier IIIA Conv	1592/4	1961–63	£3,600	£1,700	£650
Rapier IV/V	1592/ 1725/4	1963–67	£2,000	£700	£250
Alpine I–II	1494/4	1959–62	£6,000	£3,500	£1,800
Alpine III	1592/4	1963	£6,500	£4,000	£1,250
Alpine IV	1592/4	1964	£6,500	£4,000	£1,250
Alpine V	1725/4	1965–68	£7,000	£4,000	£1,250
Harrington Alpine	1592/4	1961	£8,000	£4,750	£1,250
Harrington Le Mans	1592/4	1962–63	£10,000	£6,500	£3,000
Tiger Mk 1	4261/8	1964–67	£15,000	£10,000	£6,000
Tiger Mk 2	4700/8	1967	£13,000	£8,000	£6,000
Rapier Fastback	1725/4	1967–76	£1,100	£700	£250
Rapier H120	1725/4	1968–76	£1,500	£800	£300

Talbot

A known continuous history can add value to and enhance the enjoyment of a car.

◄ **1930 Talbot Darracq Saloon,** full sunroof, Rotax headlamps, original instruments, restored, fitted with flashing indicators, finished in black with red wire wheels, interior trim in need of attention.
£10,500–11,550 UMC

1947 Talbot-Lago T26 Four-Seat Cabriolet, 4.5 litre, six-cylinder engine, 170bhp, Wilson pre-selector gearbox, independent front suspension by transverse leaf spring, hydraulic brakes, box-section chassis, right-hand drive, restored, finished in yellow and black, black leather upholstery, original apart from new wings.
£40,000–45,000 BKS

In the 1920s, Antonio Lago was based in London, where he became well-known for his LAP overhead-valve conversions. After a spell with the Wilson Self-Changing Gear Company, he joined the Sunbeam-Talbot-Darracq concern in 1933. When that company failed two years later, he was able to raise the capital to salvage part of it and launch SA Automobiles Talbot. Lago used his firm's successful participation in sports car racing to enhance its reputation and, by 1939, Talbot had become an established constructor of *Grands Routiers*, which were bodied by leading French coachbuilders.

◄ **1950 Talbot-Lago T26 Record,** 4482cc, 6-cylinder inline engine, twin carburettors, 170bhp, Wilson 4-speed pre-selector gearbox, 4-wheel hydraulic drum brakes, centre-lock wire wheels, left-hand drive, restored, finished in Aubergine, beige interior trim.
£25,000–30,000 Pou

TALBOT Model	ENGINE cc/cyl	DATES	CONDITION		
			1	2	3
25hp & 25/50	4155/4	1907–16	£35,000	£25,000	£15,000
12hp	2409/4	1909–15	£22,000	£15,000	£9,000
8/18	960/4	1922–25	£8,000	£5,000	£2,000
14/45	1666/6	1926–35	£16,000	£10,000	£5,000
75	2276/6	1930–37	£22,000	£12,000	£7,000
105	2969/6	1935–37	£30,000	£20,000+	£15,000

Higher value for tourers and coachbuilt cars.

Toyota

Although Toyota had been making cars in Japan since 1935, the company's products were little known in the UK until the 1960s. The first Toyota sold in Britain was the Corona 1500, which arrived in 1965 with little fanfare. If it provoked any comment at all, it was usually patronising, jingoistic ridicule. But it was a sign of things to come when James Bond forsook his traditional Aston Martin for a Toyota 2000 GT in *You Only Live Twice*, even though they had to chop the roof off to accommodate the strapping Sean Connery. Although the 2000 GT was only produced in very limited numbers – around 337 – it served its purpose as an attention-getter, while Toyotas moved more and more into the mainstream with a comprehensive line-up of saloons, sporting coupés, 4x4s and working vehicles.

1968 Toyota Crown M555 Saloon, 2263cc, 6-cylinder engine, finished in blue, good condition.
£800–950 TEC

1973 Toyota Crown MS63 Custom Estate, 2563cc, 6-cylinder engine, alloy wheels.
£800–950 TEC

1974 Toyota Crown MS75 Hardtop, 2563cc, 6-cylinder engine, finished in metallic light blue, good condition.
£1,500–1,800 TEC

1977 Toyota Celica TA23 ST, 1600cc engine, alloy wheels, finished in silver, good condition.
£1,800–2,200 TEC

1978 Toyota Celica TA23 ST, 1600cc engine, finished in red, good condition.
£1,800–2,200 TEC

1987 Toyota MR2, 1587cc, mid-mounted 4-cylinder engine, alloy wheels, sunroof, finished in red, black interior trim, good condition.
£5,000–6,000 TEC

TOYOTA Model	ENGINE cc/cyl	DATES	CONDITION 1	2	3
Celica TA22 & TA23 Coupé	1588/4	1971–78	£3,400	£1,800	£500
RA28 Liftback	1968/4	1971–78	£3,500	£1,500	£400
Crown MS65, MS63, MS75, Saloon, Estate, Coupé	2563/6	1972–75	£2,500	£1,000	£500
Plus a premium of £200–500 for a Twin-Cam GT, and £200–400 for the Coupé.					

Triumph
FROM BIKES TO CARS

In the glory years of the 1950s and 1960s, Triumph's TR roadsters stood out as worthy, best-of-breed contenders in the no-nonsense sports-car stakes. From the bluff-fronted TR2 to the chisel-chinned TR6, they were as true-Brit as sports cars could be. Yet the company that provided so many memorable motoring sensations for the tweed, cravat and corduroy crew was actually founded by expatriate Germans.

Nuremberg-born Siegfried Bettman arrived in Britain in the 1880s. Eventually, he teamed up with fellow German Mauritz Schulte and, in 1890, they moved to Coventry to build bicycles. Their first cycles were known as Bettmans, but the canny German soon chose the name Triumph for his products because the word was readily understood throughout Europe. As the cycle boom petered out, Triumph turned to motorcycles, the first machine appearing in 1902. By 1914, Triumph was one of the most prominent names in the business.

During WWI, Triumph supplied 30,000 motorcycles to the British Army. In the post-war boom, new car manufacturers sprouted up all over the place, but Bettman bided his time until 1923, when the first Triumph motor car finally appeared. This was the conventional 10/20hp model, capable of 52mph. It was soon followed by the more powerful 55mph 13/35, and the bigger 2169cc 15, which was no faster.

Triumph's first really successful car was the diminutive Super Seven, unveiled in 1927. Not only was it intended to rival the Austin 7, but it was also designed by the same man, Stanley Edge. The Super Seven was launched at the right time, when the looming Depression fuelled demand for small, cheap machines. The 832cc Super Seven, in most spartan form, cost less than £150 and 17,000 were built up to 1932.

The little Super Seven helped carry Triumph through the difficult times of the early 1930s, but then sales of small Triumphs began to slip away and the new, larger, six-cylinder Scorpion was flimsy and gutless. In fact, one wag quipped that the car was called Scorpion because 'those who bought it thought they'd been stung.'

Triumph's cars, which had been so profitable, were in danger of dragging down the motorcycle business. Consequently, Bettman stepped down as managing director. Among the new blood was a young Donald Healey, who joined as technical chief.

The model line-up expanded haphazardly, with names like Gloria, Southern Cross, Dolomite and Vitesse. Triumph was moving upmarket, pitching against the saloons, sporting saloons and sports cars of Riley, Rover and SS (Jaguar). But it wasn't selling enough and losses continued. In 1936, the motorcycle business was sold to fund expansion plans, and Bettman went with it as chairman. Car manufacturing limped along until June 1939, when the business closed after making a total of 47,000 cars.

That might have been the end of the story, but in 1944 Sir John Black acquired the remains of Triumph for his Standard Motor Company. What he got was a name, some residual goodwill – and little else.

The first fresh post-war designs from Standard-Triumph were both launched under the Triumph banner. The slab-sided 1800 saloon was a quirky razor-edged concoction, but the Triumph Roadster was far more appealing and, with its pastiche of sports-car styling, also signalled Black's sporting aspirations; in fact, the car's initials were soon adopted for a new sporting breed, the TR Triumphs, which blazed an export trail, particularly in the USA.

1948 Triumph Roadster 1800, crashed 1980s, barn-stored since, severely damaged nearside front wing, bodywork dented and scratched, chassis, wing undersides and floor sound, non-original front seats, finished in red, black interior.
£3,750–4,500 BKS

Triumph Milestones

1902   Triumph Cycle Co Ltd builds its first motorcycle.
1909   Triumph builds 3,000 motorcycles.
1923   First Triumph motor car launched in April.
1923   Motorcycle production up to 15,000 a year.
1930   Motorcycle production up to 30,000 a year.
1930   Triumph Cycle Company becomes Triumph Motor Company.
1931   Triumph workforce numbers 3,000 at six sites in Coventry.
1936   Triumph motorcycle business sold in January to fund expansion of car business.

1939   In June, Lloyd's Bank calls in receivers at Triumph.
1944   Sir John Black's Standard Motor Company acquires Triumph name.
1955   TR3 becomes the first British volume-production car fitted with front disc brakes as standard.
1961   Leyland takes over Standard-Triumph.
1968   Leyland merges with British Motor Holdings to form British Leyland Motor Corporation.
1981   Triumph Acclaim is the last 'Triumph', but really it's a mildly modified Honda Ballade.
1984   Austin-Rover drops Triumph name from catalogue

◄ **1949 Triumph 2000 Roadster,** 2088cc, finished in maroon, tan interior, unrestored, in need of some refurbishment.
£4,250–5,000 H&H
Launched in 1946, the 1800 Roadster had a Standard-built 1776cc overhead-valve engine and four-speed gearbox (also supplied to Jaguar for its 1 litre saloon), along with independent front suspension and aluminium coachwork. Unusually, it featured a dickey seat, a common feature of pre-war cars. It was not revised until 1948, when it received the 2.1 litre engine, three-speed gearbox, and rear axle of the newly-introduced Standard Vanguard. When Roadster production ceased in 1949, a total of 4,501 cars had been built.

Triumph TR2 (1953–55)

Engine: Four-cylinder, overhead-valve, twin SU carburettors, 1991cc.
Power output: 90bhp at 4,800rpm.
Top speed: 105mph.
0–60mph: 12 seconds.
Production: 8,628.
If ever there was a sports car that epitomised the British bulldog spirit, it must be the Triumph TR2. Spend a minute in that cosy cockpit and your dress sense will change. You'll start smoking a pipe, wearing corduroys, cravat and flat cap, and sprouting a wing-commander's handle-bar moustache. It's as true-Brit as a car can be, born in the golden

age of British sports cars, but aimed at the lucrative US market, where the Jaguar XK120 had already scored a hit. The TR2 is no conventional beauty certainly, but with its bluff-fronted, honest demeanour it was a worthy best-of-breed contender in the budget sports car arena and the cornerstone of a stout sporting tradition.
TR2 titbits: A carefully tuned pre-production TR2, with rudimentary streamlining, was officially timed at a whisker under 125mph on the Jabbeke motorway in Belgium. The Triumph sporting tradition became firmly established when TR2s came first and second in the 1954 RAC Rally.

► **1955 Triumph TR2,** 1991cc, completely restored, reconditioned radiator, new panels, floors, spare wheel compartment, rear panel and front wing, black Everflex-type hood, finished in BMW red, black interior, bodywork in good condition.
£8,750–9,750 H&H

TRS AND BEYOND

In March 1953, the TR2 emerged as a winner at the Geneva motor show and began a stout sporting TR tradition. The similarly styled TR3 of 1955 offered a little more power; then, in 1956, front disc brakes appeared, followed by 'real' door handles. The TR4 of 1961 was a watershed. Although based on an improved TR3 chassis, it sported smart – even modern – bodywork, courtesy of Michelotti, and wind-up windows. In 1965, the TR4A introduced independent rear suspension in place of the old live rear axle. Until then, the handling of TRs had been of the entertaining variety; now they were becoming competent. The TR5 took the TR4A's body and added a fuel-injected, 2498cc, six-cylinder engine in place of the earlier four. Finally, in 1969, Karmann revised the Michelotti styling to create the straight-edged TR6. All TRs were huge export successes, and the TR6 was the biggest hit of the lot. Of the 94,619 produced from 1969 to 1976, ten times as many were exported as stayed at home, most going to America.

But the TRs weren't the only sporting Triumphs. From 1961 to 1980, the pretty Spitfire pitched in against the MG Midget. There were distinguished saloons, too. In 1959 came the cheap and cheerful, separate-chassis, four-cylinder Herald, with its front-hinged bonnet that gave legendary access. The Vitesse was a punchier six-cylinder variant, distinguished by quad headlamps. Both were also available as convertibles. The 2000 saloon of 1963 and the later 2.5PI were refined saloons that offered an alternative to the Rover P6. The Dolomite and Toledo met the need for small saloons. And, of course, from 1970 to 1977, there was the Stag.

But what of Standard, the company that revived Triumph after the war? Shortly after the Leyland take-over of Standard-Triumph in 1961, Standard gently faded away. For a while, Triumph seemed favoured in the British Leyland pecking order, until Rover joined the fold in 1967. Throughout the 1970s, Triumph was starved of cash to develop new cars, and by 1980 the company had been renamed Austin-Rover Group. Triumph's last gasp under the new regime was the Acclaim, not really a Triumph at all, but a rebadged and barely modified Honda Ballade. The once-proud marque faded away in 1984, leaving a legacy of honest bulldog-spirited sports cars and post-war saloons that were always sensible and sometimes had real flair.

1956 Triumph TR3, left-hand drive, restored 1990–92, new silencer, finished in green, black upholstery. **£8,250–9,100 BKS**

Launched in late 1955, the TR3 was an improved version of the acclaimed TR2, from which it differed visually by the addition of an 'egg-crate' grille. Mechanical improvements included larger-bore SU carburettors and better porting to increase the power output of the rugged, reliable 1991cc four-cylinder engine. In the autumn of 1956, the TR3 became the first series-production British car to be fitted as standard with front disc brakes, and by the time the model was supplanted by the redesigned TR3A, early in 1958, production had reached 13,378, over 90 per cent of which went for export.

TRIUMPH Model	ENGINE cc/cyl	DATES	CONDITION 1	2	3
TLC	1393/4	1923–25	£6,000	£4,000	£1,500
TPC	2169/4	1926–30	£6,000	£4,000	£2,000
K	832/4	1928–34	£4,000	£2,000	£1,000
S	1203/6	1931–33	£5,000	£3,000	£1,500
G12 Gloria	1232/4	1935–37	£6,000	£4,000	£2,000
G16 Gloria 6	1991/6	1935–39	£7,000	£4,500	£2,000
Vitesse/Dolomite	1767/4	1937–39	£14,000	£10,000	£6,000
Dolomite	1496/4	1938–39	£7,000	£4,000	£2,000

◄ **1958 Triumph TR3A,** 1991cc, overdrive gearbox, wire wheels, left-hand drive, restored 1997–98, engine and gearbox rebuilt, all other mechanical components overhauled as necessary, new floor panels, all brightwork replaced or replated as required, resprayed in Signal red, Oatmeal interior, excellent condition. **£10,500–11,750 BRIT**

The TR3A was the ultimate development of what are now described as the 'sidescreen' TRs. It remained in production until late 1961, when it was superseded by the completely redesigned TR4.

▶ **1960 Triumph TR3A,** 2 litre engine, 100bhp, overdrive gearbox, Girling front disc brakes, Phase III Vanguard rear axle, rack-and-pinion steering, restored 1995–98, TR6 wire wheels, twin aero screens, finished in white, red interior. **£9,000–10,000 BKS**

1960 Triumph TR3A, 1960cc, wire wheels, completely restored using mainly new parts, engine bay detailed to concours standard, bare-metal respray in red, unregistered, BMIHT certificate, history file. **£11,000–12,500 H&H**

◄ **1963 Triumph TR4,** 2138cc, overdrive gearbox, new stainless steel exhaust, brightwork rechromed, finished in red, black interior trim, seats reupholstered, new carpets. **£4,500–5,500 H&H**

▶ **1963 Triumph TR4,** 2138cc, 4-cylinder engine, completely restored to concours standard, finished in Sebring white, black interior trim, history file. **£8,000–9,000 BRIT**

Superseding the TR3A in November 1961, the Michelotti-styled TR4 represented a major leap forward in sports car design compared with its predecessor. Gone were the sliding sidescreens in favour of wind-up windows, while the cockpit was vastly superior in terms of comfort. Under the skin, however, the rugged wet-liner engine and basic chassis frame remained.

▶ **1963 Triumph TR4,** 2138cc, original right-hand drive, unfinished restoration project, engine and gearbox rebuilt, most parts included to permit completion, finished in red, black and red interior.
£1,200–1,400 H&H

TRIUMPH Model	ENGINE cc/cyl	DATES	CONDITION 1	2	3
1800/2000 Roadster	1776/ 2088/4	1946–49	£14,000	£8,000	£5,000
1800	1776/4	1946–49	£4,000	£2,000	£1,000
2000 Renown	2088/4	1949–54	£4,000	£2,000	£1,000
Mayflower	1247/4	1949–53	£2,000	£1,000	£500
TR2 long door	1247/4	1953	£10,000	£8,000	£5,000
TR2	1247/4	1953–55	£9,000	£6,000	£5,000
TR3	1991/4	1955–57	£9,000	£8,500	£3,500
TR3A	1991/4	1958–62	£11,000	£8,500	£3,500
TR4	2138/4	1961–65	£9,000	£6,000	£3,000
TR4A	2138/4	1965–67	£9,000	£6,500	£3,000
TR5	2498/6	1967–68	£9,000	£7,500	£4,000
TR6 (PI)	2498/6	1969–74	£8,000	£7,500	£3,500
Herald	948/4	1959–61	£1,000	£400	£150
Herald FHC	948/4	1959–61	£1,500	£550	£300
Herald DHC	948/4	1960–61	£2,500	£1,000	£350
Herald 'S'	948/4	1961–64	£800	£400	£150
Herald 1200	1147/4	1961–70	£1,100	£500	£200
Herald 1200 FHC	1147/4	1961–64	£1,400	£800	£300
Herald 1200 DHC	1147/4	1961–67	£2,500	£1,000	£350
Herald 1200 Est	1147/4	1961–67	£1,300	£700	£300
Herald 12/50	1147/4	1963–67	£1,800	£1,000	£250
Herald 13/60	1296/4	1967–71	£1,300	£600	£200
Herald 13/60 DHC	1296/4	1967–71	£3,500	£1,500	£500
Herald 13/60 Est	1296/4	1967–71	£1,500	£650	£300
Vitesse 1600	1596/6	1962–61	£2,000	£1,250	£550
Vitesse 1600 Conv	1596/6	1962–66	£3,500	£1,800	£600
Vitesse 2 litre Mk I	1998/6	1966–68	£1,800	£800	£300
Vitesse 2 litre Mk I Conv	1998/6	1966–68	£4,500	£2,200	£1,000
Vitesse 2 litre Mk II	1998/6	1968–71	£2,000	£1,500	£300
Vitesse 2 litre Mk II Conv	1998/6	1968–71	£5,000	£2,500	£600
Spitfire Mk I	1147/4	1962–64	£2,000	£1,750	£300
Spitfire Mk II	1147/4	1965–67	£2,500	£2,000	£350
Spitfire Mk III	1296/4	1967–70	£3,500	£2,500	£450
Spitfire Mk IV	1296/4	1970–74	£5,000	£2,500	£350
Spitfire 1500	1493/4	1975–78	£3,500	£2,500	£750
Spitfire 1500	1493/4	1979–81	£5,000	£3,500	£1,200
GT6 Mk I	1998/6	1966–68	£5,000	£4,000	£1,200
GT6 Mk II	1998/6	1968–70	£6,000	£4,500	£1,400
GT6 Mk III	1998/6	1970–73	£7,000	£5,000	£1,500
2000 Mk I	1998/6	1963–69	£2,000	£1,200	£400
2000 Mk III	1998/6	1969–77	£2,000	£1,200	£500
2.5 PI	2498/6	1968–75	£2,000	£1,500	£900
2500 TC/S	2498/6	1974–77	£1,750	£700	£150
2500S	2498/6	1975–77	£2,500	£1,000	£150
1300 (FWD)	1296/4	1965–70	£800	£400	£150
1300TC (FWD)	1296/4	1967–70	£900	£450	£150
1500 (FWD)	1493/4	1970–73	£700	£450	£125
1500TC (RWD)	1296/4	1973–76	£850	£500	£100
Toledo	1296/4	1970–76	£850	£450	£100
Dolomite 1500	1493/4	1976–80	£1,350	£750	£125
Dolomite 1850	1854/4	1972–80	£1,450	£850	£150
Dolomite Sprint	1998/4	1976–81	£5,000	£4,000	£1,000
Stag	2997/8	1970–77	£9,000	£5,000	£2,000
TR7	1998/4	1975–82	£4,000	£1,200	£500
TR7 DHC	1998/4	1980–82	£5,000	£3,500	£1,500

◀ **1968 Triumph TR4A,** 2138cc, overdrive gearbox, wire wheels, spotlamps, tonneau cover, rear-seat conversion, original right-hand drive, finished in royal blue, black interior trim, 6,200 miles recorded, 3 owners, excellent condition throughout. **£8,750–9,750 H&H**

1969 Triumph TR6, completely restored, mechanics overhauled, new panels, resprayed in red, new interior trim, excellent condition. **£7,500–8,500 BARO**

1972 Triumph TR6, 2498cc, 6-cylinder engine, 150bhp, completely restored over last 2 years, finished in red, black interior trim, concours condition. **£8,750–9,750 BRIT**

Successor to the TR5, which was the first of the TR range to utilise a six-cylinder, fuel-injected engine, the TR6 enjoyed a production run of seven years. As with all TR sports cars, the TR6 was enjoyable to drive and offered an excellent combination of value for money, sure-footed handling and good performance.

1972 Triumph TR6, 2498cc, 150bhp, finished in white, black hood, good condition. **£9,000–10,000 BLE**

► **1975 Triumph TR6,** 2498cc, 6-cylinder engine, 150bhp, overdrive gearbox, restored, Minilite-type alloy wheels, finished in British Racing green, interior trimmed in black vinyl. **£7,500–8,500 BRIT**

Triumph TR6 (1969–76)

From the original TR2 of 1953, beloved of the cravat-and-corduroy crew, Triumph's sporting roadwear kept broadly abreast of the times and, in the late 1960s, combined polo-neck smartness with a touch of chest-wig brawn in the clean-cut and butch TR6. Some think the TR6 granite-jawed handsome, others find it almost thuggish. Whatever, it's just about as hairy-chested as the classic TRs got with its 2.5 litre six-cylinder engine which, in fuel-injected form, heaved you along with 150 galloping horses.

The TR6 may look true-Brit, but its crisp lines came courtesy of Germany's Karmann, who squared off the friendly curves of the TR4 created in 1964 by Italian 'haute car-turier' Michelotti. The TR6 was by far the most prolific of the TR2–6 series. More than 78,000 of the 94,619 TR6s were exported to the US, where legislators emasculated the bulldog Brit. Many US TR6s have found their way back to the UK, but US-spec. cars had carbs instead of fuel injection together with other performance wilting mods. Know what you're buying and pay less for a US-spec. car.

Pick of the bunch: Beefiest and best are pre-1973 British-spec. TR6s, which pumped out 152bhp. After that, a revised fuel-injection system reduced power output to a less thrilling 125bhp.

1978 Triumph TR7, restored 1992, engine and gearbox rebuilt, uprated springs and adjustable shock absorbers, bare-metal respray in Inca yellow, BMIHT certificate.
£1,200–1,500 BRIT

1981 Triumph TR7 Convertible, 1998cc, 5-speed manual gearbox, completely restored 1990, 6,067 miles covered since, finished in metallic green with tan interior, excellent condition throughout.
£3,200–3,800 H&H

▶ **1981 Triumph TR7 Convertible,** 5-speed manual gearbox, factory tow bar, finished in gold, 1 owner, fewer than 7,500 miles covered since 1982, 1 of last produced, very good to excellent condition throughout.
£4,250–4,750 BKS

Introduced in 1975, the TR7 abandoned the TR's traditional separate chassis in favour of unitary construction. It also adopted the 2 litre, four-cylinder engine and powertrain of the contemporary Dolomite in place of the preceding six.

1965 Triumph Vitesse Convertible, alternator, electronic ignition, spare engine, resprayed in 2-tone green, BMIHT certificate.
£1,500–1,800 BARO

◀ **1968 Triumph Vitesse Convertible,** 1998cc, 6-cylinder engine, 95bhp, c100mph top speed, restored over past 2 years, new stainless steel exhaust, overdrive gearbox rebuilt, new braking system, new door skins and rear wings, new sills and floors, hood and tonneau in excellent condition, finished in Wedgwood blue and white, black interior trim, in need of cosmetic attention and a new grille, 43,000 miles recorded, history file.
£1,500–1,800 H&H

1963 Triumph Vitesse Special, 1998cc, wire wheels, aero screens, all mechanical parts overhauled at time of conversion, bodywork completely handbuilt in aluminium, finished in black, brown interior trim, complete with workshop manual written by builder, excellent condition throughout.
£2,400–2,800 H&H

1976 Triumph Spitfire, 1493cc, 4-cylinder engine, 4-speed gearbox, left-hand drive, finished in yellow, black hood and interior, very good condition.
£3,500–4,000 PALM

◄ **1973 Triumph 2000 Mk II Saloon,** 1998cc, 6-cylinder engine, 90bhp, good condition.
£1,100–1,300 HMM

1972 Triumph 2.5PI Saloon, 2498cc, 6-cylinder engine, fuel injection, finished in dark blue, good condition.
£1,750–2,100 BARO

◄ **1973 Triumph Dolomite,** 1854cc, finished in blue, blue interior trim, 78,648 miles recorded, 3 owners, very good condition throughout.
£700–800 H&H

Triumph produced the Dolomite in the early 1970s. With the 1800 twin-carburettor engine, it was capable of over 100mph.

Miller's
Starter Marque

Starter Triumphs: *Herald and Vitesse saloons and convertibles; Spitfire; Dolomite, Toledo and variants.*

- The Herald's a top-down winner when it comes to budget wind-in-the-hair motoring – an Italian-styled four-seater convertible with a 25ft turning circle that's tighter than a London taxi's and an engine that's so accessible it's like having your own inspection pit. They are very modestly priced, too. Of course, it's not all good news. The Herald's performance is hardly shattering, particularly with the early, rather asthmatic 948cc Standard 10 engine. It's also prone to rust, and the handling was legendary – for being so darned awful, in the earlier models at least. In the wet and in sudden throttle-off conditions, the car's high-pivot, swing-axle rear suspension would pitch it suddenly into unpredictable oversteer.
- But who'd be daft enough to try to race a Herald on public roads? What's more relevant is the smiles per mile as you and your family potter along over hill and dale burning fossil fuel at a miserly 35–40mpg.
- Heralds do fray quite ferociously, so you'll want to inspect the separate chassis, which provides its structural strength. The front-hinged bonnet is both a strength and weakness. It gives unrivalled access to front running gear and engine, but once the rot sets in, it can flap around like a soggy cardboard box.
- Finally, because of its separate chassis, the Herald saloon is one car that can be safely turned into a convertible. The roof literally unbolts and several rag-top conversion kits are available.
- **Pick of the bunch:** The Herald's certainly no winged messenger, so avoid early cars with the puny 948cc engine and go for at least the 1147cc or, preferably, one of the last 1296cc cars.
- The Herald's chassis formed the basis of a number of sporting Triumphs, including the twin-headlamp Vitesse. Similar in looks to the Herald, but with 1600 and 2000cc engines, the Vitesse will heave you along with plenty more urge – almost to 100mph in 2 litre form. The chassis also featured in the pretty little two-seat Spitfire, again with wonderful engine access provided by a front-hinged, one-piece, wing-and-bonnet assembly. The Spitfire ran from 1961 to 1980, which means that there are plenty to choose from.

1980 Triumph Dolomite 1300, 1296cc, finished in blue, black interior, 10,200 miles recorded, 2 owners, very good condition throughout.
£1,500–1,800 H&H

1976 Triumph Dolomite Sprint, 1998cc, automatic transmission, engine rebuilt, new competition radiator, finished in Honeysuckle yellow, brown interior, 62,000 miles recorded, 2 owners, very good condition throughout.
£1,200–1,400 H&H

1972 Triumph Stag, manual/overdrive gearbox, hard and soft tops, finished in Mallard, black interior, unused for 12 years, completely original, 1 owner, excellent condition throughout.
£9,000–10,000 BKS

1973 Triumph Stag, 2997cc V8 engine, alloy wheels, restored 1990, new exhaust system, black lined mohair hood, finished in white, original brown interior in excellent condition.
£5,000–6,000 BRIT

1974 Triumph Stag, 2997cc V8 engine, automatic transmission, power steering, hard and soft tops, finished in yellow, black interior trim, 59,000 miles recorded, very good condition throughout.
£6,000–7,000 H&H

◀ **1976 Triumph Stag,** 2997cc V8 engine, automatic transmission, finished in Russet, 1 family ownership, 48,000 miles recorded, original, very good unrestored condition.
£4,750–5,500 BRIT

▶ **1977 Triumph Stag,** 2997cc V8 engine, 145bhp, automatic transmission, finished in Pimento red, beige vinyl interior, 56,000 miles recorded.
£4,250–4,750 BRIT

1977 Triumph Stag, 2997cc V8 engine, restored, engine rebuilt, stainless steel exhaust system, electronic ignition, Kenlowe fan, new front and rear wings, new door skins, bumpers rechromed, finished in Flamenco red, black interior trim, 58,900 miles recorded, excellent condition.
£6,000–7,000 H&H

> A known continuous history can add value to and enhance the enjoyment of a car.

1978 Triumph Stag, automatic transmission rebuilt, hardtop, excellent condition.
£8,000–9,000 UMC

1981 Triumph Acclaim Convertible, converted from saloon, new hood, remote alarm, original Triumph radio, finished in red, good condition throughout.
£700–825 BARO

The Acclaim was the first car to come out of the British Leyland/Honda marriage and was nothing more than a Triumph-badged Honda. However, it was a reliable workhorse and proved a popular addition to BL's range at the time.

Turner

◀ **1959 Turner 950,** 950cc, BMC A-series engine, 90mph top speed, fibreglass bodywork, restored, very good condition.
£4,250–4,750 HMM

The Turner was one of many limited-production, kit-built sports cars that appeared during the 1950s. To many, these represented a cheap way to sports-car ownership. Over 170 Turners were produced. Early publicity work carried out by the company employed a young model who later became an international radio and TV star, Petula Clark. She was given a car with the registration number PET 1.

TVR

1991 TVR S3 Convertible, 2.9 litre V6 engine, Targa roof panels retrimmed, OZ Racing alloy wheels, anti-theft immobiliser, finished in Charcoal grey, well maintained.
£7,000–8,000 BARO

TVR Model	ENGINE cc/cyl	DATES	CONDITION 1	2	3
Grantura I	1172/4	1957–62	£4,000	£3,000	£2,000
Grantura II	1558/4	1957–62	£4,500	£3,000	£2,000
Grantura III/1800S	1798/4	1963–67	£5,000	£3,000	£2,200
Tuscan V8	4727/8	1967–70	£12,000	£7,000	£6,000
Vixen S2/3	1599/4	1968–72	£5,000	£3,000	£1,500
3000M	2994/6	1972–79	£7,000	£4,000	£3,000
Taimar	2994/6	1977–79	£7,500	£5,000	£3,500

Vanden Plas

Restored values

The cost of a professional restoration will have an influence on, but no direct relation to, a car's market value. A restored car can have a market value lower than the cost of its restoration.

◀ **1979 Vanden Plas 1500,** 1500cc, 4-cylinder engine, finished in Champagne gold, Chestnut hide interior, walnut dash, door cappings and picnic tables, 72,600 miles recorded.
£900–1,075 BRIT

Vauxhall

The Griffin may be a mythical beast, but from modest beginnings the cars that sport this ancient English heraldic emblem have proliferated to become an enduring fact of life for millions of motorists in Great Britain and around the world. The company's first car was produced in 1903 and, in the Edwardian and Vintage years, the sporting Prince Henry and 30/98 models stood out as serious road-going rivals to the 3 litre Bentleys, worthy of mention alongside Invictas and Bugattis. In 1925, the firm's poor finances led to General Motors taking control and successfully moving the marque down market into solid middle-class territory with successful models like the H-Type 10 and the J-Type 14. In the 1950s, the transatlantic influence really became prominent with the gaudy Crestas and F-Type Victors, so beloved today of ageing teddy boys. In this period, Vauxhall's product range also expanded rapidly and aspired to compete head-to-head and model-to-model with Ford's UK offerings. For many British car buyers, the choice was a straight 'either/or' between, say, a Vauxhall Cresta and Ford Zephyr/Zodiac, and later between a Vauxhall Viva and Ford Anglia or Escort. Although America's General Motors had owned Vauxhall and a majority shareholding in German car-maker Opel since the 1920s, these European cousins operated independently of one another until the 1960s, when the model lines began to converge until most design input came from Germany.

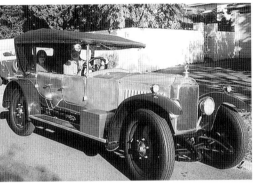

1923 Vauxhall 14/40 Princeton Tourer, 2297cc, 4-cylinder engine, 2-wheel brakes, polished aluminium coachwork, maroon wings, new black cloth hood and side curtains, black leatherette upholstery, new carpets, never completely restored, original specification throughout, good mechanical condition.
£15,000–18,000 BRIT

The Vauxhall Iron Works of London began building cars in 1903. During 1905, the company moved to Luton, and at this time the characteristic fluted bonnet appeared – a Vauxhall trade mark that was to endure until the 1960s. The company's range expanded steadily, the first four-cylinder models appearing during 1906, followed by a six-cylinder vehicle in 1910. The chief engineer at this time was the celebrated Lawrence Pomeroy, who was responsible for the legendary Prince Henry C-Type and 30/98 models. The outbreak of WWI saw production turning to War Office requirements. When hostilities ceased in 1918, the company began producing the 30/98 again together with a new smaller model, the 14/40.

1934 Vauxhall Light 12/6 Four-Door Saloon, 1530cc, 6-cylinder engine, manual gearbox, finished in brown and black, dark brown interior trim and upholstery, 59,700 miles recorded, 2 owners, very good condition.
£4,250–4,750 H&H

1923 Vauxhall 30/98 Velox Fast Tourer, completely restored, finished in dark blue with black wings, excellent condition.
£100,000–115,000 BKS

This 30/98, driven by its first owner, R.F. Summers, recorded 102mph during the 1923 Speed Week at Boulogne, proving to be the fastest of all the Vauxhalls in that event. But Mr Summers' Vauxhall, one of the earliest examples of the new 110bhp OE version of the 30/9, was not just a highly-tuned racer; late in 1923, he took this car over the steepest passes in Lakeland, accompanied by motor mountaineer George Abraham, who wrote a breathless account for *The Autocar*: 'ER-807 climbed the notorious Hard Knott and Wrynose passes without difficulty, and was then set the task of making a nonstop ascent of Hard Knott, its twelve hairpins requiring speedy attack.'

1929 Vauxhall 20/60 R-Type Saloon, 2916cc, 6-cylinder engine, Scintilla magneto, long-range driving lamps, pillar-mounted semaphore indicators, partially restored and resprayed 1986, new fuel tank, rewired, wheels recently rebuilt, original brown leather seats and headlining, 10,300 miles recorded.
£10,000–11,000 BRIT

When introduced in 1927, the 20/60 was powered by a 2.7 litre engine, but this became 2.9 litres from 1929. A variety of coachwork was available, the most popular being the Bedford saloon, as fitted to this example.

Miller's Starter Marque

Starter Vauxhalls: *PA Cresta/Velox, 1957–62; F-Type Victor, 1957–61.*

- As our price table shows, all Vauxhalls of the 1950s and 1960s are affordable, but two models that really stand out for their glamorous styling are the Detroit-inspired PA Cresta/Velox and the F-Type Victor, both representing a kind of mid-Atlantic meeting between Uncle Stan and Uncle Sam, and very appealing today to anyone nostalgic for the 1950s.
- They look for all the world like classic Yank tanks, yet their flanks clothe ordinary British mechanicals and running gear that generally are readily available and easy to maintain. The earlier E-Type Cresta, Velox and Wyvern also offer a touch of star-spangled razzmatazz, but their numbers have thinned to a level where they are not quite as practical as the subsequent PA. Later cars, like the PB Cresta and FB Victor are also practical buys; compared to the extravagant PA, they are almost muted.
- The glorious PA Cresta is a monster by British standards, a genuine six-seater with enough body rock 'n' roll to please any Elvis fan. Mechanically, they offer little to worry about with their strong 2.2 and 2.6 litre engines, while ancillaries like front discs, starter motors and dynamos are straight from the MGB.
- **Pick of the PAs:** Some prefer the looks of the pre-1960 models, with their three-piece rear windows, although later models have slightly more eager 2.6 litre lumps in place of the earlier 2.2.
- But the bodies are a different matter. Legend has it that PA Crestas rusted so rapidly that by the time they reached the end of the Luton production line they would have failed today's MoT test. Actually their resistance to rust was pretty much in line with other cars of the era. The big difference is that there's just more metal to rust. When you go to look at one, take a metal detector, because a festering rust box will be a labour of love rather than a sound proposition.
- The F-Type Victor delivers a Detroit dream in a UK-sized package. Compared to contemporary saloon rivals, it was a fine car to drive with a tough and flexible engine. The mechanicals are all pretty sturdy, but the early cars really did have a deserved reputation for rusting, as their bodyshells offered more mud traps than a Florida swamp. In fact, by the end of 1959, Vauxhall was already receiving corrosion complaints; in response, the company added underseal and splash panels.

1935 Vauxhall Big Six BXL Limousine, coachwork by Grosvenor, 3180cc, 6-cylinder engine, brightwork replated, resprayed 1996 in black, original brown leather interior trim and woodwork refurbished, new headlining and carpets.
£3,250–3,900 BRIT

In the wake of the successful Cadet VYL and VX series came the Big Six with two engine options: 2.4 and 3.2 litres. These models were available with a choice of coachwork and were of modern appearance, displaying considerable American influence. The largest variant of the Big Six was the BXL, with a 130in wheelbase and the 3.2 litre engine as standard. Limousine coachwork was invariably by Martin Walter or Grosvenor.

1936 Vauxhall DX 16/80 Three-Position Drophead Coupé, 4-seat coachwork by Salmons, restored, finished in cream and blue with black wings, new brown leather upholstery.
£5,000–6,000 BKS

By the end of 1934, Vauxhall's famous Light Six series, the ASY and ASX types, had been replaced by a new and far more modern range – the 12hp DYL and 14hp DX, powered by a 1781cc straight-six. With the introduction of the new cars came independent front suspension for the first time on a popular British car. The D-series models were largely responsible for Vauxhall's sales record of over 25,000 vehicles in 1935.

1937 Vauxhall 25hp, 3215cc, 6-cylinder engine, 80bhp, restored, finished in grey, very good condition.
£5,000–6,000 MVT

1977 Vauxhall VX2300 Estate, 2279cc, 4-cylinder engine, 4-speed manual gearbox, finished in white, blue interior trim and upholstery, 34,500 miles recorded, 1 owner, excellent condition all round.
£1,700–2,000 H&H

VAUXHALL Model	ENGINE cc/cyl	DATES	CONDITION 1	2	3
D/OD	3969/4	1914–26	£35,000	£24,000	£18,000
E/OE	4224/4	1919–28	£90,000+	£60,000+	£35,000
Eighty	3317/6	1931–33	£10,000	£8,000	£5,000
Cadet	2048/6	1931–33	£7,000	£5,000	£3,000
Lt Six	1531/6	1934–38	£5,000	£4,000	£1,500
14	1781/6	1934–39	£4,000	£3,000	£1,500
25	3215/6	1937–39	£5,000	£4,000	£1,500
10	1203/4	1938–39	£4,000	£3,000	£1,500
Wyvern LIX	1500/4	1948–51	£2,000	£1,000	£500
Velox LIP	2200/6	1948–51	£2,000	£1,000	£500
Wyvern EIX	1500/4	1951–57	£2,000	£1,320	£400
Velox EIPV	2200/6	1951–57	£3,000	£1,650	£400
Cresta EIPC	2200/6	1954–57	£3,000	£1,650	£400
Velox/Cresta PAS/PAD	2262/6	1957–59	£2,850	£1,300	£300
Velox/Cresta PASY/PADY	2262/6	1959–60	£2,700	£1,500	£300
Velox/Cresta PASX/PADX	2651/6	1960–62	£2,700	£1,300	£300
Velox/Cresta PASX/PADX Est	2651/6	1960–62	£2,700	£1,300	£300
Velox/Cresta PB	2651/6	1962–65	£1,600	£800	£100
Velox/Cresta PB Est	2651/6	1962–65	£1,600	£800	£100
Cresta/Deluxe PC	3294/6	1964–72	£1,500	£800	£100
Cresta PC Est	3294/6	1964–72	£1,500	£800	£100
Viscount	3294/6	1964–72	£1,700	£900	£100
Victor I/II	1507/4	1957–61	£2,000	£1,000	£250
Victor I/II Est	1507/4	1957–61	£2,100	£1,100	£300
Victor FB	1507/4	1961–64	£1,500	£900	£200
Victor FB Est	1507/4	1961–64	£1,600	£1,000	£300
VX4/90	1507/4	1961–64	£2,000	£900	£150
Victor FC101	1594/4	1964–67	£1,600	£900	£150
Victor FC101 Est	1594/4	1964–67	£1,800	£1,000	£200
101 VX4/90	1594/4	1964–67	£2,000	£1,500	£250
VX4/90	1975/4	1969–71	£1,000	£600	£100
Ventora I/II	3294/6	1968–71	£1,000	£375	£100
Viva HA	1057/4	1963–66	£1,000	£350	£100
Viva SL90	1159/4	1966–70	£1,000	£350	£100
Viva Brabham	1159/4	1967–70	£2,000	£1,000	£800
Viva	1600/4	1968–70	£500	£350	£100
Viva Est	1159/4	1967–70	£500	£400	£100

1974 Vauxhall Viva SL Saloon, 1256cc, 4-cylinder engine, new exhaust system, 6,895 miles recorded, original, excellent condition.
£1,200–1,400 BRIT

1979 Vauxhall Viva HC GLS Saloon, 1256cc, 4-cylinder engine, 4-speed manual gearbox, finished in metallic light blue, blue interior, excellent condition throughout.
£1,200–1,400 H&H

Vauxhall Viva HA (1963–66)

Engine: Four-cylinder, 1057cc.
Power output: 44bhp at 5,000rpm (HA): 58bhp at 5,000rpm (HA 90).
Transmission: Four-speed manual, all-synchromesh.
Brakes: Drums all-round, front discs optional at £12 extra; front discs standard on HA 90.
Top speed: 79mph (85mph, HA 90).
0–60mph: 20+ seconds.
Production: 321,332.
Price when new: £528.

As Vauxhall's first post-war entry into the growing small-car market, the Luton car maker had high hopes for the Viva, and sales got off to a brisk start, notching up 100,000 in the first 10 months. In place of flashy style, image or sizzling performance,

Vauxhall concentrated on value for money, pricing the Viva pretty much on a par with the Ford Anglia and well below the Cortina, Morris 1100 and Triumph Herald. Other than that, the Viva had a big boot and light controls, which prompted the marketing hacks to target women, perhaps imagining the 'fairer sex' to be more susceptible. 'The Viva concept centres around what a woman expects to find in a car', ran one brochure, although beyond being 'nice and slow', it's difficult to imagine what other feminine virtues the Viva possessed. The Viva was, in effect, an Anglicised version of the Opel Kadett and, although never the zenith of automotive style, sold well, swaying buyers on value for money and sheer common sense.

Venturi

◀ **1991 Venturi 260,** 2.8 litre V6 engine, 5-speed manual gearbox, air conditioning, finished in Rossini red, Crema leather interior, 40,000 miles recorded.
£13,000–16,000 BARO

The Venturi was built in very limited numbers, being powered by a 2.8 litre Renault V6 engine mounted amidships, allied to a handbuilt body. This car was originally the UK dealer's demonstrator.

Volga

A known continuous history can add value to and enhance the enjoyment of a car.

◀ **1962 Volga Four-Door Saloon,** finished in black, grey upholstery, original, in need of complete restoration.
£250–500 S

This Russian Volga saloon previously saw duty as a film car.

Volkswagen

The Volkswagen Beetle may be the best-selling car in the world – a true people's car – but it had a long and painful birth. In the early 1930s, Herr Hitler's vision for mass master-race motoring began to take shape when he entrusted Dr Ferdinand Porsche with the project. Some 630 or so Beetles were made before hostilities disrupted production. Back then, they were propaganda wagons too, named *KdF-Wagen*, after the slogan of the Hitler Youth, '*Kraft durch Freude*', which means strength through joy. When production resumed in 1945, the Beetle, now a more friendly Volkswagen, gathered an irresistible momentum, notching up 10,000 sales in 1946, 100,000 in 1950 and a million by 1955. In 1972, it overtook the Model T Ford's production record of 15 million. Today, the amazing story of the world's most popular car isn't finished yet, as every car that rolls off the remaining South American production lines adds to a 21-million-plus production record that's unlikely ever to be beaten. The Volkswagen story isn't all about the Beetle though. The Beetle-based Karmann Ghia adds a bit of sporting style to the basic father-car and remains practical and affordable, and of course the Golf GTi has become a latter-day icon.

◀ **1947 Volkswagen Beetle Saloon,** air-cooled flat-4 engine, retaining many original features including semaphore indicators, left-hand drive, finished in black, beige cloth interior believed of later origin, good condition throughout.
£7,500–9,000 S

Plans for a *Volksauto*, with distinctive aerodynamic body and a rear-mounted, flat-four engine to save space, were announced as early as 1934. Dr Porsche designed the 'People's Car' along the lines of his famous rear-engined GP Auto Union, and no model has ever had a longer production life than the Beetle, produced continuously from 1945 and outselling even the Model T Ford.

VOLKSWAGEN Model	ENGINE cc/cyl	DATES	CONDITION 1	2	3
Beetle (split rear window)	1131/4	1945–53	£5,000	£3,500	£2,000
Beetle (oval rear window)	1192/4	1953–57	£4,000	£2,000	£1,000
Beetle (sloping headlamps)	1192/4	1957–68	£2,500	£1,000	£600
Beetle Cabriolet	1192/4	1954–60	£6,000	£4,500	£2,000
Beetle 1500	1493/4	1966–70	£3,000	£2,000	£1,000
Beetle 1302 LS	1600/4	1970–72	£2,500	£1,850	£850
Beetle 1303 S	1600/4	1972–79	£3,000	£2,000	£1,500
1500 Variant/1600	1493/ 1584/4	1961–73	£2,000	£1,500	£650
1500/1600	1493/ 1584/4	1961–73	£3,000	£2,000	£800
Karmann Ghia/I	1192/4	1955–59	£5,000	£3,000	£1,000
Karmann Ghia/I DHC	1192/4	1957–59	£8,000	£5,000	£2,500
Karmann Ghia/I	1192/4	1960–74	£5,500	£3,000	£1,800
Karmann Ghia/I DHC	1192/4	1960–74	£7,000	£4,500	£2,000
Karmann Ghia/3	1493/4	1962–69	£4,000	£2,500	£1,250

1974 Volkswagen Beetle Cabriolet, 1584cc, flat-4 engine, recently refurbished, new hood, finished in black, excellent condition.
£5,500–6,600 BRIT

1979 Volkswagen Beetle Cabriolet, fitted with GT wheels, factory optional air conditioning and heated rear window, left-hand drive, finished in Diamond silver, black hood and interior.
£8,000–9,000 COYS

◄ **1972 Volkswagen 1600E Fastback,** 1584cc, fuel injection, finished in metallic turquoise, black interior trim, little use in last 4 years, 26,000 miles recorded, original condition throughout.
£6,000–7,000 H&H

Miller's is a price GUIDE not a price LIST

1962 Volkswagen Microbus, 1192cc, flat-4 engine, 40bhp, 4-speed manual gearbox, 4-wheel hydraulic drum brakes, Safari windows, original luggage rack, tip-out windscreens, California roof, completely restored, finished in sky blue with a white roof.
£15,000–18,000 RM

Miller's Starter Marque

Starter Volkswagen: *Beetle, 1945 to date.*

- The Volkswagen Beetle is one bug they just can't find a cure for; it has been produced continuously from 1945.
- The fact that the Beetle is still in production means that cheap spares are readily available for most models other than very early cars. That buzzing, air-cooled, four-cylinder engine is well nigh unburstable too, and in mechanical terms, the cars are easy to work on. One fact says it all: the world record for an engine swap – drive up to drive away – is just over three minutes.
- If you're a classic purist, there's first-of-breed purity of either the 1131cc, 1945–53 split-screen cars or the 1953–57, oval-window 1200cc cars. For driveability and less-onerous ownership costs, a good mid-way motor is the 1500cc Bug produced from 1966 to 1970. It's old enough to be a classic, fast enough to keep up and still pure in design.
- The body's the Beetle's bug, though. Although the wings bolt on and virtually every body panel is available, there are a lot of Beetle bodywork bodgers. Check very closely where the body attaches to the floorpan, just behind the front wheels and immediately ahead of the rear wheels: severe rust here can make the vehicle unsafe.

Volvo

Although Sweden's premier car maker was founded in 1927, it wasn't until the post-war era that Volvos reached a wider international audience, initially with the PV444 and PV544, which earned admiration both for the accomplished roadholding that made it a rally winner and for the solid build quality that has become a Volvo hallmark. In the later 1950s, the 121 continued in the same mould and endured through various model designations (122/131/132/123GT) up to 1970. Today, they are still enjoyed in daily use as robust and stylish classic workhorses. Perhaps the most unlikely Volvo is the P1800 sports car, a one-time flight of fancy by the sober Swedes. It's certainly stylish, robust too, and terminally typecast as the 'Saint' Volvo after co-starring alongside Roger Moore in the long-running 1960s TV series. In estate form, it's an uncommonly practical sports car.

◀ **1963 Volvo P1800,** 1780cc, 4-cylinder engine, finished in dark blue, red interior, 38,000 miles recorded, 2 owners, very good condition.
£5,750–6,500 BRIT

Volvo P1800 (1961–73)

Engine: Four-cylinder, overhead-valve, 1778cc; 1985cc, 1968–73.
Power output: 100–124bhp.
Top speed: 105–115mph.
0–60mph: 9.7–13.2 seconds.
Price when new: £1832.12s.9d.
They called it the 'second sexiest car launch of 1961' – after the E-Type Jaguar – and in its way this sleek Swede has always played a supporting role. It was terminally type-cast as the 'Saint' Volvo after co-starring alongside Roger Moore in the long-running

TV series, but although Moore went on to big-screen Bond stardom, the P1800 remained stereotyped as a London mews dweller's sports car with more go than show and a boot that you could actually put things in. Toward the end of its life, it became more practical still with the introduction of the P1800ES sports-estate. With a production run totalling just over half the E-Type's, the P1800 is relatively rare, always distinctive and about as practical as a classic sports car can be. Affordable too, as MGB money could bag you a svelte-looking Swede.

▶ **1964 Volvo P1800S,** Swedish-built example, early-type 'boomerang' front bumpers, Webasto fabric sunroof, brakes partially refurbished, finished in Signal red, black vinyl interior, 20,000 miles recorded, in need of brake master-cylinder overhaul.
£3,750–4,500 BKS

Based on the 121 saloon, the P1800 sports coupé was a radical departure for the conservative Swedish concern. Initially, it was built by Jensen Motors.

VOLVO Model	ENGINE cc/cyl	DATES	CONDITION 1	2	3
PV444	1800/4	1958–67	£4,000	£1,750	£800
PV544	1800/4	1962–64	£4,000	£1,750	£800
120 (B16)	1583/4	1956–59	£3,000	£1,000	£300
121	1708/4	1960–67	£3,500	£1,500	£350
122S	1780/4	1960–67	£4,500	£1,500	£250
131	1780/4	1962–69	£4,000	£1,500	£350
221/222	1780/4	1962–69	£2,500	£1,500	£300
123GT	1986/4	1967–69	£3,000	£2,500	£750
P1800	1986/4	1960–70	£4,500	£2,500	£1,000
P1800E	1986/4	1970–71	£4,200	£2,500	£1,000
P1800ES	1986/4	1971–73	£4,800	£3,000	£1,000

◄ **1972 Volvo P1800ES,**
1986cc, 4-cylinder engine,
fuel injection, finished in
red, restored, good
condition throughout.
£3,000–3,500 H&H

**The P1800ES sports
estate adds a high
degree of practicality to
a sports car.**

Westfield

◄ **1989 Westfield SE,** 1600cc, overhead-camshaft,
4-cylinder Ford engine, twin 40DCOE carburettors, BCF
2 camshaft, 108bhp, 4-speed gearbox, 109mph top
speed, 0–60mph in 7.3 seconds, converted to unleaded
fuel, full weather equipment, finished in green and yellow,
red upholstery, stored 1993–99, 579 miles recorded.
£6,000–7,000 BKS

When production of the last Series 4 Lotus 7 ceased
in 1973, Caterham Car Sales, which had enjoyed sole
marketing rights, took over the factory jigs and moulds,
and in 1974 relaunched an updated Series 3 Lotus,
marketed under the Caterham name. There were many
imitators, too, among them Chris Smith, who
manufactured the Westfield in the West Midlands. The
design was modified to avoid legal complications, but
essentially the Westfield was the same as the Lotus 7.

► **1989 Westfield SE,**
1620cc, Ford 4-cylinder
crossflow engine rebuilt to
Stage 2 spec., Piper 285/2
camshaft, Mexico head,
balanced and lightened
flywheel, twin Weber
40DCOE carburettors,
130bhp, Sierra 5-speed
manual gearbox, Ford
Escort Mk 2 rear axle,
21,000 miles recorded,
finished in Wine red with
yellow stripe, 2 owners.
£5,750–6,750 BRIT

Willys-Knight

◄ **1928 Willys-Knight Model 70A Four-Door
Saloon,** left-hand drive, finished in blue and
black, black upholstery, bodywork in good
condition, interior fair.
£5,000–6,000 BKS

**Head of Overland (later Willys-Overland)
since 1907, John North Willys first put his
name on an automobile in 1914, when he
adopted Charles Knight's sleeve-valve
engine to create a new car – the Willys-
Knight. Production continued until 1933.**

Wolseley

In some ways, Wolseley ended up where it had begun, for it was Herbert Austin who set the wheels in motion for car manufacture at what was then the Wolseley Sheep Shearing Machine Company. Austin left in 1905, but through an ironic twist of fate, Wolseley and Austin were reunited when Austin and Morris merged in 1952 to form the British Motor Corporation. Although Wolseley was overshadowed at BMC by its big brothers, its contribution to British motoring was still important as one of the early pace setters. The first four-wheeled Wolseley motor car was produced around 1900, and in 1901 Wolseley car manufacturing was taken over by armaments firm Vickers. Early Wolseley products usually possessed well-engineered engines that didn't always receive the chassis and running gear to match. Financial difficulties

led to the company's acquisition in 1927 by William Morris, and after 1935 Wolseleys served as upmarket Morrises with superior interiors and overhead-valve engines. After the 1952 merger of Austin and Morris, Wolseley survived as a BMC brand until 1975. BMC-era Wolseleys offer enthusiasts a little more distinction and pampering than provided by the starker, plain-Jane Austin and Morris versions.
The Wolseley Hornet, produced from 1961 to 1969, was even more distinctive. Based on the Mini's bodyshell, it was distinguished by upmarket appointments and an extended boot, which had no Austin or Morris counterpart, although the Riley Elf had the same feature. Produced in far fewer numbers than the conventional Mini, the Hornet makes a really distinctive and rather posher alternative.

1932 Wolseley Hornet 12hp Four-Door Saloon, completely restored 1996, engine, gearbox and rear axle rebuilt, suspension and brakes overhauled, rewired, brightwork rechromed, finished in black, new blue interior trim, headlining and carpets, paintwork in need of minor cosmetic attention, believed 1 of only 6 examples surviving.
£5,000–6,000 BKS

Introduced in 1930, the Hornet featured Wolseley's bevel-driven, overhead-camshaft six-cylinder engine in a lengthened Morris Minor chassis. Its power-to-weight ratio was exemplary among contemporary 1.3 litre cars, the smooth and flexible six pulling from walking pace to over 60mph. The model was revised for 1932 with a shortened and repositioned chain-driven overhead-cam engine, thus improving cabin space, and a four-speed 'silent third' gearbox.

1969 Wolseley 1300, finished in dark green, 26,000 miles recorded, good condition.
£1,700–2,000 WILM

Restored values

The cost of a professional restoration will have an influence on, but no direct relation to, a car's market value. A restored car can have a market value lower than the cost of its restoration.

WOLSELEY Model	ENGINE cc/cyl	DATES	CONDITION 1	2	3
8	918/4	1939–48	£3,000	£2,000	£1,000
10	1140/4	1939–48	£3,500	£2,000	£1,000
12/48	1548/4	1939–48	£4,000	£2,000	£1,250
14/60	1818/6	1946–48	£4,500	£2,500	£1,500
18/85	2321/6	1946–48	£6,000	£3,000	£2,000
25	3485/6	1946–48	£7,000	£4,000	£2,500
4/50	1476/4	1948–53	£2,500	£1,000	£450
6/80	2215/6	1948–54	£3,000	£1,500	£750
4/44	1250/4	1952–56	£2,500	£1,250	£750
15/50	1489/4	1956–58	£1,850	£850	£500
1500	1489/4	1958–65	£2,500	£1,000	£500
15/60	1489/4	1958–61	£2,000	£700	£400
16/60	1622/4	1961–71	£1,800	£800	£400
6/90	2639/6	1954–57	£2,500	£1,000	£500
6/99	2912/6	1959–61	£3,000	£1,500	£750
6/110 MK I/II	2912/6	1961–68	£2,000	£1,000	£500
Hornet (Mini)	848/4	1961–70	£1,500	£750	£400
1300	1275/4	1967–74	£1,250	£750	£400
18/85	1798/4	1967–72	£950	£500	£250

Commercial Vehicles

1961 Austin A55 ½ Ton Pick-up, 1.5 litre B-series engine, 4-speed manual gearbox with column-change, bench seat, restored 1997, finished in green with matching interior trim, 25,660 miles recorded, excellent condition throughout.
£7,000–8,000 BKS

The first medium-sized Austin to employ unitary construction and the last to feature a body style unique to the marque, the new Cambridge debuted in 1954. In 1.5 litre form, the model was produced until 1958, although commercial derivatives continued until 1971.

1951 Bristol KSW Double-Decker Bus, Bristol AVW engine, Eastern Coachworks body, seating for 55 passengers, 35mph top speed.
£9,500–10,500 HMM

1959 Chevrolet Apache 32 Long-Stepside Pick-up, 235.5cu.in, 6-cylinder inline engine, 135bhp, 4-speed manual gearbox, semi-elliptic leaf-spring suspension, 4-wheel hydraulic drum brakes, factory-fitted special-equipment farm bumper, left-hand drive, finished in turquoise and white, white interior, fewer than 740 miles recorded 3 owners, original.
£14,100–15,600 C

▶ **1986 Ford Transit/Hanlon Ambulance,** restored to original condition 1997, Northamptonshire Ambulance Service livery.
£2,000–2,500 BAm

1963 Austin 152 (J2) Paralanian Motor Caravan, 1489cc B-series engine, finished in 2-tone brown, very good original condition.
£2,750–3,250 BMC

1972 Bedford CF Bristolian Motor Caravan, gearbox reconditioned, finished in green and cream, very good condition.
£2,500–3,000 CCa

1927 Ford Model T Dropside Truck, 2890cc, 4-cylinder engine, older restoration, good condition.
£4,500–5,500 BRIT

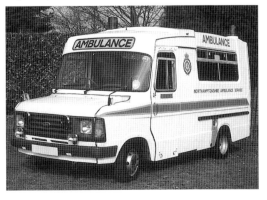

1959 Morris Minor Pick-up, later 1098cc, overhead-valve, 4-cylinder engine, twin SU carburettors, 56bhp, 4-speed manual gearbox, torsion-bar independent front suspension, leaf-spring rear, Austin-Healey Sprite front disc brakes, left-hand drive, new tilt, finished in yellow, black interior, 87,000 miles recorded.
£5,875–6,500 C

1970 Morris Minor 1000 Van, 1098cc, 4-cylinder engine, 4-speed gearbox, finished in green with Ashford Borough Council crest, little use since 1976, rear wheel arches in need of attention.
£600–700 LF

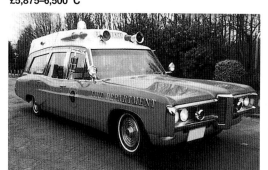

1968 Pontiac Ambulance, coachwork by Superior, 400cu.in V8 engine, 17mpg, lengthened Bonneville/Parisienne chassis (21ft overall), restored, equipped with oxygen, stretcher trolley, 'gum-ball machine' rotating beacon and sirens, lighting converted to UK-legal spec., finished in red and white.
£12,000–14,000 BKS

1947 Reliant Regent Pick-up, 750cc, completely restored, finished in green and black, grey interior trim, noisy gearbox, otherwise excellent condition.
£1,800–2,150 H&H

Children's Cars

1950s Austin J40 Pedal Car, finished in blue, in need of restoration.
£400–500 E

Bugatti Type 35 Children's Car, by Crosthwaite & Gardner, electric drive, aluminium body, original badges.
£2,500–3,000 STE

◄ **1953 Kidillac Pedal Car,** by Gendron, child's version of Cadillac Eldorado convertible, heavy-gauge pressed-steel construction with plastic fittings, vinyl upholstery, Perspex windscreen, working lights and horn, completely restored.
£1,600–2,000 CARS

1930s Chrysler Airflow Pedal Car, by Steelcraft, Perspex windscreen and wind deflectors, chrome bonnet mascot and wheels, dummy convertible hood, vinyl seat, completely restored.
£800–900 CARS

1953 Hot Rod Pedal Car, by Garton, pressed-steel construction, completely restored, resprayed in black with yellow/red flame pattern, non-original chrome greyhound bonnet mascot.
£1,000–1,250 CARS

1950 Merry-Go-Round Car, all wood construction, in need of restoration.
£280–350 PC

Jeep Tow Truck Pedal Car, by Hamilton, all-steel construction, completely restored, new wheels and tyres.
£1,200–1,500 CARS

As a rusted relic, the value of this pedal car would be £150–200.

1960s De Dion Bouton Pedal Car, by Triang, heavy-gauge pressed-steel panels on tubular frame, restored, finished in green with yellow and red trim, plastic detailing, wood and vinyl upholstered seat, bulb horn, authentic sounding crank handle.
£250–300 CARS

1960s Ferrari Pedal Car, by MG, completely restored, finished in red, white interior trim.
£500–600 PC

Mercedes 500SL Child's Car, 2-seater, 2.2hp motor, forward and reverse gears, governable 5–15mph speed.
£2,250–2,500 STE

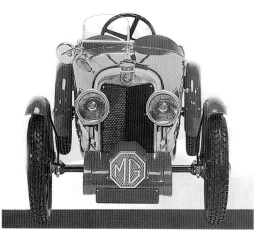

MG K3 Magnette Pedal Car, simulated supercharger, wire wheels, treaded tyres, aero screen, finished in red.
£2,250–2,500 STE

1980s Mickey Mouse Child's Car, 12 volt electric motor, moulded-plastic body, steel chassis, rubber bumpers and wheels, finished in red and blue.
£125–150 CARS

1959 Vanwall Grand Prix Pedal Car, by Triang, heavy-gauge pressed-steel construction, wire wheels, spring suspension, Perspex windscreen, plastic steering wheel, completely restored, finished in red.
£400–500 CARS

1930s Fire Truck Pedal Car, by Steelcraft, ladder, bell, working headlamps, completely restored, finished in red with yellow coachlining and logos.
£1,000–1,250 CARS

MGB Roadster Pedal Cars, fibreglass bodywork, steel chassis, solid rubber treaded tyres, polished aluminium front and rear bumpers, authentic MG grille, working headlamps and indicators, padded, leathercloth seat, acrylic windscreen, Bakelite steering wheel.
£750–800 each CARS

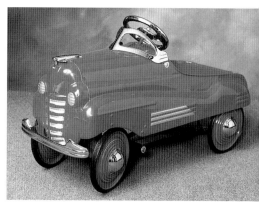

1948 Pontiac Roadster Pedal Car, by Murray, pressed-steel construction, chrome fittings, completely restored, finished in red and silver.
£1,000–1,250 CARS

1951 Taxi Cab Pedal Car, by Murray, pressed-steel construction, chrome fittings, bulb horn, completely restored, finished in yellow with new decals.
£1,200–1,500 CARS

1934 Tri-Plane Pedal Car, by Steelcraft, completely restored, some non-original parts, finished in red to represent Baron von Richtofen's WWI Fokker triplane.
£2,500–3,000 CARS

1960s Wolseley Pedal Car, by Triang, pressed-steel construction, authentic Wolseley chrome grille, opening bonnet, dummy engine, working headlights and horn, opening boot, chrome wire wheels and hubcaps, solid rubber tyres, original blue and white finish, vinyl upholstered seat.
£450–500 CARS

◀ **1960s Police Pedal Car,** by Mobo, original Perspex windscreen, working illuminated 'Police' bonnet sign, dummy grille and boot, pressed-steel disc wheels with inserted rubber treads, finished in dark blue, plastic steering wheel with horn button, original shipping carton.
£350–400 CARS

Replica, Kit & Reproduction Cars

◀ **1989 Dax Tojeiro Cobra Replica,** 5.3 litre, double-overhead-camshaft, Jaguar V12 engine, mechanical components taken from 1978 donor vehicle, Revolution alloy wheels, chrome side pipes, roll bar, finished in red with white stripes, magnolia leather interior, excellent condition throughout.
£13,000–15,000 BARO

▶ **1990 Dax Tojeiro Cobra 427 Replica,** 5.3 litre Jaguar V12 engine, 4-speed manual gearbox with overdrive, suspension and running gear from 1978 XJ6L, stainless steel side exhausts, Halibrand-style alloy wheels, over £19,000 spent on new parts, finished in Ford Galaxy blue, leather interior trim, fewer than 10,000 miles since completion, good condition throughout.
£10,500–12,000 BKS

1986 Gravetti Cobra Replica, 3528cc Rover V8 engine, Jaguar suspension, Halibrand wheels, hood, tonneau cover and sidescreens, finished in Midnight blue, fibreglass bodywork in good condition.
£10,000–12,000 BRIT

Southern Roadcraft Cobra Replica, 350cu.in Chevrolet V8 engine, 750cfm Holley carburettors, electronic ignition, 300bhp, 3-speed automatic transmission, knock-off alloy wheels, chrome roll bar, finished in red, grey interior trim, excellent condition throughout.
£10,500–12,500 H&H

Ford GTD40 Mk III Replica, 5 litre, mid-mounted V8 engine, knock-off alloy wheels, finished in dark blue, good condition.
£14,000–16,000 WILM

◀ **1989 LR Roadsters Jaguar XK-SS Replica,** 3781cc Jaguar engine, all-synchromesh manual gearbox with overdrive, ventilated front disc brakes, independent rear suspension with inboard disc brakes, replica Dunlop-type wheels, spaceframe chassis, accurate fibreglass bodyshell, finished in British Racing green, tan interior.
£14,000–16,000 H&H

▶ **1980 Stardust Jaguar D-Type Replica,** 2.5 litre Triumph 6-cylinder engine, triple Weber carburettors, 200bhp, Ford Escort Mk 1/2 running gear, competition clutch, twin electric cooling fans, stainless steel hoses, 6JJx15 wheels, fibreglass bodywork, finished in silver, polished-aluminium interior, three-point racing harnesses, first registered 1998, very good condition throughout.
£6,000–7,000 BKS

1985 Kougar Sports, 3781cc, Jaguar 6-cylinder engine, all parts rebuilt or refurbished as required, recent respray in Jaguar Indigo blue, c6,000 miles covered since completion.
£10,000–11,000 BRIT

Kougar Sports Mk I, 4.2 litre Jaguar 6-cylinder engine, triple 2in SU carburettors, custom-built stainless steel exhaust system, 4-speed Jaguar manual gearbox, race-spec. suspension, chrome roll bar, finished in ivory, racing harnesses.
£8,000–9,000 BARO

◄ **1998 Kougar Sports,** 3.8 litre Jaguar 6-cylinder engine, triple SU carburettors, manual gearbox with overdrive, limited-slip differential, engine rebuilt and converted to unleaded fuel, new clutch, master cylinder and brake servo, finished in red, red-piped black leather interior, three-point harnesses, c100 miles covered since completion.
£8,250–9,250 BKS

► **1991 Southern Roadcraft Daytona Spyder Replica,** 5343cc, Jaguar V12 engine and running gear, 1977 Jaguar XJ12 donor vehicle, all components reconditioned or replaced as required, finished in red, c2,500 miles covered since completion, good mechanical condition.
£8,000–9,000 BRIT

◄ **1995 Southern Roadcraft Daytona Spyder Replica,** 5343cc Jaguar V12 engine, built at a cost of c£43,000, finished in metallic Gunmetal grey, black duck hood, interior trimmed in grey hide, good condition throughout.
£8,500–10,000 BRIT

► **1978 Gazelle Two-Seat Sports,** 1500cc, Volkswagen 4-cylinder engine and running gear from 1970 donor vehicle, converted to right-hand drive, vinyl hood and sidescreens, finished in dark brown and cream, tan leather interior, good mechanical condition.
£3,750–4,500 BRIT

The Gazelle was inspired by the 1930s Mercedes SSK sports car.

Restoration Projects

1937 Austin 7 Van, chrome-radiator model, partially restored.
£2,250–2,750 UMC

1918 Ford Model T, right-hand drive, in need of complete restoration.
£900–1,000 TUC

c1906 Darracq Rolling Chassis, twin-cylinder engine, wooden artillery wheels, steering column, bulkhead, seat frame, fuel tank, steering wheel, all controls connected, box fitted to rear, bodyplate bearing the inscription 'E. Rousseau, C. Baudier – constructeur, Seine', no documentation.
£2,700–3,200 BKS

1937 Fiat Topolino Coupé, 570cc engine, finished in red and black, red interior, complete, 'barn discovery', in need of complete restoration.
£500–600 H&H

◀ **1967 Jaguar Mk II 3.4 Saloon,** 3442cc, overdrive gearbox, engine runs, clutch seized, new fuel pump and coil, various new panels fitted 1980s, including doors and wings, but not painted, virtually complete, plus 4 wire wheels, finished in gold, red interior, 'barn discovery'.
£450–540 H&H

1948 Lagonda 2.6 Litre Sports Saloon, coachwork by Tickford, cruciform chassis, all-independent suspension, coils and wishbones at the front, torsion bars at the rear, inboard rear brakes, no engine, in need of complete restoration.
£400–500 BKS

The Lagonda 2.6 Litre was W.O. Bentley's last design. In all, 550 examples were made, together with a further 450 examples of a rebodied 3 litre version.

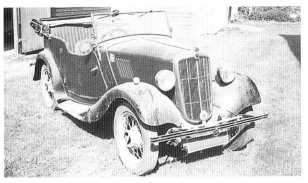

◀ **c1935 Morris Eight Two-Door Tourer,** 918cc sidevalve engine, electric fuel pump, Bishop cam steering, hydraulic brakes, hydraulic shock absorbers, wire wheels, box-section chassis, finished in maroon, red leather interior, 'barn discovery'.
£1,000–1,200 **BKS**

1927 Rolls-Royce 20hp Running Chassis, radiator, bonnet, bulkhead, instruments, 5 wire wheels, engine runs well, chassis can be driven.
£9,000–10,000 **RCC**

1927 Rolls-Royce 20hp Four-Door Saloon, coachwork by Park Ward, 4-speed manual gearbox with right-hand change, 4-wheel servo-assisted brakes, correct chassis/engine pairing, coachwork and vertical-shuttered radiator believed to have come from a 1933 20/25hp model, no inlet/exhaust manifolds, seats, interior trim or instruments, in need of complete restoration.
£2,500–3,000 **BKS**

1936 Jaguar SS 2½ Litre Saloon, 2500cc engine, finished in black, brown interior, mechanically complete, body and chassis in good condition, no windscreen, sunroof panel, side lamps, radiator badge, steering wheel or front and rear bumpers, 30,844 miles recorded.
£5,750–7,000 **H&H**

1950s Thames Trader, ex-Royal Air Force field and airport ambulance, accommodation for 6 stretcher patients, in need of complete restoration.
£400–475 **BAm**

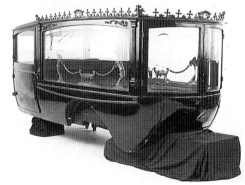

Woodall Nicholson Hearse Coachwork, thought to have come from a Rolls-Royce Silver Ghost, complete from bulkhead back, filigree-work with cross motif on roof, cut-glass windows, chrome-plated interior fittings.
£6,000–7,000 **BKS**

Microcars

1983 Bambi Bubble Car, single gullwing door, single central headlamp, finished in beige, black interior, good condition throughout.
£1,000–1,200 BKS

The acquisition of a 1960s Peel P50 microcar is said to have inspired the Bambi's creator, Alan Evans, to come up with a more modern version of the concept for the 1980s. A single-seat three-wheeler like the Peel, the Bambi was powered by a 50cc, single-cylinder two-stroke moped engine and weighed a mere 235lb. The inevitably modest performance was more than offset by the extremely frugal fuel consumption of around 100mpg. After a number of design alterations and changes of engine supplier, the Bambi ceased production after around 30 cars had been made.

1959 Messerschmitt KR200 Kabinenroller, recently restored, reconditioned engine, new wiring loom, floor, side panels and side windows, finished in silver, new blue interior trim piped in white, excellent condition throughout.
£8,000–9,000 BKS

Introduced in 1953 as the Fend, after its co-designer Fritz Fend, the Messerschmitt microcar was soon being marketed under its manufacturer's name, the change coinciding with a switch from the original's 148cc Fichtel & Sachs engine to a 174cc unit. Mounted at the rear, the single-cylinder two-stroke produced a modest 9bhp, which was enough to propel the lightweight, aerodynamic KR175 to around 55mph. Tandem seating and handlebar controls were retained for the 191cc KR200 of 1955, which featured revised bodywork and a floor-mounted accelerator and clutch. Production ceased in 1964 after 30,000 KR200s had been made.

▶ **1964 Trojan Cabin Cruiser,** restored, good condition throughout.
£4,500–5,000 HMM

The Trojan marque dates back to the 1920s, when the company's unconventional cars had a loyal following. In 1961, Trojan took over the manufacture of the Heinkel bubble car, which had gone out of production in Germany, naming it the Trojan 200.

1959 BMW 600, restored, good condition.
£4,500–5,000 HMM

1961 Isetta Trycycle, 300cc rear-mounted engine, 4-speed gearbox, completely restored, finished in yellow, excellent condition throughout.
£2,750–3,300 BARO

1961 Messerschmitt KR200 Cabriolet, 191cc, electric starter, electrically-operated reverse gear, floor-mounted accelerator and clutch pedals, 62mph top speed, double-dip headlamps, flashing indicators, recently restored, engine rebuilt, new body panels, finished in pale blue, new black hood and black interior with white-piped seats and panels.
£5,250–6,500 BKS

1927 Peugeot 190S Commerciale, 719cc, 4-cylinder engine, restored, finished in red and black, double-duck black hood, serviceable sidescreens, interior trimmed in red and black vinyl, mechanics in good condition.
£3,250–3,750 BRIT

Introduced in 1927, the Peugeot 190 was a sturdy little car in the best French light-car tradition. Based on a conventional chassis, it was available as a saloon, coupé and torpedo 'commerciale' – basically a utility tourer.

1916 Ford Model T Van, finished in green, older restoration, good condition.
£6,000–7,000 TUC

1934 Dennis Light Pump Fire Engine, 4150cc petrol engine, older restoration, rear-mounted pump, ladder, hand-operated bell and other period fire equipment, good condition throught.
£7,000–8,000 BKS

The Dennis Light Pump was a four-man appliance favoured by rural brigades and did not carry its own water supply. This example, with Braidwood-style coachwork, was supplied new to the Avon India Rubber Company, of Melksham, Wiltshire, and in WWII it served with the NFS in Southampton Docks.

1980 Mini Pick-up, 1300cc engine, 4-speed gearbox, front-wheel drive, completely restored, new front wings, door skins, front floor well and inner and outer sills, bed lined with aluminium checker-plate, bare-metal respray in metallic British Racing green, interior trimmed in grey with wood veneered dashboard and door pockets, excellent condition throughout.
£2,250–2,750 H&H

1948 Bedford 30cwt Lorry, 2 owners from new, restored, finished in brown and black, good condition, history file.
£4,000–5,000 UMC

1950s Pontiac Station Wagon Pedal Car,
manufactured by Murray, pressed-steel construction,
chrome fittings, completely restored.
£1,000–1,250 CARS

Willys Jeep Pedal Car, manufactured by Hamilton,
pressed-steel construction, restored, finished with new
decals and general's insignia.
£750–900 CARS

US Air Mail Biplane Pedal Car, manufactured by
Steelcraft, restored, finished in RFC WWI colours,
some non-original parts.
£2,500–3,000 CARS

1950s Austin J40 Pedal Car, early version with flying 'A'
mascot, restored, finished in red, cream interior,
working lights, very good condition.
£1,250–1,500 BKS

c1936 Triang Chrysler Air Flow Pedal Car, restored,
good condition.
£1,750–2,000 PC

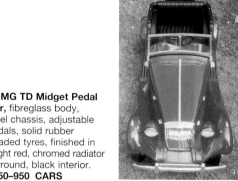

▶ **MG TD Midget Pedal
Car,** fibreglass body,
steel chassis, adjustable
pedals, solid rubber
treaded tyres, finished in
bright red, chromed radiator
surround, black interior.
£850–950 CARS

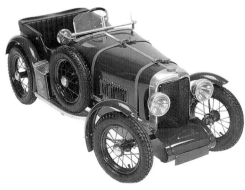

Bentley Speed 6 Children's Car, built of aluminium
and wood, finished in British Racing green,
mahogany running boards, leather bonnet straps.
£2,300–2,700 STE

Rolls-Royce Silver Ghost Children's Car, half-scale
replica, 24 volt electric motor, forward and reverse
variable speeds, rack-and-pinion steering, foot and hand
brakes, imitation engine under the bonnet, opening
doors, finished in silver with nickel-plated brightwork,
deep-buttoned black leatherette upholstery, front seats
fold to allow an adult to drive, 1 of 3 built.
£7,000–8,000 BRIT

1942 M14 International Half-Track, completely restored, original tracks, working twin Maxen turret with deactivated guns, good condition.
£7,000–8,000 MVT

1942 White Scout Car, 5.2 litre, 6-cylinder engine, 4-wheel drive, restored, deactivated machine-gun, full-length canvas hood, good condition.
£6,500–7,500 MVT

c1942 Dodge WC53 ¾-Ton Carryall, 230cu.in, 6-cylinder engine, 92bhp, 4-speed gearbox, single-speed transfer box, 4-wheel drive, restored, finished in 337th Bomb Squadron USAAF colours, good condition.
£9,000–10,000 MVT

The WC53 Carryall was developed as a light cargo and personnel carrier.

1943 Ford Jeep, restored, finished in WWII US Army colours, rifle scabbard, radio, antenna, spare wheel, hood, jerrican, excellent original condition.
£6,750–7,500 BKS

Although associated with Willys-Overland, the original Jeep was developed by American Bantam, formerly American Austin. Designed to meet the US Army's requirement for a rugged, go-anywhere, four-wheel-drive vehicle, Bantam's prototype Jeep was up and running by 1940. The Pentagon, however, doubted the firm's ability to meet the military's demands, so the major contracts went to Willys and Ford. Produced by the million, the Jeep saw service in every theatre during WWII.

1943 Ward La France M1A1 Wrecker, 6-cylinder engine, 145bhp, 6-wheel drive, 14 ton all-up weight, restored, good condition.
£5,000–6,000 MVT

c1943 Chevrolet C15A 15cwt GS, 216cu.in, 6-cylinder engine, 85bhp, 4-wheel drive, very good condition.
£4,000–4,500 MVT

The C15A chassis was fitted with many body types, among them office, wireless, personnel, AT tractor and water tanker.

◀ **1944 Diamond T 4 Ton Truck,** 5.29 litre, 6-cylinder engine, air brakes, 6-wheel drive, deactivated machine-gun on ring mount, restored, new canvas hood and sidescreens to cab, new rear tilt, excellent condition.
£7,000–8,000 MVT

1954 Humber FV 1601 1 Ton CT Truck, 4259cc, Rolls-Royce B60 engine, 120bhp 5-speed and reverse gearbox, 4-wheel drive, restored, finished in British Army colours, good condition.
£1,500–1,800 MVT

c1955 Leyland Martian 10 Ton Medium Tractor, 6490cc, 8-cylinder, Rolls-Royce B81 engine, 215bhp, 6-wheel drive, used as artillery tractor, accommodation for crew of 12, completely restored, excellent condition.
£3,000–3,500 MVT

1958 Reo M35 A1 Truck, 331cu.in, 6-cylinder, overhead-valve petrol engine, restored, finished in US Army colours, good condition.
£3,000–3,500 PC

c1958 Ferret Scout Car, 4258cc, 6-cylinder engine, 96bhp, 5-speed pre-selector gearbox, forward/reverse transfer box, independent coil-spring suspension, original.
£3,500–4,200 RRM

1958 Ferret 2/4 Scout Car, 4258cc engine, turret with deactivated machine-gun, restored, finished in United Nations colours, good condition.
£4,000–5,000 IMPS

c1960 Reo M35 2½ Ton Truck, 331cu.in, 6-cylinder engine, 127bhp, 5-speed and reverse gearbox, 2-speed transfer box, 6-wheel drive.
£2,500–3,000 MVT

The Reo M35 was introduced in 1950 and continued in production until the 1980s. It was also assembled under licence by Kaiser Jeep, Studebaker, White and AM General.

◄ **1965 Austin Gipsy,** 2200cc engine, 90in short-wheelbase model, independent suspension all-round, restored, good condition.
£1,500–1,800 MVT

Production of the Austin Gypsy began in 1958 and continued for ten years. The amalgamation of Austin with Rover to form British Leyland sounded its death knell, as there was room for only one 4x4 in the organisation, and that was the Land Rover.

A Georges Richard advertising poster, some surface damage, on linen, mounted on a frame, c1898, 59 x 42in (150 x 106.5cm).
£230–270 BKS

A Samson Tyres advertising poster, on linen, mounted on a frame, c1905, 64 x 48in (162.5 x 122cm).
£400–450 BKS

After Maurice Neuman, a lithographic Guiels & Cie advertising poster, on linen, mounted on a frame, 1899, 77 x 50in (195.5 x 127cm).
£1,700–2,000 BKS

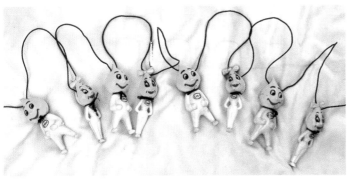

A set of Esso fairy lights, 1950s, each 4in (10cm) high.
£350–400 EDO

A Mido 18ct gold gentleman's wristwatch, in the form of a Bugatti radiator, cross-hatched silvered dial, original buckle and glass, stamped 206774 to the reverse, good original condition.
£15,000–18,000 BKS

A plaster promotional Mr Bibendum, inscribed 'Michelin Tires', original condition, minor damage, c1911, 32in (81.5cm) high.
£1,600–2,000 BKS

A nickel-silver Rolls-Royce Spirit of Ecstasy mascot, inscribed 'Rolls-Royce Limited Feb 6th 1911', signed 'Charles Sykes', mounted on display base, 9½in (24cm) high.
£500–600 BKS

A Finnigan's French Flapper mascot, by C. George, mounted on wooden base, c1920s, 8½in (21.5cm) high.
£375–425 ChA

A bull's head car mascot, 1930s.
£140–160 ATF

A glass Butterfly Girl mascot, by Red
Ashay, good condition, c1928.
£1,400–1,650 BKS

**This was the first of a series of
mascots made by the company.**

A hollow-cast bronze Telcote Pup
mascot, mounted on a wooden
base, 1920s, 5in (12.5cm) high.
£500–600 BKS

◄ A gilt bronze Coq mascot,
by Theophile Schneider,
mounted on original radiator cap,
impressed 'THS' emblem, 1910–15.
£3,500–4,000 BKS

A silvered bronze Malkovsky mascot,
by Jan Martel, depicting the ballet
dancer in cubist style, excellent
unrestored condition, signed, c1920.
£7,000–8,000 BKS

An opalescent amber glass Perche mascot, by René
Lalique, moulded 'R. Lalique' and etched 'R. Lalique
France', c1929.
£3,700–4,300 BKS

**The Perche was one of the few coloured glass
mascots produced by René Lalique.**

A Hohm Ecoleauto training car, working engine, 3-speed
and reverse gearbox, clutch, differential, hand and foot
brakes, suspension, steering and lights, all in working
order, mounted on wooden base, good condition,
1940–50s, 48in (122cm) long.
£1,000–1,200 BKS

**The Ecoleauto was produced after WWII to show
student drivers the basics of the car. The prototype
designed by Hohm was used by the German military
to train their personnel during the 1930s.**

A 1:20-scale model of a 1925 Vauxhall
30/98 Wensum Tourer, polished metal finish,
excellent condition.
£1,700–2,000 BKS

A 1:20-scale model of a 1913 Mercer Series 35J
Raceabout, brass fittings, good condition.
£2,200–2,600 BKS

A pair of Price's Motorine Motor Oil pump globes, 1930s, each 7½in (19cm) high.
£350–400 MSMP

A Welsh Dragon petrol pump globe, 1950s, 18½in (47cm) high.
£450–500 MSMP

A Super Fina glass petrol pump globe, moulded with raised lettering, 1950s, 19in (48.5cm) high.
£350–400 MSMP

A Gilbert and Barker hand-operated petrol pump, complete with dials, sight glass, hose and nozzle, completely restored, Shell livery, wired for lighting, fitted with reproduction Sealed Shell globe, early 1920s.
£900–1,100 BKS

A Gilbert and Barker hand-operated petrol pump, completely restored, original except for globe, 1920, 96in (244cm) high.
£750–850 TPS

A Cleveland Premium glass petrol pump globe, 1960s, 26in (66cm) high.
£250–300 MSMP

A Bartholomew honey leather map case, containing a set of linen-backed Bartholomew's maps, distance measuring instrument under lid, leather open reading folio, matching and complete leather-cased map set for Scotland with linen-backed maps, contour road book, c1910.
£1,000–1,200 BKS

A Louis Vuitton cabin trunk, LV material-covered, with leather edges, brass corners and locks, leather carrying handles, wooden struts, quilted lattice lid, 2 lift-out trays with straps and brass ties, 1920s.
£3,700–4,300 BKS

An Alexander Clark crocodile skin-covered vanity case, lined with watered silk, fitted with silver accessories, including brushes, silver-topped bottles and manicure set, complete and hallmarked for 1912–13.
£2,300–2,700 BKS

A French black leather-covered vanity case, with internal black leather travelling miniature suitcase, fitted with silver-topped perfume bottles, manicure set, brush, bevel-edged freestanding mirror, complete, excellent condition, c1920.
£500–600 BKS

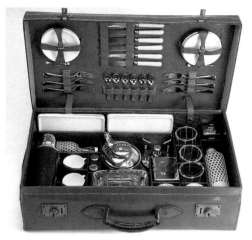

A honey leather-cased 6-person picnic set, including kettle and burner, fully-fitted wooden interior with 2 wicker-covered bottles, Coracle butter and preserves ceramic jars, cutlery fitted under lid, restored, excellent condition.
£2,300–2,800 BKS

An Abercrombie and Fitch wicker-cased 6-person picnic set, including 4 matching Coracle ceramic-based sandwich boxes, 2 wicker-covered bottles, 6 wicker-covered glasses, butter pot, 6 plates, cutlery and plates housed in lid, excellent condition, 1920s.
£750–850 BKS

◄ A Louis Vuitton wardrobe trunk, LV material-covered, with brass corners, locks, wooden rails, leather carrying handle, fully fitted interior, all drawers intact, 2 hat drawers, drawer with divisions for jewellery, leather straps for boots, support rail with 8 wooden shirt and jacket hangers, trouser hanger, unmarked original condition, 1920s.
£6,000–7,000 BKS

A Brexton wicker 4-person picnic basket, late 1960s, good condition.
£70–80 PPH

A French Texaco double-sided enamel sign, 1938, 24 x 23in (61 x 58.5cm).
£250–280 EDO

A fibreglass moulded Mickey Mouse petrol sign, 1950s, 42in (106.5cm) high.
£300–350 EDO

An Esso Lady enamel sign, 1960s, 16in (40.5cm) high.
£70–80 EDO

A Shell double-sided, illuminated, stained-glass garage advertising sign, 4 small panes with cracks, otherwise in excellent condition, together with 2 Mazda light bulbs, c1918, 26¼in (66.5cm) diam.
£2,900–3,400 S

Racing & Rallying

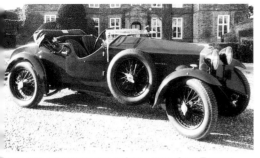

1929 OM 665S Superba 15/60hp Two-Seat Tourer, restored 1980s, further work 1996–97, finished in dark blue, black leather interior trim, ex-Tourist Trophy and Brooklands Double Twelve, good condition throughout.
£60,000–70,000 BKS

The OM 665S was one of Italy's great sporting cars of the 1920s. With a 2 litre, sidevalve six-cylinder engine, this model enjoyed a distinguished racing career, the high point of which was a 1–2–3 walk-over in the first Mille Miglia in 1927. One of only six overhead-valve conversions built to comply with the homologation requirements of the 1929 Ulster Tourist Trophy Race, this car was first raced in the 1929 Brooklands Double Twelve. Entered by British OM concessionaire L. C. Rawlence, the three-car OM équipe won a team award in that event. Of an estimated 350–370 OMs imported into the UK, only 30 or so survive. A mere four of these have overhead-valve engines: two 2.2 litre cars and two 2 litre cars.

> A known continuous history can add value to and enhance the enjoyment of a car.

1932 Alvis Speed 20 Racing Four-Seater, coachwork by Carbodies, removable cowl over rear seats, fold-flat windscreen, driver's Brooklands aero screen, cycle-style wings, Brooklands fishtail silencer, quick-release fuel filler cap with wide racing filler pipe.
£68,000–76,000 BKS

London dealer Charles Follett had tried the prototype Alvis Speed 20 late in 1931 and seen the potential in the car for competition use. He persuaded the Hon. Brian Lewis and Sir Henry 'Tim' Birkin of the virtues of Alvis's new 2½ litre model and plans were made to build a car for Lewis and Birkin to campaign in the 1932 TT. Captain G.T. Smith-Clarke at Alvis was a little frustrated at the restrictions placed on racing modifications by the TT regulations, and Birkin wanted the car to be fitted with a Villiers supercharger, which Alvis would not agree to. The outcome was that the car was not ready for the TT. However, development continued, Carbodies being commissioned to build the coachwork, which was finished in Birkin red. The car was tested on the outer circuit at Brooklands, but Birkin never took delivery. R. F. Oats, service manager at Folletts and himself a Brooklands driver, had the car briefly before it was supplied to wealthy amateur driver Sir Ronald Gunter of Wetherby Park who, with Dr Benjafield of Bentley fame, entered the car in the 1933 JCC International Trophy race at Brooklands.

1931 Bentley 4½ Litre Supercharged Racing Two-Seater, unique spring-steel coachwork by Vanden Plas, rebuilt on 10ft 10in 3 Litre chassis 1950s, Amhurst Villiers Mk IV supercharger, ventilated front brake drums, string-bound leaf springs, Hartford shock absorbers, fishtail exhaust, fork-mounted Zeiss headlamps, louvred bonnet sides and top, fold-flat windscreen, side-mounted spare, finished in dark blue, black leather upholstery.
£280,000+ BKS

Certainly the most famous, and arguably the most charismatic, of all vintage Bentleys were the supercharged Le Mans cars created by Sir Henry 'Tim' Birkin. Although 50 factory 4½ Litre supercharged cars were produced to facilitate homologation for the endurance race, there were only ever five Birkin team 'blowers'. This car was the final example to be built, and although it was never raced, it has all the charisma of those cars and retains considerable originality.

◄ **1950 Nardi-Danese Prototype Racing Single-Seater,** 750cc, flat-twin BMW engine.
£11,000–12,500 BKS

This interesting little car was built by the great Enrico Nardi - close friend and sometime colleague of the legendary Enzo Ferrari, and in 1939–40 co-constructor of what was, in effect, the very first Ferrari competition car. This single-seater is understood to have been a unique prototype built by Enrico Nardi and his collaborator, Renato Danese, in those post-war years and it was used extensively in Italian mountain-climb events by his young friend Gino Munaron (including setting fastest time on the 1953 and 1954 Sassi-Superga events) before being superseded.

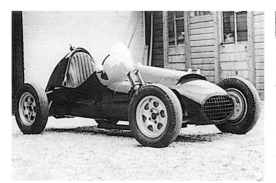

1952 Aston-Butterworth Formula 2 Single-Seater,
exhaust valve system redesigned to use conventional
Cosworth poppets closed by double coil springs and
collets, 4 racing Amal carburettors, tuned for petrol
instead of methanol, original MG gearbox, ENV drop-
gear final drive, Alfa Romeo Guilietta front drum brakes,
original Cooper rear brakes.
£29,000–34,000 BKS

This Grand Prix car combines a Cooper Mk I chassis
with the ground-breaking, air-cooled, swing-valve
Butterworth flat-four racing engine. The engine offered
around 140bhp and fitted neatly in the front of Bill
Aston's F2 prototype. It drove via an MG TC gearbox
to an ENV final-drive, which offered quick-change
drop gears to allow speedy regearing. Butterworth
continued to develop the engine through the mid-
1950s, ultimately with daring all-swing-valve induction.

1967 McLaren M4A Formula 2 Single-Seater,
1600cc, 4-cylinder engine, completely restored 1996,
race-ready condition.
£38,000–46,000 COYS

The first production single-seater manufactured
by McLaren was the M4A of 1967. It featured an
aluminium monocoque with coil-spring-and-
wishbone suspension located by radius arms. It was
powered by the 1600cc Ford Cosworth FVA engine
and was fitted with a Hewland FT200 gearbox.

1968 Merlyn Mk10 Formula 3 Single-Seater, 997cc,
Ford-Cosworth MAE engine, spaceframe chassis,
outboard suspension, race-ready condition.
£15,000–16,500 BKS

▶ **1969 Hawke DL2 Formula Ford,** 1600cc engine,
race-ready condition.
£9,000–11,000 Car

1953 Cooper Mk VII Single-Seater, 500cc, air-cooled
Norton Manx engine, spaceframe chassis, restored,
very original.
£11,500–12,750 Car

1959 Cooper-Climax T51 Monoposto Single-Seater,
2.7 litre, double-overhead-camshaft, rear-mounted,
4-cylinder inline engine, twin Weber carburettors,
250bhp, 4-speed manual gearbox, transverse-leaf-spring
and double-wishbone suspension front and rear, 4-wheel
disc brakes, tubular spaceframe chassis, finished in dark
green with white stripes.
£73,000–80,000 C

In the short space of ten years, the company founded
by Charles Cooper and his son, John, revolutionised
the world of motor racing, and by the end of the 1958
season had produced a machine capable of beating
the might of the European Grands Prix teams. The 2.5
litre engine they chose began life as an auxiliary fire-
pump motor. This car is thought to be one of four
1959 works cars, and subsequently it went on to race
in the Australian Tasman series with larger engine.

1968 Tecno-Cosworth Formula 2 Single-Seater,
1600cc 'cascade' gear Cosworth FVA engine, finished in
red, excellent condition.
£16,000–19,000 BKS

1971 Elden Mk 8 Formula Ford Single-Seater, 1600cc, ex-Tony Brise works car 1971, historic race winner 1995, race-ready condition.
£14,000–16,000 Car

This is the car in which Tony Brise began his racing career, winning 23 races with it in 1971. Subsequently, he went on to race in F1, but was killed in Graham Hill's aircraft accident in 1975.

▶ **1978 Dulon MP21 Formula Ford 1600 Single-Seater,** Scholar engine rebuilt 1995, finished in red, lots of spares including an extra chassis, excellent condition.
£3,750–4,500 H&H

1980 March 802 Formula 2 Rolling Chassis, Hewland FT200 5-speed transaxle, no engine, skirts in need of replacing, otherwise very original, ex-Mike Thackwell works car.
£7,750–8,750 BKS

1980 Fittipaldi F8 Formula 1 Single-Seater, assembled from spares for exhibition use, no engine, empty Hewland FGB gearbox casing, Skol livery, autographed by Keke Rosberg.
£8,000–10,000 BKS

1983 Osella FA 1D Formula 1 Single-Seater, Cosworth engine rebuilt 1992, aluminium monocoque with carbon-fibre reinforcement, rocker-arm suspension all-round, excellent condition throughout.
£35,000–40,000 BKS

1985 March 85B Formula 3000 Rolling Chassis, no engine or gearbox, Camel livery.
£4,000–4,800 BKS

Although a March 85B F3000 model beneath the skin, this car has been converted cosmetically to resemble the Lotus 99T-Honda with which Ayrton Senna won the opening two rounds of the 1987 season, and which carried him to third place in the World Championship.

1985/86 Lola-Haas Formula 1 Single-Seater, Hart 415T 4-cylinder turbocharged engine, kevlar composite monocoque, pushrod double-wishbone suspension all-round, excellent condition, ex-Alan Jones.
£25,000–30,000 COYS

By 1985, Lola had become a prolific and very successful producer of racing cars for lower formulae, sports racing and American Indycar racing. It was this link that brought the name back to Grand Prix racing. Carl Haas, as well as being Lola's long-time American importer, ran an Indycar team in partnership with actor Paul Newman. When Haas decided to try F1, he had the car dawn up by Lola designers and manufactured by the FORCE concern. This car, the first chassis, made its debut at the Italian Grand Prix in Monza, where it was driven by former World Champion Alan Jones.

1986 Benetton B186 Formula 1 Single-Seater, 1499cc, 4-cylinder, turbocharged BMW M12/13 engine, 6-speed gearbox, carbon-fibre monocoque, suspension by double wishbones with inboard pullrods at the front and pushrods at the rear, ex-Gerhard Berger/Teo Fabi.
£40,000–45,000 COYS

In 1985, the Toleman Grand Prix team was taken over by the Italian Benetton family. The first Benetton F1 car was the B186, and although outwardly similar in appearance to that of the Toleman TG 185, it was a very different car. The well-financed team had a successful first season with drivers Teo Fabi and Gerhard Berger scoring points in a number of races, Berger finally winning Benetton's first Grand Prix in Mexico City. This car was the original development car and used as the spare at the first race of the year; later, it was driven in six Grands Prix.

Auction prices

Miller's only includes cars declared sold. Our guide prices take into account the buyer's premium, VAT on the premium, and the extent of any published catalogue information relating to condition and provenance. To identify cars sold at auction, cross-refer the source codes at the ends of photo captions with the Key to Illustrations on page 330.

▶ **1996 Jordan 196 Formula 1 Single-Seater Show Car,** fitted with engine frame, gearbox casing, titanium driveshafts, carbon-fibre wishbones and suspension arms, OZ Racing wheels with Goodyear Eagle slick tyres, Benson & Hedges livery, ex-Rubens Barrichello.
£20,000–23,000 S

1950 Jaguar XK120 Lightweight Roadster, 3400cc, aluminium bodywork, original left-hand drive, completely restored at a cost of over £20,000, Salisbury axle, disc brakes, new chrome wire wheels, finished in silver, red leather interior, ex-Dave Gilmour of Pink Floyd.
£49,000–54,000 H&H

1954 Jaguar XK120 Competition Roadster, left-hand drive, Rocket alloy wheels, aero screens, roll bar, finished in green, tan leather interior.
£15,800–17,500 BKS

1955 Frazer Nash Sebring, 2 litre, Bristol BS1 6-cylinder engine, double-wishbone-and-coil-spring independent front suspension, de Dion rear axle.
£140,000–154,000 BKS

This Frazer Nash competed on three occasions in the classic 24-hour *Grand Prix d'Endurance* on France's Sarthe circuit, in 1955, 1956 and 1957. It was built originally for enthusiastic owner-driver and test pilot Dickie Stoop. In 1955, he and co-driver Marcel Becquart finished in tenth place at 146.090km/h, the highest average speed ever recorded by a Frazer Nash at Le Mans; in doing so, they covered 3,506.160km.

1956 Aston Martin DB3S, 3 litres, recently restored, original engine and upholstery, excellent condition.
£400,000+ BKS

One of the most evocative and best-regarded of all 1950s motor racing movies is the British-made drama *Checkpoint*, based on the Mille Miglia Italian road race and the fortunes of a beleaguered team campaigning this very car. The movie starred such stalwart British actors as Anthony Steel – the square-jawed and handsome hero – Stanley Baker – the darkly sinister villain – and James Robertson Justice, who was a genuine pre-war racer and associate of the Whitney Straight racing team, as the company owner.

◄ **1957 Ferrari 250 GT Series I Cabriolet/'Café Racer',** coachwork by Pininfarina, cut-down plastic windscreen, competition-style bonnet fasteners, completely restored 1984.
£330,000+ BKS

This car was ordered new by Dominican playboy diplomat Porfirio Rubirosa. As soon as he saw the Pininfarina *Spyder Competizione* prototype body, he decided that he had to have something similar and commissioned a unique 'café racer' body. 'Café racer' is an unkind term in the circumstances, as the car could have won races, and 'Rubi' had competed at the highest level in sports cars. It was the 12th of only 42 Series I 250 GT Cabriolets to be built.

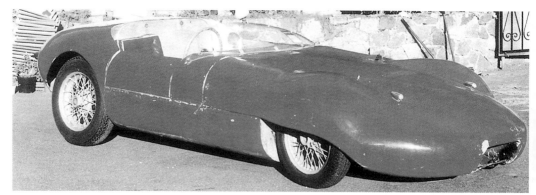

1959 Kieft Climax, 1098cc, Coventry Climax FWA engine, MGA gearbox, Triumph-derived front suspension, de Dion coil-sprung rear axle, inboard disc brakes, spaceframe chassis, little use since 1964, fair condition.
£14,000–16,000 COYS

This car was the last sports-racer to be built by Kieft.

► **1963 Marina Sports-Racer,** built by Mann brothers, 6700cc Rolls-Royce engine, Cooper F1 suspension, road-registered.
£65,000–75,000 Car

1993 Aston Martin DBR2 Replica Sports-Racing Two-Seater, 4 litre, double-overhead-camshaft, 6-cylinder Aston Martin engine, original DBR2 cylinder head, triple Weber carburettors, 5-speed ZF manual gearbox, knock-off wire wheels, finished in metallic grey, well maintained, excellent condition.
£122,000–134,500 BKS

1970 McLaren-Chevrolet M8D Group 7 Can-Am Two-Seater, 6.3 litre V8 engine, 640bhp, race-ready condition.
£165,000–182,000 BKS

This car was driven by Dan Gurney to take the pole and win at the first Can-Am round of 1970, at Mosport Park in Canada. Gurney recalled how '…that McLaren really did have an extra dimension in roadholding and handling which gave it a real advantage through twisty road sections where the driver could really go to work in real confidence.'

1971 Lola T290, 285bhp Hart BDG engine, Hewland FT 200 gearbox, both recently rebuilt, FIA papers, race-ready condition.
£47,000–53,000 COYS

1971 Chevron B19 Sports-Racing Prototype, FVC engine, FT200 gearbox, restored 1998, spare set of wheels, finished in green and yellow, race-ready, excellent condition throughout.
£58,000–69,000 COYS

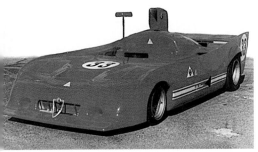

1974 Alfa Romeo Tipo 33TT12 Sports-Racing Prototype, coachwork by Autodelta, 483bhp engine, restoration completed 1994, correct Autodelta parts used throughout, mechanics overhauled, rewired, new fibreglass bodywork.
£110,000–125,000 BKS

In 1964, Alfa Romeo established Autodelta under the direction of Carlo Chiti. At first, Autodelta ran modified production cars and specials, which were based on production components. Then, for 1967, Alfa Romeo and Autodelta jointly produced a bespoke sports-racer, the *Tipo* 33. The car began with a 2 litre V8 in a tubular chassis, but this car has a 3 litre flat-12. In sports car racing, Alfa Romeo began 1974 at Monza, where Mario Andretti, partnered by Arturo Merzario, led an Alfa Romeo 1–2–3. The following season, Alfa's effort was masterminded by Willi Kausen's team; the *Tipo* 33TT12 took wins at Dijon, Monza, Spa, Watkins Glen, the Osterreichring, the Nürburgring and the Targa Florio. Finally sorted in its 12-cylinder incarnation, the '33' won the World Championship, crowning its nine-year racing career. This car was run and crashed in the 1974 Targa Florio.

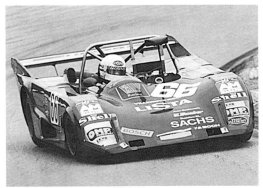

1978 Lola T297 Sports-Racer, 4-cylinder, 16-valve, BMW M12/6 engine, 300bhp, monocoque construction, stored for a number of years, restored 1997.
£38,000–44,000 COYS

A known continuous history can add value to and enhance the enjoyment of a car.

1978 Lola T492 Sports 2000, 2000cc, good condition throughout, race-ready.
£14,000–16,000 Car

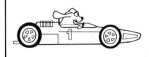

1962 Marcos 'Luton' Gullwing, 1300cc, fibreglass bodywork, gullwing doors, always used for racing, good condition, race-ready.
£12,000–14,000 Car

1963 Marcos Gullwing, 1150cc, fibreglass bodywork, gullwing doors, winner of 1963 Autosport Championship driven by Steve Minoprio.
£14,000–16,000 Car

1964 Alpine M64, 1149cc, mid-mounted, 4-cylinder engine, 115bhp, 5-speed gearbox, all-independent suspension, 5-wheel disc brakes, magnesium wheels, fibreglass bodywork, 1 of 3 built, ex-Le Mans.
£70,000–77,000 Pou

◄ **1965 Ferrari 250 LM Berlinetta,** coachwork by Scaglietti, 3285cc, overhead-camshaft V12 engine, 6 Weber 38DCN carburettors, 320bhp, 5-speed manual gearbox, 4-wheel disc brakes, all-independent double-wishbone suspension, centre-lock wire wheels, tubular-steel frame, finished in red, excellent condition.
£1,400,000 + RM

1966 Jaguar E-Type Competition Coupé, 3.8 litres, triple Weber 45DCOE carburettors, restored, little use since, engine, gearbox, brakes and suspension rebuilt, rewired, new windscreen, bare-metal respray in British Racing green, new instruments, Recaro seats.
£25,000–28,000 BKS

◀ **1968 TVR Tuscan,** 302cu.in, Ford V8 engine, 4-bolt main bearings, 4 twin-choke downdraught Weber carburettors, 400bhp, all-independent suspension, multi-tubular chassis, heavily modified for competition use, fibreglass bodywork, finished in blue and white, stored 1984–98, refurbished, race-ready.
£7,500–9,000 COYS

1970 Ferrari 512 S Sports Prototype Competition Spyder, 5 litre, double-overhead-camshaft V12 engine, fuel injection, roof converted to open-cockpit Spyder form, restored 1989, engine rebuilt, new brake discs, finished in red and white, quantity of spares, race-ready.
£750,000+ BKS

◀ **1972 Ferrari 246 GT/C Dino,** chassis number 3558, competition camshafts, 195bhp, aluminium bodywork, red, white and blue NART livery.
£40,000–45,000 COYS

A very small number of Dinos were factory-built as competition cars, being given lightweight aluminium coachwork. The most notable entrant of racing Dinos was Luigi Chinetti's North American Racing Team (NART), which entered one in the Le Mans 24-hour race.

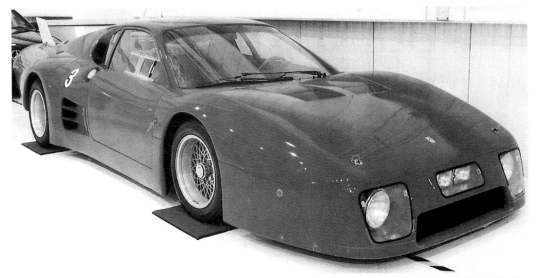

1977/78 Ferrari 512 BB Le Mans Competition Coupé, 4942cc engine, dry-sump lubrication, converted to Series 3 LM form 1980s, using all correct parts, finished in Rosso Corsa, black interior, raced in the USA 1984–93, very good condition throughout.
£80,000–90,000 BKS

Although conceived as a road car, the Berlinetta Boxer demonstrated its competition potential when a race-prepared 512 BB LM finished first in the IMSA category at the 1981 Le Mans 24-hour race. The Le Mans bodywork was in aluminium and fibreglass with sliding Plexiglas windows, and the chassis was equipped with uprated suspension, brakes and wheels. The LM engine incorporated forged racing pistons, special camshafts, lightened and balanced conrods, special valves, twin oil coolers and a racing exhaust system. With power in excess of 500bhp and a weight of around 1,200kg (1,100kg for Series 3 cars), the 512 BB LM boasted a formidable power-to-weight ratio, making for stupendous acceleration and a 320km/h top speed.

◄ **1981 Porsche Carrera 924GTR,** 1997cc, overhead-camshaft, turbocharged 4-cylinder engine, 400bhp, 5-speed manual gearbox, 4-wheel disc brakes, all-independent suspension, museum displayed from new, original condition.
£40,000–45,000 RM

Only 17 Porsche 924GTRs were built, and most were entered in classic endurance races. Many of the cars available today are either seriously battle-worn or have been completely rebuilt, losing much of their originality. Thus this particular car is quite unusual.

1989 Aston Martin AMR-1 Group C Sports Prototype, 6 litre Callaway V8 engine, unused for some years, completely restored, ex-works/Brian Redman/David Leslie, race-ready condition. 1 of 5 works AMR-1 Group C Coupés built for the 1989 World Endurance Championship racing season.
£133,500–147,000 BKS

Behind the wheel of this very car – in the 115-lap Brands Hatch Trophy World Championship-qualifying race on 23 July, 1989 – the great Brian Redman and Scots star David Leslie stormed home into fourth place overall, beaten only by two of the season's dominant Sauber-Mercedes C9s and the formidable Joest team's Porsche 962C – handled by drivers of the calibre of Jochen Mass, Jean-Louis Schlesser, Bob Wollek and Mauro Baldi. This Brands Hatch result was not only the best of the Protech Aston Martin works team's career, but it also bore terrific testimony to the enormous ground-effects power that the team had harnessed in this much-developed AMR-1 design, which proved to be so well suited to the testing Kent circuit. This particular car was the most successful of the five AMR-1s built.

1991 Ferrari F40 LM Competition Berlinetta, coachwork by Pininfarina, 1 of only 3 equipped with all aerodynamic modifications, front wheel tunnels and grilles, reprofiled biplane rear stabiliser, anti-dive front and anti-squat rear suspension geometry, adjustable anti-roll bars front and rear, Lockheed racing disc brakes, magnesium wheels, digital instrumentation, real-time data acquisition system, used for only 50 hours, 1 owner.
£225,000+ BKS

Introduced in 1988 to celebrate 40 years of Ferrari production, the F40 was the ultimate supercar. A mid-engined, two-seater coupé, it was developed from the limited-production 288 GTO. The quad-cam, 3 litre V8, with four valves per cylinder, employed twin IHI turbochargers to liberate 478bhp at 7,000rpm. The one-piece plastic body was bonded to the tubular-steel chassis to create a lightweight, very rigid structure . The doors, bonnet, boot lid, and other removable panels were of carbon-fibre. The LM, also known as the *Evoluzione*, differed from the road car by having, among other things, a reinforced chassis, a deeper front air dam and larger, cockpit-adjustable rear wing, racing interior, stiffer suspension, uprated brakes, competition gearbox, wider wheels and a specially prepared engine that produced 700–780bhp. Only 17 F40 LMs were built by the factory.

1993 Jaguar XJ220S, 3498cc, 24-valve V6 engine, 680bhp, 5-speed close-ratio manual gearbox, all-independent suspension, 4-wheel disc brakes, carbon-fibre body, lightweight competition alloy wheels, 1 of 6 XJ220S models produced.
£180,000–200,000 RM

1965 Alfa Romeo GTA 1600 Group 4, coachwork by Bertone, full-race engine, racing exhaust system, oil cooler, 5-speed close-ratio gearbox, limited-slip differential, adjustable rear suspension, BWA alloy wheels, competition fuel and oil tanks, Plexiglas side windows, finished in red, full-race interior, roll cage, Tipo 33-style racing seat, original. **£24,000–27,000 BKS**

Campaigned by official works driver Romano Martini, this car's impressive contemporary race record includes nine first-in-class wins. It was a works entry in the 1969 Nürburgring six-hour race, driven by Andrea de Adamich.

◄ **1971 Fiat 500L,** 667cc engine, twin-choke Dell'Orto carburettors, 37bhp, 5-speed gearbox, Koni adjustable suspension, track widened, 4-wheel ventilated disc brakes, chassis reinforced, 170km/h top speed, electric windows, seatbelts, rev-counter, oil temperature and pressure gauges, compass, altimeter, MoMo steering wheel, OMP seats, central locking, television, mobile phone, mini-bar, restored 1995, excellent condition throughout. **£8,000–9,000 BKS**

This much-modified Fiat 500 won the 1600km 1997 Rome–Paris Non-Stop Race in a time of 16 hours.

1985 Citroën BX 4TC Group B, turbocharged, 4-wheel drive, pneumatic suspension with ride-height control, finished in white with red and blue stripes, black and grey cloth upholstery, 2,128km recorded, excellent condition throughout. **£13,000–16,000 BKS**

Military Vehicles

1939 Humber Snipe Staff Car, 4.8 litre, 6-cylinder engine, 'balloon' tyres, roof rack, restored, good condition.
£4,500–5,300 MVT

1940 Bedford Truck, 5600cc, 6-cylinder engine, 4-speed manual gearbox, completely restored, 300 miles covered since, finished in beige and brown, grey interior.
£2,250–2,750 H&H

c1940 Humber FWD 4x4 Heavy Utility, 4 litres, 85bhp, metal-skinned wooden-framed bodywork, restored, RAF markings.
£7,500–9,000 MVT

▶ **c1941 Bedford MW Fire Engine,** 3519cc, 6-cylinder engine, 71bhp, 4-speed manual gearbox, ladder, rotating beacon.
£3,000–3,750 MVT

c1940 Churchill Heavy Tank, 12-cylinder sidevalve engine, 350bhp, 40 ton all-up weight, unrestored, not running.
£8,000–10,000 MVT

c1940 Humber FWD 8cwt, 4086cc, 6 cylinder engine, 4-wheel drive, restored, RAF markings.
£4,000–5,000 MVT

The removable rear canvas cover of this truck can also be used as a tent, the frame having folding legs.

1942 Austin D-series Truck, 4 litre, 6-cylinder engine, 4-wheel drive.
£3,000–3,500 **BAm**

c1942 Humber Mk II Light Reconnaissance Car,
4086cc, 6-cylinder engine, 87bhp, 4-speed manual
gearbox, 2-speed transfer box, 4-wheel drive.
£7,000–8,250 **MVT**

**The Mk II Humber Light Reconnaissance Car was
used by both the Royal Air Force and the British
Army from 1941 onward.**

1942 Northwestern Aircraft Tractor, Dodge engine,
torque converter, restored, finished in yellow with US Air
Force markings, very good condition.
£1,000–1,200 **MVT**

◀ **c1942 Bedford
QL Refueller,**
3519cc petrol
engine, 72bhp,
4-speed manual
gearbox, 2-speed
transfer box,
4-wheel drive, in
need of restoration.
£2,000–2,400 **MVT**

1942 Ford GPW Jeep, completely
restored, good condition.
£4,000–4,500 HMM

1943 Willys MB Jeep, in need of restoration.
£1,800–2,150 MVT

> **Cross Reference**
> See Colour Review

1943 Willys MB Jeep, 2.2 litre petrol
engine, completely restored, fitted
with all period accessories.
£5,000–5,500 MVT

c1943 Bantam ½ Ton Jeep Trailer, restored, canvas cover, good condition.
£480–580 MVT

► **1943 Karrier K6 3 Ton Truck,**
4086cc, 6-cylinder engine, 80bhp,
4-speed manual gearbox, 2-speed
transfer box, 4-wheel drive, winch.
£4,000–5,000 MVT

c1943 Diamond T 12 Ton Prime Mover, Trailer and Buick Hellcat Tank, truck with 6-cylinder engine, 185bhp,
Rogers drawbar trailer, Tank with 9-cylinder, air-cooled radial engine, 3-speed gearbox with 3-speed transfer box
driving front sprockets.

Prime Mover	£6,000–8,000
Trailer	£4,800–6,000
Tank	£16,000–20,000 **MVT**

c1943 Canadian Chevrolet C8A Heavy Utility (HUP), 6-cylinder engine, 85bhp, 4-speed manual gearbox, single-speed transfer box, 4-wheel drive, fitted with personnel carrier bodywork.
£5,600–7,000 MVT

c1944 Bedford QLT 3 Ton Troop Carrier, 3519cc, 6-cylinder engine, 72bhp, restored, very good condition.
£2,800–3,500 MVT

c1944 Austin K6A/ZH Breakdown Gantry 6x4, 3995cc, 6-cylinder engine, 82bhp, 4-speed manual gearbox driving rear wheels, restored, very good condition.
£3,500–4,000 MVT

1944 Dodge WC51, 230.2cu.in, 6-cylinder, sidevalve petrol engine, 4-speed manual gearbox, single-speed transfer box, front-axle disconnect, semi-elliptic leaf springs, restored, good condition.
3,600–4,200 IMPS

Restored values

The cost of a professional restoration will have an influence on, but no direct relation to, a car's market value. A restored car can have a market value lower than the cost of its restoration.

▶ **c1944 GMC 2½ Ton Truck,** 270cu.in, 6-cylinder engine, 6-wheel drive, from Swiss Army reserve, low mileage.
£2,250–2,750 WITH

1952 Fordson Thames 3 Ton E4 FV 13303 Truck, 3924cc, sidevalve V8 engine, 87bhp, 4-speed manual gearbox, 2-speed transfer box, 4-wheel drive.
£2,200–2,750 MVT

c1952 Bedford RLB FV 13100 Truck, 4927cc, overhead-valve 6-cylinder engine, 110bhp, 4-speed manual gearbox, 2-speed transfer box, restored, very good condition.
£1,600–2,000 MVT

c1955 International M62 Wrecker, 6-wheel drive, 20 ton rear winch, 10 ton front winch, hydraulic slewing crane, excellent condition.
£3,500–4,000 MVT

c1958 Tatra OT 810 Half-Track, 11.8 litre, air-cooled V8 diesel engine, 120bhp, 4-speed gearbox, 2-speed transfer box, leaf-spring suspension, bogies on torsion bars.
£6,500–8,000 MVT

This half-track was made by the Czech Tatra company and was based on the WWII German Sd.Kfz 251.

c1960 Ford/Kaiser Mutt, body by Fruehauf, 141.5cu.in, 4-cylinder engine, 71bhp, 4-speed gearbox, 2-speed transfer box, 2- or 4-wheel drive, coil-spring suspension.
Gun   £1,200–1,500
Jeep   £2,500–3,000 PC

▶ 1959 Reo M54 2½ ton Truck, 331cu.in, 6-cylinder engine, 5-speed manual gearbox, 2-speed transfer box, air/hydraulic brakes, restored.
£4,000–5,000 PC

c1960 Ferret Mk 2 Scout Car, 4258cc, Rolls-Royce B60 engine, 5-speed pre-selector gearbox, forward/reverse transfer box, manually-operated turret for medium machine-gun, recently released from Army storage, unissued.
£6,000–7,500 WITH

c1964 Volvo L3304 Reconnaissance Vehicle, B18A 4-cylinder engine, 68bhp, 4-speed manual gearbox, 2-speed transfer box, 4-wheel drive, limited-slip differential, semi-elliptic leaf springs, direct from Swedish Army reserve.
£3,200–4,000 WITH

Tractors

c1938 Fordson Standard, complete, in need of light restoration.
£600–700 PC

1947 Ferguson TEA 20, petrol model, self-starter, original extra implements guide, 1 owner, in need of respray.
£900–1,000 BKS

The 'grey Fergie' has been part of farming life around the world for over 50 years, and even today examples are to be found in use on many farms.

A known continuous history can add value to and enhance the enjoyment of a tractor.

◀ 1960 Fordson Super Dexta, original, good condition.
£700–800 PC

1958 Massey Ferguson 35, original, in need of light restoration.
£700–800 PC

1962 Fordson Super Major, original except seat, in need of minor restoration.
£900–1,000 PC

Horse-Drawn Vehicles

1850s **Farm Cart,** in need of restoration.
£800–950 **A&H**

19thC Shelbourne Landau, to fit 14.2hh upwards single or pair, pole, handbrake, full and three-quarter-elliptic springs, finished in burgundy with black and yellow coachlining, buttoned leather upholstery, black hood with window to front, excellent condition.
£3,500–4,000 **TSh**

c1880 Estate Van, full and semi-elliptic springs, iron-shod wheels, drop tailboard, canvas canopy over slatted wooden framework, handbrake, marked 'Earl of Strafford Wrotham Park Middlesex', in need of complete restoration.
£400–500 **TSh**

▶ **c1880 Hooded Phaeton or Chaise,** by Thaler of Austria, to fit 13.2–15.2hh single or pair, full and three-quarter-ellliptic springs, rotating patent dash allowing conversion of carriage type, finished in green with light green and black coachlining, buttoned dark green cloth upholstery.
£2,300–2,700 **TSh**

c1880 Opera Bus, by Hooper & Co of London, triple-hinged front leather canopy, expansive dash, deep front seat, carved dub ends, small floral motifs to turntable ends, luggage rails, original, in need of complete restoration.
£900–1,100 **TSh**

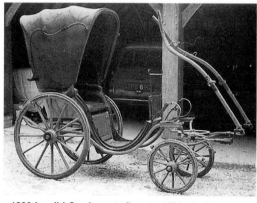

c1890 Invalid Carriage, to fit up to 13hh, double perch and C-springs, shafts, 3-position black leather folding hood, finished in green, black upholstery, good original condition.
£375–450 **TSh**

◀ **c1897 Stanhope-Style Phaeton,** by Windover of London, to fit 12.2–14hh single, pair or team, elliptic springs, handbrake, patent dash and splash boards, finely-carved dub ends, repainted in black and burgundy with yellow coachlining, buttoned navy cloth upholstery, show condition.
£3,300–4,000 TSh

Bullock Cart, by Bristol Wagon & Carriage Works, bolt-on shafts, iron-shod wheels, deeply cranked axle, drop tailboards at each end, original condition.
£500–600 TSh

Kühlne Show Phaeton, to fit 15.2–17hh pair or team, elliptic springs, foot and hand disc brakes, louvred side panels, finished in blue, black leather upholstery and dashboard.
£5,000–6,000 TSh

Drop-Front Phaeton, by Studebaker of USA, to fit 14–15hh, elliptic springs, carved dub ends, patent leather dash, new 2-position hood with small rear window, finished in dark blue with light blue undercarriage, grey melton upholstery, excellent condition.
£6,750–7,750 TSh

c1910 Spindle-Back Gig, to fit 12.2–13.2hh, dennett springs, 14-spoke Warner wheels, turned spindles to the seat, finished in dark blue with cream coachlining, black leather upholstery.
£1,300–1,600 TSh

◀ **American Hooded Sociable,** to fit 14.2–16hh, black folding hood and side curtains, finished in maroon with red coachlining, buttoned red velour upholstery.
£6,500–7,500 TSh

Automobile Art

Alan Fearnley, a 1930s wet evening scene in London's West End, oil on canvas, signed and dated '93', framed, 16 x 19in (40.5 x 45.5cm).
£2,400–2,800 BKS

R.J. Lawrie, a snow scene depicting a vintage Bentley being chased by the local hunt, watercolour, framed, 15 x 21in (38 x 53.5cm).
£750–850 BKS

After Meonier, 2 pictures depicting a couple meeting over a garden wall and subsequently being identified together, some cropping, glazed, 20 x 15in (51 x 38cm).
£1,000–1,200 BKS

François Chevalier, *A l'Attaque*, depicting Stuck driving the Auto Union at the Virage de la Gare during the 1936 Monaco Grand Prix, black ink with white and red on blue Canson paper, signed and dated, 19¾ x 25½in (50 x 65cm).
£140–165 BKS

After Roy Nockolds, The French Grand Prix of 1954, Fangio in the Mercedes-Benz W196, colour lithographic print finished by colourist Nicky Hales, 17 x 21in (43 x 53.5cm).
£110–130 BKS

◄ Michael Turner, Jack Brabham winning the 1960 Portuguese Grand Prix in a Cooper T53-Climax 4 and gaining his second World Championship in the process, mixed media, signed and dated '60', framed, 22 x 18in (56 x 45.5cm).
£2,000–2,250 BKS

After Roy Nockolds, Dick Seaman driving his Mercedes-Benz at the 1938 German Grand Prix, hand-coloured lithographic print, 23 x 32in (58.5 x 81.5cm).
£140–160 BKS

Ayrton Senna, full-colour limited-edition print, from an original by Benjamins, numbered 1/350, inscribed 'To Cathy' and signed by Senna.
£2,500–2,900 GPT

◀ Tony Upson, large mural depicting a 1957 Maserati 250F, acrylic on board, framed, 48 x 96in (122 x 244cm).
£1,750–2,000 BKS

▶ Dion Pears, Dan Gurney driving the Brabham BT7 ahead of John Surtees in the Ferrari 158 at the 1964 French Grand Prix, mixed media, signed, framed, 23 x 29in (58.5 x 73.5cm).
£680–780 BKS

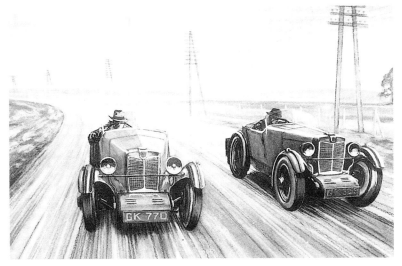

◀ Roy Nockolds, 2 MG M-Type Midgets speeding down a country road, watercolour, signed and dated, framed, 16 x 19in (40.5 x 48.5cm).
£1,400–1,600 BKS

Bryan de Grineau, The Motor Mannequin, depicting scenes from the 1932 Torquay Concours d'Elegance, probably published in *The Motor* magazine, pen and ink with whitening, signed and dated '32', 21 x 15in (53.5 x 38cm).
£500–600 BKS

Text at the base of this image includes 'no Concours d'Elegance is complete without its professional Motor Mannequins to show off the bodywork of the cars and bedazzle the eyes of the judges'.

 André Nevil, a stone-printed lithographic print, printed in reverse, mirror-image date and signature, original dated 1905.
£350–400 BKS

A preliminary sketch depicting a speeding racing car on a mountain road, French, pen, ink and wash on cartridge paper, signature indistinct, dated '05', 16 x 22in (40.5 x 56cm).
£250–300 BKS

Dion Pears, The Private Entrant, depicting the privately-owned Ferrari GTO driven by Grana and Bulcari being passed by Carlo Abate's winning Porsche in the 1963 Targa Florio, oil on canvas, manuscript-style signature, framed, 20 x 40in (51 x 101.5cm).
£650–750 BKS

Tony Smith, Juan Manuel Fangio driving his 1957 Maserati 250F, oil on board, signed, framed, 12¼ x 25¼in (31 x 64cm).
£600–700 S

Tony Upson, a large mural depicting an Alfa-Romeo racing car, acrylic on board, framed, 48 x 96in (122 x 244cm).
£1,000–1,200 BKS

Bob Murray, Stratos Encounters Elephants, depicting a Lancia Stratos meeting a herd of elephants during the 1977 Safari Rally, watercolour and gouache, signed, framed, 22 x 27½in (56 x 70cm).
£200–240 BKS

Posters

Jean Colin, a Marchal advertising poster, '*mieux voir – mieux marcher*', laid on linen, c1952, 61 x 44⅛in (155 x 13cm).
£330–370 S

A Tydol Triple X Gasoline advertising canvas banner, depicting a girl on ice skates, very good condition, c1930, 60 x 35in (152.5 x 89cm).
£175–200 BKS

◀ A Shell Circuit de Vitesse d'Agadir advertising poster, depicting Mike Sparken, a race-winner in a 3 litre Ferrari, signed by the driver, 22½ x 15in (57 x 38cm).
£115–130 BKS

Jacques Ramel, '*Grand Prix d'Europe Automobile Monaco 22 Mai 1955*' official chromolithographic advertising poster, 47¼ x 31½in (120 x 80cm).
£700–800 BKS

After Michael Turner, an advertising poster for the 25th Monaco Grand Prix in 1967, framed.
£180–210 BKS

A poster depicting Damon Hill, Jacques Villeneuve and Jean Alesi, issued to celebrate the drivers' respective 1st, 2nd and 3rd placings in the 1996 Argentinian Grand Prix, signed by Hill.
£450–550 BKS

Cross Reference
See Colour Review

After Michael Turner, an advertising poster for the Monaco Grand Prix 9–10 May 1970, mounted, framed and glazed.
£150–175 BKS

Automobilia

A silver-plated pewter card tray, relief-decorated with a Mercedes-style car in a country scene, 1903, 9in (23cm) wide.
£325–360 PC

A silver-plated brass matchbox cover, depicting a veteran car, 1906, 3in (7.5cm) wide.
£50–60 PC

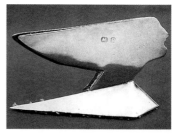

A silver menu holder, in the form of a bonnet mascot, hallmarked, 1930s, 2in (5cm) high.
£100–120 BCA

A Redex dispenser, 1950s, 16in (40.5cm) high.
£160–185 JUN

A Champion service stand for cleaning and testing spark plugs, 1940s, 41¾in (106cm) high.
£75–90 CRC

A Sinclair C5 single-seat three-wheeler, battery-powered electric motor, auxiliary pedal-and-chain drive, moulded plastic body, unused, c1985.
£450–540 AH

The Motor Car Card Game, comprising 40 cards, 1960s.
£10–12 BCA

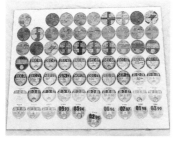

◀ A collection of road tax discs, 1930–99, 1931 missing, each 3in (7.5cm) diam.
£1–10 each PC

A Union Motoring Spirit metal petrol can, rusted, 1920, 13in (33cm) high.
£250–300 MSMP

A flask, modelled as a Bentley radiator shell, 1950, 8in (20.5cm) high.
£225–250 MSMP

◀ Three American fold-out road maps, 1940s.
£5–7 each RTT

▶ A Braimes force-feed oil can, 1950, 12in (30.5cm) long.
£6–7 **BLM**

A W.B. Dick & Co metal oil jug, 1920s, 9in (23cm) high.
£30–35 **LE**

▶ A cold-painted bronze model of a Ferrari Testarossa, on a marble base, 27in (68.5cm) wide.
£1,400–1,600 **BKS**

◀ Gordon Chism, Knight Errant, a bronze depicting Stirling Moss correcting a power slide in a Maserati 250F, on a wooden base, 1 of a limited edition of 50 sculptures, 21¾in (55.5cm) long.
£1,000–1,200 **BKS**

A Shell oil can, French, 1935, 11in (28cm) high.
£40–50 **EDO**

▶ An H. G. Allard & Co can of motor and tractor oil, 1930s.
£60–70 **JUN**

A Luvax shock absorber oil can, with spout, 1930–50, 9in (23cm) high.
£5–6 **BLM**

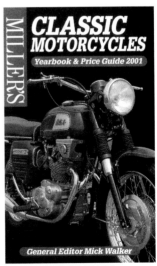

A Dartmouth Pottery model of an MGB GT, 1970s, 15in (38cm) long.
£25–30 PC

A double pack of Daimler advertising playing cards, 1920s.
£15–18 COB

A bronze showroom display figure of the Rolls-Royce Spirit of Ecstasy mascot, originally created by Charles Sykes, on a metal base, 23¾in (60.5cm) high.
£650–750 BKS

A bronze Farman Icarus inkwell, depicting a winged Icarus perched on a rock flanked by 2 birds, their wings covering two inkwells, on a green marble base, from the boardroom of Farman Automobile Company in Paris, signed 'Colin George', foundry stamp for Contenot-Lelievre.
£3,500–4,000 BKS

An Aster oil dispenser, French, 1950, 65in (165cm) high,
£1,800–2,000 EDO

A Royal Insurance Co Road Risks Illustrated Motor Prospectus, c1925.
£10–12 RTT

◀ A Pontiac brochure and handbook, 1960.
£35–40 pair COB

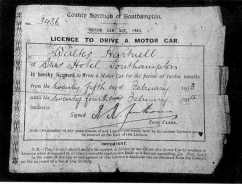

◀ A driving licence, issued by County Borough of Southampton, 1913.
£5–6 COB

▶ A Redex petrol additive tin, c1930.
£15–18 WAB

BADGES

A Steering Wheel Club enamelled car badge, late 1950s, 5in (12.5cm) high.
£225–250 LE

A Royal Automobile Club Associate badge, Royal Scottish Automobile Club centre, numbered 'A151', 1908, 3¼in (8.5cm) high.
£100–120 PC

A Veteran Motor Car Club of America enamelled car badge, on a turned wooden base, 1960s, 4in (10cm) high.
£40–45 DHA

An AC Automobiles Club enamelled badge, 1930s, 3¾in (9.5cm) high.
£90–100 GIRA

A Brooklands Automobile Racing Club member's label badge set, in original box, 1912, box 3in (7.5cm) wide.
£180–220 LE

► A Brooklands Automobile Racing Club enamelled badge, numbered '838', correct mounting stud and nut, excellent condition, c1930.
£700–850 BKS

A Circuit Routier Francorchamps enamelled badge, late 1950s, 3in (7.5cm) diam.
£180–200 DRJ

A Royal East African Automobile Association chrome badge, 1950s, 5in (12.5cm) high.
£30–40 JUN

A set of 7 Goodwood marshals' armbands, 1960s, each 8in (20.5cm) long.
£50–60 LE

A Junior Car Club enamelled badge, numbered 'J243', 1930s, 4½in (11.5cm) high.
£120–140 PC

An Order of the Road enamelled badge, with rare Instructor's motif, good condition, 4¼in (11cm) high.
£40–45 PC

A white metal and enamel Goodwood car badge, 1957–58, 4in (10cm) high.
£110–130 LE

A Commercial Motor Users Association brass radiator cap, 1920s, 6in (15cm) high.
£110–130 JUN

Princess Victoria Mary's (later Queen Mary) Royal Automobile Club life member's badge, the centre with an entwined 'VM' in silver on a royal blue ground, the obverse with the head of King Edward VII, finished in gold and surmounted by the King's crown, on an embossed over-cap, c1910.
£5,000–6,000 BKS

A Brooklands Automobile Racing Club committee member's enamelled badge, un-numbered, very rare, 1920–1930s.
£1,500–1,800 CARS

An enamelled Motor Racing Enterprises Association car badge, late 1950s, 4in (10cm) high.
£150–170 LE

A white metal and enamel Aintree car badge, 1958, 5in (12.5cm) high.
£110–130 LE

▶ A set of 3 enamelled lapel badges, British Racing & Sports Car Club, British Automobile Racing Club, NSCC, 1960s.
£30–35 each LE

COMPONENTS

A pair of handed nickel-plated acetylene gas lamps, by Herman Riemann of Germany, tubular carbide container cover, water control valve, removable heat ventilator and trumpet bezels, replated, small repair to one hinge, labelled 'Germania', good condition, c1905.
£350–400 BKS

A pair of handed Lucas Burbury oil side lamps, stepped oil reservoir covers, carrying bails, polished reflectors and patented spring clips, minor repairs, otherwise very good condition, c1906.
£450–500 BKS

A Stephan Grebel pillar-mounted spotlamp, Stephan Grebel etched glass and adjustable swivel mounting, restored, 1920–32.
£750–850 BKS

A Lucas PLG40 tribar top-hinged spotlamp, mounting bracket, original glass and cup washer, restored, 1928–29.
£900–1,100 BKS

A matched pair of Marchal pillar-mounted combination electric projector/side lamps, sunburst plano condenser lenses, restored, c1930, 12in (30.5cm) diam.
£1,500–1,800 BKS

A Mintex brake tester, 5½in (14cm) high.
£40–45 DRJ

▶ A pair of Lucas QK596 headlamps, restored, moulded U-formation speed lenses, correct stone-guards, original-pattern wiring, correct Lucas factory markings.
£2,400–2,800 BKS

▶ A Hattersley & Davids dry air pump, 20in (51cm) long.
£55–70 DRJ

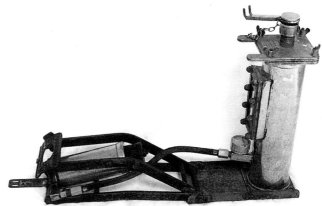

A Michelin Man portable air compressor, damaged, 1930s, 11in (28cm) long.
£170–200 JUN

A Walben Replacement Parts tin, for English, American and Continental vehicles, complete, original, 1930s, 12⅛in (30.5cm) long.
£20–24 SW

A Lamborghini Miura front body buck and framework, c1966.
£600–700 BKS

A Jones nickel-plated 60mph combination speedometer and odometer, 5-window mileage recorder, 3-window trip, dial in good condition, bowden cable missing, c1908, dial 5in (12.5cm) diam.
£280–330 BKS

A Jones nickel-plated 50mph combination speedometer and odometer, 5-window mileage recorder, 3-window trip, dial in good condition, bowden cable missing, c1912.
£150–170 BKS

A Jaeger chronometric rev-counter, late 1920s, 3¼in (8.5cm) diam.
£325–360 BCA

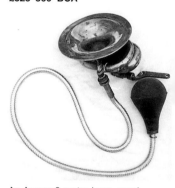

An Aurora 2 motor horn, good working order, c1900, trumpet 8in (20.5cm) diam.
£400–450 PC

A Panhard & Levassor 4hp, 2-cylinder Phenix engine, 80 x 120mm bore and stroke, missing 1 piston and conrod, otherwise internally complete, restored, mounted on display stand, 1897.
£1,000–1,200 BKS

A Ferrari Dino 246 V6 engine, complete with carburettors and exhaust manifolding, unused, rebuilt, mounted on a stainless steel display pedestal.
£6,000–7,000 BKS

▶ A Bosch dashboard dimmer switch, 1930s, 1½in (4cm) high.
£120–140 BCA

A Louis Blériot silver-plated acetylene gas lamp, complete with screw-off condenser bowl, carbide container, carrying bail, stabilising feet, polished reflector, very good condition, c1910, 8¾in (22cm) diam.
£500–600 BKS

A French Autovox brass double-turn, exhaust-assisted car horn, with expansion chamber, mounting bracket and label, extension and rubber bulb missing, c1908.
£60–66 BKS

A pair of Lucas rear lamps, model no. ST44/n, with original lenses, excellent original condition.
£1,500–1,650 BKS

An electric projector, having a rear-facing adjustable bulb, polished optically correct reflector, Stephan Grebel engraved front convex glass, original chromium-plating, mounted on a pillar with mechanical hand controls and sandwich bracket for mounting on a windscreen, c1930, 8in (20.5cm).
£2,500–2,750 BKS

A pair of Powell & Hanmer nickel-plated oil side lamps, carrying bails, patented rim clips, oil reservoirs, bevelled-edge front glasses, burners and circular P&H name plates, c1912.
£700–770 BKS

A pair of Salsbury & Son spun-brass acetylene gas projectors, stabilising feet, hinged bezels, bezel locking pin, uncracked Mangin rear reflectors, burners, patented glare-reducing 'Anti Dazlo' Type-B, stepped moulded-glass front lenses, excellent condition, c1909, lenses 7½in (19cm) diam.
£1,000–1,100 BKS

A pair of Badger Brass polished brass 'Solar' model no. 816 acetylene gas lamps, threaded carbide containers, patented water control tube, gas feed, saddle water reservoir, double-convex front glass, red diamond-cut rear warning jewel, good condition, c1903, 13in (33cm) high.
£525–580 BKS

◄ A pair of Merryweather & Sons brass-trimmed steel oil-burning Fire Engine side lamps, bevelled-edge front and side glasses, silvered reflectors, rear hinged doors, slide-out oil reservoirs, correct Raydyot porcelain burners, taper-slot mounting brackets, excellent condition, c1900, 14in (35.5cm) high.
£435–480 BKS

A British Windmill mascot, c1910,
6½in (16.5cm) high.
£225–250 ChA

A chrome emu mascot, 1950s,
4in (10cm) high.
£70–80 DHA

An Austrian Bergman satyr and goat
mascot, c1918, 9in (23cm) high.
£2,750–3,250 ChA

A silvered bronze Ballot trumpeter
mascot, La Renommée, by Emile
Peynot, original trumpet, excellent
original condition, 1922.
£1,200–1,400 BKS

A pathfinder mascot,
in the form of an
American Indian, 1925,
6in (15cm) high.
£275–305 DRJ

A nickel-bronze sitting Oriental
female mascot, by Hansi Siercke,
on original shop-display oak base,
signed, stamped, c1920.
£2,000–2,300 BKS

A chromed bronze Casimir Brau leaping horse
mascot, larger of 2 sizes produced, excellent
original condition, c1929.
£1,900–2,200 BKS

A French silvered bronze
mascot of a Ruffony nude
on a broomstick, on a
wooden base, inscribed,
signed, c1925.
£1,600–1,800 BKS

A French solid nickel trumpeter
mascot, La Renommée, by Virgil
Maury, signed, c1920.
£4,750–5,500 BKS

◄ A solid nickel Bouledogues à la
Chaine mascot, by Marvel, mounted
on original radiator cap, stamped
'G.E.' and numbered, good original
condition, 1922.
£3,500–4,000 BKS

A French nickel St George and the Dragon mascot, on turned wooden base, signed, c1920.
£1,100–1,300 BKS

A bronze fat policeman mascot, original painting to the body, impressed registration marks, 1930s.
£225–275 BKS

A German Archer with Bow mascot, signed L.F. Rozqliet, on an early radiator cap, dated 1910.
£1,000–1,200 BKS

A silvered bronze Puss in Boots mascot, by Antoine Bofill, MAM foundry stamping to the base, signed, non-original cane, c1910.
£4,000–5,000 BKS

A nickel-plated Isotta-Fraschini Spirit of Triomphe mascot, by Frederick Bazin, correct mounting bolt and nut, on a turned wooden base, c1920.
£1,750–2,000 BKS

A nude trumpeter mascot, by Podiebrad, signed, 1920s.
£1,000–1,200 BKS

A Hispano-Suiza flying stork mascot, by F. Bazin, on original base, inscribed, 1930s, 8in (20.5cm) long.
£575–675 BKS

A French elephant and barrel mascot, signed, on a wooden base, c1920.
£200–250 BKS

A chrome-plated Pixie and Lamp mascot, by Asprey of London, late 1920s.
£400–500 BKS

A French seated elephant mascot, by Hippolyte Auguste Moreau, signed, 1920s.
£200–250 BKS

A nickel French Art Deco pelican mascot, by Hippolyte-Francois Moreau, glass eyes, signed, 1920s, 7in (18cm) high.
£750–850 BKS

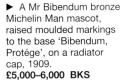

► A Mr Bibendum bronze Michelin Man mascot, raised moulded markings to the base 'Bibendum, Protége', on a radiator cap, 1909.
£5,000–6,000 BKS

◄ A nickel-plated Mickey Mouse mascot, on a black wooden base, numbered, mid-1930s, 6in (15cm) high.
£1,300–1,500 BKS

Mascots • AUTOMOBILIA

A French Latil elephant's head mascot, by F. Bazin, on wooden base, signed, 1920s.
£1,400–1,600 S

A set of 4 variations of the Vulcan Blacksmith mascot, 2 with integral caps, good original condition, 1902–28.
£250–300 BKS

A solid nickel Icarus mascot, by F. Gordon-Crosby, mounted on a wooden plinth, signed, late 1920s.
£500–600 BKS

A nickel-plated brass Bentley Flying 'B' mascot, on a later radiator cap, pre-1930s, 8in (20.5cm) wide.
£300–350 BKS

A gilt bronze Le Coq Victorieux mascot, by Edouard Guy, on heavy brass French radiator cap over a wooden base, signed, c1918.
£700–800 BKS

A display of 11 Rolls-Royce mascots of various periods, in a chromium-plated Rolls-Royce Phantom I radiator shell, mahogany-lined interior.
£2,500–3,000 BKS

A silver-plated Schneider Trophy seaplane mascot, 1929, 8in (20.5cm) long.
£250–300 COB

A bronze ape mascot, by Edouard Marcel Sandoz, on an oak display base, 1 of only 2 mascots created by the sculptor, signed, c1910.
£1,500–1,800 BKS

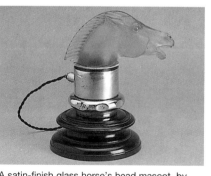

A satin-finish glass horse's head mascot, by René Lalique, correct Breves Galleries illuminated mount, moulded 'R Lalique' to base, excellent condition, c1930, 7in (18cm) high.
£4,300–4,800 BKS

◄ A glass cock's head mascot, by René Lalique, Breves Galleries illuminated mount, moulded 'Lalique France', c1929.
£550–650 BKS

An aluminium lighthouse mascot, with working light and original wiring, the reverse with a thermometer, signed 'P. Rossi', mounted on ebonised base, c1922, 8in (20.5cm) high.
£350–400 **BKS**

A dark grey glass Coq Nain mascot, with blood red centre, moulded 'R. Lalique France' to base, excellent original condition.
£2,500–3,000 **BKS**

A nickel-plated bronze Donald Duck car mascot, numbered beneath base, mounted on period radiator cap, c1932, 3¾in (9.5cm) high.
£750–825 **BKS**

A glass Chrysis-style mascot, in the form of a nude female, by Red Ashay, mounted on a metal and wooden display base, original condition, 1930s.
£1,400–1,650 **BKS**

A seated elephant mascot, French, mounted on a wooden base, c1922.
£200–240 **BKS**

▶ A bronze Squirrel mascot, by Maxime Le Verrier, c1920, 6½in (16.5cm) high.
£350–400 **BKS**

A bronze Rolls-Royce 40/50hp mascot, cushion-mounted on a small dais with 'Rolls-Royce Limited 6/9/11' and 'Charles Sykes', signs of original nickel plating, original threaded mounting stud, pre-1914, 7½in (19cm) high.
£1,850–2,250 **BKS**

▶ A chromium-plated kneeling lady Rolls-Royce mascot, mounted on new chromium-plated internal-thread radiator cap, 3½in (9cm) high.
£250–275 **BKS**

▶ A French silvered bronze Bronco mascot, in the form of a cowboy riding a horse, mounted on a jewelled nickel radiator cap, c1920.
£3,250–4,000 **BKS**

A nickel-plated bronze Mickey Mouse mascot, numbered beneath base, early 1930s, 3¾in (9.5cm) high.
£850–950 **BKS**

MODELS

A collection of 56 handbuilt 1/43-scale models representing every Monaco winner from 1929 until 1998, with display boxes, plinths and driver/car information plaques.
£5,000–6,000 BKS

A Mebetoys limited-edition scale model of an Alfa Romeo Tipo 159, on a wooden base with polished plaque, 1951.
£140–160 BKS

A limited-edition 1/8-scale model of an Aston Martin DBR Le Mans, correct green paint, numbered '14', in glazed case with wooden base, 1960s.
£500–600 BKS

A silver model of a Maserati 250F, by Theo Fennel, detailed engine, on a polished marble base, applied maker's seal, in presentation case, hallmarked London 1991, 10⅞in (27.5cm) long.
£2,500–3,000 S

A scratch-built 1/12-scale model of the 1990 Ferrari 641/2 driven by Alain Prost, numbered 5 of a limited edition of 10, rear light fitting, windscreen and Scuderia Ferrari badging, advertising logos, cast-alloy-style wheels, slick racing tyres correctly chalked, detailed instrument panel, authentic suede bucket seat with matching harness and head support, on a dark mahogany base, plaque with signature of Michele Conti, inscribed 'Ferrari 641/2 1990, 100 Vittorie, Alain Prost, Telaio 119, No. 05/10'.
£2,800–3,400 BKS

A silver model of an Alfa Romeo Monza, by Theo Fennel, detailed engine, on a polished marble display base, hallmarked London 1992, 9½in (24cm) wide.
£1,900–2,300 S

A Bellini model racing car model, in display case, 1960–70, 10in (25.5cm) long.
£2,500–3,000 S

Cross Reference
See Colour Review

A 1/43-scale model of the BMW M3 E30 raced by Alan Jones in 1993, Benson & Hedges livery.
£55–65 DRAK

A Minichamps model of Michael Schumacher's Ferrari F310B, in display case, signed by Schumacher, 1997, 9¾in (25cm) long.
£150–175 GPT

l. A tinplate Citroën car, finished in red , *faux* chromed radiator, windscreen, working steering and handbrake, clockwork motor in working order, André Citroën's signature to the underside, good condition, c1930.
£850–950 BKS
r. A Gunthermann saloon with roll-back roof, finished in yellow and ochre, maroon seats, working clockwork motor, automatic brake that applies when the car is lifted from the floor, chauffeur missing, boot and soft roof complete, c1930.
£1,000–1,100 BKS

A scratch-built 1/8-scale model of an Auto Union Type-D racing car, opening engine cover, engine, Roots supercharger, twin Solex carburettors and triple cam covers, chromed wire wheels, de Dion-type rear suspension, detailed fascia and interior, finished in silver, signed, on a mirrored base with glass case.
£4,350–4,800 BKS

A Domo of Italy remote-controlled model of a Maserati 8CTF, steel-bodied, forward and reverse gears, finished in red, in original wooden box with full operating instructions, late 1950s.
£5,000–5,500 BKS

A Wedico of Germany radio-controlled 'big rig' truck and trailer, aluminium bodywork, working steering, suspension, lights and horns, imitation engine sound, detachable trailer, full complement of batteries, radio control unit.
£975–1,075 BKS

l. A Tipp Co tinplate Mercedes-Benz open tourer, as used by the German dictator Adolf Hitler, clockwork motor, finished in black, *faux* chromed windscreen, radiator, running boards and wheel hub covers, working steering, complete with 4 original elastolin figures including one of Adolf Hitler with sprung arm, c1935.
£2,000–2,400 BKS
r. A Tipp Co tinplate troop carrier in army camouflage, clockwork motor, working steering, nickel-plated caterpillar tracks, 9 elastolin figures, c1937.
£1,150–1,275 BKS

A scratch-built model of a 1938 Alfa Romeo Mille Miglia, finished in red, resin panelling, solid chrome detailing, real leather seat, aluminium floorpan, spoked wheels.
£6,900–7,600 BKS

A Michele Conti 1/10-scale scratch-built model of a 1963 Iso Grifo, opening doors, bonnet and boot, handbuilt engine, cockpit interior clad in leather, wooden dashboard, gold-finished chrome wheels, on a mahogany base with signed brass plaque.
£5,750–6,350 BKS

PETROL PUMPS

An Avery Hardoll
hand-operated petrol
pump, 1920s.
£100–120 CRC

◀ A Gilbert &
Barker hand-
operated pot-
belly petrol pump,
complete with all
dials, sight glass,
hose and nozzle,
restored, Shell
livery, wired for
lighting, fitted with
reproduction
Sealed Shell
globe, early 1920s.
£900–1,000 BKS

▶ An Avery
Hardoll 2-stroke
pump, unrestored,
1958, 15¾in
(40cm) high.
£200–250 CRC

◀ A Power Shell Economy clock-
face petrol pump, 1960s,
86in (218.5cm) high.
£325–375 PC

An Avery Hardoll electric clock-face
pump, rewired, repainted plastic
globe, 1960, 72in (183cm) high.
£325–360 TPS

A Tockheim petrol pump, marked in
litres with barrel dials, repainted in
red and white Butler livery, 1970,
60in (152.5cm) high.
£200–250 TPS

GLOBES

A Shell Mex petrol pump globe, 1920s.
£450–500 MSMP

An Azur petrol pump globe, 1925, 20in (51cm) high.
175–200 EDO

A Carless Coalene Mixture petrol pump globe, 1930s, 17in (43cm) high.
£2,500–3,000 MSMP

A pair of Shell Motor Oil globes, 1930s, 8in (20.5cm) high.
£350–400 each MSMP

◀ A Power Petrol pump globe, 1930s, 19in (48.5cm) high.
£275–325 MSMP

▶ A Triple Shell (Heavy) petrol pump globe, 1930s, 8in (20.5cm) high.
£350–400 MSMP

A set of 3 oil pump globes, Duckham's N.O.L. E.P. 140 Transmission Oil, Gargoyle Mobiloil 'A' and Morrisol Engine Oil, 1930s, each 7½in (19cm) high.
£350–400 each MSMP

A Jet 100 petrol pump globe, 1950s, 18in (45.5cm) high.
£225–250 MSMP

A Power Diesel pump globe, 1950s, 19in (48.5cm) high.
£275–325 MSMP

▶ A Fina Green Paraffin glass pump globe, 1960s, 17in (43cm) high.
£140–160 MSMP

PICNIC SETS, VANITY CASES & TRAVEL GOODS

A Drew & Sons wooden table/games six-person picnic set, leather-lined interior, kettle and matching burner, leather-covered thermos flask, wicker-covered drinks bottle, 6 drinking glasses, 6 china cups and saucers, butter and preserves jars, spirit flask, condiment bottles, milk bottle, sandwich boxes, full complement of cutlery, 6 rectangular gilt-edge plates, pack of c1909 playing cards, lid opens to form a green baize table top.
£5,250–6,250 BKS

A G. W. Scott & Sons four-person picnic set, wicker hamper, copper kettle and burner, heavy ceramic-based sandwich box, twin drinks bottles, glasses, 4 enamel cups and saucers, 4 matching enamel plates, food boxes and spirit bottle, cutlery, vesta case, good original condition, c1920.
£2,200–2,500 BKS

A Drew & Sons two-person cocktail set, faux crocodile travelling case, 2 nickel-lidded sandwich boxes, leather-covered oval thermos flask, 2 cut-glass drinking vessels, drinks flask, milk bottle, 2 gilt-edged plates, cocktail mixing spoon, 2 knives, 2 forks, 2 spoons, original condition, 1923.
£1,400–1,700 BKS

A Coracle four-person picnic set, black suitcase-style hamper, ceramic-based sandwich box, leather-covered thermos flask, drinks bottles, glasses, plates and period cutlery, excellent original condition 1920s.
£1,000–1,200 BKS

A Harrods combination vanity set and overnight case, in honey leather, silver assayed bottles, complete with all fittings, original condition, 1930.
375–425 BKS

A Drew & Sons nickel cocktail set, comprising cocktail mixer flask, 4 stacking tumblers with gilt interiors, 3 spirit flasks, 4 plates, excellent original condition, c1909.
£250–300 BKS

A Brexton four-person picnic set, 1950s, 13 x 19in (33 x 48.5cm).
£75–90 PPH

A Brexton four-person picnic set, complete, original condition, late 1950s, 16in (40.5cm) wide.
£80–95 PPH

◄ A W. Leuchars two-person tea set, after Christopher Dresser, kettle and matching burner with stand, gilt-lined strainer and milk and sugar containers, 2 Royal Worcester cups and saucers, double doors with gilt teaspoons and sugar tongs.
£450–500 BKS

A Dupont man's vanity set, black hide case, 4 scent bottles, folding mirror, shoe horn, comb, leather boxes for valuables, large wallet box, stud box, complete, original condition, 1920s.
£850–950 BKS

A Davis & Co two-person tea set, leatherette-covered drop-front box, kettle and burner, milk jug, sugar bowl with gilt lining, clear glass milk bottle, spoons, tea box, porcelain cups and saucers, c1905, 11in (28cm) wide.
£600–750 BKS

An Alexander Clark vanity set, blue leather case, 8-day silver assayed travelling clock, brushes, silver-lidded glass vanity bottles, mirror, shoe horn, original tooth and clothes brushes, 1920s.
£1,400–1,650 BKS

An H. Greaves wicker four-person fold-front picnic set, original kettle and burner, sandwich box, vesta case, white china cups with gilt handles, matching saucers, lid doubles as a serving tray with nickel-plated liner, c1905.
£1,000–1,100 BKS

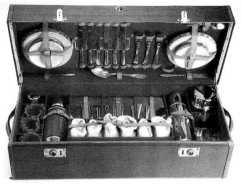

A German six-person picnic set, green case with leather edges, ice bucket, heavy nickel cutlery, 2 thermos flasks, 4 sandwich boxes, bone china cups and saucers, complete, original condition.
£2,500–2,750 BKS

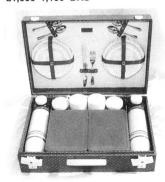

A Brexton four-person picnic set, 1950s, 19in (48.5cm) wide.
£80–90 PPH

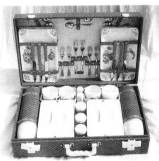

A Brexton six-person picnic set, complete including unusual ceramic trays, 1950s, 22in (56cm) wide.
£200–240 PPH

A Brexton four-person, blue-cased picnic set, complete, late 1960s, 16in (40.5cm) wide.
£80–90 PPH

A Coracle six-person picnic set, 3 tin sandwich boxes, cutlery, cups and saucers, rectangular plates, kettle and burner, glasses, condiment accessories, some items replaced or matched.
£1,800–2,000 BKS

◄ A Drew & Sons six-person fold-front wicker picnic set, oval kettle, burner and stand, stacking sandwich boxes, 6 enamel plates, large serving plate, gilt-rimmed fine china cups, matching saucers, full set of cutlery, heavy glass drinks bottles, 6 stacking drinking tots, c1910.
£1,500–1,750 BKS

ENAMEL SIGNS

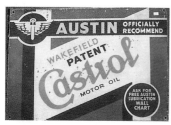

A Castrol printed tin sign, 1930s,
12 x 18in (30.5 x 45.5cm).
£130–145 MSMP

A pair of Gargoyle Mobiloil enamel
signs, 1930s, 19in (48.5cm) high.
£450–500 each MSMP

An AA single-sided Grantham sign,
1st series, poor condition, c1905,
24in (61cm) diam.
£175–200 MSMP

An AA hotel double-sided sign,
1950s, 31 x 22in (78.5 x 56cm).
£100–120 JUN

A South Eastern and Chatham Railway
Company cast-iron road bridge
weight-limit sign, missing 2 weight
plates, c1920, 50in (127cm) high.
£130–145 TPS

A Thelson Motor Oils single-sided
enamel sign, good condition, 1930s,
48in (122cm) wide.
£140–155 MSMP

A Zenith Carburetter Service
double-sided illuminated glass
sign, 2 bulbs, 1950s.
£250–275 MSMP

A Dunlop enamel sign, 1920s,
30 x 20in (76 x 51cm)
£400–500 JUN

A BP Motor Spirit double-sided enamel sign, c1920s,
24 x 16in (61 x 40.5cm).
£100–125 JUN

A Shell double-sided enamel sign, 1920,
24 x 18in (61 x 45.5cm).
£500–550 BRUM

A Shell Lubricating Oils double-sided pennant sign, 1920–30, 19 x 22in (48.5 x 56cm).
£650–720 MSMP

A Shell Motor Oil double-sided sign, 1920–30, 19in (48.5cm) high.
£350–400 MSMP

A Caltex double-sided enamel sign, 1950, 39in (99cm) diam.
£150–180 EDO

An *Autocar* magazine cloth advertising banner, slight damage and staining, c1920, 46½ x 220in, (118 x 560cm).
£325–360 S

▶ A Morris Commercial Sales & Service Depot illuminated box sign, 1930s, 30in (76cm) wide.
£450–550 MSMP

◀ A National Benzole Mixture enamel petrol pump sign, 1920s, 8 x 8in (20.5 x 20.5cm).
£60–70 JUN

An Esso lady advertising sign, 1960s, 73in (185.5cm) high.
£350–400 EDO

A Fordson Tractors single-sided enamel sign, good condition, c1930, 36in (91.5cm) high.
£175–195 MSMP

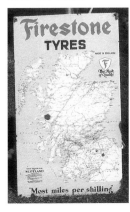

▶ A Firestone Tyres enamel road-map sign, 48 x 29in (122 x 73.5cm).
£240–270 JUN

WATCHES & CLOCKS

◀ A Ferrari limited-edition moulded plastic clock, numbered 9/50, issued by Ferrari Owners' Club.
£40–50 CARS

▶ A pair of watches, in the shape of steering wheels, 1 with BMW logo, the other with Ford Mustang logo, 1970s.
£130–150 each LE

BOOKS

Jack Brabham, *Jack Brabham's Motor Racing Book*, 1st edition, signed by Jack Brabham and John Cooper, 1960.
£45–50 GPCC

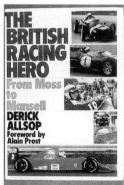

Derick Allsop, *The British Racing Hero From Moss to Mansell*, signed by Allsop and drivers Allison, Ashley, Attwood, Bell, Needell, Piper, Redman, Salvadori, Stewart and Thompson, 1st edition, 1990.
£70–80 GPCC

Alan Jones and Keith Botsford, *Alan Jones Driving Ambition*, signed by Alan Jones, 1981.
£60–70 GPCC

Bette Hill, *The Other Side of the Hill, Life with Graham*, signed by Bette Hill, 1978.
£40–45 GPCC

Michael Riedner, *Mercedes-Benz W196, Last of the Silver Arrows*, signed by Mercedes drivers Herrmann and Kling, 1990.
£70–80 GPCC

David Hodges, *A–Z of Formula Racing Cars,* 1991.
£40–50 GPCC

▶ Denis Jenkinson, *The Racing Driver, The Theory and Practice of Fast Driving,* 1969.
£20–25 GPCC

◀ Jack C. Fox, *The Illustrated History of The Indianapolis 500, 1911–1984,* 1984.
£60–75 GPCC

Paolo D'Alessio, *Obrigado Ayrton, Simply the Best*, signed by Ayrton's sister Viviane Senna, 1994.
£50–55 GPCC

Motor Racing Memorabilia

RACE SUITS & HELMETS

A Griffin helmet, worn by Graham Hill during the 1974 season, decorated in the colours of the London Rowing Club, dark blue with 8 white 'oar' flashes, visor, 1 button missing, leather chin strap.
£7,000–8,000 S

A pair of Bluebird land/water speed record overalls, worn by a member of the support team, with Union Jacks and BP sponsor's badge, 'BP Racing Services' on back, 1963–64.
£550–660 MUL

A Simpson helmet, worn by Keke Rosberg during the 1980 season, in blue and white, hole cut in chin guard for microphone, visor.
£2,300–2,700 S

A Sparco race suit, worn by Eddie Irvine while driving for Jordan in 1995, red with embroidered driver's name, Union Jack and shamrock on right hip pocket, sponsors' logos and patches.
£1,100–1,300 S

A Formula 1 race suit, worn by Ukyo Katayama while driving for Minardi at the European Grand Prix, Jerez, 1997, white, black and yellow with driver's name and Japanese flag on belt, signed on right breast.
£1,900–2,300 S

A helmet visor, signed by Johnny Herbert, 1994.
£135–165 GPT

A Stand 21 race suit, worn by Ayrton Senna during the 1989 season, red with Brazilian flag on belt, embroidered sponsors' patches, handwritten 'AS 6' to inside of neckline.
£5,000–6,000 S

▶ A Sparco race suit, worn by Giancarlo Fisichella while driving for Jordan during the 1997 season, yellow with name and Italian flag on right hip pocket, signed on pocket.
£1,000–1,200 S

A Stand 21 race suit, worn by Mark Blundell while driving for Ligier at the British Grand Prix, 1993, blue and white with name and Union Jack on belt, signed 'Best Wishes M Blundell', dated 'British Grand Prix 93'.
£900–1,100 S

A limited-edition replica Michael Schumacher Bell helmet, signed on visor, 1 of 100, 1995.
£2,500–2,750 GPT

A replica Mario Andretti Bell helmet, in silver and red, sponsors logos, 'Arrivederci Mario 1994' sticker, clear visor signed by Andretti.
£1,100–1,300 S

A Bell Racestar helmet, signed by World Champions and various other drivers, including Nigel Mansell, Ayrton Senna, Niki Lauda, James Hunt, Michael Schumacher, Mika Häkkinen and Damon Hill, visor bearing 'Legends in Time' sticker, some wear and smudging, helmet bag, 1992.
£3,000–3,500 S

A Bell helmet, worn by Riccardo Patrese during the 1987 season, in blue and white with sponsors' logos, radio leads, microphone and speakers, visor.
£2,500–3,000 S

A replica Alain Prost Arai crash helmet, by Mike Fairholme Designs, in red, white and blue, sponsors' logos, visor, blue Arai helmet bag, 1993.
£2,500–3,000 S

A Shoei helmet, worn by Jean Alesi while driving for Ferrari in 1992, in black, red, blue and white, sponsors' logos.
£5,000–6,000 BKS

A Team Tyrrell Elf belt, 1974–75.
£40–45 LE

▶ A Sparco race suit, worn by Ralf Schumacher during his first test drive for Jordan, yellow with driver's name and German flag on right hip pocket, signed on the pocket, late 1996.
£1,100–1,300 S

A pair of Ferrari race gloves, worn by Eddie Irvine, signed and framed, 1998.
£400–450 GPT

Cross Reference
See Colour Review

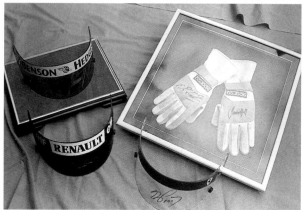

▶ A pair of Sparco driver's race gloves, signed by Damon Hill and Heinz-Harald Frentzen, framed, together with 3 helmet visors, signed by various drivers.
Gloves   £450–495
Visors   £350–750 each GPT

A Sparco race suit, worn by Rubens Barrichello while driving for Jordan during the 1994 season, red with name and Brazilian flag on left hip pocket, signed on left leg.
£900–1,000 **S**

A Sparco race suit, worn by Gerhard Berger during the 1997 season, light blue with driver's name and national flag on belt.
£1,100–1,250 **S**

A Nomex race suit, worn by Alain Prost while driving for McLaren during 1985, left breast and rear Marlboro patches missing.
£1,100–1,250 **BKS**

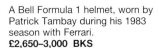

A Sparco race suit, worn by Ralf Schumacher during 1998, yellow with black cuffs and ankles, embroidered driver's name and German flag on right hip pocket, together with a Jordan certificate of authenticity signed by Trevor Foster.
£1,600–1,800 **S**

A helmet visor signed by Ralf Schumacher, in display case.
£325–375 **GPT**

A Bell Formula 1 helmet, worn by Patrick Tambay during his 1983 season with Ferrari.
£2,650–3,000 **BKS**

A replica 1998 Alexander Wurz Bieffe crash helmet, signed by the driver in silver pen to the crown, dark tinted visor, together with a signed translation of a letter from Wurz regarding the helmet, 3 photographs and a Bieffe helmet box.
£950–1,050 **S**

An Arai helmet, worn by Nigel Mansell during the 1991 season, dated 8.91 on inspector's sticker inside lining, 2 original sponsors' stickers removed, 2 Crookes Healthcare stickers, complete with visor and Arai helmet bag.
£3,000–3,500 **S**

▶ An Arai Formula 1 helmet, worn by Damon Hill during his 1993 season with Williams, full radio system, used at Hungarian and Italian Grands Prix.
£5,150–5,675 **BKS**

COMPONENTS

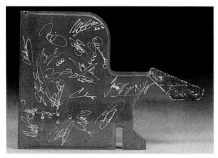

A Simtek S941 rear wing end-plate, painted metallic purple, signed by 19 drivers including Michael Schumacher, Jacques Villeneuve, Mika Häkkinen, Damon Hill, David Coulthard, Heinz-Harald Frentzen and Johnny Herbert, 1994.
£475–575 S

A limited-edition replica Honda McLaren steering wheel, as used by Ayrton Senna, 1 of 40 produced, framed.
£750–850 GPT

A 1994 Ferrari 041 V12 Formula 1 engine, 3.5 litres, double overhead camshafts per bank of 6 cylinders, 5 valves per cylinder, Magneti Marelli electrics, chromium-plated exhaust manifolds, c775bhp at 15,000rpm, mounted on display stand, used for the first 8 races of the 1994 season in the Ferrari 412T1 driven by Jean Alesi and Gerhard Berger.
£32,000–36,000 BKS

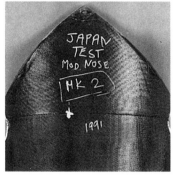

A nosecone top panel from Ayrton Senna's McLaren MP4/6, used during testing in Japan, moulded carbon-fibre, underside inscribed 'Japan Test Mod Nose Mk2 1991', top decorated with sponsors' logos and bearing the World Champion's number 1, slight damage, 56½in (144cm) long.
£5,500–6,500 S

PHOTOGRAPHS

A signed photograph of Ayrton Senna, helmeted and seated in a racing car, together with a letter dated 8th March 1994, to Hamlin, thanking him for his letter and forwarding the photo.
£325–375 VS

► A signed colour photograph of Jacques Villeneuve, taken at Melbourne in 1997, the first race of the season in which he became World Champion, 8 x 11½in (20.5 x 29cm).
£40–45 VS

◄ A signed colour photograph of Jacques Villeneuve and Heinz-Harald Frentzen, both in Williams Renault cars, at the European Grand Prix in Jerez, 1997, the year that Villeneuve became World Champion, 9½ x 7in (24 x 18cm).
£75–90 VS

Dealer prices

Miller's guide prices for dealer cars take into account the value of any guarantees or warranties that may be included in the purchase. Dealers must also observe additional statutory consumer regulations, which do not apply to private sellers. This is factored into our dealer guide prices. To identify dealer cars cross-refer the source codes at the ends of photo captions with the Key to Illustrations on page 330.

TROPHIES & RALLY PLAQUES

A silver-plated trophy presented to Tommy Wisdom for winning his class in an Aston Martin during the 1952 Mille Miglia, applied with enamel 'Club 1000 Miglia' badge, the base with plate engraved with the driver and '3–4 Maggio 1952 Classe 0 Litre 2000cmc', on circular display base, 9in (23cm) high.
£1,350–1,500 BKS

Miller's is a price GUIDE not a price LIST

A Moët & Chandon rostrum champagne bottle, signed by Giancarlo Fisichella and inscribed 'Canada '97'.
£325–400 GPT

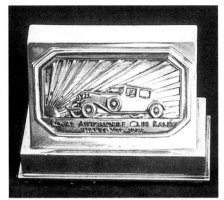

A silver Royal Automobile Club Rally, Hastings trophy, 1933.
£80–100 DRJ

A set of 5 Monte Carlo Rally finisher's awards, 1960s–1980s.
£230–260 each LE

The Southport Cup, a silver trophy presented to the winner of the concours d'elegance at the 1928 Southport Trials and Concours d'Elegance, mounted on a wooden base, together with a period photograph of the winning vehicle, marks for Connard and Son Ltd, Birmingham, 1928, 7in (18cm) high.
£365–405 BKS

A Brooklands enamelled car badge, awarded to R.E.L. Feathersonhaugh for achieving an average speed of over 120mph on the outer banking at Brooklands while driving the ex-Straight Duesenberg single-seater with Dick Seaman, very good original condition, marked 'Spencer London' to the rear, slight wear.
£3,450–3,800 BKS

◄ A trophy presented by the *President du Conseil Régional de la Sarthe* to the winner of the 1973 *24 Heures du Mans* endurance race, modelled as a vapour car manufactured by Amédée Bollée, on a marble base, brass presentation plate, 17¾in (45cm) long.
£375–405 BKS

A Holland Tulip Rally finisher's award, 1956, 3½in (9cm) diam.
£65–80 LE

The United States Grand Prix winner's chequered flag from Watkins Glen, signed by race winners from 1961 to 1980, including Innes Ireland, Jim Clark, Graham Hill, Jackie Stewart, Jochen Rindt, Emerson Fittipaldi, Francois Cevert, Ronnie Peterson, Carlos Reutemann, Niki Lauda, James Hunt, Gilles Villeneuve and Alan Jones, 19¼in (49cm) square.
£2,800–3,400 S

Key to Illustrations

Each illustration and descriptive caption is accompanied by a letter code. By referring to the following list of Auctioneers (denoted by *), dealers (•), Clubs, Museums and Trusts (§), the source of any item may be immediately determined. Inclusion in this edition no way constitutes or implies a contract or binding offer on the part of any of our contributors to supply or sell the goods illustrated, or similar articles, at the prices stated. Advertisers in this year's directory are denoted by †.

If you require a valuation, it is advisable to check whether the dealer or specialist will carry out this service and if there is a charge. Please mention Miller's when making an enquiry. A valuation by telephone is not possible. Most dealers are willing to help you with your enquiry; however, they are very busy people and consideration of the above points would be welcomed.

A&H	•	Architectural & Historical Salvage, Spa Street, Ossett, Wakefield, Yorkshire WF5 0HJ Tel: 01924 262831
AC	§	Association of American Car Clubs UK, PO Box 2222, Braintree, Essex CM7 9TW Tel/Fax: 01376 552478
AH	*	Andrew Hartley, Victoria Hall Salerooms, Little Lane, Ilkley, Yorkshire LS29 8EA Tel: 01943 816363
AHE	§	Association of Healey Owners, John Humphreys, 2 Kingsbury's Lane, Ringwood, Hampshire BH24 1EL
AS	•	Ashted Service Station of Kenilworth, The Willows, Meer End Road, Kenilworth, Warwicks CV8 1PU Tel: 01676 532289
ATF	•	A. T. Fletcher (Enthusiast & Collector).
BAm	§	British Ambulance Society, Paul M Tona, 5 Cormorant Drive, Hythe, Hampshire SO45 3GG Tel: 023 8084 1999
BARO/ WeR	*†	Barons, Brooklands House, 33 New Road, Hythe, Southampton, Hampshire SO45 6BN Tel: 023 8084 0081
BB(S)	*	Butterfield & Butterfield, 220 San Bruno Avenue, San Francisco CA 94103, USA Tel: 00 1 415 861 7500
BC	•†	Beaulieu Garage Ltd, Beaulieu, Brockenhurst, Hampshire SO42 7YE Tel: 01590 612999
BCA	•	Bealieu Cars Automobilia, Beaulieu Garage, Brockenhurst, Hampshire SO42 7YE Tel: 01590 612999
BERK	§	Berkeley Enthusiasts Club, Phil James, 55 Main Street, Sutton Bonington, Loughborough, Leicestershire LE12 5PE
BKS	*†	Robert Brooks (Auctioneers), 81 Westside, London SW4 9AY Tel: 020 7228 8000
BLE	•	Ivor Bleaney, PO Box 60, Salisbury, Wiltshire SP5 2DH Tel: 01794 390895
BLK	•	Blackhawk Collection, 1092 Eagles Nest Place, Danville, California 94506-5872, USA Tel: 00 1 925 736 3444
BLM	•	Bill Little Motorcycles, Oak Farm, Braydon, Swindon, Wiltshire SN5 0AG Tel: 01666 860577
BRIT	*	British Car Auctions Ltd, Classic & Historic Automobile Division, Auction Centre, Blackbushe Airport, Blackwater, Camberley, Surrey GU17 9LG Tel: 01252 878555
BRUM	•	Fred Brumby Tel: 01487 842999
C	*	Christie, Manson & Woods Ltd, The Jack Barclay Showroom, 2–4 Ponton Road, Nine Elms, London SW8 5BA Tel: 020 7389 2217
Car	•†	Chris Alford, Newland Cottage, Hassocks, East Sussex BN6 8NU Tel: 01273 845966
CARS	•†	C.A.R.S. (Classic Automobilia & Regalia Specialists), 4–4a Chapel Terrace Mews, Kemp Town, Brighton, East Sussex BN2 1HU Tel: 01273 60 1960
CC	•	Collectors Cars, Drakeshill, Birmingham Road, Kenilworth, Warwickshire CV8 1PT Tel: 01926 857705
CCa	§	The Classic Camper Club, PO Box 3, Amlwch, Anglesey LL68 9ZE Tel/Fax: 01407 832243
CGC	*†	Cheffins Grain & Comins, 2 Clifton Road, Cambridge CB2 4BW Tel: 01223 358731
ChA	•	Chapel Antiques, The Chapel, Chapel Place, Tunbridge Wells, Kent TN1 1YR Tel: 01892 619921
COB	•	Cobwebs, 78 Northam Road, Southampton, Hampshire SO14 0PB Tel: 023 8022 7458
COHN	•	Terry Cohn, Rotherwood Lodge, Jumps Road, Churt, Surrey GU10 2JZ Tel: 01252 795000
COR	•†	Claremont Corvette, Snodland, Kent ME6 5NA Tel: 01634 244444
COYS	*	Coys of Kensington, 2/4 Queens Gate Mews, London SW7 5QJ Tel: 020 7584 7444
CPUK	§	Club Peugeot UK, Peter Vaughan, 41 Hazelwood Drive, Bourne, Lincolnshire PE10 9SZ
CRC	§	Craven Collection of Classic Motorcycles, Brockfield Villa, Stockton-on-the-Forest, Yorkshire YO3 9UE Tel: 01904 488461/400493
DHA	•	Durham House Antiques Centre, Sheep Street, Stow-on-the-Wold, Glos GL54 1AA Tel: 01451 870404
DRAK	•	John Drake, 5 Fox Field, Everton, Lymington, Hampshire SO41 0LR Tel: 01590 645623
DRJ	•	The Motorhouse, D. S. & R. G. Johnson, Thorton Hall, Thorton, Bucks MK17 0HB Tel: 01280 812280
E	*	Ewbank, Burnt Common Auction Room, London Road, Send, Woking, Surrey GU23 7LN Tel: 01483 223101
EDO	•	Evariste Doublet, 30 Rue de la Gare, 19100 Lisieux, Normandie, France Tel: 00 33 0231317979
FCO	§	Ford Cortina 1600E Owners Club, Dave Marston, 23 Cumberland Road, Bilston, West Midlands WV14 6LT Tel: 01902 405055
FEO	§	Ford Executive Owners Register, George Young, 31 Brian Road, Chadwell Heath, Romford, Essex RM6 5DA
FHD	•†	F. H. Douglass, 1a South Ealing Road, Ealing, London W5 4OT Tel: 020 8567 0570
FORD	•	Affordable Classics, The Old Garage, 22 Ridgewell Road, Great Yeldham, Halstead, Essex CO9 4RG Tel: 01787 237887
FOS	•	Foskers, U5 Brands Hatch Circuit, Scratchers Lane, Fawkham, Kent DA3 8NG Tel: 01474 874777
GIRA	•	Girauto, Porte d'Orange, 84860 Caderousse, France Tel: 00 33 04 90 51 93 72
GPCC	•	Grand Prix Database, David Hayhoe, 43 New Barn Lane, Ridgewood, Uckfield, East Sussex TN22 5EL Tel: 01825 764918
GPT	•†	Grand Prix Top Gear, The Old Mill, Mill End, Standon, Hertfordshire SG11 1LR Tel: 01279 843999

H&H *† H & H Classic Auctions Ltd, Whitegate Farm, Hatton Lane, Hatton, Warrington, Cheshire WA4 4BZ Tel: 01925 730630

HAL • John & Simon Haley, 89 Northgate, Halifax, Yorkshire HX1 1XF Tel: 01422 822148

HMM §† Haynes Motor Museum, Sparkford, Yeovil, Somerset BA22 7LH Tel: 01963 440804

IMP § Imp Club, 27 Brookside Road, Stratford-on-Avon, Warwickshire CV37 9PH

IMPS § Invicta Military Vehicle Preservation Society, 58 Ladds Way, Swanley, Kent BR8 8HW Tel: 01322 408738

JUN •† Junktion, The Old Railway Station, New Bolingbroke, Boston, Lincolnshire PE22 7LB Tel: 01205 480068

KHP • Kent High Performance Cars, Unit 1–2, Target Business Centre, Bircholt Road, Parkwood Industrial Estate, Maidstone, Kent ME15 9YY Tel: 01622 663308

KI * Kruse International, PO Box 190, 5400 County Road 11A, Auburn, Indiana 46706, USA Tel: 00 1 219 925 5600

KING • King Classic Cars. Tel: 01273 508486

KOLN * Auction Team Koln, Postfach 50 11 19, 50971 Koln, Germany Tel: 00 49 0221 38 70 49

LE • Laurence Edscer, Flat B, Semple Mews, Semple House, Gardeners Lane, Romsey, Hants SO51 6AD Tel: 023 8081 4665

LEW * Lewes Auction Rooms (Julian Dawson), 56 High Street, Lewes, East Sussex BN7 1XE Tel: 01273 478221

LF * Lambert & Foster, 77 Commercial Road, Paddock Wood, Kent TN12 6DR Tel: 01892 832325

LOM • Lombarda Sport Ltd, 2 Railway Mews, Notting Hill, London W10 6HN Tel: 020 7792 9773

MEE • Nicholas Mee & Company Ltd, 36-38 Queensgate Place Mews, London SW7 5BQ Tel: 020 7581 0088

MINI § Mini Cooper Register, Philip Splett, Public Relations Officer, Burtons Farm, Barling Road, Barling Magna, Southend, Essex SS3 0LZ

MoR § Morris Register, Michael Thomas (Secretary), 14 Meadow Rise, Horam, East Sussex TN21 0LZ Tel: 01435 810133

Mot • Motospot, North Kilworth, Nr Lutterworth, Leicestershire LE17 6EP Tel: 01455 552548/0850 450269

MSMP • Mike Smith Motoring Past, Chiltern House, Ashendon, Aylesbury, Bucks HP18 0HB Tel: 01296 651283

MUL • Mullock & Madeley, The Old Shippon, Wall-under-Heywood, Church Stretton, Shropshire SY6 7DS Tel: 01694 771771

MVT § MVT, PO Box 6, Fleet, Hampshire GU13 9PE

P(E) * Phillips, Alphin Brook Road, Alphington, Exeter, Devon EX2 8TH Tel: 01392 439025

PALM *† Palm Springs Exotic Car Auctions, 602 East Sunny Dunes Road, Palm Springs, California 92264, USA Tel: 00 1 760 320 3290

PC   Private Collection

PM • Pollard's Motorcycles, The Garage, Clarence Street, Dinnington, Sheffield, Yorkshire S25 7NA Tel: 01909 563310

PMB •† Pooks Motor Bookshop, Fowke Street, Rothley, Leicestershire LE7 7PJ Tel: 0116 237 6222

PORT • Portfield Sports & Classics Ltd, Quarry Lane, Chichester, West Sussex PO19 2NX Tel: 01243 528500

Pou * Poulain Le Fur Commissaires Priseurs Associes, 20 Rue de Provence, 75009 Paris, France Tel: 00 33 01 42 46 81 81

PPH • Period Picnic Hampers Tel: 0115 937 2934

RCC •† Real Car Co Ltd, Snowdonia Business Park, Coed y Parc, Bethesda, Gwynedd LL57 4YS Tel: 01248 602649

RIL § Riley RM Club, Mrs J Manders, Y Fachell, Ruthin Road, Gwernymynydd, North Wales CH7 5LQ

RM * RM Classic Cars, 825 Park Avenue West, Chatham, Ontario, Canada Tel: 00 1 519 352 4575

RRM • RR Motor Services Ltd, Bethersden, Ashford, Kent TN26 3DN Tel: 01233 820219

RTT • Rin Tin Tin, 34 North Road, Brighton, East Sussex BN1 1YB Tel: 01273 672424/733689

S * Sotheby's, 34–35 New Bond Street, London W1A 2AA Tel: 020 7293 5000

SAB § Saab Owners Club of GB Ltd, John Wood (Membership Secretary), PO Box 900, Durham DH1 2GF Tel: 01923 229945 Membership Hotline 070 71 71 9000

SJR • Simon J Robinson (1982) Ltd, Ketton Garage, Durham Road, Coatham, Munderville, Darlington, Co Durham DL1 3LZ Tel: 01325 311232

STE •† Stevenson Brothers, The Workshop, Ashford Road, Bethersden, Ashford, Kent TN26 3AP Tel: 01233 820363

SW • Spinning Wheel Garage, Sheffield Road, Sheepbridge, Chesterfield, Derbyshire S41 9EH Tel: 01246 451772

TALA • Talacrest, 74 Station Road, Egham, Surrey TW20 9LF Tel: 01784 439797

TEC § Toyota Enthusiasts Club, c/o Secretary/Treasurer Billy Wells, 28 Park Road, Feltham, Middlesex TW13 6PW Tel/Fax: 020 8898 0740

TEN * Tennants, The Auction Centre, Harmby Road, Leyburn, Yorkshire DL8 5SG Tel: 01969 623780

TEN * Tennants, 34 Montpellier Parade, Harrogate, Yorkshire HG1 2TG Tel: 01423 531661

TPS • Trevor's Pump Shop, 2 Cement Cottages, Station Road, Rainham, Kent ME8 7UF Tel: 01634 361231

TSh * Thimbleby & Shorland, 31 Great Knollys Street, Reading, Berkshire RG1 7HU Tel: 01734 508611

TUC •† Tuckett Bros, Marstonfields, North Marston, Bucks MK18 3PG Tel: 01296 670500

TWY • Twyford Moors Classic Cars, Unit C Burnes Shipyard, Old Bosham, Nr Chicester, West Sussex PO18 8LJ Tel: 01243 576586

UMC •† Unicorn Motor Company, Brian R. Chant, M.I.M.I., Station Road, Stalbridge, Dorset DT10 2RH Tel: 01963 363353

VIC •† Vicarys of Battle Ltd, 32 High St, Battle, East Sussex TN33 0EH Tel: 01424 772425

VIN • Vintage & Sports Car Garage Ltd, 47 West Street, Harrietsham, Kent ME17 1HX Tel: 01622 859570

VS * T. Vennett-Smith, 11 Nottingham Road, Gotham, Notts NG11 0HE Tel: 0115 983 0541

WAB • Warboys Antiques, Old Church School, High Street, Warboys, Cambridge PE17 2SX Tel: 01487 823686

WCL • Waterside Classics Ltd, 3 Alleysbank Road, Farmeloan Estate, Rutherglen, Glasgow, Scotland G73 1AE Tel: 0141 647 0333

WILM • Wilmington Classic Cars, Lewes Road, Wilmington, Polegate, East Sussex BN26 5JE Tel: 01323 486136

WITH • Witham Specialist Vehicles, Honey Pot Lane, Colsterworth, Grantham, Lincolnshire NG33 5LY Tel: 01476 861361

YEST • Yesterday's, V.O.F. Yesterday's, Maaseikerweg 202, 6006 AD Weert, Netherlands. Tel: 00 31 0475 531207

Glossary

We have attempted to define some of the terms that you will come across in this book. If there are any terms or technical expressions that you would like explained or you feel should be included in future, please let us know.

Aero screen A small, curved windscreen fitted to the scuttle of a sports car in place of the standard full-width screen. Used in competition to reduce wind resistance. Normally fitted in pairs, one each in front of the driver and passenger.

All-weather A term used to describe a vehicle with a more sophisticated folding hood than the normal Cape hood fitted to a touring vehicle. The sides were fitted with metal frames and transparent material, in some cases glass.

Barchetta Italian for 'little boat', an all-enveloping open sports bodywork.

Berline *See* **Sedanca de Ville**.

Boost The amount of pressure applied by a supercharger or turbocharger.

Boxer Engine configuration with horizontally-opposed cylinders.

Brake A term dating from the days of horse-drawn vehicles. Originally the seating was fore and aft, the passengers facing inwards.

Brake horsepower (bhp) This is the amount of power produced by an engine, measured at the flywheel (*See* **Horsepower**).

Cabriolet The term Cabriolet applies to a vehicle with a hood that can be closed, folded half-way or folded right back. A Cabriolet can be distinguished from a Landaulette because the front of the hood reaches the top of the windscreen, whereas on a Landaulette, it only covers the rear half of the car.

Chain drive A transmission system in which the wheels are attached to a sprocket, driven by a chain from an engine-powered sprocket, usually on the output side of a gearbox.

Chassis A framework to which the car body, engine, gearbox, and axles are attached.

Chummy An open-top, two-door body style, usually with a single door on each side, two seats in the front and one at the rear.

Cloverleaf A three-seater, open body style, usually with a single door on each side, two seats in the front and one at the rear.

Concours Concours d'Elegance is a competition in which cars are judged by their condition. Concours has become a byword for a vehicle in excellent condition.

Cone clutch A clutch in which both driving and driven faces form a cone.

Connollising Leather treatment produced by British firm Connolly to rejuvenate and restore suppleness to old and dry leather.

Convertible A general term (post-war) for any car with a folding soft top.

Continental A car specifically designed for high-speed touring, usually on the Continent. Rolls-Royce and Bentley almost exclusively used this term during the 1930s and post-WWII.

Coupé In the early Vintage and Edwardian period, Coupé was only applied to what is now termed a Half Limousine or Doctor's Coupé, which was a two-door two-seater. The term is now usually prefixed by Drophead or Fixed-Head.

Cubic capacity The volume of an engine obtained by multiplying the area of the bore by the stroke. Engine capacity is given in cubic centimetres (cc) in Europe and cubic inches (cu.in) in the USA. 1 cubic inch equals 16.38cc (1 litre = 61.02cu.in).

de Ville A style of coachwork in which the driver/chauffeur occupies an open driving position, and the passengers a closed compartment – thus, Coupé de Ville or Sedanca de Ville. In America, these vehicles are known as Town Cars.

Dickey seat A passenger seat, usually for two people, contained in the boot of the car and without a folding hood (the boot lid forms the backrest). *See* **Rumble seat**.

Doctor's coupé A fixed or drophead coupé without a dickey seat, the passenger seat being slightly staggered back from the driver's to accommodate the famous doctor's bag.

Dog cart A form of horse-drawn vehicle originally designed for transporting beaters and their dogs to a shoot (the dogs were contained in louvred boxes under the seats; the louvres were kept for decoration long after the practice of carrying dogs in this way had ceased).

Dos-à-dos Literally back-to-back, i.e. the passenger seating arrangement.

Double-duck Double-layered fabric used in construction of folding convertible tops.

Drophead coupé Originally a two-door two-seater with a folding roof.

Dry sump A method of lubricating engines in which the oil is contained in a separate reservoir rather than in a sump at the bottom of the cylinder block. Usually, two oil pumps are used, one to remove oil from the engine to the reservoir, the other to pump it back to the engine.

Fender American term used to describe the wing of a car.

F-head An engine design in which the inlet valve is in the cylinder head, while the exhaust valve is in the cylinder block. Also referred to as inlet-over-exhaust.

Fixed-head coupé A coupé with a solid fixed roof.

Golfer's coupé Usually an open two-seater with a square-doored locker behind the driver's seat to accommodate golf clubs.

Hansom As with the famous horse-drawn cab, an enclosed two-seater with the driver out in the elements, either behind or in front of the passenger compartment.

Homologation To qualify for entry into some race series, the rules can require that a minimum number of road-going production versions of the race car are built. These are generally known as 'homologation specials'.

Hood American term used to describe the bonnet of a car.

Horsepower (hp) The unit of measurement of engine power – one horsepower represents the energy expended in raising 33,000lb by one foot in 60 seconds.

Landau An open town carriage for four people with a folding hood at each end, which would meet in the middle when erected.

Landaulette A horse-drawn Landaulette carried two people and was built much like a coupé. The roof line of a Landaulette is always angular, in contrast to a Cabriolet, and the folding hood is very often made of patent leather. A true Landaulette only opens over the rear compartment and not over the front seat at all. (Also Landaulet.)

L-head An engine design in which the inlet and exhaust valves are contained within the cylinder block. *See* **Sidevalve**.

Limousine French in origin and used to describe a closed car equipped with occasional seats and a division between the rear and driver's compartments.

Monobloc engine An engine with all its cylinders cast in a single block.

Monocoque A method of constructing a car without a separate chassis, structural strength being provided by the arrangement of the stressed panels. Most modern, mass-produced cars are built in this way.

Monoposto Single-seater (Italian).

Nitrided Used to describe engine components, particularly crankshafts, that have been specially hardened to withstand the stresses of racing or other high-performance applications.

OHC Overhead camshaft, either single (SOHC) or double (DOHC).

OHV Overhead valves.

Phaeton A term dating back to the days of horse-drawn vehicles and used to describe an open body, sometimes with a dickey or rumble seat for the groom at the rear. It was an owner/driver carriage and designed to be pulled by four horses. A term often misused during the Veteran period, but still in common use, particularly in the USA.

Post Vintage Thoroughbred (PVT) A British term created by the Vintage Sports Car Club (VSCC) to describe selected models made in the vintage tradition between 1931 and 1942.

Roadster A two-seater, open sporting vehicle, the hood of which is removed completely rather than being folded down, as on a drophead coupé. Early versions without side windows.

Roi des Belges A luxurious open touring car with elaborately contoured seat backs, named after King Leopold II of Belgium. The term is sometimes incorrectly used to describe general touring cars.

Rotary engine A unique form of car engine in which the cylinders, pistons and crankshaft of the normal reciprocating engine are replaced by a triangular rotor that rotates about an eccentric shaft within a special waisted chamber. One or more rotor/chamber assemblies may be used. On the whole, the engine has a third of the number of parts of a comparable reciprocating engine. The engine was designed by Dr Felix Wankel and has been used in a range of sports cars by Mazda.

RPM Engine revolutions per minute.

Rumble seat An American term for a folding seat for two passengers, used to increase the carrying capacity of a standard two-passenger car. *See* **Dickey seat**.

Runabout A low-powered, lightweight, open two-seater from the 1900s.

Saloon A two- or four-door car with four or more seats and a fixed roof.

Sedan *See* **Saloon**.

Sedanca de Ville A limousine body with an open driving compartment that can be covered with a folding or sliding roof section, known in America as a Town Car.

Sidevalve Used to describe an engine in which the valves are located in the cylinder block rather than the head.

Sociable A cyclecar term used to describe the side-by-side seating of the driver and passenger.

Spider/Spyder An open two-seater sports car, sometimes a 2+2 (with two small occasional seats behind the two front seats).

Station wagon American term for an estate car.

Supercharger An engine-driven pump for forcing the fuel/air mixture into the cylinders to gain extra power.

Surrey An early 20thC open four-seater with a fringed canopy. A term from the days of horse-drawn vehicles.

Stanhope A single-seat, two-wheeled horse-drawn carriage with a hood. Later, a four-wheeled, two-seater, sometimes with an underfloor engine.

Stroke The distance an engine's piston moves up-and-down within its cylinder. The stroke is invariably measured in millimetres, although in the USA, inches may be used.

Superleggera Italian for 'super lightweight' and used to describe a method of construction devised by Touring of Milan, whereby an aluminium skin was attached to a framework of steel tubes to produce a light, yet strong, structure. One of the best-known proponents of this method was Aston Martin, which employed Superleggera construction in some of its DB series cars.

Tandem A cyclecar term used to describe the fore-and-aft seating of the driver and passenger.

Targa A coupé fitted with a removable central roof section.

Tonneau A rear-entrance tonneau is a four-seater to which access is provided through a centrally-placed rear door. A detachable tonneau meant that the rear seats could be removed to make a two-seater. Today, 'tonneau' usually refers to a waterproof cover that can be fitted over the cockpit of an open car when the roof is detached.

Torpedo An open tourer that has coachwork with an unbroken line from the bonnet to the rear of the body.

Tourer An open four- or five-seater with three or four doors, a folding hood (with or without sidescreens) and seats flush with the body sides. This body style began to appear in about 1910 and, initially, was known as a torpedo (*see above*), but by 1920, the word 'tourer' was being used instead – except in France, where 'torpedo' continued in use until the 1930s.

Turbocharger An exhaust-gas-driven pump for forcing the air/fuel mixture into the engine's cylinders to produce extra power.

Unitary construction Used to describe a vehicle without a separate chassis, structural strength being provided by the arrangement of the stressed panels. *See* **Monocoque**.

Veteran All vehicles manufactured before 31 December 1918; only cars built before 31 March 1904 are eligible for the London to Brighton Commemorative Run.

Victoria Generally an American term for a two- or four-seater with a very large folding hood. If a four-seater, the hood would only cover the rear seats. In some cases, applied to a saloon with a 'bustle' back.

Vintage Any vehicle manufactured between the end of the veteran period and 31 December 1930. *See* **Post Vintage Thoroughbred**.

Vis-à-vis Face-to-face; an open car in which the passengers sit opposite each other.

Voiturette A French term used to describe a very light car, originally coined by Léon Bollée.

Wagonette A large car for six or more passengers, in which the rear seats face each other. Entrance is at the rear, and the vehicle is usually open.

Waxoyled Used to describe a vehicle in which the underside has been treated with Waxoyl, a proprietary oil and wax spray that protects against moisture.

Weymann A system of body construction employing Rexine fabric panels over a Kapok filling to prevent noise and provide insulation.

Wheelbase The distance between the centres of the front and rear wheels of a vehicle.

Directory of Car Clubs

If you would like your Club to be included in next year's directory, or have a change of address or telephone number, please inform us by 31 May 2001.

105E Anglia Owners' Club Middlesex Group, 9 Evelyn Avenue, Ruislip, Middlesex HA4 8AR Tel: 01895 672251

2CVGB Deux Chevaux Club of GB, PO Box 602, Crick, Northampton, Northamptonshire NN6 7UW

750 Motor Club Ltd, Worth Farm, Little Horsted, West Sussex TN22 5TT Tel: 01825 750760

AC Owners' Club, R A Morpeth, The Clovers, Mursley, Buckinghamshire MK17 0RT

A40 Farina Club, 2 Ivy Cottages, Fullers Vale, Headley Down, Bordon, Hampshire GU35 8NR

ABC Owners' Club, D A Hales, The Hedgerows, Sutton St Nicholas, Hereford HR1 3BU Tel: 01432 880726

Alexis Racing & Trials Car Register, Duncan Rabagliati, 4 Wool Road, Wimbledon, London SW20 0HW

Alfa Romeo 1900 Register, Peter Marshall, Mariners, Courtlands Avenue, Esher, Surrey KT10 9HZ

Alfa Romeo Owners' Club, Michael Lindsay, 97 High Street, Linton, Cambridgeshire CB1 6JT

Alfa Romeo Section (VSCC Ltd), Allan & Angela Cherrett, Old Forge, Quarr, Nr Gillingham, Dorset SP8 5PA

Allard Owners' Club, Miss P Hulse, 1 Dalmeny Avenue, Tufnell Park, London N7

Alvis Owners' Club, 1 Forge Cottages, Bayham Road, Little Bayham, Lamberhurst, Kent TN3 8BB

Alvis Register, Mr J Willis, The Vinery, Wanborough Manor, Nr Guildford, Surrey GU3 2JR Tel: 01483 810308

American Auto Club UK, 11 Wych Elm, Colchester, Essex CO2 8PR Tel: 01206 564404

Amilcar Salmson Register, R A F King, Apple House, Wildmoor Lane, Sherfield-on-Lodden, Hampshire RG27 0HA

Armstrong Siddeley Owners' Club Ltd, Peter Sheppard, 57 Berberry Close, Bournville, Birmingham, West Midlands B30 1TB

Association of American Car Clubs UK, PO Box 2222, Braintree, Essex CM7 9TW Tel/Fax: 01376 552478 email: tlsec@motorvatinusa.org.uk web: www.motorvatinusa.org.uk

Assoc of British Volkswagen Clubs, Dept PC, 76 Eastfield Road, Burnham, Buckinghamshire SL1 7PF

Association of Healey Owners, John Humphreys, 2 Kingsbury's Lane, Ringwood, Hampshire BH24 1EL

Association of Old Vehicle Clubs in Northern Ireland Ltd, Trevor Mitchell, 38 Ballymaconnell Road, Bangor, Co Down, N Ireland BT20 5PS Tel: 028 9146 7886

Association of Singer Car Owners, Anne Page, 39 Oakfield, Rickmansworth, Hertfordshire WD3 2LR Tel: 01923 778575

Aston Martin Owners' Club Ltd, Jim Whyman, AMOC Ltd, 1A High Street, Sutton, Nr Ely, Cambridgeshire CB6 2RB Tel: 01353 777353

Atlas Register, 38 Ridgeway, Southwell, Nottinghamshire NG25 0DJ

Austin 3 Litre OC, Neil Kidby, 78 Croft Street, Ipswich, Suffolk IP2 8EF

Austin A30-35 Owners' Club, Mrs C Tarsey, 3 George Street, Leighton Buzzard, Bedfordshire LU7 8JX web: www.austin.club.co.uk

Austin Atlantic Owners' Club, Lee Marshall, Wildwood, 21 Cornflower Close, Stamford, Lincolnshire PE9 2WL

Austin Big 7 Register, R E Taylor, 101 Derby Road, Chellaston, Derbyshire DE73 1SB

Austin Cambridge/Westminster Car Club, Arthur Swann, 21 Alexander Terr, Corsham, Wiltshire SN13 0BW

Austin Counties Car Club, Martin Pickard, 10 George Street, Bedworth, Warwickshire CV12 8EB

Austin Eight Register, Ian Pinniger, 3 La Grange Martin, St Martin, Jersey, Channel Islands JE3 6JB

Austin Gipsy Register 1958–1968, Mike Gilbert, 24 Green Close, Rixon, Sturminster Newton, Dorset DT10 1BJ

Austin Healey Club, Colleen Holmes, 4 Saxby Street, Leicester, Leicestershire LE2 0ND

Austin Healey Club, Mike Ward, Midland Centre, 66 Glascote Lane, Tamworth, Staffordshire B77 2PH Tel/Fax: 01827 260 644 email: sam.ward@ukgateway.net

Austin J40 Pedal Car Club, Mary Rowlands, 21 Forest Close, Lickey End, Bromsgrove, Worcestershire B60 1JU

Austin Maxi Club, Mrs C J Jackson, 27 Queen Street, Bardney, Lincolnshire LN3 5XF

Austin Seven Mulliner Register, Mike Tebbett, Little Wyche, Walwyn Road, Upper Colwall, Nr Malvern, Worcestershire WR13 6PL

Austin Seven Van Register 1923–29, N B Baldry, 32 Wentworth Crescent, Maidenhead, Berkshire SL6 4RW

Austin Sheerline & Princess Club, Ian Coombes, 44 Vermeer Crescent, Shoeburyness, Essex S53 9TJ

Austin Swallow Register, G L Walker, School House, Rectory Road, Great Haseley, Oxfordshire OX44 7JP

Austin Taxi Club, A Thomas, 52 Foss Avenue, Waddon, Croydon, Surrey CR0 4EU web: www.taxiclub.freeserve.co.uk

Austin Ten Drivers' Club Ltd, Ian M Dean, PO Box 12, Chichester, West Sussex PO20 7PH Tel: 01243 641284

Battery Vehicle Society, Keith Roberts, 29 Ambergate Drive, North Pentwyn, Cardiff, Wales CF2 7AX

Bentley Drivers' Club, 16 Chearsley Road, Long Crendon, Aylesbury, Buckinghamshire HP18 9AW

Berkeley Enthusiasts' Club, Phil James, 55 Main Street, Sutton Bonington, Loughborough, Leicestershire LE12 5PE

Biggin Hill Car Club with XJ Register of JDC, Peter Adams, Jasmine House, Jasmine Grove, London SE20 8JY Tel: 020 8778 7531

BMC J2/152 Register, 10 Sunnyside Cottages, Woodford, Kettering, Northamptonshire NN14 4HX

BMW Drivers' Club, Sue Hicks, Bavaria House, PO Box 8, Dereham, Norfolk NR19 1TF Tel: 01362 694459

Bond Owners' Club, Stan Cornock, 42 Beaufort Ave, Hodge Hill, Birmingham, West Midlands B34 6AE

Borgward Drivers' Club, Mr D C Farr, 19 Highfield Road, Kettering, Northamptonshire NN15 6HR Tel: 01536 510771

Brabham Register, Ed Walker, The Old Bull, 5 Woodmancote, Dursley, Gloucestershire GL11 4AF Tel: 01453 543243

Bristol Austin Seven Club, 1 Silsbury Hill Cottages, West Kennett, Marlborough, Wiltshire SN8 1QH

Bristol Microcar Club, 123 Queens Road, Bishopsworth, Bristol, Gloucestershire BS13 8QB Tel: 0117 964 2901

Bristol Owners' Club, John Emery, Vesutor, Marringdean Road, Billingshurst, West Sussex RH14 9HD

British Ambulance Society, Roger Leonard, General Secretary, 21 Victoria Road, Horley, Surrey RH6 9BN Tel/Fax: 01293 776636

British Ambulance Society, Paul M Tona, 5 Cormorant Drive, Hythe, Hampshire SO45 3GG Tel: 023 8084 1999

British Automobile Racing Club, Thruxton Circuit, Andover, Hampshire SP11 8PN Tel: 01264 772607 & 772696/7

British Saab Enthusiasts, Mr M Hodges, 75 Upper Road, Poole, Dorset BH12 3EN

British Salmson Owners' Club, John Maddison, 86 Broadway North, Walsall, West Midlands WS1 2QF Tel: 01922 29677

Brough Superior Club, Justin Wand, Flint Cottage, St Paul's Walden, Hitchin, Hertfordshire SG4 8ONL

Buckler Car Register, Stan Hibberd, 52 Greenacres, Woolton Hill, Newbury, Berkshire RG15 9TA Tel: 01635 254162

Bugatti Owners' Club Ltd, Sue Ward, Prescott Hill, Gotherington, Cheltenham, Gloucestershire GL52 4RD Tel: 01242 673136

Buick Club UK, PO Box 2222, Braintree, Essex CM7 9TW Tel/Fax: 01376 552478

Bullnose Morris Club, Richard Harris, PO Box 383, Hove, East Sussex BN3 4FX

CA Bedford Owners' Club, G W Seller, 7 Grasmere Road, Benfleet, Essex SS7 3HF

Cambridge-Oxford Owners' Club, 32 Reservoir Road, Southgate, London N14 4BG

Capri Club International, 18 Arden Business Centre, Arden Road, Alcester B49 6HW

Capri Club International, North London Branch, 12 Chalton Road, Edmonton, London N9 8EG Tel: 020 8364 7845/020 8804 6326

Capri Drivers' Association, Mrs Moira Farrelly, Secretary, 9 Lyndhurst Road, Coulsdon, Surrey CR5 3HT

Citroën Car Club, PO Box 348, Bromley, Kent BR2 2QT Tel: Membership 01689 853999 General fax/ansphone: 07000 248 258 email: members@citroencarclub.org.uk web: www.citroencarclub.org.uk

Citroën Traction Owners' Club, Peter Riggs, 2 Appleby Gardens, Dunstable, Bedfordshire LU6 3DB

Clan Owners' Club, Chris Clay, 48 Valley Road, Littleover, Derbyshire DE23 6HS Tel: 01332 767410

Classic and Historic Motor Club Ltd, Tricia Burridge, Stream Cottage, Yarley Cross, Wells, Somerset BA5 1LS Tel: 01749 675404

Classic Camaro Club, PO Box 2222, Braintree, Essex CM7 9TW Tel/Fax: 01376 552478

The Classic Camper Club, PO Box 3, Amlwch, Anglesey LL68 9ZE Tel/Fax: 01407 832243 Mobile: 07780 618499 email: Classic.CamperClub@btinternet.com web: www.ClassicCamperClub.co.uk

Classic Chevrolet Club, PO Box 2222, Braintree, Essex CM7 9TW Tel/Fax: 01376 552478

Classic Corvette Club (UK), Ashley Pickering, The Gables, Christchurch Rd, Tring, Hertfordshire HP23 4EF

Classic Z Register, Jon Newlyn, 11 Lawday Link, Upper Hale, Farnham, Surrey GU9 0BS

Club Alpine Renault UK Ltd, 1 Bloomfield Close, Wombourne, Wolverhampton, West Midlands WV5 8HQ

Club Lotus, Lotus Lodge, PO Box 8, Dereham, Norfolk NR19 1TF Tel: 01362 694459

Club Marcos International, Mrs I Chivers, 8 Ludmead Rd, Corsham, Wiltshire SN13 9AS Tel: 01249 713769

Club Peugeot UK, Peter Vaughan, 41 Hazelwood Drive, Bourne, Lincolnshire PE10 9SZ

Club Peugeot UK, Club Regs 504 Cab/Coupe, Beacon View, Forester Road, Soberton Heath, Southampton, Hampshire SO32 3QG Tel: 01329 833029

Club Triumph, Derek Pollock, 86 Waggon Road, Hadley Wood, Hertfordshire EN14 0PP Tel: 020 8440 9000

Club Triumph Eastern, Mr D A Davies, 72 Springwater Rd, Eastwood, Leigh-on-Sea, Essex SS9 5BJ

Clyno Club, Swallow Cottage, Langton Farm, Elmesthorpe, Leicestershire LE9 7SE

Commercial Vehicle and Road Transport Club, Steven Wimbush, 8 Tachbrook Road, Uxbridge, Middlesex UB8 2QS

Connaught Register, Duncan Rabagliati, 4 Wool Road, Wimbledon, London SW20 0HW

Cortina Mk II Register, Mark Blows, 78 Church Avenue, Broomfield, Chelmsford, Essex CM1 7HA

Cougar Club of America, Barrie S Dixon, 11 Dean Close, Partington, Greater Manchester M31 4BQ

Crayford Convertible Car Club, 58 Geriant Road, Downham, Bromley, Kent BR1 5DX Tel: 020 8461 1805

Crossley Register, 7 Manor Road, Sherborne St John, Nr Basingstoke, Hampshire RG24 9JJ

Crossley Register, Malcolm Jenner, Willow Cottage, Lexham Road, Great Dunham, Kings Lynn, Norfolk PE32 2LS

DAF Owners' Club, S K Bidwell, 56 Ridgedale Road, Bolsover, Chesterfield, Derbyshire S44 6TX

Daimler and Lanchester Owners' Club, PO Box 276, Sittingbourne, Kent ME9 7GA Tel: 07000 356285 email: daimleruk@aol.com

Datsun Owners' Club, Jon Rodwell, 28 Langton Park, Wroughton, Wiltshire SN4 0QN Tel: 01793 845271 web: www.datsunworld.com

De Tomaso Drivers' Club, Phil Stebbings, Founder and Club Secretary, Flint Barn, Malthouse Lane, Ashington, West Sussex RH20 3BU Tel/Fax: 01903 893870

Delage Section of the VSCC Ltd, Peter Jacobs, Clouds' Reach, The Scop, Almondsbury, Bristol BS32 4DU

Delahaye Club GB, A F Harrison, 34 Marine Parade, Hythe, Kent CT21 6AN Tel: 01303 261016

Dellow Register, Douglas Temple Design Group, 4 Roumelia Lane, Bournemouth, Dorset BH5 1EU Tel: 01202 304641

DeLorean Owners' Club, c/o Chris Parnham, 14 Quarndon Heights, Allestree, Derby DE22 2XN

Diva Register, Steve Pethybridge, 8 Wait End Road, Waterlooville, Hampshire PO7 7DD Tel: 023 9225 1485

DKW Owners' Club, David Simon, Aurelia, Garlogie, Skene, Westhill, Aberdeenshire, Scotland AB32 6RX

Droop Snoot Group, 41 Horsham Avenue, Finchley, London N12 9BG Tel: 020 8368 1884

Dunsfold Land Rover Trust, Dunsfold, Surrey GU8 4NP Tel: 01483 200058

Dutton Owners' Club, Rob Powell, 20 Burford Road, Baswich, Stafford, Staffordshire ST17 0BT Tel: 01785 56835

Early Ford V8 Club, 12 Fairholme Gardens, Cranham, Upminster, Essex, RM14 1HJ Tel: 01708 222729

East Anglia Fighting Group, 206 Colchester Road, Lawford, Nr Manningtree, Essex Tel: 01206 395177

Elva Owners Club, Roger Dunbar, 8 Liverpool Terrace, Worthing, W Sussex BN11 1TA Tel/Fax: 01903 823710 email: roger.dunbar@elva.com web: www.elva.com

Enfield & District Veteran Vehicle Trust, Whitewebbs Museum, Whitewebbs Road, Enfield, Middlesex EN2 9HW Tel: 020 8367 1898

ERA Club, Guy Spollon, Arden Grange, Tanworth-in-Arden, Warwickshire B94 5AE

F & FB Victor Owners' Club, Wayne Parkhouse, 5 Farnell Road, Staines, Middlesex TW18 4HT

F-Victor Owners' Club, Alan Victor Pope, 34 Hawkesbury Drive, Mill Lane, Calcot, Reading, Berkshire RG3 5ZR Tel: 01635 43532

Facel Vega Car Club, Mr M Green, Secretary, 17 Stanley Road, Lymington, Hampshire SO41 3SJ

Fairthorpe Sports Car Club, Tony Hill, 9 Lynhurst Crescent, Uxbridge, Middlesex UB10 9EF

Ferrari Club of GB, Betty Mathias, 7 Swan Close, Blake Down, Kidderminster, Worcestershire DY10 3JT Tel: 01562 700009

Ferrari Owners' Club, Peter Everingham, 35 Market Place, Snettisham, Kings Lynn PE31 7LR

Fiat 130 Owners' Club, Michael Reid, 28 Warwick Mansions, Cromwell Crescent, London SW5 9QR Tel: 020 7373 9740

Fiat 500 Club, Janet Westcott, Secretary, 33 Lionel Avenue, Wendover, Aylesbury, Buckinghamshire HP22 6LP

Fiat Dino Register, Mr Morris, 59 Sandown Park, Tunbridge Wells, Kent TN2 4RT

Fiat Motor Club (GB), Mrs S Robins, Hon Membership Sec, 118 Brookland Rd, Langport, Somerset TA10 9TH

Fiat Osca Register, Mr M Elliott, 36 Maypole Drive, Chigwell, Essex IG7 6DE Tel: 020 8500 7127

Fiesta Club of GB, S Church, 145 Chapel Lane, Farnborough, Hampshire GU14 9BN

Fire Service Preservation Group, Andrew Scott, 50 Old Slade Lane, Iver, Buckinghamshire SL0 9DR

Five Hundred Owners' Club Association, David Docherty, Oakley, 68 Upton Park, Chester, Cheshire CH2 1DQ Tel: 01244 382789

Ford 105E Owners' Club, Sally Harris, 30 Gower Road, Sedgley, Dudley, West Midlands DY3 3PN Tel: 01902 671071

Ford Avo Owners' Club, D Hensley, 11 Sycamore Drive, Patchway, Bristol, Gloucestershire BS12 5DH

Ford Capri Enthusiasts' Register, Glyn Watson, 7 Louis Avenue, Bury, Lancashire BL9 5EQ Tel: 0161 762 9952

Ford Classic and Capri Owners' Club, 1 Verney Close, Covingham, Swindon, Wiltshire SN3 5EF Tel: 01793 523574

Ford Corsair Owners' Club, Mrs E Checkley, 7 Barnfield, New Malden, Surrey KT3 5RH

Ford Cortina 1600E Owners' Club, Dave Marston, 23 Cumberland Road, Bilston, West Midlands WV14 6LT Tel: 01902 405055

Ford Cortina Owners' Club, Mr D Eastwood, 52 Woodfield, Bamber Bridge, Preston, Lancashire PR5 8ED Tel: 01772 627004 after 6pm

Ford Escort 1300E Owners' Club, Robert Watt, 65 Lindley Road, Walton-on-Thames, Surrey KT12 3EZ

Ford Executive Owners' Register, George Young, 31 Brian Road, Chadwell Heath, Romford, Essex RM6 5DA

Ford GT Owners' Club, c/o Riverside School, Ferry Road, Hullbridge, Hockley, Essex SS5 6ND

Ford Mk II Independent O C International, B & J Enticknap, 173 Sparrow Farm Dr, Feltham, Middlesex TW14 0DG Tel: 020 8384 3559 Fax: 020 8890 3741

Ford Mk III Zephyr & Zodiac Owners' Club, John Wilding 10 Waltondale, Telford, Shropshire TF7 5NQ Tel: 01952 580746

Ford Mk IV Zephyr & Zodiac Owners' Club, Richard Cordle, 29 Ruskin Drive, Worcester Park, Surrey KT4 8LG Tel: 020 8649 0685

Ford Model T Ford Register of GB, Mrs Julia Armer, 3 Strong Close, Keighley, Yorkshire BD21 4JT

Ford Sidevalve Owners' Club, 30 Earls Close, Bishopstoke, Eastleigh, Hampshire SO50 8HY

Ford Y&C Model Register, Bob Wilkinson, 9 Brambleside, Thrapston, Northamptonshire NN14 4PY

Frazer-Nash Section of the VSCC, Mrs J Blake, Daisy Head Farm, South Street, Caulcott, Bicester, Oxfordshire OX6 3NE

Friends of The British Commercial Vehicle, c/o BCVM, King Street, Leyland, Preston, Lancashire PR5 1LE

The Gentry Register, Barbara Reynolds, General Secretary, Barn Close Cottage, Cromford Road, Woodlinkin, Nottinghamshire NG16 4HD

Gilbern Owners' Club, Alan Smith, Hunters Hill, Church Lane, Peppard Common, Oxfordshire RG9 5JL Tel: 01491 628379

Gordon Keeble Owners' Club, Ann Knott, Westminster Road, Helmdon, Brackley, Northamptonshire NN13 5QB Tel: 01280 702311

Guernsey Motorcycle & Car Club, c/o Graham Rumens, Glenesk, Sandy Hook, St Sampsons, Guernsey, Channel Islands GY2 4ER

Gwynne Register, H K Good, 9 Lancaster Avenue, Hadley Wood, Barnet, Hertfordshire EN4 0EP

Heinkel Trojan Owners' & Enthusiasts' Club, Y Luty, Carisbrooke, Wood End Lane, Fillongley, Coventry, Warwickshire CV7 8DF

Heinz 57 Register, Barry Priestman, Secretary, 58 Geriant Road, Downham, Bromley, Kent BR1 5DX

Hermon Enthusiasts' Club, 6 Westleton Way, Felixstowe, Suffolk IP11 8YG Tel: 01394 272774

Hillman, Commer & Karrier Club, A Freakes, Capri House, Walton-on-Thames, Surrey KT12 2LY

Historic Caravan Club, Barbara Bissell, Secretary, 29 Linnet Close, Lodgefield Park, Halesowen, West Midlands B62 8TW Tel: 0121 561 5742

Historic Commercial Vehicle Society, HCVS, Iden Grange, Cranbrook Road, Staplehurst, Kent TN12 0ET

Historic Grand Prix Cars Association, 106 Gifford Street, London N1 0DF Tel: 020 7607 4887

Historic Lotus Register, Victor Thomas, President, Badgers Farm, Short Green, Winfarthing, Norfolk IP22 2EE Tel: 01953 860508

Historic Rally Car Register RAC, Martin Jubb, 38 Longfield Road, Bristol, Gloucestershire BS7 9AG

Historic Sports Car Club, Cold Harbour, Kington Langley, Wiltshire SN15 5LY

Historic Volkswagen Club, Rod Sleigh, 28 Longnor Road, Brooklands, Telford, Shropshire TF1 3NY

Holden UK Register, G R C Hardy, Clun Felin, Wolf's Castle, Haverfordwest, Pembrokshire, Dyfed, Wales SA62 5LR

Honda S800 Sports Car Club, Chris Wallwork, 23a High Street, Steeton, Yorkshire BD20 6NT Tel: 01535 653845

Hotchkiss Association GB, Michael Edwards, Wootton Tops, Sandy Lane, Boars Hill, Oxford, Oxfordshire OX1 5HN Tel: 01865 735180

HRG Association, I J Dussek, Churchers, Church Road, Upper Farringdon, Alton, Hampshire GU34 3EG

Humber Register, R N Arman, Northbrook Cottage, 175 York Road, Broadstone, Dorset BH18 8ES

Imp Club, Michelle Sozanska, 27 Brookside Road, Stratford-on-Avon, Warwickshire CV37 9PH Tel/Fax: 01789 414789

Invicta Military Vehicle Preservation Society, 58 Ladds Way, Swanley, Kent BR8 8HW Tel: 01322 408738

Isetta Owners' Club, 19 Towcester Road, Old Stratford, Milton Keynes, Buckinghamshire MK19 6AH Tel: 01908 569103

Jaguar Car Club, R Pugh, 19 Eldorado Crescent, Cheltenham, Gloucestershire GL50 2PY

Jaguar Drivers' Club, JDC, Jaguar House, 18 Stuart Street, Luton, Bedfordshire LU1 2SL Tel: 01582 419332

Jaguar Enthusiasts' Club, 176 Whittington Way, Pinner, Middlesex HA5 5JY Tel: 020 8866 2073

Jaguar/Daimler Owners' Club, 130/132 Bordesley Green, Birmingham, West Midlands B9 4SU

Jensen Owners' Club, Brian Morrey, Selwood, Howley, Nr Chard, Somerset TA20 3DX Tel: 01460 64165

Jowett Car Club, Ian Priestly, 626 Huddersfield Road, Wyke, Bradford, Yorkshire BD12 8JR

JU 250 Register, Stuart Cooke, 34 Thorncliffe Drive, Darwen, Lancashire BB3 3QA

Junior Zagato Register, Kenfield Hall, Petham, Nr Canterbury, Kent CT4 5RN Tel: 01227 700555

Jupiter Owners' Auto Club, Steve Keil, 16 Empress Avenue, Woodford Green, Essex IG8 9EA Tel: 020 8505 2215

K70 Register, SAE to: Steve Bood, 25 Cedar Grove, Penn Fields, Wolverhampton WV3 7EB

Karmann Ghia Owners' Club, Astrid Kelly, 7 Keble Rd, Maidenhead, Berkshire SL6 6BB Tel: 01628 39185

Kieft Racing & Sports Car Club, Duncan Rabagliati, 4 Wool Road, Wimbledon, London SW20 0HW

Lagonda Club, Colin Bugler, Hon Secretary, Wintney House, London Road, Hartley Wintney, Hook, Hampshire RG27 8RN Tel/Fax: 01252 845451

Lancia Motor Club, Dave Baker, Mount Pleasant, Penrhos, Brymbo, Wrexham, Clwyd, Wales LL11 5LY

Land Rover Register (1947–1951), Membership Secretary, High House, Ladbrooke, Leamington Spa, Warwickshire CV33 0BT

Land Rover Series 3 Owners' Club Ltd, 23 Deidre Avenue, Wickford, Essex SS12 0AX Tel: 01268 560818

Land Rover Series One Club, David Bowyer, East Foldhay, Zeal Monachorum, Crediton, Devon EX17 6DH

Land Rover Series Two Club Ltd, Laurence Mitchell Esq, PO Box 251, Barnsley S70 5YN

Landcrab Owners' Club International, 5 Rolston Avenue, Huntington, York YO31 9JD

Lea Francis Owners' Club, R Sawers, French's, High St, Long Wittenham, Abingdon, Oxfordshire OX14 4QQ

Lincoln-Zephyr Owners' Club, Colin Spong, 22 New North Road Hainault, Ilford, Essex IG6 2XG

London Bus Preservation Trust, Mike Nash, 43 Stroudwater, Weybridge, Surrey KT13 0DT

London Vintage Taxi Association, Steve Dimmock, 51 Ferndale Crescent, Cowley, Uxbridge, Berkshire UB8 2AY

Lotus Cortina Register, Andy Morrell, 64 The Queens Drive, Chorleywood, Rickmansworth, Hertfordshire WD3 2LT

Lotus Drivers' Club, Lee Barton, 15 Pleasant Way, Leamington Spa, Warwickshire CV32 5XA Tel: 01926 313514

Lotus Seven Club, Julie Richens, PO Box 7, Cranleigh, Surrey GU6 8YP

Manta A Series Register, Mark Kinnon, 112 Northwood Avenue, Purley, Surrey CR8 2EQ

Marcos Owners' Club, 62 Culverley Road, Catford, London SE6 2LA Tel: 020 8697 2988

Marendaz Special Car Register, John Shaw, 107 Old Bath Road, Cheltenham, Gloucestershire GL53 7DA Tel: 01242 526310

Marina/Ital Drivers' Club, Mr J G Lawson, 12 Nithsdale Road, Liverpool, Lancashire L15 5AX

Maserati Club, Michael Miles, The Paddock, Old Salisbury Road, Abbotts Ann, Andover, Hampshire SP11 7NT Tel: 01264 710312

Masters Club, Barry Knight, 2 Ranmore Avenue, East Croydon, Surrey CR0 5QA

Matra Enthusiasts' Club, MEC, 19 Abbotsbury, Orton Goldhay, Peterborough, Cambridgeshire PE2 5PS Tel: 01733 234555

Mercedes-Benz Owners' Association, Upper Birchetts House, Langton Road, Langton Green, Tunbridge Wells, Kent TN3 0EG Tel: 01892 860928

Mercedes-Benz Owners' Club, Northern Ireland Area Organiser, Trevor Mitchell, 38 Ballymaconell Road, Bangor, Co Down, Northern Ireland BT20 5PS email: info@onpublications.com

Messerschmitt Owners' Club, Mrs Eileen Hallam, Birches, Ashmores Lane, Rusper, West Sussex RH12 4PS Tel: 01293 871417

Metropolitan Owners' Club, Nick Savage, The Old Pump House, Nutbourne Common, Pulborough, West Sussex RH20 2HB Tel: 01798 813713

MG Car Club, 7 Chequer Lane, Ash, Canterbury, Kent CT3 2ET Tel: 01304 240380/01304 813863

MG Octagon Car Club, Unit 19, Hollins Business Centre, Rowley Street, Stafford, Staffordshire ST16 2RH Tel: 01785 251014

MG Owners' Club, Octagon House, Swavesey, Cambridgeshire CB4 5QZ Tel: 01954 231125

MG 'Y' Type Register, Mr J G Lawson, 12 Nithsdale Road, Liverpool, Lancashire L15 5AX

Midas Owners' Club, Steve Evans, 8 Mill Road, Holyhead, Anglesey LL65 2TA

Midget & Sprite Club, Nigel Williams, 15 Foxcote, Kingswood, Bristol, Gloucestershire BS15 2TX

Military Vehicle Trust, PO Box 6, Fleet, Hampshire GU13 9PE

Mini Cooper Club, Mary Fowler, 59 Giraud Street, Poplar, London E14 6EE

Mini Cooper Register, Philip Splett, Public Relations Officer, Burtons Farm, Barling Road, Barling Magna, Southend, Essex SS3 0LZ

Mini Marcos Owners' Club, Roger Garland, 28 Meadow Road, Worcester, Worcestershire WR3 7PP Tel: 01905 58533

Mini Moke Club, Paul Beard, 13 Ashdene Close, Hartlebury, Herefordshire DY11 7TN

Mini Owners' Club, 15 Birchwood Road, Lichfield, Staffordshire WS14 9UN

Mini Seven Racing Club, Mick Jackson, 345 Clay Lane, South Yardley, Birmingham, West Midlands B26 1ES

Mk I Consul, Zephyr & Zodiac Club, 180 Gypsy Road, Welling, Kent DA16 1JQ Tel: 020 8301 3709

Mk I Cortina Owners' Club, R J Raisey, 51 Studley Rise, Trowbridge, Wiltshire BA14 0PD

Mk II Consul, Zephyr & Zodiac Club, 170 Conisborough Crescent, Catford, London SE6 2SH

Mk II Granada Owners' Club, Paul Farrer, 58 Jevington Way, Lee, London SE12 9NQ Tel: 020 8857 4356

Model A Ford Club of Great Britain, Mr S J Shepherd, 32 Portland Street, Clifton, Bristol, Gloucestershire BS8 4JB Tel: 0117 973 9355

Morgan Sports Car Club, Carol Kennett, Old Ford Lodge, Ogston, Higham, Derbyshire DE55 6EL

Morgan Three-Wheeler Club Ltd, Dennis Plater, Holbrooks, Thoby Lane, Mountnessing, Brentwood, Essex CM15 0TA Tel: 01277 352867

Morris 12 Club, D Hedge, Crossways, Potton Road, Hilton, Huntingdon, Cambridgeshire PE18 9NG

Morris Cowley & Oxford Club, Derek Andrews, 202 Chantry Gardens, Southwick, Trowbridge, Wiltshire BA14 9QX

Morris Marina Owners' Club, Nigel Butler, Llys-Aled, 63 Junction Road, Stourbridge, West Midlands DY8 4YJ

Morris Minor Owners' Club, Jane White, 127–129 Green Lane, Derby, Derbyshire DE1 1RZ

Morris Minor Owners' Club, Northern Ireland Branch, Mrs Joanne Jeffery, Secretary, 116 Oakdale, Ballygowan, Newtownards, Co Down, Northern Ireland BT23 5TT

Morris Register, Michael Thomas, Secretary, 14 Meadow Rise, Horam, East Sussex TN21 0LZ Tel: 01435 810133 web: www.morrisregister.co.uk

Moss Owners' Club, David Pegler, Pinewood, Weston Lane, Bath, Somerset BA1 4AG Tel: 01225 331509

Motorvatin' USA American CC, T Lynn, PO Box 2222, Braintree, Essex CM7 6TW Tel/Fax: 01376 552478

Naylor Car Club, Mrs F R Taylor, Registrar, c/o Naylor Brothers Restoration, Airedale Garage, Hollins Hill, Shipley, Yorkshire BD17 7QN

Nobel Register, Mike Ayriss, 29 Oak Drive, Syston, Leicester, Leicestershire LE7 2PX

Norfolk Military Vehicle Group, Fakenham Road, Stanhoe, Norfolk PE31 8PX Tel: 01485 518052

North East Club for Pre-War Austins, Tom Gatenby, 9 Townsend Crescent, Morpeth, Northumberland NE61 2XW

North London MG Club, 2 Duckett Road, Harringey, London N4 1BN Tel: 020 8366 6655/020 8341 7436

North Thames Military Vehicle Preservation Society, 22 Victoria Avenue, Grays, Essex RM16 2RP

Nova Owners' Club, Ray Nicholls, 19 Bute Avenue, Hathershaw, Oldham, Lancashire OL8 2AQ

NSU Owners' Club, Rosemarie Crowley, 58 Tadorne Rd, Tadworth, Surrey KT20 5TF Tel: 01737 812412

Ogle Register, Chris Gow, 108 Potters Lane, Burgess Hill, West Sussex RH15 9JN Tel: 01444 248439

Old Bean Society, P P Cole, 165 Denbigh Drive, Hately Heath, West Bromwich, West Midlands B71 2SP

Opel GT UK Owners' Club, Dean Hayes, 11 Thrale Way, Parkwood, Rainham, Kent ME8 9LX Tel: 01634 379065

Opel Vauxhall Drivers' Club, The Old Mill, Dereham, Norfolk NR20 5RT

Panhard et Levassor Club GB, Martin McLarence, 18 Dovedale Rd, Offerton, Stockport, Cheshire SK2 5DY

Panther Enthusiasts' Club UK, George Newell, Secretary, 91 Fleet Road, Farnborough, Hampshire GU14 9RE Tel: 01252 540217

Pedal Car Collectors' Club (PCCC), c/o A P Gayler, 4/4a Chapel Terrace Mews, Kemp Town, Brighton, East Sussex BN2 1HU Tel/Fax: 01273 601960 email: cars@kemptown-brighton.freeserve.co.uk web: www.carsofbrighton.co.uk; eurosurf.pcc.com

Piper (Sports & Racing Car) Club, Clive Davies, Pipers Oak, Lopham Rd, East Harling, Norfolk NR16 2PE Tel: 01953 717813

Porsche Club Great Britain, Robin Walker, c/o Cornbury House, Cotswold Business Village, London Road, Moreton-in-Marsh, Gloucestershire GL56 0JQ Tel: 01608 652911/01296 688760

Post Office Vehicle Club, 7 Bignal Rand Drive, Wells, Somerset BA5 2EU

Post-War Thoroughbred Car Club, 87 London Street, Chertsey, Surrey KT16 8AN

Post-Vintage Humber Car Club, Neil Gibbins, 32 Walsh Crescent, New Addington, Croydon, Surrey CR0 0BX Tel: 01689 849851

Potteries Vintage & Classic Car Club, B Theobald, 78 Reeves Avenue, Cross Heath, Newcastle, Staffordshire ST5 9LA

Pre-1940 Triumph Owners' Club, Jon Quiney, 2 Duncroft Close, Reigate, Surrey RH2 9DE

Pre-67 Ford Owners' Club, Alistair Cuninghame, 13 Drum Brae Gardens, Edinburgh, Scotland EH12 8SY Tel: 0131 339 1179

Pre-50 American Auto Club, Alan Murphy, 41 Eastham Rake, Wirral, Merseyside L62 9AN Tel: 0151 327 1392

Pre-War Austin Seven Club Ltd, Stephen Jones, 1 The Fold, Doncaster Road, Whitley, Nr Goole, Yorkshire DN14 0HZ

Quattro Owners' Club, David Preece, Coombe Cottage, Coombe Lane, Cradley, Worcester WR13 5JF Tel: 01886 880777

Radford Register, Chris Gow, 108 Potters Lane, Burgess Hill, W Sussex RH15 9JN Tel: 01444 248439

Railton Owners' Club, Barrie McKenzie, Fairmiles, Barnes Hall Road, Burncross, Sheffield, Yorkshire S35 1RF Tel: 01742 468357

Range Rover Register, Chris Tomley, Cwm/Cochen, Bettws, Newtown, Powys, Wales SY16 3LQ

Rapier Register, D C H Williams, Smithy, Tregynon, Newtown, Powys, Wales SY16 3EH Tel: 01686 650396

Rear Engine Renault Club, R Woodall, 346 Crewe Road, Cresty, Crewe, Cheshire CW2 5AD

Register of Unusual Micro-Cars, Jean Hammond, School House Farm, Hawkenbury, Staplehurst, Kent TN12 0EB

Reliant Kitten Register, Brian Marshall, 16 Glendee Gardens, Renfrew PA4 0AL

Reliant Owners' Club, Graham Close, 19 Smithey Close, High Green, Sheffield, Yorkshire S30 4FQ

Reliant Sabre & Scimitar Owners' Club, PO Box 67, Teddington, Middlesex TW11 8QR Tel: 020 8977 6625

Renault Freres, J G Kemsley, Yew Tree House, Jubliee Road, Chelsfield, Kent BR6 7QZ

Renault Owners' Club, J Henderson, 24 Long Meadow, Mansfield Woodhouse, Mansfield, Nottinghamshire NG19 9QW

Riley MC Ltd, J Hall, Treelands, 127 Penn Road, Wolverhampton WV3 0DU

Riley Register – Pre 1940 Cars, J A Clarke, 56 Cheltenham Road, Bishops Cleeve, Cheltenham, Gloucestershire GL52 4LY

Riley RM Club, Mrs J Manders, 'Y Fachell', Ruthin Road, Gwernymynydd, North Wales CH7 5LQ

Ro80 Club GB, Mr Alec Coutts, 46 Molivers Lane, Bromham, Bedfordshire MK43 8LD

Rochdale Owners Club, Alaric Spendlove, 7 Whitley Avenue, Crownhill, Plymouth, Devon PL5 3BQ Tel: 01752 791409

Rolls-Royce Enthusiasts' Club, Peter Baines, The Hunt House, Paulerspury, Northamptonshire NN12 7NA

Ronart Drivers' Club, Simon Sutton, Membership Secretary, Orchard Cottage, Allan Lane, Fritchley, Belper, Derbyshire DE56 2FX Tel: 01773 856901

Rover P4 Drivers' Guild, 54 Ingaway, Lee Chapel Sth, Basildon, Essex SS16 5QR Tel: 01268 413395

Rover P5 Owners' Club, G Moorshead, 13 Glen Ave, Ashford, Middlesex TW15 2JE Tel: 01784 258166

Rover P6 Owners' Club, M Jones, 48 Upper Aughton Rd, Birkdale, Southport PR8 5NH Tel: 01704 560929

Rover SD1 Club, PO Box 12, Owlsmoor, Sandhurst, Berkshire GU47 4WZ Tel: 01344 761791

Rover Sports Register, Cliff Evans, 8 Hilary Close, Great Boughton, Chester, Cheshire CH3 5QP

Royal Automobile Club, PO Box 700, Bristol, Gloucestershire BS99 1RB Tel: 01454 208000

Saab Enthusiasts' Club, PO Box 96, Harrow, Middlesex HA3 7DW Tel: 01249 815792

Saab Owners' Club of GB Ltd, John Wood, PO Box 900, Durham DH1 2GF Tel: 01923 229945 Membership Hotline: 070 7171 9000

Scimitar Drivers' Club International, Steve Lloyd, 45 Kingshill Park, Dursley, Gloucestershire GL11 4DG Tel: 01245 320734

Scootacar Register, Stephen Boyd, Pamanste, 18 Holman Close, Aylsham, Norwich, Norfolk NR11 6DD Tel: 01263 733861

Sebring OC, D Soundy, Hill House, Water Lane, Chelveston, Northamptonshire NN9 6AP

Simca Owners' Register, David Chapman, 18 Cavendish Gardens, Redhill, Surrey RH1 4AQ

Singer Owners' Club, Martyn Wray, 11 Ermine Rise, Great Casterton, Stamford, Lincolnshire PE9 4AJ Tel: 01780 62740

Small Ford Club, 115 Woodland Gardens, Isleworth, Middlesex TW7 6LU Tel: 020 8568 3227

Solent Austin Seven Club Ltd, F Claxton, 185 Warsash Road, Warsash, Hampshire SO31 9JE

South Devon Commercial Vehicle Club, Bob Gale, Avonwick Station, Diptford, Totnes, Devon TQ9 7LU Tel: 01364 73130

South Hants Model Auto Club, C Derbyshire, 21 Aintree Rd, Calmore, Southampton, Hampshire SO40 2TL

South Wales Austin Seven Club, Mr H Morgan, Glynteg, 90 Ammanford Road, Llandybie, Ammanford, Wales SA18 2JYX

Spartan Owners' Club, Steve Andrews, 28 Ashford Drive, Ravenhead, Nottinghamshire NG15 9DE Tel: 01623 793742

Split Screen Van Club, Mike & Sue Mundy, The Homestead, Valebridge Road, Burgess Hill, West Sussex RH15 0RT Tel: 01444 241407

Sporting Escort Owners' Club, 26 Huntingdon Crescent, Off Madresfield Drive, Halesowen, West Midlands B63 3DJ

Sporting Fiats Club (Formerly Fiat Twin-Cam Register), Freepost (MID D2062), Leamington Spa, Warwickshire CV33 9BR

Stag Owners' Club, c/o The Old Rectory, Aslacton, Norfolk NR15 2JN

Standard Motor Club, Tony Pingriff, 57 Main Road, Meriden, Coventry, West Midlands CV7 0LP

Star, Starling, Stuart & Briton Register, D E A Evans, New Wood Lodge, 2A Hyperion Road, Stourton, Stourbridge, West Midlands DY7 6SB

Sunbeam Alpine Owners' Club, Pauline Leese, 53 Wood Street, Mow Cop, Stoke-on-Trent, Staffordshire ST7 3PF Tel: 01782 5198652

Sunbeam Rapier Owners' Club, Ruth Kingston, Wayside, Depmore Lane, Kingsley, Nr Warrington, Cheshire WA6 6UD

Sunbeam Talbot Alpine Register, Derek Cook, 47 Crescent Wood Road, Sydenham, London SE26 6SA

Sunbeam Talbot Darracq Register, R Lawson, West Emlett Cottage, Black Dog, Crediton, Devon EX17 4QB

Sunbeam Tiger Owners' Club, Brian Postle, Beechwood, 8 Villa Real Estate, Consett, Co Durham DH8 6BJ Tel: 01207 508296

Surrey Classic Vehicle Club, 55a Ditton Road, Surbiton, Surrey KT6 6RF Tel: 020 8390 3570

Swift Club & Swift Register, John Harrison, 70 Eastwick Drive, Bookham, Leatherhead, Surrey KT23 3NX Tel: 01372 452120

Tame Valley Vintage & Classic Car Club, Mrs S Ogden, 13 Valley New Road, Royton, Oldham, Lancashire OL2 6BP

Tornado Register, Dave Malins, 48 St Monica's Ave, Luton, Bedfordshire LU3 1PN Tel: 01582 37641

Toyota Enthusiasts' Club, c/o Secretary/Treasurer, Billy Wells, 28 Park Road, Feltham, Middlesex TW13 6PW Tel/Fax: 020 8898 0740

TR Drivers' Club, Bryan Harber, 19 Irene Road, Orpington, Kent BR6 0HA

TR Register, 1B Hawksworth, Southmead Ind Park, Didcot, Oxfordshire OX10 7HR Tel: 01235 818866

Trident Car Club, David Rowlinson, 23 Matlock Cres, Cheam, Sutton, Surrey SM3 9SS Tel: 020 8644 9029

Triumph 2000/2500/2.5 Register, Alan Crussell, 10 Gables Close, Chalfont St Peter, Buckinghamshire SL9 0PR Tel: 01494 873264 email: t2000register@compuserve.com web: www.kvaleberg.com/t2000.html

Triumph Dolomite Club, 39 Mill Lane, Upper Arncott, Bicester, Oxfordshire OX6 0PB Tel: 01869 242847 (am)

Triumph Mayflower Club, T Gordon, 12 Manor Close, Hoghton, Preston, Lancashire PR5 0EN

Triumph Razoredge Owners' Club, Stewart Langton, 62 Seaward Avenue, Barton-on-Sea, Hampshire BH25 7HP Tel: 01425 618074

Triumph Roadster Club, J Cattaway, 59 Cowdray Park Rd, Little Common, Bexhill-on-Sea, E Sussex TN39 4EZ

Triumph Spitfire Club, Mr Cor Gent, Anemoon 41, 7483 AC Haaksbergen, The Netherlands

Triumph Sporting Owners' Club, G R King, 16 Windsor Road, Hazel Grove, Stockport, Cheshire SK7 4SW

Triumph Sports Six Club Ltd, 121B St Mary's Road, Market Harborough, Leicestershire E16 7DT

Triumph Stag Register, M Wattam, 18 Hazel Close, Highcliffe, Dorset BH23 4PS

Trojan Owners' Club, Derrick Graham, President, Troylands, St Johns, Earlswood Common, Redhill, Surrey RH1 6QF Tel: 01737 763643

Turner Register, Dave Scott, 21 Ellsworth Road, High Wycombe, Buckinghamshire HP11 2TU

TVR Car Club, c/o David Gerald, TVR Sports Cars Tel: 01386 793239

United States Army Vehicle Club, Dave Boocock, 31 Valley View Close, Bogthorn, Oakworth Rd, Keighley, Yorkshire BD22 7LZ

United States Army Vehicle Club, Simon Johnson, 7 Carter Fold, Mellor, Lancashire BB2 7ER

Unloved Soviet Socialist Register, Julian Nowill, Earlsland House, Bradninch, Exeter, Devon EX5 4QP

Vanguard 1 & 2 Owners' Club, R Jones, The Villa, The Down, Alviston, Avon BS12 2TQ Tel: 01454 419232

Vauxhall Cavalier Convertible Club, Ron Goddard, 47 Brooklands Close, Luton, Bedfordshire LU4 9EH

Vauxhall Owners' Club, Roy Childers, 31 Greenbanks, Melbourn, Nr Royston, Cambridgeshire SG8 6AS

Vauxhall PA/PB/PC/E Owners' Club, G Lonsdale, 77 Pilling Lane, Preesall, Lancashire FY6 0HB Tel: 01253 810866

Vauxhall Viva OC, Adrian Miller, The Thatches, Snetterton North End, Snetterton, Norwich, Norfolk NR16 2LD Tel: 01953 498818 email: adrian@vivaclub.freeserve.co.uk

Vauxhall VX4/90 Drivers' Club (FD/FE 1972–1978), 1 Milverton Drive, Uttoxeter, Staffordshire ST14 7RE

Vectis Historic Vehicle Club, Nigel Offer, 10 Paddock Drive, Bembridge, Isle of Wight PO35 5TL

Veteran Car Club Of Great Britain, Jessamine Court, High Street, Ashwell, Baldock, Hertfordshire SG7 5NL Tel: 01462 742818

Vintage Austin Register, Frank Smith, The Briars, Four Lane Ends, Oakerthorpe, Alfreton, Derbyshire DE55 7LH Tel: 0773 831646

Vintage Sports-Car Club Ltd, The Secretary, The Old Post Office, West Street, Chipping Norton, Oxfordshire OX7 5EL Tel: 01608 644777 email: wiggle@globalnet.co.uk

Volkswagen '50–67' Transporter Club, Peter Nicholson, 11 Lowton Road, Lytham St Annes, Lancashire FY8 3JD Tel: 01253 720023

Volkswagen Cabriolet Owners' Club (GB), Emma Palfreyman, Secretary, Dishley Mill, Derby Road, Loughborough, Leicestershire LE11 0SF

Volkswagen Owners' Club (GB), PO Box 7, Burntwood, Walsall, West Midlands WS7 8SB

Volvo Enthusiasts' Club, Kevin Price, 4 Goonbell, St Agnes, Cornwall TR5 0PH

Vulcan Register, D Hales, The Hedgerows, Sutton Street, Nicholas, Herefordshire HR1 3BU Tel: 01432 880726

VW Type 3 & 4 Club, Jane Terry, Pear Tree Bungalow, Exted, Elham, Canterbury, Kent CT4 6YG

Wartburg Owners' Club, Bernard Trevena, 55 Spiceall Estate, Compton, Guildford, Surrey GU31 Tel: 01483 810493

Wolseley 6/80 & Morris Oxford MO Club, Don Gould, 2 Barleyfield Close, Heighington, Lincoln LN4 1TX Tel: 01652 635138

Wolseley Hornet Special Club 1930–1935, Wolseley Hornet Sports & Specials, Ms Chris Hyde, Kylemor, Crown Gardens, Fleet, Hampshire GU13 9PD

Wolseley Register, M Stanley, Chairman, 1 Flashgate, Higher Ramsgreave Road, Ramsgreave, Nr Blackburn, Lancashire BB1 9DH

XR Owners' Club, PO Box 47, Loughborough, Leicestershire LE11 1XS Tel: 01509 882300 web: www.xrownersclub.co.uk

Yankee Jeep Club, 8 Chew Brook Drive, Greenfield, Saddleworth, Lancashire OL3 7PD

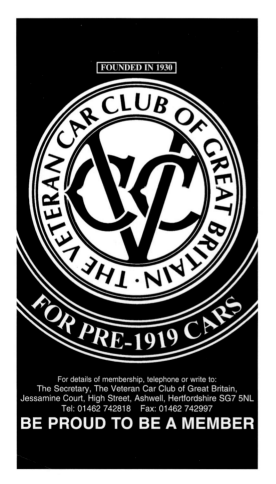

Directory of Auctioneers

Barons, Brooklands House, 33 New Road, Hythe, Southampton, Hampshire SO45 6BN
Tel: 023 8084 0081

British Car Auctions Ltd, Classic & Historic Automobile Division, Auction Centre, Blackbushe Airport, Blackwater, Camberley, Surrey GU17 9LG Tel: 01252 878555

Brooks, Robert (Auctioneers), 81 Westside, London SW4 9AY Tel: 020 7228 8000

Mervyn Carey, Twysden Cottage, Benenden, Cranbrook, Kent TN17 4LD
Tel: 01580 240283

Central Motor Auctions Plc, Central House, Pontefract Road, Rothwell, Leeds, Yorkshire LS26 0JE Tel: 0113 282 0707

Cheffins Grain & Comins, 2 Clifton Rd, Cambridge, Cambridgeshire CB2 4BW
Tel: 01223 358731

Christie's International Motor Cars Ltd, The Jack Barclay Showroom, 2–4 Ponton Road, Nine Elms, London SW8 5BA

Classic Automobile Auctions BV, Goethestrasse 10, 6000 Frankfurt 1, Germany
Tel: 00 49 69 28666/8

Coys of Kensington, 2–4 Queens Gate Mews, London SW7 5QJ Tel: 020 7584 7444

Dickinson Davy & Markham, Wrawby Street, Brigg, Humberside DN20 8JJ
Tel: 01652 653666

Eccles Auctions, Unit 4, 25 Gwydir Street, Cambridge CB1 2LG Tel: 01223 561518

Evans & Partridge, Agriculture House, High Street, Stockbridge, Hampshire SO20 6HF
Tel: 01264 810702

Thomas Wm Gaze & Son, 10 Market Hill, Diss, Norfolk IP22 3JZ Tel: 01379 651931

H & H Classic Auctions Ltd, Whitegate Farm, Hatton Lane, Hatton, Warrington, Cheshire WA4 4BZ Tel: 01925 730630

Andrew Hartley, Victoria Hall Salerooms, Little Lane, Ilkley, Yorkshire LS29 8EA
Tel: 01943 816363

Kidson Trigg, Estate Office, Friars Farm, Sevenhampton, Highworth, Swindon, Wiltshire SN6 7PZ Tel: 01793 861000

Kruse International, PO Box 190, 5400 County Road 11A, Auburn, Indiana 46706, USA
Tel: 00 1 219 925 5600

Lambert & Foster, 77 Commercial Road, Paddock Wood, Kent TN12 6DR
Tel: 01892 832325

Lawrences Auctioneers, Norfolk House, 80 High Street, Bletchingley, Surrey RH1 4PA
Tel: 01883 743323

Thomas Mawer & Son, The Lincoln Saleroom, 63 Monks Road, Lincoln LN2 5HP
Tel: 01522 524984

Mealy's, Chatsworth Street, Castle Comer, Co Kilkenny, Republic of Ireland
Tel: 00 353 56 41229

Morphets of Harrogate, 6 Albert Street, Harrogate, Yorkshire HG1 1JL
Tel: 01423 530030

Neales, 192–194 Mansfield Road, Nottingham NG1 3HU Tel: 0115 962 4141

John Nicholson, The Auction Rooms, Longfield, Midhurst Road, Fernhurst, Surrey GU27 3HA Tel: 01428 653727

Onslow's, The Depot, 2 Michael Road, London SW6 2AD Tel: 020 7371 0505

Palm Springs Exotic Car Auctions, 602 East Sunny Dunes Road, Palm Springs, California 92264, USA Tel: 00 1 760 320 3290

Palmer Snell, 65 Cheap Street, Sherborne, Dorset DT9 3BA Tel: 01935 812218

J R Parkinson Son & Hamer Auctions, The Auction Rooms, Rochdale Road (Kershaw Street), Bury, Lancashire BL9 7HH
Tel: 0161 761 1612/761 7372

Phillips, Blenstock House, 101 New Bond Street, London W1Y 0AS
Tel: 020 7629 6602

Phillips, 20 The Square, Retford, Nottinghamshire DN22 6BX
Tel: 01777 708633

Phillips, Alphin Brook Road, Alphington, Exeter, Devon EX2 8TH
Tel: 01392 439025

Phillips Scotland, 207 Bath Street, Glasgow, Scotland G2 4HD Tel: 0141 221 8377

RM Classic Cars, 825 Park Ave West, Chatham, Ontario, Canada Tel: 00 1 519 352 4575

Rogers Jones & Co, The Saleroom, 33 Abergele Road, Colwyn Bay, Wales LL29 7RU Tel: 01492 532176

Martyn Rowe, The Truro Auction Centre, Calenick Street, Truro, Cornwall TR1 2SG
Tel: 01892 260020

RTS Auctions Ltd, Unit 1 Alston Road, Hellesden Park Industrial Estate, Norwich, Norfolk NR6 5OS
Tel: 01603 418200

Russell Baldwin & Bright, Fine Art Salerooms, Ryelands Road, Leominster, Herefordshire HR6 8NZ Tel: 01568 611122

Silver Collector Car Auctions, E204, Spokane, Washington 99207, USA Tel: 00 1 509 326 4485

Sloan's Auctioneers & Appraisers, Miami Gallery, 8861 NW 18th Terrace, Suite 100, Miami, Florida 33172, USA
Tel: 00 1 305 592-2575

Sotheby's, 34–35 New Bond Street, London W1A 2AA Tel: 020 7293 5000

G E Sworder & Sons, 14 Cambridge Road, Stansted Mountfitchet, Essex CM24 8BZ
Tel: 01279 817778

Taylors, Honiton Galleries, 205 High Street, Honiton, Devon EX14 8LF Tel: 01404 42404

Thimbleby & Shorland, 31 Great Knollys Street, Reading, Berkshire RG1 7HU
Tel: 01734 508611

Wealden Auction Galleries, Desmond Judd, 23 Hendly Drive, Cranbrook, Kent TN17 3DY
Tel: 01580 714522

Wellers Auctioneers, The Salesroom, Moorfield Road, Slyfield Green, Guildford, Surrey GU1 1SG Tel: 01483 447447

World Classic Auction & Exposition Co, 3600 Blackhawk Plaza Circle, Danville, California 94506, USA Tel: 00 1 925 736 3444

Directory of Museums

Bedfordshire
Shuttleworth Collection,
Old Warden Aerodrome, Nr Biggleswade
SG18 9EP Tel: 01767 627288
Europe's biggest collection of flying pre-1940 aircraft,
also veteran and vintage vehicles including 15 motorcycles.
Restaurant, gift shop. Open daily 10–3pm (4pm Mar–Oct).

Stondon Museum,
Station Road, Lower Stondon, Henlow SG16 6JN
Tel: 01462 850339
Over 320 transport exhibits including Bentleys and over
30 motorcycles. Coffee shop. Open every day 10–5pm.

Cheshire
Mouldsworth Motor Museum,
Smithy Lane, Mouldsworth, Chester
CH3 8AR Tel: 01928 731781
Over 60 cars, motorcycles and early bicycles in
a 1937 Art Deco building. Open Sundays March–end
November 12–5pm inc bank holidays & weekends and
also Wednesdays 1–5pm, all July and August.

Cornwall
Automobilia Motor Museum,
The Old Mill, Terras Road, St Stephen,
St Austell PL26 7RX Tel: 01726 823092
Around 50 vehicles from 1900 to 1966, plus about 10
motorcycles. Café, shop and autojumble. Open every day
except Saturday in April, May and October 10–4pm,
June–September every day 10–5pm.

Cumbria
Cars of the Stars Motor Museum,
Standish Street, Keswick CA12 5LS
Tel: 01768 73757

Lakeland Motor Museum,
Holker Hall & Gardens, Cark-in-Cartmel,
Nr Grange-over-Sands, South Lakeland LA11 7PL
150 classic and vintage cars, tractors, cycles and engines
including about 40 motorcycles. A collection of rare
models and replicas of Donald Campbell's Bluebird cars
and boats. Open end March to end October,
Sunday–Friday 10.30–4.45pm, closed Saturday. Hall,
gardens and grounds.

Western Lakes Motor Museum,
The Maltings, Brewery Lane, Cockermouth
Tel: 01900 824448
Located in Jennings Castle Brewery beneath the walls of
Cockermouth Castle. Some 45 cars and 17 motorcycles
from Vintage to Formula 3. Coffee shop, parking in town.
Open March–October, 10–5pm daily. Closed January,
other dates weekends only.

Derbyshire
The Donnington Collection,
Donnington Park, Castle Donnington
DE74 2RP Tel: 01332 810048

Gloucestershire
Bristol Industrial Museum,
Princes Wharf, City Docks, Bristol BS1 4RN
Tel: 0117 925 1470
Railway exhibits, boats, workshops plus lorries and cars
made at Bristol. Open Tuesday–Sunday 10–5pm.

The Bugatti Trust,
34 ᵗʰ Hill Gotherington, Cheltenham
977201

Cotswold Motoring Museum & Toy Collection,
Sherbourne Street, Bourton-on-the-Water,
Nr Cheltenham GL54 2BY Tel: 01451 821 255
Largest collection of advertising signs in the world, plus
toys and motorcycles. The home of the Brough-Superior
Co and of 'Brum', the small, open 1920's car that has a
TV series. Disabled entrance, museum shop and café.
Open daily February–November 10–6pm.

Greater Manchester
Manchester Museum of Transport,
Boyle Street M8 8UW Tel: 0161 205 2122

Hampshire
National Motor Museum,
Brockenhurst, Beaulieu SO42 7ZN
Tel: 01590 612123/612345
Over 200 cars, 60 motorcycles and memorabilia.
Gardens, information centre, monorail, veteran bus and
car rides, model railway, special events including the
world famous autojumbles. Restaurant, shops and
facilities. Open daily from 10am, closed December 25.

Humberside
Bradford Industrial Museum,
Moorside Mills, Moorside Road,
Bradford BD2 3HP
Tel: 01274 631756
General industrial museum including many engineering
items, Jowett cars, Panther and Scott motorcycles, a
steam roller and Bradford's last tram. Open
Tuesday–Friday and Bank Holidays 10–5pm.

Northern Ireland
Ulster Folk and Transport Museum,
Cultra Manor, Holywood, Co Down BT18 0EU
Tel: 028 90 428 428
Folk museum, railway collection and road transport
galleries featuring every kind of road vehicle. Tearooms,
gift shop, and free parking. Open all year round
10.30–5/6pm, Sundays 12–6pm, closed Christmas.

Republic of Ireland
Kilgarvan Motor Museum,
Kilgarvan, Co Kerry Tel: 00 353 64 85346

Isle of Man
Manx Motor Museum,
Crosby Tel: 01624 851236

Port Erin Motor Museum,
High Street, Port Erin Tel: 01624 832964

Kent
Historic Vehicles Collection of C M Booth,
Falstaff Antiques, 63–67 High Street,
Rolvenden TN17 4LP
Tel: 01580 241234
A private museum consisting mainly of Morgan three-
wheelers but some motorbikes. An interesting collection
plus memorabilia, at the rear of the antique shop. Open
Monday–Saturday 10–6pm.

Ramsgate Motor Museum,
West Cliff Hall, Ramsgate CT11 9JX
Tel: 01843 581948
Founded 1982, dedicated to the history of motoring, every
vehicle set out in scenes depicting the past. Open
April–November 10.30–5.30pm, winter Sundays 10–5pm.

SEUMS

Lancashire

British Commercial Vehicles Museum,
King Street, Leyland, Preston PR5 1LE
Tel: 01772 451011 Fax: 01772 423404

Bury Transport Museum,
Castlecroft Road, off Bolton Street, Bury
Tel: 0161 764 7790

Middlesex

Whitewebbs Museum of Transport,
Whitewebbs Road, Enfield EN2 9HW
Tel: 020 8367 1898
Collection of commercial vehicles, cars and 20–30 motorcycles. Ring for opening times.

Norfolk

Caister Castle Motor Museum,
Caister-on-Sea, Nr Great Yarmouth
Tel: 01572 787251
Private collection of cars and motorcycles from 1893. Tearoom, free car park. Open daily mid-May to end September, closed Saturday.

Nottinghamshire

Nottingham Industrial Museum,
Courtyard Buildings, Wallaton Park
Tel: 0115 915 3910

Scotland

Grampian Transport Museum,
Alford, Aberdeenshire AB33 8AE
Tel: 019755 62292 Fax: 019755 62180
email: info@gtm.org.uk
Displays and working exhibits tracing the history of travel and transport in the locality. Open April 2–Oct 31 10–5pm.

Moray Motor Museum,
Bridge Street, Elgin IV30 2DE Tel: 01343 544933
Interesting collection of cars and motorcycles, memorabilia and diecast models. Open daily Easter–October 11–5pm.

Museum of Transport,
Kelvin Hall, 1 Bunhouse Road, Glasgow G3 8DP
Tel: 0141 357 3929
A museum devoted to the history of transport on the land. Café, gift shop, disabled access. Open daily 10–5pm, Sunday 11–5pm except December 25 and January 1.

Myreton Motor Museum,
Aberlady, Longniddry, East Lothian EH32 0PZ
Tel: 01875 870288
Collection of cars, motorcycles, commercials and WWII military vehicles. Established 1966. Open daily at 10am except Christmas Day. Parties and coaches welcome.

National Museum of Scotland,
Granton Centre, 242 West Granton Road,
Edinburgh EH1 1JF Tel: 0131 225 7534

Shropshire

Midland Motor Museum,
Stanmore Hall, Stourbridge Road,
Bridgnorth WV15 6DT Tel: 01746 762992
Collection of 60 cars and 30 motorcycles. Museum shop. Open daily 10.30–5pm except Christmas and Boxing Days.

Somerset

Haynes Motor Museum,
Sparkford, Yeovil BA22 7LH
Tel: 01963 440804
Haynes Publishing Co museum with vintage, veteran and classic cars and motorcycles. 250 cars and 50 motorcycles. Café, shop. Open daily summer 9.30–5.30pm, winter 10–4pm except Christmas, Boxing and New Year's Days.

Surrey

Brooklands Museum,
Brooklands Road, Weybridge KT13 0QN
Tel: 01932 857381
Motorsport and aviation museum including historic racing cars and aircraft. About 20 motorcycles pre-WWII. Monthly auction events. Tearooms and museum shop. Open daily except Mondays, Good Friday and Christmas 10–5pm summer, 10–4pm winter.

Dunsfold Land Rover Museum,
Dunsfold GU8 4NP Tel: 01483 200567

East Sussex

Bentley Motor Museum,
Bentley Wild Fowl Trust, Harvey's Lane, Ringmer, Lewes BN8 5AF Tel: 01825 840573

Foulkes-Halbard of Filching,
Filching Manor, Filching, Wannock, Polegate
BN26 5QA Tel: 01323 487838
Fax: 01323 486331
About 100 cars dating from 1893 to 1993, also 30 motorcycles including American pre-1940s bikes ex-Steve McQueen. Open Easter–October Thursday, Friday, Saturday and Sunday 10.30–4pm.

Tyne & Wear

Newburn Hall Motor Museum,
35 Townfield Gardens, Newburn NE15 8PY
Tel: 0191 264 2977
Private museum of about 50 cars and 10 motorcycles. Restaurant. Open daily 10–6pm, closed Mondays.

Wales

Llangollen Motor Museum,
Pentrefelin, Llangollen LL20 8EE
Tel: 01978 860324
20-plus cars and approx 10 motorcycles. Model vehicles, signs, tools and parts. Reference library, shop. Open every day 10–5pm Easter–September.

Madog Car & Motorcycle Museum,
Snowdon Street, Porthmadog Tel: 01758 713618
15 cars and nearly 70 motorcycles plus memorabilia. Open Monday–Saturday 10–5 May–September.

Warwickshire

Heritage Motor Centre,
Banbury Road, Gaydon CV35 0BJ
Tel: 01926 641188 web: www.heritage.org.uk

Museum of British Road Transport,
St Agnes Lane, Hales Street, Coventry CV1 1PN
Tel: 024 7683 2425 Fax: 024 7683 2465
email: museum@mbrt.co.uk
web: www.mbrt.co.uk

West Midlands

Black Country Living Museum,
Tipton Road, Dudley DY1 4SQ
Tel: 0121 557 9643

Wiltshire

Atwell-Wilson Motor Museum,
Downside, Stockley Lane, Calne SN11 0QX
Tel: 01249 813119
Over 60 cars plus vintage, post vintage and classic motorcycles. Open Monday–Thursday and Sunday, April–October 11–5pm, November–March 11–4pm and Good Friday.

Science Museum Transport Museum,
Red Barn Gate, Wroughton, Nr Swindon SN4 9NS
Tel: 01793 814466

Index to Advertisers

Bibliography

Baldwin, Nick; Georgano, G. N.; Sedgwick, Michael; and Laban, Brian; *The World Guide to Automobiles*, Guild Publishing, London, 1987

Colin Chapman *Lotus Engineering*, Osprey, 1993.

Flammang, James M; *Standard Catalog of Imported Cars*, Krause Publications Inc, 1992.

Georgano, G. N.; ed: *Encyclopedia of Sports Cars*, Bison Books, 1985.

Georgano, Nick; *Military Vehicles of World War II*, Osprey 1994.

Harding, Anthony; Allport, Warren; Hodges, David; Davenport, John; *The Guinness Book of the Car*, Guinness Superlatives Ltd, 1987

Hay, Michael; *Bentley Factory Cars*, Osprey, 1993.

Hough, Richard; *A History of the World's Sports Cars*, Allen & Unwin, 1961.

Isaac, Rowan; *Morgan*, Osprey, 1994.

McComb, F. Wilson; *MG by McComb*, Osprey, 1978.

Nye, Doug; *Autocourse History of the Grand Prix Car 1966–1991*, Hazleton Publishing, 1992.

Posthumus, Cyril, and Hodges, David; *Classic Sportscars*, Ivy Leaf, 1991.

Robson, Graham; *Classic and Sportscar A–Z of Cars of the 1970s*, Bay View Books, 1990.

Sedgwick, Michael; Gillies, Mark; *Classic and Sportscar A–Z of Cars of the 1930s*, Bay View Books, 1989.

Sedgwick, Michael, Gillies, Mark; *Classic and Sportscar A–Z of Cars 1945–70*, Bay View Books, 1990.

Sieff, Theo; *Mercedes Benz*, Gallery Books, 1989.

Vanderveen, Bart; *Historic Military Vehicles Directory*, After the Battle Publications, 1989.

Willson, Quentin; Selby David, *The Ultimate Classic Car Book*, Dorling Kindersley, 1995.

Index

Italic page numbers denote colour pages; **bold** numbers refer to information and pointer boxes